Kings *of the* Sea

CHARLES II, JAMES II AND THE ROYAL NAVY

J D DAVIES

Seaforth
PUBLISHING

Title pages: The surrender of *Royal Prince*
during the Four Days' Battle, 1666.
Willem van de Velde the Younger.
(Rijksmuseum, Amsterdam)

For Peter and Diane Le Fevre

First published in Great Britain in 2017 by
Seaforth Publishing,
A division of Pen & Sword Books Ltd,
47 Church Street,
Barnsley S70 2AS

www.seaforthpublishing.com

British Library Cataloguing in Publication Data
A catalogue record for this book is available from the British Library

ISBN 978 1 84832 400 8 (hardback)
ISBN 978 1 84832 402 0 (epub)
ISBN 978 1 84832 401 5 (kindle)

Typeset and designed by Steve Dent
Printed and bound in China by Imago

Contents

Preface and Acknowledgements

TO THE BEST OF MY RECOLLECTION, I first conceived the idea of writing a book rather like this one over thirty years ago, when I was locked in Samuel Pepys's library. This was not quite the dire emergency, nor the unexpected proof of the feasibility of time travel, that it might sound. Pepys's glorious bequest to his old Cambridge college, Magdalene, stands four-square alongside the River Cam, and contains many of the great man's papers, contained within exactly 3,000 of his books, no more, no less – arranged, uniquely, in order of size, from the smallest to the largest. When I was working there extensively in the 1980s, the library opened to the public for an hour in the morning, from 11.30 to 12.30, and another in the afternoon, from 2.30 to 3.30; but by prior arrangement, researchers could continue to work through the two hours in between, when the doors of the library were firmly bolted. This necessitated either a very early lunch or a very late one, not to mention unwavering faith in the fire-prevention facilities of Magdalene College, Cambridge, and it is hardly surprising that this delightful laissez-faire policy eventually fell foul of the relentless advance of 'elf 'n' safety'. But the two hour lock-in, alone with Samuel Pepys's books, many of them full of the letters written by him to, or sent to him from, the likes of King Charles II and King James II, gave ample time for one's thoughts to wander in all kinds of directions. One of them involved contemplation of a paradox. In many periods of history, and in many topics of historical study, the role of monarchs has probably been studied more exhaustively than their actual importance often merits, contributing to an over-whelmingly 'top-down' view of history (and, yes, an often overwhelm-ingly male one too, for that is what monarchs usually were). The naval history of late seventeenth-century Britain is a marked exception. There, if anything, the monarchs have been placed in the background, and in some books, their contributions appear nearly invisible, overshadowed by an even more dominant figure. That person is regarded almost universally as the driving force behind all that happened in the navy of his day, the individual responsible for all that was good and important, the unim-peachable authority for all that took place in naval affairs. I got to know this person very well: after all, I was often locked in his library.

The feeling that Samuel Pepys was, perhaps, not quite as responsible for all that happened in the navy of the Restoration era as posterity believes (essentially because Pepys told posterity what to believe, and posterity duly complied), and that the contributions to naval history of the Stuart brothers, Charles and James, have been somewhat neglected, stayed with me in the years that followed. Indeed, several of the themes and ideas explored in this book first saw the light of day in a number of essays and articles, most of them published in obscure academic journals and collections of essays: which is a polite way of saying 'nobody read them'. But during the years that followed, other priorities always intervened to take me away from this book.

Now, though, it's time to set the record straight; and in attempting to do so, I've accumulated many debts. The staffs of the vast majority of the libraries and archives listed in the notes were overwhelmingly helpful and efficient, and I won't succumb to the considerable temptation to name and shame the tiny minority who weren't. Instead, I'll take this opportunity to commend Amsterdam's Rijksmuseum in the warmest possible terms for its decision to make images of its entire collection available for free use, for any purpose, by anyone – in marked contrast to those many British and American institutions which still think it acceptable to charge an arm and a leg to reproduce images for which they do not hold the copyright. Historians, and, indeed, authors, academics from other disciplines, and other professionals in general, have been complicit in this cartel for too long, as they have in those that control academic publishing, and this tacit collaboration with inexcusable corporate avarice should cease.

I would like to thank Susanna Plummer, house manager at Doddington Hall, for making the Gunman paintings available to me, and the Pepys Librarian, Master and Fellows of Magdalene College, Cambridge, for permitting access to the Pepys papers. Sam McLean helped to sharpen and refine my thinking about both the seventeenth-century Royal Navy and Star Wars. Although the ideas we've brainstormed about naval ideology will ultimately appear in a different book, my conversations with Alan James and Gijs Rommelse have helped to shape and clarify several of the themes that appear in this one. My critical readers were Ann Coats, Richard Endsor, Frank Fox, and Peter Le Fevre, my long-time colleagues in attempting to convince the wider world of the importance and innate interest of the Restoration Navy, and to whom I have been indebted for many years in more ways than I can say. Professor Steve Murdoch of the University of St Andrews provided invaluable input for several of the chapters; and, as with all of my books, be they fiction or non-fiction, my partner Wendy provided both indispensable critical advice, and an infallible ability to pull me out of the depths of the seventeenth century and back into the real world (despite, in the case of this title, being in the throes of writing her own book, her first).

Finally, though, I return to Peter Le Fevre. I first encountered Peter some time in 1983, when I was undertaking one of my first research visits to what was then still called the Public Record Office at Kew. I had ordered up some of the miscellaneous items in ADM106, an astonishing archive-within-an-archive which contains a huge amount of material, often barely catalogued and sometimes barely touched; indeed, there are some who say that Indiana Jones's quests for the lost Ark of the Covenant and the Holy Grail might have been over in rather shorter order had he known about ADM106. These particular items consisted of sets of large boxes, which were stacked behind the staff desk. The first I knew that Peter, probably the only other person in the building (staff included) who knew exactly what they were, had spotted these and had determined to seek out the person who'd ordered them, was when a large shadow fell across my desk, and a voice boomed out, 'What are you looking at those for?' That was the beginning of a close friendship which has endured for over thirty years, during which Peter's generosity, support, and infallibly sound advice have been second to none. I dedicate this book to him, and his wife Diane, with gratitude and affection.

J D Davies
Bedfordshire, Trafalgar Day 2016

Introduction

A T SOME POINT during the afternoon of 30 June 1675, the King of England disappeared. In many European states of the period, this would have triggered immediate panic. Kings were still regarded by many as little gods upon Earth; the entire political and social order was based, to some extent, on *knowing where they were*. Both before and since the seventeenth century, there have been countless instances where the sudden disappearance of a head of state has triggered anything from bouts of religious hysteria, to rioting in the streets, to full-scale revolutions. But for at least some of those who knew about it, King Charles II's disappearance on 30 June probably caused little more than a mild frisson of concern, perhaps no more than a few disapproving shakes of the head.

Because the king had gone sailing.

Yet again.

The royal cruise of 1675 involved seven royal yachts and three small frigates. This flotilla set off from Gravesend on 26 June, with the king aboard the Sixth Rate man-of-war *Greyhound*. A further eight warships, including the Third Rate *Harwich* and two fireships, joined them in the Downs. Bad weather delayed progress, causing the 'disappearance' of the flotilla not once, but several times; the *Katherine Yacht* lost touch entirely, and was believed to have been lost, while the yacht carrying the Speaker of the House of Commons had to turn back from the Downs. Progress was so slow that the royal party missed the principal object of the voyage, namely attending the launch of the great new First Rate man-of-war *Royal James* at Portsmouth Dockyard on 29 June. As it was, the other ships in the royal flotilla lost sight of the *Greyhound* during the 'very stormy and dark weather' on the night of 29/30 June, when they were on the west side of the Isle of Wight – a coast notorious for shipwrecks. The vessels sighted each other again in the morning, and the yachts carrying the king's brother and heir, the Duke of York, and Charles II's eldest illegitimate son, the Duke of Monmouth, went into Portsmouth. But once again, there was no sign of the *Greyhound*, which the others expected to make for the Isle of Wight.

By early evening, none of the fires which would have signalled a sighting of the ship flying the royal standard could be seen anywhere on the island. At eight the next morning, both James and Monmouth set sail to see if they could find the king. Whether either, or both, wondered

Royal yachts at sea in a strong wind, with a warship flying the royal standard. Willem van de Velde the younger. (© National Maritime Museum, Greenwich, London, BHC0891)

for even the most fleeting moment whether Charles had drowned in a catastrophic shipwreck, which would have meant that James was already King of England, Scotland, and Ireland, will never be known. In fact, the *Greyhound* had lain-to 'in very rough weather' off Dunnose Head until the morning of 1 July, when Charles got ashore in a shallop. He was met by the governor of the island, the outspoken, buccaneering old admiral, Sir Robert Holmes, who took him off to a 'good dinner' at Yarmouth, where the Duke of York eventually caught up with him. Charles finally came into Portsmouth harbour at one in the morning on 2 July. The Venetian ambassador said of the king's disappearance that 'anxiety was universal', and that his reappearance was greeted by 'unspeakable relief'.[1] Despite the alarm that had been caused, one courtier reported that 'this stormy voyage has not at all discouraged his Majesty from the sea, and all he can be persuaded to is only to change his ship and return in the *Harwich*, a good Third Rate frigate, but he will by no means hearken to any proposition of returning by land, notwithstanding all manner of conveniences and supplications have been proposed to him'.[2]

This dramatic voyage was by no means the only, nor the most ambitious, royal voyage of the reign. In July 1671, the king and Duke of York went overland to Portsmouth, where they viewed the new warships *St Michael, Royal James* and *Edgar*. They and their retinues then embarked in seven yachts, which, with six escorting warships, sailed for Plymouth, where they arrived on the 17th; the extended voyage also saw the royal flotilla call at Dartmouth. The king's informality during this expedition startled many, and still 'shocks historians accustomed to the near scripted progress of most baroque monarchs'; he arrived at Portsmouth unexpectedly early, and left Plymouth so abruptly that the mayor and corporation had to pursue him to Mount Edgcumbe in their own boat in order to take formal leave.[3] Describing this voyage, the chief minister, the Earl of Arlington, said of his king (revealing a little of his nervousness in the process), 'twenty leagues [by sea] are more pleasing to him than two by land. It is a new exploit for kings, but I hope God will bless him in it …'[4] The year 1677 saw another expedition to Plymouth. The royal party arrived at Portsmouth on 10 August, where the king and Duke of York inspected the new fortifications and the ships under construction in the dockyard, before sailing on to Plymouth, where they arrived on the 16th. The king inspected the Royal Citadel and dined at Mount Edgcumbe House before sailing for home on the 18th.[5] So impressed was he by the experience that he vowed to repeat the trip every other year, and it has been suggested that only the subsequent political crisis of several years' duration prevented him doing so.[6]

As well as these substantial voyages, the king and his brother regularly sailed down the Thames to Sheerness or the Nore and back, outings so frequent that they rarely attracted any comment or attention at all. Moreover, these were not decadent pleasure cruises where downtrodden mariners worked the yacht while the king dallied with his latest mistress in the stern cabin. Charles and James often took the helms themselves, taking great delight in racing each other. On 1 October 1661, the diarist John Evelyn witnessed a race between the royal siblings:

> I sailed this morning with His Majesty in one of his yachts (or pleasure boats), vessels not known among us till the Dutch East India Company [*sic*] presented that curious piece to the King, being very excellent sailing vessels. It was on a wager between his other new pleasure boat, built frigate-like, and one of the Duke of York's, the

wager £100; the race from Greenwich to Gravesend and back. The King lost it going, the wind being contrary, but saved stakes in returning. There were divers noble persons and lords on board, his Majesty sometimes steering himself. His barge and kitchen boat attended. I brake fast this morning with the King at return in his smaller vessel [*Bezan*], he being pleased to take me and only four more, who were noblemen, with him, but dined in his yacht, where we all eat together with His Majesty.[7]

'Messing about on boats' was an integral part of the macho, competitive culture of the Restoration court, along with the similarly energetic male pursuits of hunting, horse racing and fornicating.[8] So when one poet described King Charles in distinctly North Korean terms as Britain's 'great pilot', he was using the term both literally and metaphorically.[9]

Even so, the potentially history-changing implications of the royal passion for the sea were very real, even on the jaunts downriver. In July 1662, the king was caught

in a furious gale at the mouth of the Thames … the mast was broken, the sails torn, the sailors dismayed, and all in disorder he was thrown on the banks of Lie [*sic;* presumably Leigh-on-Sea in Essex] … and was obliged to stay there for several hours exposed to the fury of the waves, until the tide fell and the wind dropping, he could reach a safer place.[10]

The dangers were illustrated even more dramatically by the loss of the *Gloucester*, on 6 May 1682. This was not some tiny, fragile royal yacht, but a powerful 60-gun Third Rate man-of-war. She was carrying the Duke of York and a large party of courtiers back to Leith, where James was to retrieve his wife, left behind when their previous sojourn at Holyrood ended unexpectedly with his summons back to London. The voyage should have been routine, through one of the best known and most frequented seaways in British waters. But somehow, a catastrophic navigational error was made, and the ship struck the Lemon and Oare sandbank off Great Yarmouth.

The mistake was largely James's own fault: he seems to have taken command himself, having lost confidence in the *Gloucester*'s highly experienced pilot James Aires, and ordered a course change that proved fatal. About 130 passengers and crew were killed, including the Earl of Roxburgh, Lord Hopetoun and James's brother-in-law, James Hyde. Those who escaped included the Marquis of Montrose, Samuel Pepys (who was sailing in the escorting *Katherine Yacht*, not the *Gloucester*) and John Churchill, the future Duke of Marlborough. Above all, James, Duke of York, survived the shipwreck, albeit only just. He stayed aboard the ship until very nearly too late, and then had to climb out of one of the stern windows, with Churchill having at swordpoint to hold off the press of men trying to clamber into the duke's boat.[11] The conclusion to be drawn from all this is inescapable: the lives of Charles and James Stuart were threatened more immediately, and much more often, by the vagaries of the sea, than by the bullets and daggers of potential assassins.

Despite all of this, historians have largely written the sea, and the navy in particular, out of the stories they choose to tell about the reigns of Charles II and James II. One weighty, academic, and highly acclaimed modern study of the Restoration era makes not one reference to the navy – *not one* – in over five hundred pages of text. The same book has an index entry that would be laughable, were it not so depressing: 'Armed Forces: see Army, Militia'.[12] But it is by no means alone. References to the navy in several other modern histories of the period are as elusive as confirmed sightings of the Yeti or the Loch Ness monster; the late Professor Kevin Sharpe barely mentioned it in the lumbago-inducing 849 pages of his mighty tome on the representation and imagery of the later Stuart monarchy, even though the sorts of naval examples presented in this book would have perfectly complemented and enhanced his arguments. Even more astonishingly, several books and doctoral theses that purport to be about the so-called 'British Atlantic world', a topic very much à la mode in historical circles, convey the impression that this 'world' contained no such things as navies. This cavalier degree of omission seriously skews perceptions of seventeenth-century Britain. For most of that period, the navy was by far the largest spending department of the state, with about a third of English national revenue going towards it in a 'quiet' year like 1675 and over half in a war year like 1665;[13] its dockyards were, by a considerable distance, the largest industrial establishments in the country; and when fully mobilised, its population made it the third largest 'city' in the British Isles. Ignoring it, simply because a historian does not understand it, does not regard it as important, does not fancy getting to grips with its very large body of unfamiliar and sometimes difficult source material, or even, perhaps, does not approve of it on moral or political grounds, means that a distorted, incomplete, and ultimately inadequate picture of national history is being presented to that historian's readers.[14] Perhaps the closest modern analogy would be writing a history of modern Britain and completely omitting any mention of the National Health Service.*

* Or, as Nicholas Rodger memorably said of the even more shocking neglect of the navy by many historians of the eighteenth century, 'it must have been as difficult as writing a history of Switzerland without mentioning mountains, or writing a novel without using the letter "e"'. It is, perhaps, indicative of this state of affairs that during the last twenty years or so, the 'military and naval' section of the Institute of Historical Research in London has gradually moved, via several intermediate incarnations, from a pleasant and spacious top-floor room, with excellent views of Bloomsbury, to a gloomy, cramped and windowless corner of the basement.

Above, left: Grinling Gibbons's statue of King Charles II at the Royal Hospital, Chelsea. *(Author's photograph)*

Above, right: King James II. Cornelis van Dalen, after Simon Luttichuys. *(Rijksmuseum, Amsterdam)*

For the simple fact is that the priorities of Charles II and James II, especially the former, were not necessarily those which historians think they should have had. Eager young would-be academics, writing weighty but nearly unreadable theses about, say, obscure aspects of Parliament or religion, and then spending their careers writing weighty but nearly unreadable books and articles about, say, obscure aspects of Parliament or religion, naturally tend to assume that their own subjects are the be-all and end-all of the period, and that the Stuart kings, therefore, should have regarded them with precisely the same gravity. Charles II in particular has often been condemned by historians holding eminent tenured positions in august universities on the grounds that his work rate seems to have been vastly inferior to that which they would expect from themselves, and even from some of their more feckless undergraduates; even today, the Protestant work ethic has a lot to answer for.[15]

To be fair, though, there is plenty of reason to adopt such a critical view. For instance, Lorenzo Magalotti, an Italian traveller and thus an entirely disinterested contemporary observer, provided the damning judgement that Charles's 'fiercest enemies are diligence and business … [he] hates implacably all sorts of work, and loves with the greater enthusiasm every kind of play and diversion'.[16] Bishop Gilbert Burnet, who knew the king rather better, stated baldly that 'he hated business, and could not be easily brought to mind any'; while his pursuit of pleasure, such as going to watch the horse racing at Newmarket for extended periods twice a year, regardless of political and national circumstances, was often both hugely inconvenient to the conduct of government and crassly insensitive to the sufferings of his subjects.[17]

Such evidence made Ronald Hutton, one of the king's most recent biographers, develop such an intense dislike of his 'monumentally selfish' subject that he came to find the entire experience 'genuinely depressing'; he even hoped that his work would reveal 'a monarch so unpleasant that he could never be made a credible hero again'.[18] In so doing, Hutton, like most modern historians, comprehensively threw out the baby with the bathwater, belittling Charles's role in naval affairs as an insignificant hobby, not really something that should have been part of the CV of a respectable and serious seventeenth-century ruler.[19] (Conversely and tellingly, Tsar Peter the Great is almost unanimously praised by historians – and not just Russian ones – for having possessed very much the same level of technical knowledge of, enthusiasm for, and involvement with, his ships and fleets, as Charles II did; and few would quibble with Peter's 'CV' as a monarch, apart, perhaps, from those sections of it that involve mass executions and the torture of his own son.) Earlier historians, many of whom were more sympathetic to Charles, and who, in many cases, did give due weight to his role in naval affairs, are now hopelessly unfashionable and, in some cases, politically incorrect in spades.[20] Moreover, for almost every historian who has written about Charles during the last 150 years, their contemporary role models – conscious or subconscious – of how British monarchs should behave were, and are, conscientious to the point of workaholic, monogamous to the point of suburban, and prim to the point of cloistered: two astonishingly durable women, Victoria and Elizabeth II, and two exceptionally earnest Georges. The reigns of two hedonistic Edwards, the true heirs of Charles II, were far too brief to register on historical orthodoxy.[21]

Because British historians have invariably compared Charles almost exclusively with other British monarchs, he has, perhaps, suffered in comparison with his European contemporaries and near-contemporaries. As this book will attempt to demonstrate, not only was Charles's passion for, and commitment to the development of, his navy similar to that of Peter the Great, his concern for reputation – or, as the French might put it, *gloire* – was, at least at times, not dissimilar to that of Louis XIV. It may also be worth pointing out that while Charles has often been damned by the prurient for having a succession of mistresses and a vast brood of illegitimate children (fourteen at least), Louis XIV, *Louis le Grand, le Roi Soleil*, had virtually the same number of both. But, *naturellement*, the French have always tended to be rather more relaxed about such things.

Ultimately, then, kingship, like so many other things, is very much in the eye of the beholder.

King Charles is a notoriously difficult character to fathom: a man who intrigued, confused and infuriated contemporaries and posterity alike. The traditional one-word monikers, like 'enigma', 'libertine', and 'dissembler', do little to explain the personality of this complex, devious, remarkably self-aware man, at once the most public and most private of monarchs.[22] Even his sternest critics often had to qualify their more stinging judgements. Burnet's barbed comment about the king hating business seems damning when taken out of context, but even the critical bishop added a crucial caveat in the very same sentence: 'when it was necessary, and he was set to it, he would stay as long as his ministers had work for him', and this more nuanced assessment is particularly apposite to the king's role in naval affairs.[23] Moreover, Charles was king de facto from the age of thirty to his death at fifty-four, and as with any human being, it would be dangerous to assume that he did not change in at least some ways during the course of twenty-four years. Lorenzo Magalotti only observed the king briefly and from a distance, and inevitably compiled much of what he wrote from the court gossip he picked up. Pepys, who knew Charles much better, often bemoaned his sovereign's lack of attention to business and addiction to pleasure, but most of these comments also come from a relatively brief period in 1666/67, when the depths of the national crisis seemed to require some sort of a superman, or, failing that, a rather more dynamic and omniscient monarch, perhaps a cross between the biblical Solomon, Shakespeare's Henry V and the historical Elizabeth I. Pepys even recycled a particularly salacious piece of court gossip, to the effect that someone really needed to take the king to one side and tell him that he was the only man who could put things right, if only he would stop '[spending] his time in employing his lips and his prick about the court'.[24] But even if both Pepys and Magalotti were correct in stating that Charles was an idle hedonist in 1666, 1667 or 1668, that might not necessarily have been the case ten or twelve years later. Charles himself said in 1681, following the traumas of the Exclusion Crisis and his brush with death two years earlier, that he intended henceforward to be firmer and bolder – and the evidence of the last years of his reign strongly suggests that he was true to his word.[25] In many of his public utterances, and in his actions, the older Charles was a much more dynamic and decisive creature than his pleasure-loving younger incarnation.

It can be a surprise to modern sensibilities to learn that many contemporaries actually preferred James, Duke of York, at least before he came to the throne as James II of England and VII of Scots: inflexible and humourless he might have been, a man who saw things (notably loyalty to himself) in distinctly black-and-white terms, but people generally knew where they stood with him, at least in comparison with his brother.[26] Quite simply, James Stuart was considerably more predictable than his elder sibling. The Duke of York was a soldier first and foremost, a man with a highly developed, very nearly medieval, sense of honour, and a proven track record of tremendous personal bravery in battle, 'more himself … in the middle of a desperate service than at other times'. If some of these traits seem unfamiliar and unattractive to us now, they certainly would not have done so in the late seventeenth century, when even relatively un-martial aristocrats and gentlemen were still given essentially medieval funerals, complete with standards, helms, and gauntlets.[27] For those who remembered Charles I, and looked back fondly to the peaceful years of his reign before the Civil War, the martyr's younger son would have seemed very much more like his father than the elder. Come to that, even some of those who remembered the last religiously driven soldier to rule Britain, Oliver Cromwell, and the military and naval glories of his rule, might have found James II rather easier to comprehend than Charles II.

King Charles freely admitted that he hated writing and did as little of

Above, left: King Charles II. *(Richard Endsor collection)*

Above, right: Samuel Pepys. *(Richard Endsor collection)*

it as possible, yet for historians, written evidence is usually all they have to call upon, and thus all that matters. A historical figure who usually kept his real opinions firmly to himself, who invariably worked informally, and who depended above all on *simply talking to people,* is always likely to be underestimated: literally written out of the record because s/he inconsiderately left too few written records for historians to work with. Charles often gave purely verbal orders, to his brother in the 1660s and to Pepys in the 1670s; but the fact that he did so makes it difficult accurately to assess his role in naval affairs, and properly to assign responsibility for decisions.[28] Again, on 14 July 1673, the king spent the entire morning talking to the Earl of Anglesey 'about his affairs and intentions', but neither man actually recorded what was said.[29]

In this as in so many other ways, James II was the opposite of his brother, writing more than enough – including a partial autobiography – for history to come to the very nearly unanimous judgement that he was either stupid, or unbelievably deluded, or both.[30] Moreover, the brilliant naval administrator who served them both wrote very nearly an entire library's worth, so it is perhaps hardly surprising that historians have found comfort in the sheer vastness (and generally meticulous organisation) of Samuel Pepys's papers, so much more like their assumptions about what a serious body of work should look like – and even less surprising that, as a result, they have usually accepted unquestioningly Pepys's facts, figures, opinions and prejudices. Meanwhile, general readers and enthusiasts for the Stuart age have usually come to Pepys either by way of his diary, and are won over immediately by the likeable, ever so slightly pompous, lascivious, eternally curious, achingly (but not entirely) self-aware author; or they come first to the biographies of the man in question, most of which present their subject as a deeply sympathetic hero whose views, and outlook on life, are, on the whole, to be taken as gospel. Perhaps because of all this, Samuel Pepys occupies a unique position in Restoration England, better known, and certainly better loved, than many who were, by any definition, significantly greater than him. Consequently, it is a curious fact that there is no Isaac Newton Club, no Christopher Wren Society, no League of Admirers of the Earl of Rochester (thankfully), certainly no Charles II Society;* but there is a Samuel Pepys Club.

This is equally true when one considers the naval history of the age. Generally speaking, such epochs are usually defined by fighting men: Drake for the Elizabethan period, Nelson for – well, what can only be described as the age of Nelson. But this is emphatically not true of the seventeenth century. Outside of Bridgwater in Somerset, the birthplace of Robert Blake, it is very unlikely that any 'man in the street' anywhere in the British Isles or beyond would be able to name any admiral of the

* Fortunately, though, there is an Aphra Behn Society and a Purcell Society.

period, although one seaman who never served in the Royal Navy, Henry Morgan, might have a respectable amount of name recognition, if only among rum drinkers. Instead, and uniquely, the one name associated with the navy of the age is that of a civil servant. Over the winter of 2015/16, the National Maritime Museum in Greenwich devoted a major exhibition to Pepys, and rightly so; but one wonders how many other bureaucrats have ever been honoured in this way at major national institutions, and how long we will have to wait before the NMM (or any other national museum) devotes an exhibition to an individual sea-officer of the seventeenth century.

If Pepys had not left us the diary, it is quite likely that those very few writers, historians and interested readers who might have heard about him at all would have damned him as a fairly unsavoury specimen of Restoration degeneracy. True, within his own world, the naval administration, later generations of ink-slingers knew the scale of his achievement, and admired his legacy: in the year after Nelson's death and over a century after his own, Pepys was still remembered in the Navy Office as 'a man of extraordinary knowledge in all that related to the business of that department, of great talents, and the most indefatigable industry'.[31] And there is no doubt that Pepys is a seminally important figure in British naval history, a remarkably capable and methodical individual who did much to shape the navy of his day, and, indeed, that of centuries to come. But by his own admission, Pepys was also corrupt by the standards of his age, let alone ours: there is simply no other explanation for the increase of his personal wealth in seven and a half years from virtually nothing to £7,500, according to figures he recorded himself, at a time when his official salary was £350 a year.[32] (It is, perhaps, significant that at the end of the seven and a half years in question, he suddenly stopped recording the amounts, perhaps because he realised how embarrassing and incriminating the information was becoming.) The difference, of course, is that Pepys used the diary to justify his 'perquisites' to himself, often by relying on tortuous self-deception and outrageous double standards, and his justifications, rather than being critically challenged, have usually been accepted by posterity as yet another of his charming foibles.[33]

Pepys was also a brazen nepotist, shamelessly promoting his brother, his brother-in-law, several of his best friends, and at least one man he had cuckolded: but in Restoration England, he was hardly unique in any of that. Nor was he unique in his dogmatic partisanship, his blinkered prejudices, and his readiness to traduce his opponents by twisting and, if necessary, inventing evidence. What was different about Pepys was the sheer scale on which he operated, amassing arrays of facts and figures that battered his enemies into submission, and bringing forward every piece of salacious hearsay he could find so as to blacken the reputation of someone he disliked.[34] It is, perhaps, no surprise that in his own day he had very many more enemies than friends, and was both a difficult colleague and a self-righteous, inflexible superior.[35] Quite what sort of a subordinate he was to the two men who are the focus of this book is one of the themes which runs through the pages that follow.

In order to place the naval activities of Charles II and James II in proper context, this book examines the entire history of the Stuart family's interest in the sea, both before and after the two reigns in question. Such a study reveals that the royal brothers' deep and genuine interest in their navy did not emerge out of thin air, and was not unique to them; several previous Stewart and Stuart monarchs, including their father, King Charles I, had been strongly committed to their navies. Moreover, the connection between the senior line of the Stuart dynasty and naval warfare did not end with the downfall of James II in 1688/89. Every Jacobite attempt to effect a restoration to the lost thrones, up to and including the very final one in 1759 (not 1745, as many wrongly assume), had a significant naval element to it, and the princes remembered by posterity as 'the Old and Young Pretenders' presided over what might be termed a virtually unknown 'shadow navy' in exile.

1

The Stuarts and the Sea I:
The Inheritance

IT IS, PERHAPS, A SURPRISE to realise that of all Britain's royal dynasties, the one that most truly had the sea in its blood was the much-maligned House of Stuart.

The Plantagenets were landlubbers to a man. Shakespeare's John of Gaunt might have extolled 'this sceptred isle … this precious stone set in a silver sea', but his real-life counterpart's principal castle was at Hertford. Gaunt's famous grandson, King Henry V, was born in Monmouth, and probably grew up even further from the sea (although he was subsequently responsible for what is commonly regarded as the first ever fleet review, in 1415). The House of York had its power bases at Fotheringhay in Northamptonshire, and in inland Yorkshire. True, the Tudors originally came from an island, namely Anglesey, and Henry VII grew up in sea-girt Pembroke Castle; but Henry VIII and Elizabeth I grew up and lived in and around London, with their royal progresses invariably taking them inland, very rarely to the coast, for all Henry's avowed enthusiasm for his navy. As their names suggest, the Houses of Hanover and Saxe-Coburg-Gotha originated in continental Europe, far from the ocean. Although King William IV had impeccable naval credentials – to the extent of having served with Horatio Nelson – his family did not truly take the sea to their hearts until Queen Victoria built Osborne House, with its uninterrupted view over the Solent, and sent, first, her second son, and later her two senior grandsons, into the Royal Navy. They were followed in their turn by various members of the incumbent House of Mountbatten-Windsor, as the amount of naval dress rig sported by members of the Royal Family during state occasions still reminds us.

But from its earliest days as the royal house of Scotland, and even before, the Stewart dynasty was shaped by the sea. Getting to or from Rothesay Castle on the Isle of Bute, the family's principal seat from the time of Alan, High Steward of the kingdom (died 1204) until the reign of King Robert III (1390–1406), entailed a sea voyage, as it still does.[1] Dundonald Castle, built by King Robert II (1371–90) as his favourite residence, is so close to the Ayrshire coast that it would have been possible

Rothesay Castle, Isle of Bute, the principal seat of the Stewart dynasty. *(Author's photograph)*

to see the Isle of Arran from the tops of its towers. Maritime affairs were a constant in the Stewart family's policy-making. Many of the family's personal lands were in coastal regions, and as monarchs they had to come to a modus vivendi with – or take measures against – the Macdonalds, Lords of the Isles, who, from Finlaggan on Islay, ruled a huge, semi-independent seaborne state, controlled by means of formidable galley fleets that could penetrate up the sea-lochs of the west coast of Scotland. While fifteenth-century English monarchs aspired to hold or regain vast tracts of continental France, their Scots counterparts looked for their only feasible territorial gains towards offshore islands, either those held by the Lords of the Isles and other semi-independent island chieftains, or else the Orkney and Shetland archipelagos, ruled by the Scandinavian kings of the Kalmar Union until their acquisition by Scotland in 1468/69 as part of the marriage dowry of King James III's bride. The Stewart kings also maintained an intermittent naval presence in the west and the Irish Sea, where they were able to compete on more equal terms with the English; this enabled interventions in Ireland during the first decades of the fourteenth century, and in the second Welsh War of Independence from 1400 to 1416.[2] Thus geography and political circumstances dictated that the Stewarts had to have a sound knowledge of, and a real interest in, maritime and naval affairs.[3]

The sea and naval warfare played particularly important parts in the life and reign of King James IV, who succeeded to the throne in 1488 at the age of seventeen. In 1493–95, he personally led three naval campaigns in the west, culminating in the final defeat of the last independent Lord of the Isles, and also established a naval base at Dumbarton.[4] In later years, James went to sea quite often, sometimes for short cruises to the Isle of May or up the Forth (where he established further new bases at Newhaven and Pol of Erth). In February 1506, he spent several days aboard his large new ship, *Margaret*, mingling with the crew and dining in state in the great cabin, with his silver service and two tapestries being brought aboard for the purpose; a boating tournament, with sailors 'jousting' in small craft, was laid on for his entertainment.[5] In 1502, he hired a fleet of privately owned vessels to transport Scots troops to the Baltic, thereby fulfilling his treaty obligations to the Danes. This method of raising a fleet proved less than successful, and James reacted by starting to build up a purpose-built royal fleet on the east coast. The most remarkable unit of this was the *Michael*, begun at Newhaven in 1506 and launched in 1511. There has been a great deal of myth-making about this huge ship, not the least being the notion that the best proof of her dimensions was a hawthorn hedge designed to correspond to the exact size and shape of her hull, supposedly planted by Sir William Murray of Tullibardine.[6] Even so, it is clear that she was of roughly 1,000 tons, mounted twenty-seven large cannon, and cost approximately an entire year of the King of Scots' income, making her colossal by European standards, let alone those of Scottish waters. She formed the centrepiece of a powerful fleet that consisted of thirty-eight ships by 1513, of which fifteen were true warships. This force conducted operations in Irish waters and the English Channel during James IV's brief and fateful war against his brother-in-law, Henry VIII of England, but the ships had to return to Scotland abruptly after the defeat and death of the king at the Battle of Flodden.

Model of the great Scots warship the *Michael*, Burntisland Church, Fife. *(Kim Traynor; Wikimedia Commons under Creative Commons Attribution)*

The strong interest of Scottish monarchs in naval matters was maintained during the reign of James V, who succeeded as an infant after his
father's untimely demise, and reigned as an adult from 1528 to 1542.
James embarked on several major sea voyages that were substantially
longer than anything ever undertaken by his much more famous uncle,
Henry VIII of England. In July 1536, he sailed north from Fife, went
through the Pentland Firth, and then proceeded down the west coast to
Whithorn. The purpose of this expedition is unclear, but on 1
September, when he sailed again from Kirkcaldy, he was bound for
France, reaching Dieppe eight days later. He stayed at the French court
until May, when he returned home with a new queen, the ethereally
beautiful but terminally consumptive Madeleine de Valois, and two new
warships, gifted to him by Francis I.[7] Of these, *Salamander* became his
flagship, and undertook several more voyages to France with other units
of 'this rejuvenated Scottish navy'.[8] In the years that followed, James
embarked on a significant programme of galley construction, and in 1540
he undertook another major voyage to the north and west, sailing from
Fife to Orkney, then down to Lewis, Skye, and finally to Dumbarton. In
part, at least, this was a 'showing the flag' expedition intended to overawe
the clan chiefs, who were suitably cowed. The royal flagship was elaborately decorated, and James himself sported a gold whistle, the traditional
symbol of naval command.[9] He also commissioned the first 'rutter' (navigational manual) of Scottish waters, built or otherwise acquired a number
of new warships, and ordered the construction of a new harbour at
Burntisland in Fife, defended by three blockhouses apparently intended
both as part of a broader scheme to defend the Firth of Forth from
English attack, and as one example of the significant investment that
James made in artillery and fortifications throughout his kingdom.[10] The
king's death in 1542 at the age of only thirty, like that of his father nearly
thirty years earlier, put an abrupt halt to the nascent development of what
might have become an impressive and effective Scots navy. As it was, most
of the surviving ships were destroyed during English attacks in the Forth
in 1547, and for the rest of the sixteenth century, the Stuart monarchs
relied almost exclusively on privateers to provide their naval forces.

At first sight, King James VI, who succeeded as James I of England in
1603, might seem to be one of the least nautical monarchs ever to sit on
a British throne, and, indeed, he showed little interest in naval affairs
during his purely Scottish reign. In this, as in so little else, he followed the
example of his mother, Mary, Queen of Scots, whose only significant
intervention in naval matters was the outright prohibition, in 1561, of all

Scots privateering operations.[11] James was content to leave all such matters in the hands of his Lord High Admiral, which in Scotland was a hereditary office. Throughout the 1580s – in other words, at a critical period of naval crisis, culminating in the Spanish Armada's circumnavigation of the British coast – this office was in the hands of the king's erratic cousin Francis Stewart, Earl of Bothwell, who was at various times accused of murder, piracy, treason and witchcraft.[12] Three times James promised to emulate his grandfather and great-grandfather by undertaking a maritime circumnavigation of his kingdom, and three times he failed to keep his word.[13] But James was not a complete ignoramus when it came to the sea and naval warfare. His voyages to and from Oslo in 1589/90 to claim his bride, Anna of Denmark, can be set alongside the voyages of his grandfather James V as some of the longest transits by sea undertaken by an occupant of a British throne since the early Middle Ages. Possibly uniquely among the pantheon of monarchs, James even wrote an epic poem about a sea battle: *The Lepanto*. Over one thousand lines long, this remarkable work, penned in about 1585 and published in 1591, displays a surprisingly ambiguous attitude to violence, and quite a reasonable grasp of what a sea battle was actually like.[14] Moreover, James, invariably labelled charitably as a peacemaker (his own preferred description of himself) and less charitably as a downright coward, led armies into armed combat six times – which might well be more often than any English monarch since the Wars of the Roses.[15]

King James's reign in England, from 1603 to 1625, has always been seen as a dark age in the history of the Royal Navy, and the weight of evidence that can be produced to support this point of view is certainly compelling. Corruption was endemic, as two major commissions of enquiry, in 1608 and 1618, demonstrated; but the very fact that there were two demonstrates that the problem proved intractable. Offices were sold, and phenomenal amounts of money were paid for non-existent ships.[16] Not only did James not deal decisively with the problem, he arguably exacerbated it: the 1608 enquiry was hamstrung by his refusal to allow attacks on his personal favourites, and ended with James ineffectually lecturing his naval administrators to do better in future, an admonishment that they naturally and comprehensively ignored.[17] The operational navy was very small for much of James's reign: four ships and perhaps two pinnaces patrolling the English Channel was the norm for much of the time.[18] However, unfavourable comparisons between the Elizabethan and Jacobean navies are misleading and, up to a point, unfair. The latter was very much the usual size for a peacetime service, and undertook the traditional peacetime duties; the comparison is skewed because of the overwhelming focus of English naval historical writing (and, one might add, of fiction and feature films) on the colossal war

King James I of
England, VI of Scots.
Miniature by
Nicholas Hilliard.
*(Rijksmuseum,
Amsterdam)*

during the last eighteen years of Elizabeth's reign, on the larger-than-life figures who fought in it, and on the great things they did.[19] In that sense, the Jacobean navy has suffered from the same problems of perception and neglect that beset the Royal Navy of the 1920s and the late 1940s: a substantial force doing important things, but very few people know much about it, preferring instead to focus on the rather more exciting periods immediately beforehand.

If King James's personal interest in the navy was limited at best, the same certainly could not be said of his eldest son, Henry, Prince of Wales, who developed a passionate interest in the sea and ships. It is possible that this can be dated precisely to 6 March 1604, when he was presented with a small ship of his own by the Lord High Admiral of England, the Earl of Nottingham – who, as Lord Howard of Effingham, had commanded the fleet that defeated the Spanish Armada.* Designed by Phineas Pett and built at Chatham Dockyard, the 28ft-long vessel was 'launched … with a noise of trumpets, drums, and such like ceremonies'. Not surprisingly, the gift was greeted by the ten-year-old prince 'with great delight', and he personally named it *Disdain*.[20] Three years later, Pett gave him a model ship, cementing a relationship that would endure until Henry's death; indeed, Henry's blind loyalty to Pett probably saved the latter from censure during the 1609 enquiry into corruption in the navy. Above all, Pett was responsible for building the *Prince Royal*, a colossal new ship begun in

* However, it is possible that Henry's interest in the sea was already known by this time, and that the present was thus a response, not a catalyst. A painting of the young prince in his Garter robes, made by Robert Peake in the same year and now displayed in the National Portrait Gallery of Scotland, shows a ship within the elaborate jewel in his hat; Henry had been admitted to the order in July 1603.

1608 and launched early in the morning of 25 September 1610, following a failed attempt to launch it during the previous day, when the king had been present.[21] Named after himself by the prince, it was adorned with elaborate gilding and painting that cost some £868, and contained a cabin for Henry, 'very curiously wrought with divers histories'.[22]

The prince took an active part in naval reform. He regularly inspected the ships and dockyards, carefully scrutinising the strengths and weaknesses of the former, and promoted voyages of exploration, seeing a forward maritime policy as a way of promoting the idea of an aggressively Protestant, crusading, expansionist, 'British Empire'.[23] This was reflected in court culture: the masque to celebrate his investiture as Prince of Wales in June 1610 was full of triumphalist nautical imagery, casting the prince as Meliadus, Lord of the Isles, who would eventually reign as 'Henry IX', when:

> He like great Neptune on three seas shall rove,
> And rule three realms, with triple power, like Jove.[24]

Henry, Prince of Wales. (*National Library of Scotland*)

Similarly, the tilt armour created for the prince in about 1607 featured 'mermen blowing conches, fighting tops of ships, darts, anchors, oars and tridents', with a substantial figure of Neptune at the top of the breast-plate.[25] Henry was supposed to have got the king's agreement that he would replace the ancient and corrupt Nottingham as Lord High Admiral, but the prince's premature death on 6 November 1612, aged eighteen, put paid to these ambitions.[26]

Meanwhile, and despite being much less interested or involved than his son, King James did not neglect naval affairs completely. After all, the navy was one of the largest and most obvious expressions of his regal authority, a kind of floating expression of 'the divine right of kings'. He named ships, and attended launches: indeed, he expressed his support for English overseas expansion and the newly founded (1600) East India Company by attending the launch of at least two merchantmen, the *Trade's Increase* and *Peppercorn*, in 1610.[27] Thanks to James, the navy gained its first *St George* – an obvious nod to the sensibilities of his adopted kingdom – as well as a matching *St Andrew*, suggesting that, even in 1622, James's dreams of a 'united kingdom' had not vanished altogether. With his peace policy stuttering by that time, and Europe consumed by warfare, James also brought back the great Elizabethan names *Swiftsure*, *Triumph* and *Victory*, perhaps to remind Englishmen of past glories and to remind foreigners of what an English navy could do. And although it did rela-tively little during James's reign, apart from mundane patrol duties, some of its actions were of considerable importance; in particular, piracy conducted by English and Scots ships in each other's waters was success-fully suppressed.[28] There were some impressive set-piece voyages, too, to remind other European princes that English seapower was not quite a thing of the past. In 1613, for example, the giant new ship, the *Prince Royal*, was employed to transport the newly married Elector Frederick V of the Palatinate and his bride, King James's daughter Elizabeth, from Margate to Vlissingen, a voyage that was immortalised in several substan-tial works of art. Above all, in 1620 a squadron commanded by Sir Robert Mansel sailed as far as Algiers, the headquarters of many of the 'Barbary corsairs' whose depredations in British waters were becoming increasingly frequent and damaging. This was the first British naval inter-vention in the Mediterranean, beginning a history of engagement with the North African coast that continues to the present.

The navy's situation improved markedly after 1619, when the king's favourite, George Villiers, Duke of Buckingham, was installed as Lord High Admiral. His appointment, nearly concurrent with the 1618 commission of enquiry into naval corruption, coincided with a new imperative in the British kingdoms' international relations: what would become known as the Thirty Years War began in the same year, prompted by the election of James's son-in-law Frederick of the Palatinate to the throne of Bohemia. His subsequent overthrow, and the enforced flight into exile of James's daughter and grandchildren, gave the king a pressing and deeply personal reason to increase England's naval strength, especially after Spain, which actively supported Frederick's enemies, resumed its war with the Dutch in 1621. Two new ships, the *Reformation* and *Happy Entrance* – their names reflecting the new direction in naval policy – were launched by James in November 1619, followed by two more every year until 1623, which, together with repairs to older vessels, increased the number of serviceable ships from twenty-three in 1618 to thirty-five in 1623.[29] Indeed, and counter-intuitively, the navy at the end of James I's reign was significantly larger and more powerful than it had been at the end of Elizabeth I's. This led the veteran Secretary of State, Sir John Coke,

George Villiers, Duke of Buckingham, Lord High Admiral of England, 1619–28. *(New York Public Library)*

to claim that it was then 'much better than ever it was in my memory and exceeded the navies of former times'; Coke's memory would have gone back to his childhood in the 1570s, supposedly the beginning of the great age of Elizabethan naval primacy.[30]

As well as expanding the fleet, Buckingham and the commissioners serving under him made a number of changes that have shaped the navy ever since, such as the introduction of centrally appointed surgeons and chaplains aboard all major ships.[31] It is unclear whether the king had any personal input into these innovations, but it is unlikely that they could have proceeded without royal approval; the appointment of chaplains, in particular, was bound to have been a matter of interest for a Supreme Governor of the Church of England who prided himself on his theological skill.

The reforms made to the royal dockyards during Buckingham's admiralty, and in James's reign as a whole, were particularly important. Deptford and Woolwich took on the approximate shapes and sizes that they would retain until their closures in 1869. Two mast docks, new wharves, a rope-house, storehouses, officers' houses, a double dock and a single dock were built at Chatham between 1619 and 1623; the Medway yard, previously used simply as an anchorage, now became the navy's principal repair facility.[32] Chatham and Portsmouth were expanded beyond recognition in the eighteenth, and then again in the late-nineteenth, centuries; but it was in the old single dock at the former, excavated in 1623 and personally inspected by King James as soon as it was ready, that the keel of HMS *Victory* was laid on 23 August 1759, and from which she was launched on 7 May 1765.[33] In the dockyards, getting right the times when work began and finished – and, crucially, the timings of the breakfast and dinner (ie, lunch) breaks – were essential to good labour relations, and thus to the smooth running of what were far and away the largest industrial facilities in seventeenth-century England. The concepts of 'double time' and 'time and a half', for extra shifts worked at unsociable times, stem from the practice first adopted in seventeenth-century dockyards. Consequently, knowing the precise start and end times of work periods became essential for both employers and employees alike. Thus the royal dockyards became the first workplaces to have publicly visible clocks, placed prominently in towers that could be seen from almost anywhere in the yard. Medieval abbeys worked to the inexorable passage of the monastic hours; Stuart dockyards, and all workplaces ever since, to a centralised display of time. In this sense, the tyranny of 'clocking in and out', and, indeed, the very concept of the '9 to 5' itself, can be traced back directly to the royal dockyards of King James I.

2

———✦✦———

Civil War and Restoration

O N 25 SEPTEMBER 1637, King Charles I went to Woolwich to launch a great new ship for his navy. The vessel was a veritable leviathan: 167ft long on her lower gun deck, she would have a gross tonnage of over 1,500 tons. In operational service in later years, her draught of 23ft was more than that of any other royal ship. Fifty years after launching, her maximum complement of 815 men would still be the largest of any British man-of-war.[1] She would be the first English warship ever to mount over one hundred guns, the king having given personal direction for her armament to be increased from the originally proposed ninety.[2] Her decoration was as extraordinary as her size. The figurehead was of the Saxon King Edgar riding a galloping charger, trampling seven prostrate lesser kings. According to legend, these had rowed Edgar upon the River Dee, one of the acts by which he asserted his sovereignty over the 'four British seas' – a legal claim which had particular currency in the 1630s, when the king was keen to revive the rights supposedly handed down to him from time immemorial.* The ship's beak was adorned with the greyhounds of Henry VII, the dragon of Wales, the thistle and unicorn of Scotland, the rose and lion of England, the harp of Ireland, the lily of France (for Charles's titles still included that of King of France), the Tudor portcullis, the Prince of Wales's feathers, and the royal monograms CR and HM, for *Carolus Rex* and Henrietta Maria.[3]

The ship's sides bore another extraordinary variety of symbols. There were military objects galore, including representations of weapons and armour of all periods. The uppermost frieze contained the signs of the zodiac, alternating with the royal initials and busts of Roman emperors, surrounded by wreaths of foliage. Jupiter, Mars and Neptune appeared in several places on the hull. The stern was adorned with many sculptures and Latin inscriptions, the most prominent of which was *Qui mare, qui fluetus, ventos, navesque gubernat, Sospitet hanc arcem, Carole Magne, tuam* ('May He whom the seas and tides obey and the winds that blow and the ships Guard this, Great Charles, thy man-of-war with sustenance Divine'). The taffrail had a huge representation of Victory; above it was the ship's vast lantern, so large that, in January 1661, Pepys and eight others could squeeze inside it.[4] Other classical and royal symbols covered

* See Chapter 8.

most of the hull. What might have been Charles himself appeared as a classical hero, surrounded by the symbols of his kingdoms, including the triple feathers of his eldest son, the Prince of Wales. The monster ship cost some £65,000: no other British warship would cost as much, in either relative or absolute terms, for well over a century.[5]

Immense in all ways, the great ship was immensely controversial, too. Her construction had been funded largely by the levying of 'ship money', traditionally a form of tax levied on coastal communities to support maritime defence. But with Parliament not sitting after 1629, and the king determined to rule without it indefinitely if he could, ship money was extended to the entire country in 1635. Despite the fact that the money had, in fact, been used to send out a series of powerful fleets, it was increasingly perceived by Charles's many critics as a credible, and thus exceptionally dangerous, substitute for parliamentary taxation. Consequently, the launch of the colossus at Woolwich was hugely symbolic on many levels. Unfortunately for Charles, the launch became symbolic in other ways that he had certainly not intended. The September date was of the king's own choosing, and ran counter to all the advice he had received from the so-called experts, who argued in favour of February. 'I am not of your opinion,' Charles replied peremptorily, and gave orders for the event to go ahead on his preferred date.[6] But the launch was botched, with the flood on the king's chosen spring tide proving too shallow to accommodate the vast hull. Rather than the spectacular public ritual and royal christening intended for the great ship, she was launched with almost no ceremony, and in darkness, during the night of 13/14 October. The naming ceremony was performed by Sir Robert Mansel, to whom the king had confided the name.[7] Although once a successful fighting admiral, Mansel's rather more contemporary reputation was as an unpopular courtier who had been an astonishingly corrupt treasurer of the navy under James I, and who now held the lucrative (and blatantly exploited) monopoly on the manufacture of glass. So in many ways, the story of the launch of the new ship encapsulated several of the issues and tensions that would come to a head five years later, with the outbreak of civil war between the king and Parliament. Unsurprisingly, a number of historians identify the great ship itself as one of the causes of that war, its name, like its sheer size and astonishing decoration, epitomising the arrogant ambitions of an out-of-touch monarch: the *Sovereign of the Seas*.

The man responsible for the vast vessel, the aloof and fastidious King Charles I, might not seem a natural sailor, nor even a natural armchair

Filius sic Magni est Jacobi, hac filia Magni Henrici, soboles die (mihi quahs erit?)

A.V. DYCK PINXIT.   CUM PRIVIL. REGIS.   R.V. VOERST SCULP. LON. 1634.

King Charles I and Queen Henrietta Maria in 1634. Engraving after an original by Sir Anthony van Dyck. (*Rijksmuseum, Amsterdam*)

admiral. In fact, though, his passion for the navy rivalled that of his elder brother and his sons, and some of his exploits at sea bordered on the staggeringly reckless. In 1623, for example, the prince was returning from his extraordinary (and spectacularly unsuccessful) incognito mission to try and woo the King of Spain's daughter, and went to Santander to join the squadron that his father King James had sent to fetch him back. Charles was being rowed out in a pinnace to the flagship, lying three miles offshore to be out of range of Spanish guns, when a sudden storm threatened to blow his boat out to sea; the heir to the throne's life was saved by a whisker.[8] Undaunted, later in the same voyage, Charles insisted on casting off in rough seas at one in the morning for a five-day visit to the Isles of Scilly, contrary to the advice of all the expert seamen and the local pilots.[9]

When he ascended the throne, Charles I often visited his ships and fleets, particularly during the preparations for major expeditions. Indeed, his first public appearance as king, following his accession in March 1625, was a visit to his ships at Blackwall, and less than three months later, he sailed to France in the *Prince* to bring back his new wife, experiencing 'a great storm' which killed one of the crew.[10] In June 1627, Charles went

The return of
Charles, Prince of
Wales, from Spain in
1623, aboard the great
ship the *Prince*,
launched in 1610.
*(© National Maritime
Museum, Greenwich,
London, BHC0710)*

to Portsmouth to encourage the speedier fitting out of the fleet for a
campaign against France, visiting the *Victory, Rainbow, Warspite, Repulse*
and *Vanguard*. He dined aboard the *Triumph*, where he interrogated her
captain about the ship's sailing qualities.[11] In August and September 1628,
he went down to the Duke of Buckingham's fleet at Spithead as it
prepared to sail again for La Rochelle, and was aboard his ships every day
for a week.[12] Naval reform was close to his heart. He first became seriously involved in naval affairs in tandem with Buckingham, and as long
as the duke lived, Charles was content to delegate all naval policy,
including even strategy, to him.[13] But Buckingham's murder in 1628,
followed closely by the dissolution of Parliament in 1629, prompted the
king to take a more direct role in naval affairs. He actively promoted
further reform, notably significant changes to the Navy Board.[14] Four
very large new ships were ordered in 1631, and in the same year the king
undertook a tour of inspection of his ships and dockyards, apparently
visiting every one of the former and touring them thoroughly.[15] He
often attended ship launches, such as those of the new *Vanguard* in 1631,
the *Charles* and the *Henrietta Maria* in 1633, and the *Leopard* in 1635.[16]
Following the failed launch of the *Sovereign of the Seas* in September
1637, the king and queen dined aboard her on 6 May 1638, and Charles
was back aboard her on 12 July, this time to check on her seakeeping
qualities.[17]

Although Charles attended very few meetings of the Admiralty
commission that succeeded Buckingham, he was present for a number of
particularly important discussions. The king took on personal responsibility for the appointment of admirals and captains, often using his own
judgement to reject Admiralty recommendations; in 1629, for example,
he chose John Pennington to command a squadron blockading the Elbe,
even though his name had not been on a shortlist submitted by the

Admiralty.[18] Charles also decided the number of ships to deploy at sea, and on their individual identities. Even after the Earl of Northumberland became Lord High Admiral de facto in 1637, the king continued to issue operational orders and read many of the despatches nominally sent to the earl.[19] The launch of the *Sovereign*, and the decision to increase her arma-ment, were not the only occasions when Charles overrode the advice of experts and intervened directly in ship design and construction: in 1634,

Peter Pett and the stern of the *Sovereign of the Seas*.
(© *National Maritime Museum, Greenwich, London, BHC2949*)

for instance, he ordered that the new ships *Leopard* and *Swallow* should
have their gunports 8ft apart, thereby going against his admirals, who
argued that 9ft was the bare minimum.[20]

When the *Sovereign of the Seas* was launched, Charles, Prince of Wales, was
seven years old; his younger brother James, Duke of York and Albany, just
four. Like their almost exact contemporary, Samuel Pepys, they probably
grew up hearing their elders regale them with the legends of Elizabethan
naval triumphs.[21] Unlike Pepys, though, they might well have learned of
mythic events like the battle against the Spanish Armada and the Cadiz
raid of 1596 from actual participants. The Earl of Mulgrave, who had
commanded a ship against the Armada, lived on until 1646, but he was a
committed Parliamentarian, so his contact with the young princes, if any,
was probably minimal. But the boys, especially the elder, Charles, would
certainly have known at least some of his father's most senior naval
commanders, Sir Robert Mansel, Sir William Monson, Sir Henry
Mainwaring, Sir John Pennington and the Earl of Lindsey, several of
whom had served under such legends of Elizabeth's wars as Drake,
Cumberland, Essex and Raleigh; Mainwaring, for instance, was with
Charles when he went to Scilly and Jersey in 1646, and was given
nominal command of a warship by the prince two years later.[22] Both
Charles and James would undoubtedly have known the rather younger
nautical adventurer and polymath Sir Kenelm Digby, a Catholic who was
a confidential aide of their mother, Queen Henrietta Maria, so it is probable that he regaled them with accounts of his astonishing semi-piratical
cruise in the Mediterranean in 1627/28.[23]

In addition to encountering these living, breathing links to the sea, and
to past naval glories, the young boys were swiftly made aware of the
maritime world. At the age of four, Prince Charles was presented by the
shipbuilder Phineas Pett with a model ship, 'completely rigged and gilded
and placed upon a carriage with wheels resembling the sea', which the
boy greeted 'with a great deal of joy'.[24] In March of the following year,
the four-year-old James was named Lord High Admiral, although his age
meant that the post was held pro tem by the Earl of Northumberland.
Quite how much of the previous nautical heritage and naval pedigree of
the House of Stuart was known to the young Charles and James is a
moot point. But there is no reason why they would not have known it,
and a strong likelihood that they did. Pepys certainly knew the story of
James IV's great ships, and of the published journal of James V's voyage
around Scotland, so it would have been remarkable if the kings he served
did not share the same knowledge.[25] And, of course, both Charles and

James undoubtedly also saw themselves as the successors of Gloriana, Elizabeth I. This made them the custodians of one of the most powerful 'creation myths' of English naval success, the legacy of the desperate fight against the 'invincible' Spanish Armada: in later years, they would be reminded of the fact every time they sat in the House of Lords, the walls of which were adorned by a famous set of tapestries commemorating the battle.* By the time of the Restoration, this legacy had been reinforced (somewhat inconveniently) by the successes of the Commonwealth's navy, part of which consisted of keeping the Stuart brothers firmly ensconced in exile following the defeat of their cause during the British civil wars. These ambiguities played out shortly after the Restoration, when Charles ordered the exhumation of the republic's greatest admiral, Robert Blake, from the tomb in Westminster Abbey where he had been interred after a spectacular state funeral in 1657. Under the new dispensation, Blake's remains were dumped unceremoniously in a communal grave pit, an action which rendered at least one Victorian writer apoplectic:

> But what tongue or pen shall dare to defend the dastard spite, that dragged the courageous and honest Blake from his grave with ignominy? One of the bravest of the brave ... might surely have been allowed a quiet grave in the old abbey of Westminster; a few yards of honoured space in the country he had helped to save for a debauched and unprincipled King.[26]

But the 'debauched and unprincipled King' in question gave high command, knighthoods, and even peerages, to most of Blake's senior subordinates, and kept on many of his captains, too. The naval legacies inherited by the Stuart brothers were, indeed, many and complex.

In 1642, though, the whole question of what inheritance, if any, would eventually come to Charles and James was thrown into the melting pot. Charles (and possibly James) was at Nottingham on 22 August 1642, when his father raised his standard to mark the formal outbreak of civil war against his Parliament. The fleet on which the king had lavished so much care and money was already lost to him. A tussle over the appointment of an admiral to command the fleet set out in 1642 was won by Parliament, whose choice, the Earl of Warwick, was able to purge Royalist captains and secure the loyalty of crews who were in any case already inclined toward the Parliamentarian cause. Thereafter, Parliament's control of the sea proved vital to its success during the first Civil War. Beleaguered ports and garrisons could be supplied and relieved from the sea, Royalist ports and garrisons could be blockaded, potential foreign aid to the king was prevented, and above all, the port of London

* Charles II regularly attended debates in the Lords from 1669 onwards, establishing a precedent not followed by his successors.

was kept free of hostile blockade, thereby ensuring that the revenues of trade flowed into Parliament's coffers. Conversely, Royalist privateers operated from bases in the West Country, Ireland and the Channel Islands, but the Stuarts themselves had little direct contact with any of the small, scattered naval forces engaged on their behalf. In 1645/46, though, the Prince of Wales was given command of Royalist forces in the west, based overwhelmingly in Devon and Cornwall, and might well have learned lessons about naval strategy during that time. Indeed, he learned at first hand about the stranglehold that a naval blockade could impose: Dartmouth, the principal operating base in Great Britain for Royalist warships, was forced to surrender in January 1646, and in March, Charles and his council escaped to the Scilly Islands from Falmouth, the last major port in Royalist hands.

On 16 April 1646, the prince arrived at his next destination, Jersey, where he would remain until 25 June. This ten-week sojourn proved to be the making of Charles Stuart as a seaman. One of his mentors was the Royalist naval captain Baldwin Wake, who commanded the ship that brought him from Scilly. Wake was knighted at Elizabeth Castle, the temporary royal 'palace', on 24 April, perhaps partly because he had allowed the Prince of Wales to steer the frigate *Proud Black Eagle*, in which they sailed from Scilly, with Charles taking the helm for a couple of hours at a time. On arrival in Jersey, he issued orders for a pinnace to be built for him at St Malo, and this arrived on 8 June; but although he ordered it, he lacked the resources to pay for it, so the money was put up by the local squire, Royalist naval captain and future colleague of Samuel Pepys, Sir George Carteret, whom the prince created a knight and baronet. Fitted with twelve pairs of oars and a couple of masts, the vessel proved greatly to the young prince's liking, and he often took to the water, invariably taking the helm himself.[27] Another Royalist captain, George Bowden of Falmouth (who had defected from the Parliamentarian fleet), seems to have played a leading part in teaching Charles how to sail her.[28]

While the Prince of Wales was learning to sail, his father's cause was collapsing. The king's final defeat and surrender in 1646 (some three weeks before his son's pinnace arrived in Jersey) led to two years of tortuous, unsuccessful negotiations and increasing divisions among the victors, culminating in the outbreak of a second Civil War in the spring of 1648. The navy, which had been relatively united in Parliament's cause since 1642, was riven by both many of the discontents apparent on land and others that were specific to the seamen. In June 1648, ten warships defected to the Royalists, sailing from the Thames to the Dutch anchorage at Hellevoetsluis. The fourteen-year-old Duke of York, who had made a daring escape from house arrest at Saint James's Palace just two months earlier, hurried there from The Hague, and attempted to take command by virtue of his nominal status as Lord High Admiral. Unfortunately, his brother the Prince of Wales did not see things in the same way: it was clear to Charles that James did not have the natural authority or experience to command.[29] Instead, the Prince of Wales himself took charge of his new fleet and took it to sea, entering the Thames estuary on 29 August. The prince displayed reckless, almost manic, courage, cheerfully waving a pistol and refusing all requests to go below to greater safety.[30] But the Royalist fleet narrowly avoided being trapped between two Parliamentarian squadrons, and Charles, realising that he had no other realistic options, ordered withdrawal back to

The *Royal Escape*, formerly the *Success*, the vessel in which Charles II escaped from England in 1651. *(© National Maritime Museum, Greenwich, London, BHC3600)*

Hellevoetsluis. The failure of the second Civil War (the main Royalist field army was defeated at Preston on 17–19 August) and the increasing threat to King Charles's prospects of political or, indeed, personal survival, made it too dangerous for the Prince of Wales to remain in command at sea, so in late October, he commissioned his cousin Prince Rupert in his stead.[31] Born in Prague Castle during his parents' brief tenure as King and Queen of Bohemia, Rupert of the Rhine, as he was invariably known, was now nearly thirty. He might have been a Wittelsbach from his father's line, and a prince of the Rhine Palatinate, but he was also very much a Stuart: his name was simply a German rendering of Robert, the name of three Scottish kings (including the legendary Bruce) and of his uncle the Duke of Kintyre, the short-lived brother of the 'Winter Queen', King Charles I and Henry, Prince of Wales. A veteran of the Thirty Years War in Europe, Rupert had commanded Royalist armies to both glorious victories and terrible defeats during the civil wars. Previous experience at sea was the only credential for command of a fleet that Rupert lacked, but with competent officers under him, that hardly mattered. Arguably more significant

Prince Rupert of the Rhine (1619–82), admiral of the Royalist fleet 1648–53, joint commander of the fleet in 1666 and sole commander in 1673. *(Rijksmuseum, Amsterdam)*

was the fact that the Prince of Wales now authorised him to fly the royal standard, something that only a king had previously done; this was one of several actions taken by Charles in 1646–49, all of them in a naval context, in which he first exercised the full powers of the royal prerogative, traditionally reserved to the anointed monarch alone, even though his father still lived.[32]

On 30 January 1649, though, Charles I was beheaded at Whitehall, and shortly afterwards, the monarchy was abolished. Both the king's 'martyrdom' and the subsequent restoration of his son were marked by the Royal Navy for many years, with commemorative gun salutes still being fired by warships until well into the 1750s.[33] In the shorter term, Charles and James had to face the prospect of an indeterminate period of exile, punctuated by diplomatic or military efforts to regain their lost thrones. Meanwhile, in England, the new government, centred on the so-called Rump Parliament, began an unprecedented naval expansion that dwarfed in scale both Charles I's building programme and that undertaken by the Duke of Buckingham earlier in the century. Between 1649 and 1651, twenty new ships of the Third, Fourth and Fifth rates were built, and another thirty were approved in September 1652. In all, between 1649 and 1660, the Commonwealth regimes added over two hundred ships to the navy.[34] Attempts were made to expunge the fact that this had ever been a 'royal navy'. The *Prince Royal* of 1610 was renamed *Resolution*, and attempts were made to rechristen the *Sovereign of the Seas* as the *Commonwealth*, but the latter name never stuck; even under a republic, the name and already mythic (if completely undeserved) reputation of the colossal ship proved unshakeable.

Charles was in the Netherlands for a year, between June 1648 and June 1649, a period that saw both his attempts to exploit the revolt of the Parliamentarian fleet and his accession to the throne, at least nominally. However, the sojourn also allowed him to indulge in some pleasures, such as his brief liaison with a Welsh woman named Lucy Walter, leading to the birth of his first illegitimate child, the future Duke of Monmouth. There are also traditions of him taking up sailing once again, and learning the ways of the peculiarly Dutch craft, the *jacht*; the castle at Woerden, which he occupied as the guest of his brother-in-law, the Stadholder William II, had a set of stairs known as the '*koningstrap*', the king's stairs, because they were supposedly Charles's route down to his own yacht, on the river that flowed by the castle.[35] Charles was back in Jersey in September 1649, hoping to be able to use it as a launch pad for an intervention in Ireland. Although his stay there was very brief, he still had opportunities to hone his boat-handling skills, such as taking the helm of the pinnace built for him in 1646 and steering himself from Cotainville in Normandy to Jersey.[36] Charles then moved on to Scotland, where he

Elizabeth Castle,
Jersey, headquarters of
Charles's court in
1646 and 1649.
Engraving by
Wenceslaus Hollar,
1665. (Rijksmuseum,
Amsterdam)

was crowned King of Scots at Scone. A fraught and often humiliating alliance with the Scottish Covenanters culminated in an invasion of England, but this was defeated decisively by Cromwell's army at Worcester on 3 September 1651. After a series of escapades, Charles managed to reach the south coast, where Nicholas Tattersall, the captain of a Brighton coal smack, the *Success*, was persuaded to take him across the Channel to safety in France. After the Restoration, the *Success* was purchased, renamed *Royal Escape,* and for some twelve years was kept moored off Whitehall Palace, where the king showed her off to visitors. She was then transferred to general naval duties, was rebuilt several times, and lasted well into the eighteenth century, as did the annual pension paid to Tattersall's son.

The king's defeat at Worcester meant that the Royalist cause lingered on in only a very few, relatively insignificant, outposts. Dunnottar Castle, near Aberdeen, the last fortress holding out for the Crown in the British Isles, fell in May 1652, followed by its last territory of all, Inishboffin Island off the Galway coast, in February 1653, by which time the various pro-Royalist colonies in the Americas had all surrendered to the Commonwealth. This left only one military force in arms for the young king: the tiny Royalist fleet which Prince Rupert had commanded since 1648. For four years, this force had exerted an influence out of all proportion to its actual size. Between January and October 1649, it operated in Irish waters, forcing Parliament to send all its newly minted generals-at-sea to deal with it. Rupert then sailed for Portugal, where the simple existence of his fleet forced General Robert Blake to maintain a powerful blockading squadron off Lisbon for the best part of a year. The six ships remaining under Rupert's command then made for the Mediterranean, before crossing to the Azores in the middle of 1651, and then sailed on to West Africa in the autumn before spending most of 1652 in the Caribbean. But in September 1652, disaster struck the Royalist fleet. It was caught in a hurricane off the Virgin Islands, and three of the four remaining ships were lost; among the casualties was Rupert's brother and vice-admiral, Prince Maurice, who was never seen again. The last remnant of the Navy Royal limped back to Nantes, where it was paid off in the spring of 1653.[37] Thereafter, many privateers operated with Royalist commissions, on condition that they paid a fifth of their profits to Charles and another fifth to James; but many of the captains were distinctly dubious individuals, and the Stuart brothers only ever received a tiny percentage of the cuts to which they were nominally entitled.[38]

It is unclear when and where the young Duke of York learned to sail: even Pepys, who got to know him very well and often had informal conversations with him, had no idea.[39] The brief and unsuccessful attempt to install him as admiral during the naval revolt of 1648 was unlikely to have given him any opportunity to take a helm, but in September 1649, Charles took his younger brother with him to Jersey, subsequently installing him as governor, the future king's first experience of independent rule. The duke remained on the island until September 1650, so may well have had his first taste of sailing in exactly the same waters as his sibling.[40] Thereafter, though, James developed an exclusively military career. In April 1652, he joined the staff of France's greatest general, Marshal Turenne, and spent four years as a dashing and undoubtedly brave cavalry officer, risking his life in a number of ferocious actions. But Cromwell's treaty with France, and Charles II's parallel treaty with Spain, led to a furious argument between the two brothers. James eventually backed down and went into Spanish service, fighting against his old master Turenne; at the Battle of the Dunes, outside Dunkirk, in June 1658, he and his small Royalist army-in-exile also encountered the 6,000 Ironsides that Cromwell had provided as reinforcements to the French army.[41]

The Battle of the Dunes was followed within three months by the death of Oliver Cromwell, but despite the political instability which followed, all Royalist schemes to exploit the situation came to nothing. With no apparent prospect of an imminent restoration, James, at least, began to contemplate the prospect of life in permanent exile. Early in 1660, he accepted King Felipe IV's offer of the title *Capitán general de la armada del mar Océano*, the title that the Duke of Medina Sidonia had held when in command of the Spanish Armada; to all intents and purposes, Lord High Admiral of Spain. As he admitted in his autobiography, James was attracted to the position because of both its high status and the opportunity to pocket a fifth of the prize money taken by all Spanish warships – an important consideration for an impecunious prince with virtually no income.[42] But events in Britain were moving quickly, and the navy was playing a central part in them.

Following the resignation of Lord Protector Richard Cromwell in April 1659, factions within the increasingly isolated and unpopular governing elites of the Commonwealth struggled to assert themselves. Richard was replaced by the multiply purged remnant of the Rump Parliament which had ruled between 1649 and 1653 (and which was, in name at least, a tiny fraction of the Long Parliament originally elected in 1640). But this body soon clashed with the army generals, who ejected it. Vice-Admiral John Lawson, commanding the fleet, supported the Rump, and in December 1659, he brought his ships into the Thames to blockade London – a crucial move, because if collier fleets from Newcastle were unable to get upriver, Londoners would freeze. Meanwhile, General George Monck, who had commanded at sea during the Dutch war of 1652–54, also declared for the Rump, and brought his Scottish army into England.

Following a further series of extraordinary political shifts, in April 1660 a brand new parliament declared the monarchy restored.[43] A fleet

The departure of Charles II from Scheveningen beach, May 1660. (Rijkmuseum, Amsterdam)

commanded by Edward Mountagu, another of the Commonwealth's erstwhile generals-at-sea, arrived at Scheveningen on 14 May to bring home the royal brothers and their followers. The king and Duke of York went aboard the flagship *Naseby* on 23 May; before nightfall, the ship was rechristened the *Royal Charles*. Unfortunately, the human royal Charles immediately encountered the eternal difficulty confronting tall men aboard wooden sailing ships, and walked straight into a low beam. Samuel Pepys, Mountagu's secretary, ever one to spot an opportunity to ingratiate himself with his superiors, swiftly arranged for the piece of wood in question to be marked with a gold seal bearing the royal cipher.[44]

On 22 April 1661, the day before his coronation, King Charles II and his brother James, Duke of York, processed in state from the Tower of London to Whitehall Palace. It was a glorious day, with the sun finally shining after many weeks of rain. The royal brothers were accompanied by over a thousand men on horseback and many more on foot, including peers, judges and other officers of state, all gloriously attired for the occasion. The column was over a mile and a half long, passing through streets lined with troops, and was accompanied by drums, trumpets and streaming banners.[45] The procession passed through a series of four great triumphal arches which illustrated themes relating to the king and his reign. At Cornhill, where Pepys, now Clerk of the Acts to the Navy Board, witnessed the spectacle from the window of a flag-maker's house, the royal party passed under a 'Naval Arch', which featured representations of Mars and Neptune, beneath whom an inscription read '*Neptuno Reduci*' (To Neptune Restored). Eight women were positioned on the arch: four represented Europe, Asia, Africa and America, the others Arithmetic, Geometry, Astronomy and Navigation. On the north side of the street was a stage shaped like a ship, bearing a plaque that proclaimed:

Neptuno Britannico
Carolo II
Cujus Arbitrio
Mare
Vel Liberum, Vel Clausum

(To British Neptune
Charles II
whose dominion
over the sea
both unrestrained and confined)

The Duke of York was also honoured on the arch by being shown 'like Neptune, standing on a shell drawn by Sea-horses, before which a Triton [is] sounding, in one hand a Trident, the Reins in the other; his Motto, *Spes Altera*.'*

Charles stopped at the arch, and was addressed by a man representing the River Thames, who exalted the king as Neptune and extolled the kingdom's naval prowess. A chorus of 'sailors' then serenaded the king:

> King Charles. King Charles, great Neptune of the Main!
> Thy Royal Navy rig,
> And We'll not care a Fig
> For France, for France, the Netherlands, nor Spain.
> The Turk, who looks so big,
> We'll whip him like a Gig
> About the Mediterrane;
> His Gallies all sunk, or ta'ne.
> We'll seize on their Goods, and their Monies,
> Those Algier Sharks,
> That Plunder Ships, and Barks,
> Algier, Sally, and Tunis,
> We'll give them such Tosts
> To the Barbary Coasts,
> Shall drive them to Harbour, like Conies.
> Tan tara ran tan tan
> Tan tara ran tan tara,
> Not all the World we fear-a;
> The great Fish-Pond
> Shall be thine-a
> Both here, and beyond,
> From strand to Strand,
> And underneath the Line-a …
>
> They yield, they yield; shall we the poor Rogues spare?
> Their ill-gotten Goods,
> Preserv'd from the Floods,
> That King CHARLES, and we may share?
> With Wine then, chear our Bloods,
> And, putting off our Hoods,
> Drink to His MAJESTY bare,
> The King of all Compassion:
> On our knees next fall
> T' our Royal Admiral,
> A Hearth for His Preservation,

* 'The other hope', ie, of the kingdom.

Dear JAMES the Duke of York,
Till our Heels grow light as Cork,
The second Glory of our Nation.
Tantara ran tan ran
Tantara ran tan tara
To be the Royal Pair-a,
Let every man
Full of wine-a
Take off his Can,
Though wan, though wan,
To make his Red Nose Shine-a.[46]

In the years after 1661, such symbolism was pervasive in Restoration England. It shaped high art, music, literature and the culture of the court. It gave the country its definitive maritime icon, Britannia.* Three-masted men of war appeared on the Restoration farthing, and on the pass tokens given to scrofula sufferers being admitted to the royal presence to be touched for 'the King's Evil'.[47] All of this begs an obvious question: to what extent were these cultural allusions and grand ambitions reflected in reality, namely what the navy was, and what the navy did? Did the Stuart brothers really see themselves as 'British Neptunes', and if so, what, if anything, did they do to try and live up to the billing?

* See Chapter 8.

The only section to be completed of Charles II's Greenwich Palace, commenced in 1663, looking towards the nearby site of the royal dockyard at Deptford. *(Author's photograph)*

3

—————→←—————

His Majesty's Ships I

THE NAMING OF WARSHIPS has always been highly political, and in Britain, with the exception of one interval of eleven years, it has always been royal.[1] For many centuries, monarchs have taken personal responsibility for naming at least some of their ships, particularly the most prestigious ones. In 1183, Sverre, the Viking King of Norway, gave a speech at the launching of his new ship *Mariusuden*, explaining why he had given her that name; and his predecessors had probably been naming their ships for centuries before that.[2] Both in their names and their elaborate decoration, King Henry V's great ships, the likes of the *Holighost* and the *Grace Dieu*, reflected both his profound religiosity and his political ambitions.[3] Henry VIII personally dedicated the *Henry Grace à Dieu* on 13 June 1514, and famously named the *Mary Rose* after his favourite sister. He also named the *Virgin Mary* in 1515, dressed in a sailor's coat and carrying a large nautical whistle; a mass to bless the new ship was celebrated by the Bishop of Durham, an age-old practice that ceased when Henry broke with Rome. Warship launches then became exclusively secular affairs, a situation which persisted until an Anglican ceremony was belatedly introduced in 1875.[4] Elizabeth I attended launches, such as those of the *Due Repulse* in 1596, but it is less clear whether she actually bestowed the names herself.[5] James I was present at Woolwich on 24 September 1610 for the failed first attempt to launch the great ship which became the *Prince Royal* (she was successfully launched the following night, with Henry, Prince of Wales, performing the naming ceremony). As already noted, Charles I invariably attended launches, including the failed attempt to launch the *Sovereign of the Seas* on 25 September 1637, and his new additions to the navy's roll of names included *Unicorn*, honouring his Scottish kingdom, *Charles* and *James* after his sons, and *Henrietta Maria* after his wife. Even Oliver Cromwell complied with the tradition, attending a number of launches both before and after he became Lord Protector.[6]

An echo of all this survives to this day. The monarch still has the final say in the naming of new warships; a note listing proposed names is submitted to Queen Elizabeth 'with humble duty'.[7] Although this process has become very much a rubber stamp, it was not always so. In 1911, King George V famously vetoed Churchill's suggestion that the name *Oliver Cromwell* be given to a battleship, and His Majesty was equally unimpressed with the notion of an HMS *Pitt*; his considerable naval experience convinced him, undoubtedly correctly, that seamen would swiftly employ scatological rhyming slang to rechristen it. Some thirty years later, too, his rather less cantankerous son King George VI abandoned the tradition that the first battleship of a new reign should be named after the recently enthroned sovereign by vetoing his own name for the ship in question, which became instead a second *King George V*.* He also subsequently requested that a Loch-class frigate be named *Loch Muick*, after a favourite spot near Balmoral Castle.[8] Even more recently, the committee tasked with naming the 'D'-class Type 45 destroyers built in the first decade of the twenty-first century apparently rejected the notion of an HMS *Diana* so as not to place the queen in an invidious position.[9] Conversely, Britain's largest ever warships are named *Queen Elizabeth* and *Prince of Wales*, at least in part, to try and ensure they were not cancelled by a government that might think twice about giving such offence to HM and HRH. The queen acted as sponsor of the giant aircraft carrier named after her, maintaining the tradition that the sovereign, or else the consort, christens the very largest or most powerful ships of the navy; her mother had launched two *Ark Royals*. Thus 'Her (or His) Majesty's Ship' is not a quaint anachronism, invariably rendered as a mere acronym and taken for granted at all times; it is actually a quite literal statement of legal ownership. As one English diplomat put it in 1698, the king's ships 'in all ports and harbours whatsoever, have been considered as his royal palaces, and respected as such'.[10] King George V was wont to refer to 'my navy', as though it were a car or a corgi. Perhaps his predecessor Charles II was stretching the same point just a little when he sent a warship to Marseilles to fetch wine for his private account, or used naval canvas to patch up his birdcage in Saint James's Park, but ultimately, he was perfectly entitled to do both.[11]

All of this was demonstrated conclusively at the Restoration. On 23 May 1660, King Charles II and members of his immediate family were rowed out from the beach at Scheveningen, in the Netherlands, and boarded the *Naseby*, flagship of the fleet that had been sent to bring the king back to England after nine years in exile. The guns of every ship fired joyous salutes. Samuel Pepys kissed the king's hand, having done the same with his brother, the Duke of York, when the latter had come aboard on the previous day – the beginning of a complex professional relationship between the three men that would last for the best part of thirty years. The royal family dined, and then the king and duke perused a list of names of the ships in the fleet, changing those that reflected the triumphs and personalities of the English republic into rather more politically correct ones for a monarchy. To all intents and purposes, this was

* The king may have felt that the short intervening reign of Edward VIII muddied the waters. He also launched the ship himself, thus going against the almost universal practice (at least, universal since the first half of the nineteenth century) of having ships christened by women. King Edward VII had done the same at the launch of HMS *Dreadnought* in 1906.

Charles II's first executive act as the restored King of England, Scotland and Ireland, de facto as well as de jure; certainly his first executive act on English 'territory', as the *Naseby* most definitely was. Pepys's account makes it clear that the process was conducted exclusively by the king and the Duke of York, who was about to enter into the office of Lord High Admiral for which he had been intended from childhood:

> After dinner the King and Duke altered the name of some of the ships, viz. the *Naseby* into *Charles*; the *Richard*, *James*; the *Speaker*, *Mary*; the *Dunbar* (which was not in company with us), the *Henry*; *Winsby*, *Happy Return*; *Wakefield*, *Richmond*; *Lamport*, the *Henrietta*; *Cheriton*, the *Speedwell*; *Bradford*, the *Success*.

The name changes are all easily explicable – five of them were for the royal siblings (four of whom were present aboard the newly minted *Charles*), and *Richmond* for their distant cousin, the head of the junior Lennox Stuart line (and hereditary Lord High Admiral of Scotland), while *Happy Return*, *Speedwell* and *Success* are natural emotions reflecting the family's mood at the Restoration. On the other hand, *Speedwell* was also a traditional warship name – there had been two ships of the name in the Elizabethan navy. The displaced names were overtly political: *Naseby*, *Dunbar*, *Winceby*, *Wakefield*, *Langport*, *Cheriton* and *Bradford* were all Parliamentarian victories, and by replacing *Naseby* with the name he

De Regale Charles, Lang; 170 wijt 42 Voot.

shared with his father, the king who had been defeated in that battle, Charles could not have made a more potent symbolic statement. Similarly, the *Richard* had been named after Oliver Cromwell's son and successor, so there was an interesting symmetry in Charles renaming her after his own heir. Edward Barlow, a Mancunian seaman serving on the *Naseby/Royal Charles,* put it succinctly: 'His Majesty was pleased to new name some of the ships, which he might now call his own without fear, for he did not like the names of some of them, wherewith Crumbwell [*sic*] had named them ... they were all named anew, he not well affecting them which were traitors to the crown and which had murdered his father'.[12] Two of the new names actually duplicated ones already on the navy list, a *James* launched in 1634 and a *Success*, acquired earlier in 1660. Whether nobody thought of, or dared to inform the royal brothers about, this inconvenient clash, or whether Charles and James already knew of it and decided simply to disregard it, will probably never be known; but as a result, the existing ships had to be swiftly rechristened *Old James* and *Old Success.*

For the first fifteen years or so of Charles II's reign, naming policy closely followed the precedent laid down in May 1660: a heavy emphasis on names that honoured members of the Stuart family, the dynasty as a whole, or key players in the Restoration, together with the revival of well-established warship names which particularly revived memories of the 'glory days' of Elizabethan England. Charles followed these principles when changing the remaining interregnum names: *Marston Moor* became *York*; *Bridgwater, Anne; Torrington, Dreadnought; Tredagh* (Drogheda), *Resolution*; *Newbury, Revenge; Lyme, Mountagu; Preston, Antelope; Maidstone, Mary Rose; Taunton, Crown; Nantwich, Bredah* (where Charles had signed the declaration promising liberty of conscience which guaranteed his restoration). Entirely new names included *Royal Katherine*, after his wife; *Rupert*, after his cousin; *Cambridge* and *Edgar,* after short-lived nephews; *Monmouth*, after his eldest illegitimate son. Other revivals of Elizabethan names to set alongside the likes of the newly rebranded *Dreadnought* and *Revenge* included *Defiance* and *Warspite*. The different parts of Charles's realms were recognised by naming warships after their patron saints. The navy already had a *St George* and a *St Andrew*, but Charles added a *St Patrick*, launched in 1666, and a *St David*, launched in 1667.

Probably the most potent of the new names was that given to the second large warship ordered after the Restoration, a Second Rate built at the same time as the *Royal Katherine*, and launched at Portsmouth dockyard on 26 December 1664. During his escape after the Battle of Worcester, the king was forced at one point to spend a day hiding in a tree in the grounds of Boscobel House in Shropshire, while Parliamentarian search parties scoured the area all around. Charles II's life was saved, not by any common-or-garden tree, but by an oak, anciently revered in biblical, Greek and Druidic traditions, and already long established as one of the most potent symbols of English national identity. This ensured that after the Restoration, the oak tree was associated indissolubly with both the miraculous preservation of the king, and with the great ships built from its timbers; poets from Waller to Pope stressed such connections, and the holiday that marked both the king's birthday and his restoration was christened Oak Apple Day.[13] As one pamphleteer put it, referring to all Charles II's warships:

> These guard our prince from villains' fatal stroke,
> And every man of war's a Royal Oak.[14]

King-and-nation, tree-and-nation, and navy-and-nation, formed a sort of mystic trinity, so it was no coincidence that Charles decided to use the name *Royal Oak* for one of his largest men-of-war: she was a vast, floating, triple entendre.*

Charles II's selection of names for ships included some idiosyncratic quirks and witticisms, too. The name *Sweepstakes*, a Fifth Rate frigate launched in 1666, probably reflected the court's love of gambling, while the *Fubbs Yacht* was named after his mistress, Louise de Keroualle, Duchess of Portsmouth (specifically, it is said, after the chubbiness of her naked form!). Similarly, the *Fanfan*, Prince Rupert's personal yacht, was apparently his nickname for one of his mistresses.[15] *Saudadoes* was a Portuguese name given to what was intended to be Queen Catherine of Braganza's yacht; the queen had the right to appoint the ship's captain, although in practice her husband often recommended a preferred name to her.[16] The *Little Victory* was so-called because she was built from timbers left over from the rebuilding of the old Second Rate *Victory*. The destruction of the Second Rate *London* in March 1665, as a result of an accidental explosion, inspired the City to offer the funds for a replacement. The king named the new ship *Loyal London*, certainly a reflection of his capital's generosity, perhaps a gesture to 'let bygones be bygones'; after all, during the Civil War, London had been anything but loyal to the House of Stuart. However, a new *London* was built following the *Loyal London*'s destruction during the Dutch attack on Chatham in 1667; even a king whose relationship with his capital was increasingly frosty saw the necessity of pandering to its sensibilities by naming another great ship after it. But the new ship launched in 1670 was not given the prefix 'loyal', as the City would not pay for it. Moreover, it might be revealing that this was one of the very few launches of great ships that neither Charles nor James attended, despite the fact that it took place at Deptford, the easiest yard for them to get to.[17]

* British accounts of the Dutch attack on the Medway in 1667 invariably focus on the humiliating capture of the *Royal Charles*, but the burning of the *Royal Oak* during the same action was an equally shattering symbolic blow to national pride, and perhaps also to the self-esteem of the king.

Particularly intriguing was the choice in 1669 of the name *St Michael* for a large Second Rate, which was swiftly reclassified as a First. The name had never been used for an English warship before, and it would never be used again. (However, a similar name had been used for the greatest of all Scots warships, launched in 1511.) With the obvious exception of the national patrons, English warships since the Reformation had almost never borne the names of saints, unless they were prizes taken from the navies of Catholic states, so there were clearly special circumstances of some sort involved in the naming of the *St Michael*. For one thing, the launching ceremony was planned for Michaelmas Day, 29 September, which was one of the most important feast days in the royal liturgical calendar;[18] in the event, though, unspecified 'difficulties' forced the postponement of the launch until the next morning. However, the timing of the launch also coincided with Anglo-French negotiations for a military and naval alliance against the Dutch entering a critical phase, with Charles talking in increasingly belligerent terms of obtaining revenge for the humiliation he had suffered at Chatham in 1667, and

The *Royal Katherine* of 1664 after her armament was increased in 1673. Possibly by Isaac Sailmaker or the van de Velde studio; ship identified by Frank Fox in 2015.
(© National Maritime Museum, Greenwich, London, London, BHC0970)

The fine model of
the *St Michael* (1669),
the first that can be
positively identified as
a named ship.
*(© National Maritime
Museum, Greenwich,
London, F9219)*

with the king expressing to his most intimate confidantes an apparently sincere determination to announce his conversion to Roman Catholicism. Thus there may have been several complex reasons under-pinning Charles II's decision at this particular time to name a great man-of-war after this particular saint: Michael, the avenging archangel, the protector of Israel and patron saint of warriors, the bearer of the flaming sword of vengeance and justice; the victorious commander of the armies of the righteous in the final battle against the forces of evil.

Finally, there was one glaring omission from the list of names chosen by the king. Intriguingly, Charles did not name a ship *Henrietta Maria* after his mother, although there had been a Second Rate of that name before (launched in 1633, she was renamed *Paragon* in 1650, thereby displaying a delicious irony not always associated with the dour Puritans of the Rump Parliament; the ship was lost in 1655). Perhaps this omis-sion was a reflection of the famously strained relationship between mother and son. Conversely, Charles certainly displayed no false modesty in his selection of other warship names. By 1678, the navy had a *Charles* and a *Royal Charles*, both First Rates, along with a *Charles Yacht* and a *Charles Galley*.

In 1677, Parliament voted for the funds for a huge new construction programme of thirty ships, intended to eliminate the French navy's perceived superiority in numbers,* and the ships began to be named and launched from the spring of 1678 onwards. The first three names were essentially personal to the king. The *Lenox* was named after Charles, Duke of Richmond and Lennox, his illegitimate son by the Duchess of

* See Chapter 8.

The launch of the *Lenox* at Deptford, April 1678, with King Charles II and the Duchess of Portsmouth in attendance.
(Original painting by Richard Endsor, based on drawings by Willem van de Velde)

Portsmouth, and thus by extension probably honours the mother as well, as the names Richmond and Portsmouth were already in use. The idiosyncratic spelling seems to have been Charles's own, as both the ducal patent and all historical precedents spell the name with a double 'n'; but the infant in question was always known as 'Charles Lenox', thus providing circumstantial proof that even the precise spelling of ship names was down to the personal preference of the monarch.[19] The second, *Restoration*, was launched on 29 May 1678, the eighteenth anniversary of the event her name commemorated. The third was named *Hampton Court*, after the palace which Charles had often frequented in the 1660s, albeit rather less so in more recent years. The *Captain* (July 1678) was presumably named in honour of the Duke of Monmouth, who was appointed captain-general of the English army in April.

Before the next batch of ships was launched, the Popish Plot had erupted. An alleged deep-seated Jesuit conspiracy to kill the king and place his Catholic brother James on the throne, the story of the plot generated popular hysteria, a febrile political atmosphere, and demands for the exclusion of James from the succession. Although Charles knew very quickly that the story was a fiction, manufactured by an unsavoury bunch of fantasists and troublemakers, he realised that he needed to make appropriate gestures that pandered to Protestant and patriotic sentiment, and this seems to have extended to the choice of names for the next batch of ships. The *Anne*, named in November 1678, honoured a Protestant and legitimate member of the king's family, the Duke of York's second daughter and future queen. *Windsor Castle* was named after one of the monarchy's most obvious symbols (and, like the earlier *Hampton Court*, was pointedly given the name of a royal residence somewhere other than London), while three names recalled the Elizabethan navy, *Eagle*, *Vanguard* and *Elizabeth* herself. The *Hope*, launched on 3 March

The *Hope* of 1679; contemporary model at the Heeresgeschichtliches Museum, Vienna. (*Author's photograph*)

1679, also recalled the triumph against the Spanish Armada (a galleon of that name had fought in the action), but the timing of the launch suggests that the name might have had a double meaning, possibly to reflect the optimism surrounding the meeting of the first new parliament for eighteen years, which opened on the 6th; this was short-lived, as relations between Charles and this parliament rapidly deteriorated.

No fewer than seven ships were named in May 1679, the month in which Charles's difficult relationship with the 'first exclusion parliament' culminated in its prorogation. One, the *Sandwich*, recalled an architect of the Restoration (Edward Mountagu, Earl of Sandwich) who had been killed at the same time of year, seven years before. The *Grafton* was named after another of the king's illegitimate sons; she was followed in June by the *Northumberland*, named after the young duke's brother. The *Duchess* might have been named for the Duchess of York, the Catholic Mary of Modena, so her naming might have been a subtle gesture of defiance against the exclusionists; an alternative candidate would be the Duchess of Portsmouth, which would have been equally provocative. (Of course, it is equally possible that the name simply recognised the generic title.) *Kent* and *Essex* seem to be purely geographical names, honouring counties which made particularly substantial contributions to the Royal Navy, and they also revived the names of warships lost earlier in the reign. On the other hand, the name *Essex* might have had a double meaning which could have been a gesture towards Charles's opponents – Arthur, Earl of Essex, was a key figure in the newly remodelled Privy Council that was meant to bring about national reconciliation (and his brother was First Lord of the Admiralty at the time), while the navy's previous *Essex* had been named after Parliament's captain-general in the Civil War.

The other ships launched in the summer of 1679 were the *Berwick* (May) and the *Stirling Castle* (July). These seemingly odd choices, given Charles II's well-known dislike of all things even approximately Scottish, might have been a response to the almost exactly contemporary rebellion that culminated in the Battle of Bothwell Brig (22 June), in other words, emphasising the strength of the fortresses that faced potential rebels and thus by implication the strength of royal control of Scotland; indeed, the name *Berwick* was given at the exact moment when Charles was ordering the despatch of 1,600 troops by sea to that fortress, so the great fortress on the Tweed was clearly in the king's mind at the time.[20] Similarly, the name *Stirling Castle* could represent an assertion of royal rule after the defeat of that rebellion, by choosing the name of one of the most obvious symbols of that rule in Charles II's northern kingdom.

The two names chosen in September 1679, *Expedition* and *Bredah*, were fairly neutral, although the latter can only be a reference back to the Declaration of Breda in 1660 – a fairly odd name to choose at that point, given the suspicion of Charles for failing to implement the terms he had agreed in that document, partly those guaranteeing freedom of worship to religious dissenters. But with a new parliament due to meet in October (although it was later postponed), one that was again likely to be heavily influenced by urban dissenter opinion, the choice of name might have been a subtle signal that the king would now be more inclusive towards dissent, as he had originally promised at Breda. The *Burford*, launched in November 1679, reverted to type in the sense that it was named after one of his illegitimate sons – but interestingly, it was not named after the eldest of the brood still not to have a ship named after him, the Duke of Southampton (who never actually received this honour at all, perhaps suggesting that Charles was never wholly confident of the paternity that he had acknowledged in 1670), but after a mere earl, his son by Nell Gwyn, 'the Protestant whore', so perhaps once more this was actually a subtle nod toward Protestant sensibilities. But the most politically significant name of all was that of the *Pendennis*, launched on Christmas Day 1679, shortly after the Earl of Shaftesbury and his newly formed Whig party began a campaign of petitioning to demand that Parliament should be allowed to sit in order finally to exclude the Duke of York from the succession. The choice of this name can only have been a gesture of defiance by Charles toward his critics – Pendennis Castle was the last garrison in England to hold out for Charles I during the Civil War, surrendering only after a prolonged siege, so the name might reflect a determination to persist against overwhelming odds and regardless of the consequences. If that is so, virtually no other piece of surviving historical evidence provides such clear proof of King Charles II's thinking at the end of 1679.

In the spring of 1680, Charles seemed to return to purely geographical names, christening two ships *Exeter* and *Suffolk*. It is difficult to see a political rationale behind these names, but there is less difficulty with the other 1680 launch; in October, the month when Parliament was finally due to convene, he named the *Albemarle*, recollecting another great figure of the Restoration. Following the dissolution of the third exclusion parliament in March 1681, Charles could again select ship names that did not pander to, or reflect, the broader political situation, and which reflected his own aspirations. Thus he named the *Ossory* after one of his recently deceased close friends, *Duke* probably in honour of his brother James, whose place in the succession had now been secured, and the *Britannia* and the *Neptune*, reflecting the broader concern to assert his 'sovereignty over the seas' that had been apparent since his restoration.[*] The fact that these were the last two warship names Charles II ever chose, in 1682 and 1683 respectively – after the decisive defeat of the Whigs, and the end of the 'exclusion crisis' – is deeply revealing. For if

[*] See Chapter 8.

the king was intent on a quiet life and financial retrenchment, why did he choose names with such powerful symbolism, reflecting ambitions to achieve dominion over the oceans?

The question of how and why a particular name was chosen at a particular time is unlikely ever to be answered satisfactorily, essentially because the naming process seems to have taken place entirely in the king's head. The lack of evidence to the contrary in Pepys's papers suggests that Charles, and later James when he succeeded as king, did not consult the one man whom they might have been expected to take into their confidence on such matters. As it is, we catch only occasional glimpses of the king's thought process in action. On 14 April 1679, for instance, Pepys wrote to the Navy Board to inform them that the king had given the name *Sandwich* to the Third Rate recently launched at Deptford by mistake, he having 'from the first design of building the thirty ships determined upon conferring it upon one of the Second Rates out of the regard he is pleased out of his great goodness he bears to the memory of the late noble lord of that name', so he ordered the

The *Britannia*, launched in 1682, the last First Rate built under Charles II. Shown with the Royal Standard at the main and the Lord High Admiral's flag at the fore. *(© National Maritime Museum, Greenwich, London, London, PT2557)*

Third to be renamed *Hope* and the Second building at Harwich to be named *Sandwich*.[21] This evidence demonstrates both that the king's memory sometimes failed him (which, in itself, suggests that his plans for ship names were probably never written down), and that, from the very beginning of the huge building programme, Charles had a rough plan for the names of at least some of the thirty ships. There are some obvious 'batches': some royal palaces, some fortresses, some of his children, a couple of architects of the Restoration. There is some evidence to suggest that the king might have allocated some of the names in pairs. On 18 November 1678, for instance, the Admiralty wrote to the Navy Board:

> We are to acquaint you that his Majesty has been pleased to name his new third Rate Ship lately launched at Chatham the *Anne*,* and his new Second Rate Ship designed to be speedily launched at Portsmouth the *Vanguard*, so that you may please to take notice thereof, and cause them to be inserted in the List of His Majesty's Royal Navy by those names.[22]

* The ship, named after the Duke of York's younger daughter and future queen, had been launched without a name on 7 November. The king undoubtedly had other things on his mind at the time: popular hysteria over the newly minted Popish Plot was at fever pitch. *Anne* was burned to prevent capture during the Battle of Beachy Head, 30 June 1690, and her remains, managed by the excellent Shipwreck Museum at Hastings, are sometimes exposed at particularly low tides. They constitute the most visible remaining survival of any British warship of the later seventeenth century.

Clearly, though, some of the names given to the 'thirty ships' were responses to events that could not possibly have been envisaged in 1677, such as the death in 1680 of his friend the Earl of Ossory, and, of course, *Pendennis*, if the interpretation of this name presented earlier is correct. Charles also chose some of the names at the last minute, and in what seems to have been very short order. In July 1678, for instance, Pepys was unable to inform the Navy Board of the name of the new Third Rate about to be launched at Deptford (*Hampton Court*), as 'His Majesty has not yet determined it. But as soon as he has, you shall have it'.[23] Again according to Pepys, the king decided on the name *Eagle* for the new Third Rate about to be launched at Portsmouth only during the morning of 30 March 1679, the day before the ceremony.[24] On the other hand, the names of other ships were sent to the building yards well in advance, suggesting that the king had decided on them significantly earlier: in 1678, Harwich had the name of the *Restoration* over a week beforehand, as did Portsmouth with the *Coronation* in 1685. Some names were known even from the time the keel was laid, as was the case with the *Loyal London* in 1665 and the *Royal James* in 1675.[25]

——— ➤❖ ———

Charles II attended many launches in person, particularly at Deptford and Woolwich, which were easily accessible from London. Indeed, the available evidence suggests that he attended the majority of launches of major warships (ie, of the Fourth Rate and above), and also those of a number of lesser ones, which took place in those two yards. Pepys went with Charles and James to Woolwich on 26 October 1664 for the launch of the *Royal Katherine*, a ceremony that was also attended by the queen, after whom the ship was named.[26] On 3 March 1668, the king, the Duke of York, Prince Rupert and many noblemen went to Deptford for the launch of a new First Rate that the king named *Charles the Second*, although it was usually known as the *Royal Charles* until a new ship of that name was launched in 1673, after which it was known simply as the *Charles*.[27] Between June 1675 and June 1676, he attended the launch of the Sixth Rate *Lark* in a commercial yard at Blackwall, that of the Fourth Rate *Woolwich* at its namesake yard, and that of the Third Rate *Defiance* at Chatham; he would have been at the launch of the First Rate *Royal James* at Portsmouth too, but for the mishap described in the Introduction.[28] On 20 October 1681, he attended a launch at Woolwich, and returned to Whitehall the same evening.[29] It was clearly not practicable for him to attend all launches that took place further afield. In those circumstances, he confided the name of the new ship to a naval official, usually a Commissioner of the Navy or sometimes the master shipwright of the dockyard, who presided at the launch; in April 1679, for instance, the Second Rate *Sandwich*, building at Harwich, was named by the Controller of the Navy, the veteran admiral Sir Thomas Allin, who had an estate near Lowestoft.[30] When he could, though, the king seems to have conducted the naming ceremony himself, thus reversing what seems to have been the practice of the previous century or so, when the monarch usually watched from a gallery ashore while another, standing on the poop deck, had actually christened the ship.

Launches were spectacular affairs. The king's involvement extended to frequently specifying on which date, and indeed which tide, a ship should be launched; it was Charles I's stubbornness over this that caused the problems with the launch of the *Sovereign of the Seas*.[31] Indeed, launches were sometimes delayed by a day or two so that the king could attend, as was the case with the *Defiance* in 1676.[32] The royal party invariably went downriver by barge or, if at Chatham, in the royal yachts, joining a small fleet of similar craft that lay off the dockyard, carrying spectators.[33] Trumpeters and drummers provided rousing music and fanfares; at the launch of the *Loyal London*, for example, this was provided by a sergeant-trumpeter, eight trumpeters and a kettle drummer.[34] Jury masts flew a colourful array of flags, with the royal standard at the main, the Admiralty flag at the fore, the Union at the mizzen and the bow, the red ensign at the stern. The time-honoured procedure was for the king to stand at the forward end of the poop, drink part of a goblet of wine, and then throw the rest of the contents forward, naming the ship as he did so, before flinging the goblet itself over the side − a practice that harked back to

pagan times. The master shipwright was then given a gift of inscribed plate as a gesture of thanks from his monarch.[35] For building the First Rate *London* at Deptford in 1670, Jonas Shish received a bowl worth £22 4s 5d; for building the *Cleveland Yacht* at Portsmouth, Anthony Deane got a flagon worth £14 6s.[36] A party was laid on for those attending launching ceremonies. At the launch of the *Captain* in August 1678, Thomas Shish, the master shipwright at Woolwich, provided 'a small banquet' costing over £30 for the king and other members of the royal family who were present.[37] At this distance, it is impossible to judge whether this really was a more modest affair than the 'great banquet' laid on when the king, the Lord Mayor and the sheriffs attended the launch of the *Loyal London* in June 1666.[38] These affairs were not simply for the elite, though; the workmen who had built the ship also partook of them. The feasts became so extravagant, and thus so expensive (despite, or perhaps because of, the fact that their expense could be claimed back), with shipbuilders vying to outdo each other, that the king had to put a stop to them. For the launch of the *Windsor Castle* at Woolwich in February 1679, Charles ordered John Shish, the master shipwright, not to provide a banquet: instead, the royal household provided the dinner itself, and this became standard practice at subsequent launches, even those taking place further afield.[39] In 1687, for example, Pepys told the commissioner at Chatham not to lay on a dinner ashore at the launch of the *Sedgemoor*, as the king would be accompanied by the royal yachts, where 'care will be taken (as on like occasions there always has been) for the providing as many meals for the king as will answer the times he intends to be abroad'.[40]

King James II and VII named few ships during his brief reign, but those that he did select are deeply revealing of the king's thinking, and of the personality flaws that cost him his throne. The last of the 'thirty new ships', launched on 23 May 1685, was naturally named *Coronation* after the event that had taken place exactly thirty days earlier (and was, of course, another name that could not possibly have been chosen by Charles II back in 1677). Three Fourth Rates were launched in 1687; these were named *Deptford*, *St Albans* and *Sedgemoor*. The first of these was uncontentious, and simply mirrored Charles II's naming of a warship after Woolwich dockyard. The choice of *St Albans*, though, is more intriguing. James would hardly have honoured a middling Hertfordshire town, so it is more likely that the ship was named for Charles Beauclerk, Duke of St Albans, Charles II's seventeen-year-old illegitimate son by Nell Gwyn. Beauclerk already had a warship named after him (the *Burford*, his title before he was elevated to a dukedom), but in the summer of 1687, when the new frigate was named, there were strong rumours that he was on the point of converting to Catholicism.[41] The conversion of a son of 'the Protestant whore' would have been quite a coup for James, so it is possible that flattering the young duke by naming a second large warship in his honour was a subtle inducement for him to do so. Clearly, though, the name also commemorated England's first Christian martyr, so it might have presaged a succession of other 'saintly' ship names if James's Catholic rule had continued (thus corresponding more closely to warship naming policy in France and especially in Spain). Limited confirmation of this might be the renaming of the *Charles* as the *St George* in October 1687, when the old Second Rate of that name was discarded.* And, of course, this act certainly represented James distancing himself from his brother's distinctly egocentric naming policy.

Sedgemoor harked back to the naming policy of the Commonwealth and Protectorate, when many ships were named after Parliamentary victories of the civil war; but both then and in 1687, naming ships after battles in which Englishmen killed Englishmen was hardly a gesture of tolerance and reconciliation. Instead, choosing the name *Sedgemoor* shows James at his most autocratic, insensitive and implacable, exulting in his military triumph, and by doing so, sending out a strong message of warning to other potential rebels. Some of his courtiers thought the name inappropriate, but not for the obvious reason: 'some very loyal persons would not have had it called so, that there might not be a standing memorial to the cowardice of the royal army, who had certainly run away if the rebels had either fought or stood their ground'.[42] Perhaps curiously, James did not change the name of the Third Rate *Monmouth*, which had been named after the 'Black Duke' in 1667. This contrasts with the comparable situation in 1715, when the name of the new Fourth Rate *Ormonde* was swiftly changed to *Dragon* following the defection of the second Duke of Ormonde to the Jacobites. *Sedgemoor* did not survive long enough to present William of Orange with the dilemma of whether to rename her or not: she was conveniently wrecked in St Margaret's Bay, on the Kent coast, on 2 January 1689, barely eighteen months after she was launched. Otherwise, James was as assiduous in attending launches as his brother had been. Indeed, in the spring of 1687 he changed the order of two proposed launches so he could attend both that of the *Sedgemoor* at Chatham on 3 May and that of the *St Albans* at Deptford on the following day, a sequence that enabled him to get back to Whitehall by the morning of the fifth.[43]

Many of the Stuarts' warship names became nearly permanent fixtures in the navy lists of subsequent centuries. At the time of writing this book, for example, the Royal Navy still has a *Monmouth*, a *Northumberland*, and

* The name might also have been an indirect allusion to James himself: in John Dryden's *Albion and Albanius*, the great court masque of 1684, the character of Albanius was an explicit representation of the then Duke of York, with Albion, naturally, being the king. Although we will never know what name Charles II, had he lived, would have given the ship that his brother named *Coronation*, Albion has to be a strong possibility, both because of the recent currency of the masque and because the name occupied the same mythic and patriotic ground as the previous two names he had given to his greatest ships, *Britannia* and *Neptune*.

even a *St Albans*: 350 years on, the warships of 'egalitarian' Britain are still being named after Charles II's illegitimate children, a fact that might well have amused their progenitor.[44] The current HMS *Neptune*, a name which has been in almost continuous use since 1683, is the shore establishment at HM Naval Base, Clyde, the home of Britain's nuclear submarines. The most recent *Britannia*, the last royal yacht in an unbroken line dating back to 1660, and bearing the name first given to a warship by Charles II in 1682, enjoys retirement as a tourist attraction at Leith. Other names in current service that would have been very familiar to the Stuart brothers include *Vanguard*, *Triumph*, *Dragon*, *Kent*, *Portland*, *Richmond* and *Pembroke*. The most recent *Sovereign*, lineal successor of their father's vast status symbol, is still laid up at Devonport dockyard until Britain decides how, exactly, it will dispose of its redundant nuclear submarines, only some forty years after the issue first arose. But one element of the Stuarts' naming preferences disappeared almost overnight after the Glorious Revolution, and has never been revived: the honouring of their own personal names. The *Royal James* was renamed *Victory* in 1691, while in 1693 the *Royal Charles* became the *Queen*.

Although subsequent regimes used similar formulas to honour the monarch of the day – *Royal William*, for example, and *Royal George* – the previous monarchs of the House of Stuart and their direct heirs were so politically toxic that there was never any realistic prospect of the navy gaining new ships bearing the names of the royal siblings. Or at least, that was the case until 1944–46, when a remarkable Stuart renaissance took place. Not only were the names of the two brothers revived, but the navy also acquired a new *Royal Katherine* and *Royal Prince*. For the first and only time, it also gained a *Royal Rupert*, and, recalling the Saxon predecessor with whom they were obsessed, a *Royal Edgar*. But these were not the Second World War's equivalents of Stuart First Rates, majestically ruling the waves. The names were given to small Royal Navy base units, established in liberated France or in occupied Germany towards or after the end of the war. *Royal Edgar* was at Hamburg, *Royal Rupert* at Wilhelmshaven, and so on; *Royal Charles* was at Calais in 1944/45, and another unit with the same name was in commission at Krefeld, on the Rhine, in 1951–53, by which time the name was no longer as quaintly archaic as it had previously had been.[45]

4

His Majesty's Ships II

LARGE WARSHIPS were by far the most technologically complex, expensive, powerful, and yet desperately fragile, machines of the seventeenth century. Each one carried more guns than any European army of the age; each one cost about the same as a fort, but unlike a fort, even the mightiest First Rate man-of-war could be destroyed literally in minutes, as was the *Royal James* following a Dutch fireship attack during the Battle of Solebay (28 May 1672).[1] Designing, building and sailing such leviathans were all skills that stretched the limits of the known boundaries of human knowledge. Above all, the exact method for constructing them was known only to a closed caste of cognoscenti, who guarded their secret truths with the fanaticism of Knights Templar. But both Charles II and James II made themselves authorities in this strange, esoteric and forbidden field. One expert who had a conversation with Charles about 'the various qualities incident to the diverse and respective shapes of ships' bodies underwater' found himself 'exceedingly enlightened in some obscure points' by the king (or so he said), and went off to research his royal master's suggestions more thoroughly.[2] Pepys, who initially believed that shipbuilding was 'not hard' to master, was soon disabused. In 1665, he had to admit that a discussion about the merits and demerits of lowering the topmast abaft the mainmast was 'a business I understood not'; but the king and the Duke of York certainly did understand it, and held their own amid the assembled ranks of shipwrights and experienced captains.[3] Perhaps the closest modern analogy, which admittedly requires a quite remarkable feat of imagination, would be if two consecutive prime ministers of the United Kingdom, or presidents of the United States, possessed doctorates in astrophysics.

The king's frequent attendance at launches has already been discussed, but these were by no means the only stages in a ship's life which he oversaw personally. In the first place, he usually took the decision to build a new ship in the first place: as warships were essentially royal property, it was only natural that this should be the case. His father, Charles I, seems to have consulted nobody else before, in 1634, he privately told the shipwright Phineas Pett of his intention to build the *Sovereign of the Seas*, and Charles II followed suit, ordering his brother in August 1660 to build a new First Rate in one of the royal dockyards –

the difference being that the son's ship was never actually built.[4] The king often visited warships under construction. As early as July 1661, the Venetian ambassador noted how Charles 'frequently visits the arsenals where the ships are fitting out, as he greatly delights in watching such work'.[5] He often took a fair number of courtiers with him, as in April 1675 when he went to Woolwich to view progress on the warship that would eventually take the name of that dockyard.[6] He was again at Woolwich in September 1676, quizzing the master shipwright about the partial copper sheathing being fitted to the *Charles Galley*; her sister ship, the *James Galley*, was similarly fitted with copper in areas of high wear, over a hundred years before copper sheathing was universally adopted throughout the Royal Navy.[7] In September 1677, the king personally reported back to the Admiralty board on the condition of the *Dartmouth*, which he had recently viewed at Chatham.[8] On 6 March 1680, Charles and James were at Blackwall, inspecting the new warships under construction in the private yard of Henry Johnson, who received

The *Woolwich*, launched in her namesake dockyard in 1675. This painting by Willem van de Velde originally adorned the cabin of the *Charlotte Yacht*, as did that of the *Charles Galley* (p74), a fact established by Richard Endsor in 2008. (© *National Maritime Museum, Greenwich, London, BHC3732*)

a knighthood and was invited to dine with the royal brothers; five months later, they spent three days at Chatham.[9]

The record suggests that, overall, the king visited the royal dockyards, especially Deptford and Woolwich, several times a year during the 1670s, often in the company of the Duke of York: visits that were as frequent as every few weeks during the summer months. Charles often gave direct verbal orders for particular works to be done on individual ships, completely bypassing the established hierarchy of the navy.[10] In this way, Charles II often dealt on superficially equal, professional terms with men from very humble backgrounds. In 1677, the king asked the son of the master shipwright's assistant at Chatham to make him a model of a new yacht; this arrangement was struck without reference to the commissioner of the dockyard, Sir Richard Beach, who was distinctly miffed that his shipwrights were being diverted from their proper work, even if it was at royal behest.[11] In the following year, Charles had a conversation with William Bagwell, a shipwright who was overseeing the construction of the new *Northumberland* at Bristol,* and instructed him to fit two balconies at the ship's stern, a feature which was common in Spanish warships but a distinct innovation for the Royal Navy. In some trepidation, Bagwell asked the Navy Board for advice about what he should do.[12]

The easy, mutually respectful relationship between the royal brothers and their shipbuilders was observed at first hand by Pepys, who said of Charles and James that their:

> personal concernments for, and knowledges in, that affair [ship-building] led them not only to the giving a liberty, but even encouraging all men of that trade, beginners as well as old practisers, and even assistants and foremen as well as master-builders, nay, down to the very barge maker and boat maker, to bring their draughts to them, and themselves vouchsafed to administer occasion of discoursing and debating the same and the reasons appertaining thereto. Not only to the great and universal encouragement of the men, but improvement of their art to the benefit of the state: themselves taking delight to visit the merchant yards as well as their own, and both honour and assist with their presence no less the merchant builder at his launchings of a new ship of any tolerable consideration, and enquiring after the proofs of them at their return from sea, than his own master-builders.[13]

Pepys might have been exaggerating a little – this passage was part of a polemical jibe directed against the Stuart brothers' successor, King William III, 'a prince whose genius seems bent to land action only' – but

* Bagwell is best known for colluding in his own cuckolding at the hands of Samuel Pepys, to whom he effectively pimped his wife in order to secure his own professional advancement.

only a very little. For instance, Charles and James certainly visited merchant yards, and spent time on merchant ships, as well as their own vessels: in 1661, Charles was entertained aboard the *Richard and Martha*, which had just returned from the East Indies, and it was said that the captain would have been knighted if he had not died three days later.[14]

Charles II undoubtedly took great pride in his command of naval architecture. Once, in conversation with Pepys, the two men embarked upon:

> a discourse of the great improvement of the art of shipbuilding since the king came in; he being pleased to say, and most truly, that he has ever made it his business to try all ways for the improving of that matter, so as he believes (as I have heard him often say) that there is little left to be added by the shipwright in his craft … as to proportion, shape, and placing of masts, sails, riggings etc.[15]

Pepys was fond of trumpeting the king's mastery of the art, claiming that 'the king [was] one that understands it so well as makes it unsafe for any shipwright to approach him that is not a master of the theory of his trade, as well as the ordinary labour of it'.[16] At least one of the shipwrights in question agreed: William Sutherland, a nephew of William Bagwell, reckoned that Charles II was 'able to discourse [with] and examine most of the principal shipbuilders'.[17] Sutherland first went to sea at the age of eleven aboard the *Edgar*, and said of her that she was:

> contrived at the command of King Charles the Second, her lower body was exactly made in fashion of a river wherry, but she was monstrously built upon being near 9 foot from the poop to the top of the taffrail, and near 7 foot from the top of the Forecastle to the top of the beakhead.[18]

Another contemporary who knew the king well, Bishop Gilbert Burnet, suggested that his knowledge of such a 'mechanical' art was so complete that it was actually a little unseemly for a monarch: 'He understood navigation well: but above all he knew the architecture of ships so perfectly, that in that respect he was exact rather more than became a prince'.[19] But in a different account of the king's character, Burnet was rather more complimentary. 'He has knowledge in many things, chiefly in all naval affairs; even in the architecture of ships he judges as critically as any of the trade can do, and knows the smallest things belonging to it'.[20]

The Duke of York, and probably the king too, built up substantial collections of magnificent ship models. Although these were – and are – splendid objects to have on display, their purpose remains obscure. Some were clearly built at stages of the design process, others might have been built simultaneously with the ship itself to enable points to be demonstrated during construction, yet others might have been direct commissions. This last seems to have been the case with one of the most magnificent models of the Restoration era, and the first which can definitely be linked to a specific ship: that of the *St Michael* of 1669, now at the National Maritime Museum in Greenwich, which was probably built for her first captain, Sir Robert Holmes.[21] Whatever the models' origins, though, they were clearly objects in which their owners took pride. James showed off his collection to Cosmo III, Grand Duke of Tuscany, in 1669: the Italian was suitably impressed, and claimed that James had designed the models himself. One of James's models might be that of a Fourth Rate of fifty guns, made in 1682, held at the National Maritime Museum, and which has the triple ostrich feathers usually associated with the Prince of Wales (but actually those of the heir) at the centre of the sternpiece.[22] Inevitably, Pepys was quick to jump on the royal bandwagon, acquiring a number of models from friends like Anthony Deane and other sources; sadly, though, it is no longer possible to establish which, if any, surviving models once belonged to him.[23]

Charles delighted in drawing the draughts and dimensions of vessels in his own hand, and probably drew up the original design of the 1682 *Fubbs Yacht* himself.[24] He decided personally on the positioning of the mast on another of the royal yachts, always one of the key elements in determining a vessel's performance.[25] Indeed, when it came to ship

Ship model of the *Mordaunt* (1681). (© National Maritime Museum, Greenwich, London, London, L2369)

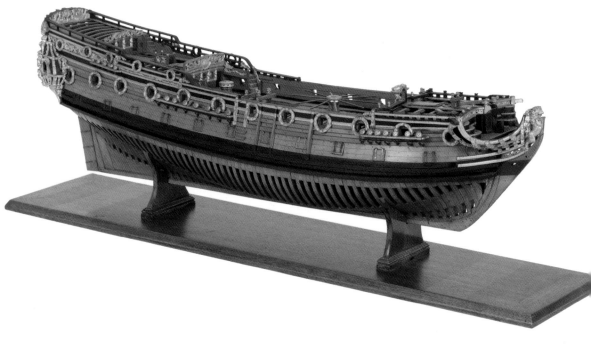

design, the king had a competitive streak of immense proportions. In 1672, the Venetian ambassador concluded a report on one of the king's many visits to the fleet by noting that:

> His Majesty's passion for naval manoeuvres have rendered him so thorough a master of the science that on several occasions he outdid the pilots, who had gained their skill by experience. He finds satisfaction at seeing four large ships, built under his own orders and of a new construction, carrying larger sails, standing a heavier sea and making more way than the others.[26]

In the following year, Charles wrote to his admiral, Prince Rupert of the Rhine, that 'I believe if you try the two sloops that were built at Woolwich which have my invention in them, they will outsail any of the French sloops'.[27] The king was more than willing to overrule the opinion of his so-called experts, as in 1680, when he thought it better to sink the old *Rainbow* to shelter the graving place at Sheerness, rather than haul her on shore as the Navy Board wished to do.[28] This was true even at times of dire national emergency: in June 1667, with the Dutch sailing up the Medway, Charles took issue with Trinity House's suggestion that block-ships should be sunk at Galleons Reach to stop the enemy reaching London, and proposed Blackwall instead, where the river was narrower (but where the risk was arguably greater, as it was much further upstream).[29]

The king encouraged those who suggested innovations. Sir William Petty, one of the most prolific and ingenious polymaths of an age that abounded in them, devised a double-bottomed ship, essentially a forerunner of the catamaran, and built two prototypes in Ireland in 1662/63, the results of which were laid before the Royal Society. The king and Duke of York were sceptical, laughing 'at Sir W Petty to his face in a most contemptible manner for his vessel'; Petty himself heard a story that 'His Majesty himself wishes ill success to my poor design of shipping'.[30] Despite this, both Charles and James were present at the launch of the third prototype at Rotherhithe in December 1664, with the king naming the craft the *Experiment*. But she foundered in the Bay of Biscay on her proving voyage, and although Petty returned to the concept later in life, the Stuarts did not, with Charles and James laying wagers that his later experiments would fail.[31] But the king's fascination with innovations never faded. In 1673, at the height of the Anglo-Dutch war, Charles encouraged both Sir Samuel Morland and the Venetian ambassador to devise new methods of weighing anchor, which he would then consider in consultation with the shipbuilders John Tippetts and Anthony Deane.[32] Following demonstrations in his presence in St James's Park, the king also encouraged Morland's project for a speaking trumpet which could supposedly project a voice over a mile or more, and examples of these were then sent to sea on royal warships; Morland's work on mechanical pumps also found favour with Charles, and led to a series of trials at Chatham.[33]

The king was always keen to witness the testing of these inventions at first hand. In May 1674, he, James and Rupert went to Sheerness to conduct sea trials with the yachts *Cleveland* and *Portsmouth*, which were allegedly 'built on a new principle, to increase their speed', and in the following month Charles went to Portsmouth to see a sailing match between two new frigates, on which the courtiers placed bets.[34] In March 1679, despite the political crisis raging all around him, the king made time to go to the trial of a new warping engine.[35] He was also keen to receive reports on the sailing qualities of his ships. In 1673, he was pleased with his cousin Rupert's report on the new First Rate *Charles*: 'a girdling this winter when she comes in will make her the best ship in England next summer'.[36] In 1678, Pepys reported Charles's reaction to a trial of several new vessels, 'where I know not whether I find him more surprised at the extraordinary performances of the *Oxford*, or pleased at the report ... of the *Royal James*, or unsatisfied to what to impute the ill-sailing of the *Woolwich*'.[37]

Consequently, the king had a clear understanding of which ships were likely to be suitable for which operations. Late in 1677, he proposed sending the frigates *Dover* and *Crown* to reinforce the Mediterranean fleet, they 'being ranked [by] the king in the top of our sailers'.[38] Such was Charles's passion for ships and shipbuilding that he sometimes pestered his subordinates relentlessly about matters that particularly interested him. The popular image of a hard-working Pepys constantly chivvying a lazy king is inverted somewhat by a letter of the former's dated 3 March 1679, where the Admiralty secretary noted that 'I find His Majesty so very earnest for the immediate going in hand with his new yacht [that he is] calling upon me almost every hour about it'.[39] Charles – and, indeed, his brother James and cousin Rupert – also frequently quizzed the Venetian ambassador about the types of vessel in the Serene Republic's navy, and about the mighty *Arsenale* itself, the largest dockyard in the world.[40]

Some of the king's personal interventions in ship design were, indeed, masterly. He invented 'bumpkins', short booms projecting from the bows to extend the lower corners of the foresail to windward, and introduced two masts – in other words, ketch rig – to the royal yachts.[41] He was an advocate of increasing the beam of warships, thereby improving their stability; in 1665, the shipbuilder William Castle increased the beam of the *Defiance*, 'the king so much desiring breadth', and he also intervened to increase the dimensions of the contemporary *Warspite*.[42] Similarly, in 1672 or 1673 he gave a verbal order to the shipbuilder Anthony Deane to increase the scantlings and dimensions of the new ships *Harwich* and *Swiftsure* from those specified in the contract.[43] According to Pepys, this command followed the visit by Charles and James to the French warship *La Superbe* when they inspected her at Spithead in 1673, and gave orders for the building of the *Harwich* to essentially the design and dimensions of the French ship, which then became the model for the twenty Third Rates built from 1677 onwards.[44] The royal brothers were certainly impressed by *La Superbe*, which was broader and carried her guns higher than her English contemporaries, but otherwise, Pepys's memory was seriously faulty. The dimensions of the *Harwich* (which had already been on order for months) were nothing like those of the French warship, but were nearly identical to those of the navy's previous Third Rate, *Edgar*, launched in 1668. Instead, the new ship that was most closely modelled on *La Superbe* was the second *Royal Oak*, launched at Deptford in August 1674; and it was the dimensions of this ship, albeit slightly reduced, that served as the model for the twenty new Third Rates.[45]

Charles was directly involved in introducing an entirely new type of warship into the navy. In 1676, he learned from Captain Thomas Willshaw that the French were building galley frigates at Toulon, following on from the prototype *La Bien Aimée* of 1672, and authorised Sir Anthony Deane's son to go there to view them and take down the dimensions. A little while later, Charles discussed the matter with the Venetian ambassador, Paolo Sarotti, whose report to the Doge and Senate gives a fascinating insight into both the genesis of the new type of warship and the relationship between the king and his two closest male relatives:

[The oars of the galley frigates] are so disposed that they and the rowers can be withdrawn inside the ship, when required, without moving them from their place and without getting in the way of the artillery and its use. His Majesty has decided to have one of this sort at built at once; the king himself told me this. The Duke of Hyorck [*sic*] remarked to me that he could have wished that the king had waited to hear how one of the [King of France's vessels] turned out. He asked me various questions about the shape and use of them. Prince Roberto [*sic*] afterwards expressly asked me to get one for him from Venice. He said, with the utmost courtesy, that they had not the remotest idea of having galleasses built, which would be of no use in these seas, but to consider the position of the oars and the artillery and other things which might throw a great deal of light upon the ship in question. They only want a drawing upon a sheet of paper.[46]

The ships that were built as a result of the royal family's deliberations, the *Charles Galley* and *James Galley*, proved highly successful in their principal task, the pursuit of fast Barbary Corsair raiders. Charles immediately decided to build two more of them, 'having a great opinion of the usefulness of such vessels', and decided on the dimensions himself, although ultimately the ships in question were never built.[47] Nevertheless, James II built a third, the *Mary Galley*, in 1687. The galley frigates required larger crews than usual and were therefore not economical to operate; they were ultimately converted to Fifth Rates and largely lost their rowing function.[48] But the essential principle of the type, a single, uninterrupted, main gun deck, became the basis of British frigate design in the eighteenth and early-nineteenth centuries: many of the famous 'star frigates' of Nelson's day were designed in this way, so the last survivors of them,

The *Charles Galley*, the navy's first galley frigate; a concept and a design attributable directly to King Charles II. Willem van de Velde. (© *National Maritime Museum, Greenwich, London, BHC3254*)

HMS *Trincomalee* at Hartlepool and HMS *Unicorn* at Dundee, are in many respects the direct lineal descendants of the *Charles Galley*, a vessel that was the personal brainchild of King Charles II.[49]

The king and duke were particularly actively involved in the project to build thirty new warships of the First to Third Rates, arguably the greatest infrastructure project that the British kingdoms undertook in the second half of the seventeenth century.* Charles made peace with the Dutch in February 1674, but the international situation remained fraught: France and the Netherlands were still at war with each other, and the appalling physical state of King Carlos II of Spain meant that a crisis over the Spanish succession could develop at any moment. However, Charles II's navy had sustained severe damage during the war, and English shipyards had also failed to keep up with the productivity of their French and Dutch counterparts. A comparative list which proved this point, albeit with some exaggeration of the figures, was drawn up by the shipbuilder Sir Anthony Deane and initially sent to the Lord Treasurer, the Earl of Danby. This paper was discussed by the Admiralty board on 16 January 1675, and subsequently presented to the king.[50] Charles was initially reluctant to accept the logic of the situation, being concerned above all to reduce the burden of debt, but he was gradually persuaded by Pepys, his new Lord Treasurer the Earl of Danby, and, perhaps, by rapidly improving national finances, due in part to the benefits of being the only neutral carrier in war-torn north European and Mediterranean waters.[51]

It was against this backdrop that, on 24 April 1675, Pepys, now MP for Castle Rising, presented to the House of Commons a paper which compared the naval strengths of the three major maritime powers. While Britain possessed ninety-two major warships, the French had ninety-six and the Dutch 136. Although many MPs immediately accepted the need for new construction to make up the shortfall, no action was taken; the 1675 session drifted into peevishness and discord, and Charles eventually prorogued it. When Parliament finally met again, in February 1677, Pepys submitted a proposal for the construction of thirty new ships, making the case in a long speech that both revealed his customary command of detail and lavished fulsome praise on his royal master:

> the king has built more ships from the stocks, than all his predecessors from the conquest; ninety, great and small, from the year 1660 to this day ... By the king's personal application to building ships, skill has been advanced, beyond any memory of man, and, perhaps, beyond any improvement. More docks have been built – No age, at one time, had so many encouragements for navigation. Has any time produced better encouragements for building ships, and provisions for flag officers?[52]

* The rebuilding of London after the Great Fire is perhaps the only challenger for the title; but unlike the building of the thirty ships, that was not centrally planned.

The language might have been Pepys's, but the underlying message – the request for funding to build thirty new men-of-war – undoubtedly came from the king.[53] Although some opposition diehards objected to the proposed amount of £600,000, fearing that it would be diverted to uses other than those specified, such as extravagant gifts for the royal mistresses, the Commons finally voted in favour of the proposition to build one First Rate of 1,400 tons, nine Seconds of 1,100 tons, and twenty Thirds of 900 tons. These were to be built within two years – an astonishing prospect, given that the previous Second Rates built during the reign, with one exception, had each taken at least three years to build, and that at a time when very little other construction was taking place. Charles became closely involved in the design process. He ordered that scantlings and dimensions should be standardised as much as possible, and specified that ships should be launched as soon as the hulls were ready, in order to clear the stocks for a new vessel.[54] He dictated that the later ships should have six or eight holes cut in their sides for firebooms.[55] He debated the best dimensions for the sole First Rate of the programme, *Britannia*, with her builder Phineas Pett; took exception to a number of the dimensions that Pepys had proposed and Parliament had agreed; decided that the new Second Rates would be provided with forecastles; and above all, insisted on increasing the dimensions of the Third Rates in particular at his own expense, to 1,600 tons for the First Rate, 1,400 for the Seconds, and 1,100 for the Thirds.[56] Or rather, he said he would increase the dimensions at his own expense: as with so many of Charles II's promises, he simply lacked the money to deliver, and had to publicly admit the fact in April 1679.[57] Nevertheless, the increased size undoubtedly made the new ships better sea-boats, as well as more effective gun platforms and also, incidentally, 'the best looking warships ever built', and several of them saw extensive active service over several decades.[58] All of this was the direct personal responsibility of King Charles II, in the form of his decision to change the dimensions to ones that he himself suggested. As the pre-eminent historian of Restoration warship construction rightly states, this does the king 'great credit for understanding ship requirements and design'.[59]

However, several of the king's ventures into the mysteries of shipwrightry were significantly less successful, and he was, perhaps, not quite the astute master of the shipwrights' art that he believed himself to be. When he launched the *Royal Katherine* in October 1664, he proclaimed her to have 'the best bow that ever he saw', and that she was 'the finest ship that has yet been built'.[60] But the *Royal Katherine* was initially an unmitigated failure. Built on experimental lines suggested by the Royal Society to test a theory of water resistance, she had only 3ft of freeboard – and that was before all of her guns and stores were put in her.

Consequently, she was so unstable that she had to be girdled at once.[61] This was by no means Charles's only misjudgement – although, of course, it could also be argued that his willingness to experiment and accept innovative ideas from the Royal Society was actually commendable, and that he was not hidebound by conventional thinking. The king enthusiastically backed the project of a renegade Dutch captain, Lauris van Heemskerck, to build a frigate that would outsail anything else on the oceans simply by building her with the grain of all the timbers laid one way: the result, *Nonsuch*, was a perfectly effective Fifth Rate which saw much action in a thirty-year career, but she was no faster than any other ship of the type.[62] Charles's enthusiasm for fitting the thirty new ships with upright stems was criticised by Pepys and the rather more knowledgeable Phineas Pett, who covertly modified the king's specifications in the ships he built, and Charles eventually came to have his own doubts about the innovation.[63] Charles also had to backtrack on his initial approval of Pett's suggestion that the draught of the thirty new ships might be reduced substantially; the other leading shipwrights, Sir John Tippetts and Sir Anthony Deane, argued strongly against this, and Charles ultimately deferred to their opinion.[64]

Above all, the eventual success of the galley frigates came only in the wake of a disastrous experiment with an out-and-out galley. This was very much Charles II's personal initiative: on 8 July 1670, he wrote to his brother directing him to give orders for the construction of two galleys for the defence of Tangier, one at the Medici arsenal in Leghorn and one at Genoa.[65] It was reported that these would be the prototypes for a squadron of six *bastardella* galleys – a sturdier variety, well suited to operating under sail – which were to be deployed against the Barbary corsairs.[66] In the end, the Genoa galley was never completed, but Leghorn's vessel was launched in 1671, and proceeded slowly to completion. Her first captain, the Frenchman Sir Jean-Baptiste du Teil, cupbearer to the Duke of York, was a colourful character with a distinctly chequered history and a complete absence of the diplomatic skills that such a unique command demanded.* The *Margaret Galley* finally went into service in 1674, fitted with one great gun, as was typical of her kind, and with a number of distinctly un-English features, such as 'one tent of canvas', 'two umbrellas of oiled cloth for the windows at the side', and an officer called '[an] agozile, [who] puts the slaves in chains and sees they do not loose them'.[67] Her oars were manned by a motley collection of the scourings of the Mediterranean slave markets, subsequently supplemented by some thirty Algonquin Indian prisoners of war.[68] It swiftly became obvious that the cost of running the galley, which was initially ranked as a Second Rate – about £18,000 a year – was completely prohibitive, and the Duke of York intervened personally to suggest that it should be dispensed with,

* Du Teil appears again, and in more detail, in Chapter 7.

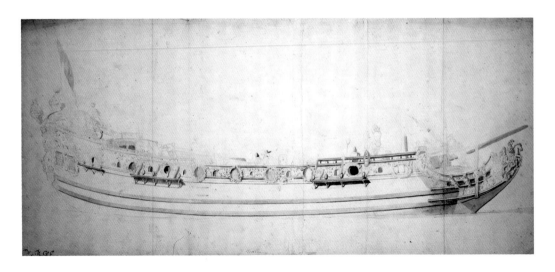

thereby demonstrating once again (as the Venetian ambassador's letter about the galley frigates also suggests) that the younger brother had a significantly more cautious and practical streak than his much more impetuous and spendthrift elder sibling. The king, already persuaded of the alternative merits of the much cheaper galley frigates, finally gave his consent in February 1676, at the same time that the first of the latter – 'a vessel of the design lately proposed by His Majesty' – was ordered.[69] The *Margaret* was laid up alongside the Tangier mole, and later sold to two senior naval officers, who presumably had her taken to pieces.[70]

The decoration of royal warships reflected the attitudes of the monarchs who commissioned them. Ships were elaborately gilded and adorned with spectacular carvings; under Charles II, the style of decoration became increasingly baroque, but even so, the cost of the work done on his last First Rate, the *Britannia* of 1682 – £895 – paled into significance compared to the £6,691 his father had spent on the astonishing display of art, mythology and royal pretensions on the *Sovereign of the Seas*, described in Chapter 2.[71] The Commonwealth had introduced a measure of austerity, notably by substituting gold paint for gold leaf, but some of the symbolism of its ship decoration was hardly less excessive than anything devised by the Stuarts. Above all, the figurehead of the *Naseby*, launched in 1655, was consciously modelled on that of the *Sovereign of the Seas*: it portrayed Cromwell trampling underfoot an Englishman, a Scotsman, an Irishman, a Frenchman, a Dutchman and a Spaniard, with a carved figure representing Fame holding above the Lord Protector's head a laurel bearing the words 'God With Us'. Although Charles II renamed the ship *Royal Charles* almost as soon as he went aboard her, the removal of the politically incorrect figurehead took rather longer. It was finally taken down and burned in December 1663, which, according to

Pepys, 'was done with so much insulting and folly as I never heard of';
Pepys disapproved of the fact that it would cost £100 to make a new one
(of Neptune), but it is difficult to see how he could really have expected
his king to have a flagship with a figurehead glorifying the man who was
principally responsible for cutting off his father's head.[72] From then on,
the most common form of figurehead was a crowned lion, an obvious
symbol of courage and aggression. But the lion also directly represented
royal ownership, given the presence of lions on the royal standard, while
St Edward's crown, which was traditionally used in the coronation, was
used as the template for that which adorned the lion figurehead from
1675 onwards.[73] The largest ships of the Restoration age had dramatic
equestrian figureheads, while *St Michael* of 1669 had a slightly ambiguous
emblem of a bird which seems to have represented the traditional
Christian symbol of sacrifice, the 'pelican in her piety'.[74]

Like both their father and their distant ancestor King James IV, Charles
II and his brother preferred to build large warships. There were sound
tactical reasons for this: large ships provided the heaviest possible broadside from a 'line of battle', the new method of fighting at sea adopted
from the First Anglo-Dutch war (1652–54) onwards. In the later wars,
British fleets consistently outgunned their Dutch opponents, the size of
whose ships was constrained by the shallow coastal waters they had to
navigate, and Charles and James, like the Commonwealth's rulers (and,
indeed, their father) before them, found it impossible to resist the imperative to cram as many guns into their ships as possible, even if it turned
them into lumbering slugs which were unable to open their lowest rank
of gunports in even a light to moderate swell (although it must be said
that these conditions were very rare, and ships carried fewer guns on
foreign deployments or in winter).[75] All of this was summed up
succinctly by James in 1664:

> It must always be expected that the Dutch will go beyond us in
> number of ships, and that they will find among their merchantmen
> many ships capable of carrying force equal or near to the king's 4th
> rates, so that the king's advantage must consist in this, that few of his
> ships shall carry greater force than greater number of theirs.[76]

But the preference for large warships was significant in other respects,
too. As had been the case with the *Sovereign of the Seas*, large warships
were hugely impressive symbols of royal authority, intended to have a
deterrent effect, and of that elusive quality which many contemporary

writers described as the '*grandezza*' of kings: hence the seemingly dispro-
portionate outlay on carving, gilding and other decoration. The colossal
men-of-war of Charles II and James II were intended to mete out
destruction on an unimaginable scale, but they were also intended to
look sensational as they did so.

A simple comparison of the strength of the fleet at the Restoration
with that at the downfall of James II clearly demonstrates the priorities
of the royal brothers, especially as it needs to be borne in mind that the
average size of warships in the largest rates, and the weight of their broadsides, also increased markedly between the two dates.[77]

Rate of ship	Number in 1660 (number built since 1649 in brackets)	Number in 1688 (number built since 1660 in brackets)
First	4 (2)	9 (8)
Second	11 (3)	11 (10)
Third	15 (15)	39 (30)
Fourth	45 (26)	43 (20)
Fifth	35	12
Sixth	20	8

Thus the proportion of the navy made up of 'great ships', the First to
Third rates, almost exactly doubled during the reigns of the Stuart
brothers. The numbers might have been even more impressive, had it not
been for the chronic financial woes of the Restoration regime. In June
1666, for instance, Charles gave an Order in Council to build ten new
ships, all of the Third Rate or above, but in the end only three were
completed.[78] Despite this, though, the navy of Charles and James was
overwhelmingly one of 'great ships', and the fact that it was so can be
attributed directly and solely to them.

5

The Royal Yachts

THE WINTER OF 1679 was harsh in more ways than one. In January, the Thames froze over, and the captains of the royal yachts, lying off Deptford and Greenwich, were ordered to take special care that their vessels were not iced in.[1] At much the same time, England's Roman Catholics were experiencing a very different kind of harshness: on 24 January, two of them were hanged, drawn and quartered at Tyburn for high treason. New revelations of the Popish Plot, an alleged Catholic conspiracy to kill the king, seemed to emerge almost daily, stirring up suspicions, popular hysteria, and mob violence. Priests were hunted down, and Catholic books and vestments were publicly burned. A squadron of Spanish galleons was reported to have set sail, intending to land an invading army at Milford Haven. To cap it all, one Sunday, 'a prodigious darkness overspread the face of the sky', and the ghost of the murdered Protestant magistrate, Sir Edmund Berry Godfrey, was said to have been seen haunting the queen's chapel at Somerset House at the exact moment when mass was being said.[2] Ordinary, law-abiding Catholics went in fear of their lives. But for a very small number of them, an unlikely lifeline was about to be provided. On or about 17 February, for instance, Thomas Keightley of Hertingfordbury, his wife Katherine, their young son William, Katherine's sister Lettice Knollys, and Dorothy Lester, a maidservant, made their way along icy roads toward Greenwich, where they hoped to find passage to safety in France.[3] This unassuming Catholic gentry family was fleeing likely imprisonment, and possibly much, much worse, thanks to three unlikely 'Oskar Schindlers': King Charles II, Samuel Pepys and Ralph Sanderson, captain of the royal yacht *Charlotte*.

Charles II's early experiences of sailing, and of the Dutch *jachts*, led him to declare an intention to build such a vessel for himself when he returned to England. Seeing an opportunity to ingratiate themselves with a monarch who was about to be restored, the civic regents of Amsterdam voted to present him with a yacht that had recently been built for the city's Admiralty, and this vessel sailed for England in August 1660.[4] Pepys had a chance to go aboard on 8 November, and found the vessel, now named the *Mary Yacht* after the king's sister (who then had little more than a month to live), 'one of the finest things that ever I saw for neatness and room in so small a vessel'.[5] The *Mary* was indeed small, less than 67ft overall, with very shallow draught and a high, elaborately decorated stern which carried a 'pavilion' or deckhouse for her passengers; she also had fan-shaped leeboards on each side, a feature that made perfect sense in Dutch canals and estuaries, but which had rather less utility in English waters.[6] Charles swiftly ordered two more yachts to purely English designs, the *Katherine* for himself and the *Anne* for his brother, as well as the smaller *Bezan*, named after her unconventional rig, and it was these vessels that John Evelyn saw race in October 1661. The new generation of yachts designed and built in England had finer lines and a deeper draught than the Dutch *Mary*, making them better sea-boats; they also discarded the leeboards and the prominent pavilion.[7] They proved their worth emphatically during a huge storm in July 1662, which they successfully weathered: 'all ends to the honour of the pleasure-boats', Pepys wrote, 'which, had they not been very good boats, they could never have endured the sea as they did'.[8] Thereafter, the yachts got progressively larger. The first English-built yacht, the *Katherine*, had a length in the keel of 49ft and a beam of 19ft; the penultimate yacht built before the revolution of 1688, the *Fubbs*, was 63ft in the keel and 21ft in the beam.[9]

The Stuart yachts formed a 'navy within a navy'. By 1685, there were about twenty of them, although only seven were truly 'royal', notionally assigned to the immediate service of the king and the royal family. Beyond this elite squadron, the *Navy Yacht*, for example, was at the service of the officers and commissioners of the Navy Board, while the *Deal*, *Queenborough* and *Isle of Wight* yachts served the three naval anchorages adjacent to their namesakes. By the end of 1661, the first *Mary Yacht* had been relegated to service as a packet boat between Dublin, Anglesey and the Dee estuary, and was ultimately wrecked on the Skerries in 1675, while the *Jemmy* was at the service of the officers of the Chatham yard.[10] The first *Katherine* was given to the Ordnance Office in 1668, followed by Charles II's sometime favourite yacht, *Cleveland*, after the king's death. One yacht was usually employed on the Irish coast, under the orders of the Lord Lieutenant; the *Portsmouth Yacht* replaced the *Monmouth Yacht* in this role in 1679, with the *Portsmouth* returning to the station again in 1687.[11] Meanwhile, the *Kitchen Yacht* was quite literally that, and provided the meals for those embarked on the other yachts during royal sailing expeditions: the specifically royal yachts were victualled by the Lord Steward's department, not the navy, so the meals provided for them were lavish. Although it was no doubt a particularly extravagant display intended to impress royal guests, the dinner provided for the new Queen

The *Cleveland Yacht*, painted by Jacob Knyff; for some time Charles II's favourite yacht. Charles is shown arriving aboard her to visit a flagship at the Nore. *(Private collection)*

of Portugal aboard the *Fubbs Yacht* in July 1687 included duck, beef, turbot, pork, bacon, quails, salmon and lobster, all washed down by claret and Rhenish wine.[12]

The king part-funded the construction of several yachts out of his own purse. He contributed £1,000 to the cost of the *Charles Yacht* in 1675, and £500 to the *Charlotte Yacht* in 1677.[13] These yachts were not automatically units of the Royal Navy; they were initially the king's private property, and were only 'taken into the list and charge' of the navy when the king ordered them to be.[14] This gave Charles carte blanche to have the yachts fitted out and adorned as he wished. The cabins of the principal yachts were elaborately decorated; from 1674 onwards, they benefited from the comprehensive programme of refurbishment of royal property undertaken by the Earl of Arlington as Lord Chamberlain, which also saw spectacular new examples of continental art, like the Verrio paintings described in Chapter 8, appearing on the walls and ceilings of the king's palaces.[15] When the *Charlotte Yacht* was built in 1677, the best marine artists of the day, Willem van de Velde the Elder and Younger, were commissioned and paid £74 to provide a set of painted panels portraying other warships built in Woolwich dockyard.[16] The *Fubbs Yacht* had a four-poster bed, gold brocade and costly silks, while in 1673 the *Katherine Yacht* was described as having 'a brave hall painted all round with works of art, gilded and decorated with carving', together with cabins 'separated by screens painted with the king's arms and gilded'.[17] The galley chimney of the first *Henrietta Yacht* was fitted with marble. The yachts had pewter chamber pots and crimson damask curtains, although the king's bed on the *Greyhound* was only 6ft by 3ft, which must have been somewhat spartan for the lofty monarch.[18] Pepys, though, vouched for the comfortable qualities of the velvet cushions provided on the *Bezan Yacht* by sleeping soundly on them as she lay at anchor in the Thames in August 1665.[19]

The yachts' exteriors were also elaborately decorated, with a profusion of sculptures and gilding. Contemporary models, such as that of the *Henrietta Yacht* of 1679, on display in the Portland Collection at Welbeck Abbey, reveal beautiful, sleek craft, gloriously gilded; on the *Henrietta*, a small 'well deck' of sorts divided the great cabin into two, providing a semi-enclosed space in which the monarch could take the air upon a damask-clad throne. Unsurprisingly, none of this came cheap. The carvings of the *Charlotte* cost over £500, the paintwork £474 3s, the gilding of the carvings on the *Isabella* over £100: these were up to three times the amounts spent on equivalent works on a Third Rate man-of-war.[20] In November 1677, the matter was taken up by the Admiralty board, with both the king and Duke of York present, because of the 'extraordinary lavishness of expense' in the carving and gilding of the duke's new yacht, the second *Mary*. Orders were given to rein in the shipwrights, but not before Charles was forced to admit that part of the problem was the verbal orders he was accustomed to give them, as in the case of the van de Velde paintings on the *Charlotte Yacht*.[21]

The specifically royal yachts were fitted out, repaired, and manned in the same ways as the other ships of the navy, and they often received their orders in the same way, too. During wartime, their speed and flexibility made them ideal despatch vessels, pressing tenders and fast troop transports; indeed, one was captured and one lost in action, both in 1673. The spaciousness of the yachts, and their easy accessibility at Greenwich and Deptford, made them ideal venues for courts martial, which were always held afloat. The fact that several of them were in permanent commission, at anchor in the Thames and ready to sail at short notice, also made them ideal vessels to deploy rapidly during unexpected emergencies, when larger warships might take significantly longer to put to sea. This was demonstrated at the beginning of February 1685, following what proved to be King Charles II's fatal stroke during the morning of Monday the 2nd. At four that afternoon, presumably acting on the Duke of York's orders, Pepys commanded the royal yachts to sail downriver prior to taking up station in the mouth of the Thames, where they were to intercept all incoming foreign vessels and detain any passengers aboard them; James clearly expected his brother's illness and possible death to be the trigger for an immediate insurrection, stoked by subversive elements arriving from abroad. Captain Christopher Gunman sailed at once with the *Mary Yacht*, anchored at Holehaven,* and began to search incoming vessels, 'but did not find what I looked for'. At the Buoy of the Nore, the *Fubbs* and *Kitchen* yachts fired at three incoming vessels and brought them

* Holehaven Creek, on Canvey Island, was the quarantine anchorage for ships arriving from plague-stricken countries.

to an anchor.[22] When, later in the year, the Earl of Argyll embarked upon a rebellion in Scotland, the ubiquitous *Kitchen* was one of the vessels sent to the Dutch coast to intercept him as he sailed, and when this mission failed, the first vessel sent north to provide a naval presence in the Firth of Clyde was the *Charlotte Yacht*.[23] Beautiful they may have been, but the royal yachts were also the rapid-response force of the later Stuart navy.

In peacetime, the principal yachts were always ultimately at the king's personal disposal, with his business – be it public or secret – taking precedence in their deployment. Individual yachts, or sometimes small squadrons of them, were used to convey royal personages, their retinues and other important foreign visitors, from and to the continent. In June 1665, for example, a royal yacht carried the Queen Mother, Henrietta Maria, out of England for the final time.[24] In 1673, Mary of Modena came over in the *Cleveland Yacht* ahead of her marriage to the Duke of York; her retinue came over in the *Monmouth Yacht*, which subsequently took her mother, the Duchess of Modena, back to Calais.[25] The duchess subsequently came to England every couple of years to visit her daughter, and her son-in-law's yacht, *Anne*, always conveyed her back and forth.[26] The royal mistresses used them often: in June 1679, for example, a yacht was sent to Calais to embark the Duchess of Cleveland.[27] In this way, the royal yachts were the almost unnoticed vehicles that facilitated some of the most important political changes of Charles II's reign. In 1662, the yachts brought over the 4,500,000 livres in silver, contained within 293 boxes, paid by Louis XIV to Charles for the purchase of Dunkirk, won by Cromwell's forces in 1658.[28] In 1670, the *Anne Yacht* brought over Henrietta, Duchess of Orléans, the sister of Charles II and the Duke of York, for the family reunion that served as a front for the signing of the secret Treaty of Dover, and subsequently took her back to France, where she died, suspiciously suddenly, only weeks later.[29] In 1677, when William of Orange came over to marry the duke's daughter, Princess Mary, four of the best royal yachts were sent to the Netherlands to collect him, escorted by two frigates. Charles flattered his nephew by giving him the new *Mary Yacht*, described by Pepys as 'the most beautiful that has been hitherto built', allowing him to fly the Union Flag – exclusively the command flag of a senior officer – and permitting him to exercise command over the little squadron.[30] In 1679, when the king banished first his brother and then his illegitimate son, Monmouth, it was a royal yacht that carried them out of England; and when James returned from exile in Scotland, first in February 1680 and then, definitively, in March 1682, he did so aboard the *Mary Yacht*.[31]

Foreign ambassadors and other dignitaries were invariably transported in the yachts. In July 1678, for example, the *Portsmouth Yacht* carried the Swedish ambassador to Den Briel; in February 1682, the *Mary Yacht*

Overleaf: The departure of Mary of Modena, second wife of James, Duke of York, from Calais, 21 November 1673. Jacob Knyff. *(© National Maritime Museum, Greenwich, London, BHC0319)*

transported the Russian ambassador to Rotterdam; in October 1683, the *Charlotte Yacht* carried the Danish ambassador to Rotterdam; and in November 1685, the same vessel brought over the Venetian ambassador from Den Briel.[32] These voyages were much more complex affairs than the mere transportation of one man. When the *Mary Yacht* brought over the new French ambassador, the Marquis d'Angeau, in the summer of 1680, she also carried four other marquises, four counts, three chevaliers, two gentlemen and the fifty-four valets that they mustered between them; the yachts were spacious, but even so, the voyage must have been uncomfortably cramped.[33] The yachts also transported British ministers and diplomats setting off on, or returning from, foreign missions. Although most of these voyages involved simply landing or embarking the dignitary in question at a suitable port in France or Flanders, some involved much longer voyages, for instance to Stockholm or Gdansk.[34] Yachts were also frequently employed to carry the goods of prominent figures from A to B. In March 1674, the *Monmouth Yacht* went to Calais to bring back some goods belonging to the king's mistress, the Duchess of Portsmouth, before sailing to Leith to bring south some plate belonging to the Duke of Lauderdale, the effective viceroy of Scotland; while in the following year, one of the yachts was ordered to bring the Duchess of Richmond's bed from Dieppe.[35] The yachts sometimes transported the dead. After the Earl of Sandwich's body was fished out of the sea following his death at the Battle of Solebay in May 1672, it was brought up to Greenwich on a yacht before being 'locked up in some private room' in Deptford dockyard 'till the day of his solemnity'.[36] In April 1679, the *Mary Yacht* brought back the corpse of Lady Mordaunt from France, attended by a mourning retinue of twenty-seven, which included eight children and such relatively lowly individuals as her butler, groom, coachman, 'serving man' and laundress.[37]

A number of the yachts were, at least nominally, at the beck and call of those after whom they were named, or their spouses. The king could call on any or all of the yachts, but at any time, he had one or more favourites: the two *Katherines*, *Charlotte* and *Cleveland* occupied this position at different times. When the second *Katherine Yacht* was ordered in 1673, she was said to be 'for His Majesty's special use'.[38] The king also had a strong liking for the Sixth Rate frigate *Greyhound*, which was sometimes used as a yacht, as in the voyage of 1675. The Duke of York's first yacht was the *Anne*, which was replaced in 1677 by the second *Mary*, named after both his daughter and his second wife; her captain always described her as 'His Royal Highness's Yacht *Mary*', not as 'His Majesty's'.[39] The *Monmouth Yacht* was available for the service of the duke of that name, although he seems to have used it relatively little, and in later years, the *Isabella* for the Duke of Grafton, Monmouth's half-brother

(Isabella was the name of his wife, the daughter of the royal minister Lord Arlington). Grafton took his yacht with him when he went out to command in the Mediterranean in 1687, but he also used it for a purpose probably unique in the annals of British royal yachts: namely, kidnapping. In March 1686, he helped his brother, the Duke of Northumberland, to abduct the latter's wife from Chelsea, then bundled her aboard the *Isabella* prior to shipping her off to a convent in Ghent. Northumberland's hasty marriage to the relatively low-born widow Katherine Lucy (reputedly the daughter of a poulterer from Bracknell) had stymied his chances of a much more lucrative match to a daughter of the fabulously wealthy Duke of Newcastle, and the two brothers seem to have colluded to remove the inconvenient Katherine from the scene. Rather like a distant relative of his in future years, though, King James II was not amused, and insisted both that Grafton should extract Katherine from her convent and that Northumberland should honour his marriage to her, which he duly did.[40]

Lenox was the private yacht of Charles Stuart, Duke of Richmond and Lennox, Lord High Admiral of Scotland, but following the duke's death in 1673, it was incorporated into the navy proper.[41] *Fanfan*, although not officially a yacht, was the personal pleasure boat of Prince Rupert, serving as the prince's despatch vessel during wartime. In 1666, it even served briefly as a flagship, when Rupert loaned it to his old colleague Sir Robert Holmes for the attack on the Dutch anchorage at the Vlie.[42] By the mid–1670s, though, the prince's sailing days were over, and the *Fanfan* was employed on general naval duties at Tangier.[43] The *Saudadoes* was meant to be Queen Catherine of Braganza's personal yacht, and at first, after its launching in 1670, she had 'frequent divertissement upon the river' in it; at her behest, too, it was sent on two voyages back to Catherine's homeland of Portugal, with the captain under orders to bring back detailed information about the state of affairs there.[44] Thereafter, particularly after the yacht was rebuilt into a Sixth Rate frigate in 1673, the queen rarely used it again; perhaps the prospect of sailing in company with the *Cleveland* and *Portsmouth* yachts, named after two of the royal mistresses, was a little unpalatable. Her successor Mary of Modena had no such emotional baggage, and made use of whichever yacht was available when she had 'some errand of hers' in mind.[45]

Naturally, given the nature of the missions that the yachts undertook and the passengers that they carried, their captains were chosen for both professional skill and outstanding discretion. By rights, such small vessels should not have had full captains at all, but those who commanded the yachts were invariably senior men, who often possessed impressive service records. The Duke of York's favourite yacht commander was Christopher Gunman, who, uniquely among his fraternity, was techni-

Captain Christopher Gunman, commander of the Duke of York's yacht until his death in 1685; the empty left sleeve betrays the loss of that hand in battle. *(Doddington Hall, Lincolnshire)*

cally a foreigner: born at Dramm in Norway, albeit to a father from Norfolk, he eventually became a naturalised English citizen in 1670. Less uniquely, he also bore the scars of war service, having lost his left hand in a ferocious single-ship combat in 1666. From 1669 to 1685, Gunman commanded James's principal yacht, first the *Anne* and then the second *Mary*. In September 1672, James offered him the chance to take command of a frigate for the winter, giving Gunman a potential opportunity to enrich himself through prize money, or to stay in the duke's yacht. Gunman chose the latter, and James promised 'to take a particular care of me'.[46] The duke was true to his word; when, ten years later, Gunman was briefly imprisoned because of his supposed part in the sinking of the *Gloucester*, James swiftly intervened to secure his release.

King Charles's favourite yacht captains were William Fazeby and Ralph Sanderson. Fazeby, a veteran cavalier, had also lost a limb, in his case a leg, during the second Dutch war; despite this, he commanded no fewer than eight yachts, almost all of them principal ones, in an unbroken career that began in 1661 and continued until after the Glorious Revolution.[47] Sanderson, who commanded four of the principal royal yachts in succession between 1674 and 1689, came from an old seafaring family of County Durham, and had previously served as master of the navy's largest warships. The yacht captains tended to live in Deptford or Greenwich, close to their vessels, because they were often sent to sea at very short notice: for example, at noon on Sunday, 10 February 1678, Pepys sent an order to the captain of the *Cleveland Yacht*, 'or any other yacht in present condition to sail', to sail for Dover on the next tide, but if that was not possible, 'you are by no means (wind and weather permitting) to omit tomorrow morning'.[48] The highly confidential and discreet nature of their work might explain how the yacht captains became wealthy men, certainly much wealthier than their regular pay alone would have permitted them to be. Gunman died suddenly in 1685 (bizarrely, he fell off Calais pier and perished of gangrene), but left £1,000 to his widow alone, in addition to substantial legacies to each of his five surviving children.[49] Fazeby received at least one payment of secret service money from Charles II, totalling nearly £400, and by the time of his death in 1711, he owned several properties in Greenwich and could bequeath £1,500 as future dowries for each of his two granddaughters.[50] However, the treatment of the yacht crews was not quite so generous. In 1682, the men of the *Cleveland* petitioned for their back pay: all had served on her for between four and six years, but had never received any wages, forcing their families to live on ever more extended credit.[51]

Despite Charles II's undoubted enthusiasm for going to sea whenever he could, the direct royal employment of the yachts was always relatively brief, and it is probable that he spent no more than about fifty nights aboard them during the entirety of his reign.[52] As the king got older, too, so his sailing expeditions became less frequent. The court's move to Windsor for much of every summer from 1674 onwards made it more difficult and time consuming for Charles to get to the yachts, which were moored at Deptford and Greenwich; an easy trip in the royal barge from Whitehall, and not too problematic from Hampton Court, but a slightly greater logistical problem from so much further upstream. The last long-distance yacht voyage took place in August 1679, when Charles sailed down to Chatham and Sheerness, then round to Portsmouth. He went ashore there, and then returned overland to Windsor. But the voyage nearly proved fatal; the king developed a fever shortly after returning, at a time when the kingdom was wracked by a crisis over the succession to the throne, and for a time his life was despaired of. Perhaps this experience made him decide to scale back his seafaring, although the vigorous tennis match he played shortly after returning from sea might have been rather more directly responsible for the crisis.[53] The king's last significant cruises were in June 1682, when he went to Chatham in the *Charlotte Yacht* to witness the launch of the First Rate *Britannia*; in September of the same year, when he tested the sailing qualities of his new yacht *Fubbs* in the Thames estuary; and in September 1683, when he went from Southampton to Portsmouth and back, conducting an extensive tour of the fortifications and ships at the latter.[54] It might have been during the September 1682 voyage in the *Fubbs* that a stiff breeze suddenly blew up off the North Foreland, compelling the royal brothers to take in sail themselves. One of the passengers, the Reverend John Gostling, sub-dean of the Chapel Royal, who possessed a 'stupendous' bass voice, was so struck by the danger (or, probably, the highly exaggerated sense of danger that a landlubber clergyman might have felt), that he wrote an anthem about the terrors of the deep, and got Purcell to compose the music for it.[55] The anthem in question, 'They that go down to the sea in ships' (Z57), certainly features a prominent bass part, and would probably have been sung by Gostling before the king in the Chapel Royal towards the end of Charles's life.[56]

The increasing rarity of Charles II's outings can be seen in the number of times when the principal yachts were employed on royal business. The *Charlotte* made five such voyages in the year from May 1679 to May 1680, four in each of the following two years, but only one in 1682/83 and none in 1683/84; the *Kitchen* made an average of six royal voyages a year between 1680 and 1683, but only three in 1683/84, and some of these voyages would have been to provide meals for 'royals' other than the king.[57] But the Duke of York continued to sail, both before and after he ascended the throne. Indeed, James even managed to obtain some sea time during the Exclusion Crisis, when his brother sent him into exile in Scotland: the *Mary Yacht* went with him, and during the first half of 1681, it took James from its berth at Leith on frequent cruises to the islands in the Firth of Forth, sometimes sailing as far as Tantallon Castle.[58] In August 1684, James and his son-in-law, Prince George of Denmark, took the *Charlotte Yacht* from Sheerness to Greenwich, and in the following month the two men sailed to Spithead. As king, James took his yachts down to the Medway in April 1686, inspecting the fortifications of Sheerness, the ships under construction at Chatham, and the regiment known as Kirke's Lambs, once of the Tangier garrison and more recently notorious for their viciousness against Monmouth's rebels in the West Country. James made a similar voyage in the following year in order to attend the launch of the *Sedgemoor*, and sailed round from Southampton to Portsmouth during his summer progress in August 1686.[59]

Increasingly, the yachts were made available for the service of anyone prominent enough or rich enough to be able to hire them for a voyage. Pepys complained that yacht voyages were traded on the Royal Exchange, and that whereas in the early days, when there were very few of them, passengers were prepared to share, by the 1680s 'nobody expects less than the appointment of a yacht to himself only'. Worse, Pepys argued that the yachts presented a security threat, 'the king's own vessels … carrying out persons (without search) he would [ie should] have kept at home, and bringing over others which he would have stayed abroad'.[60] It is impossible from the surviving evidence to establish which yacht voyages were purchased and which were for reasons of state, but it is difficult to see how the latter could have applied to such individuals as the wealthy banker Alderman Edward Backwell, who was transported to Holland by the *Cleveland Yacht* in 1681, Sir Henry Tichborne, who came across from Le Havre in 1685, or Mademoiselle Elizabeth de Cafaro, who crossed to Rotterdam in 1687.[61] The yachts were even used to carry foreigners who were not bound to or from England: in March 1674, the *Monmouth Yacht* carried the Bishop of Marseilles from Calais to Hamburg, and three months later made the same voyage with the Marquis de Béthune.[62] But other unlikely voyages probably did carry a royal imprimatur. In 1678, a yacht was ordered to Dieppe to bring across Sir Robert Tabor, 'our famous ague doctor'; Tabor had previously cured Charles II, and had just done the same for the Dauphin of France.[63] Some yacht voyages can only be regarded as bizarre, such as that undertaken by the *Charlotte Yacht* in May 1684, when she went to Rotterdam to bring over some 'French comedians'.[64] Their special status, possessing de facto 'diplomatic immunity', made the yachts ideal vehicles for other forms of activity, too. In March 1679, even the trusted Christopher Gunman was reprimanded for smuggling, a zealous customs official having discovered a substantial amount of undeclared wine aboard the *Mary Yacht*.[65]

It would be easy to paint a picture of the yachts as little more than glorified pleasure craft, serving the whims of both a cynical monarch and the idle rich who could afford to pay him for their services; indeed, the frequent description of the yachts in contemporary sources as 'pleasure boats' reinforces this impression. But this is a gross distortion of the yachts' actual role, and above all, it would ignore the two occasions when they undertook humanitarian missions that undoubtedly saved the lives of some of those fleeing persecution in their native lands. The exodus of English Catholics, including the Keightleys of Hertingfordbury, aboard the *Charlotte Yacht* in February 1679, also included the likes of the Oxfordshire gentlemen Lyster Blount and Richard Farmer; Charles Arundel, brother of one of England's principal Catholic aristocrats, Lord Arundel of Wardour, who was already in prison for treason; John Belson, the prominent Catholic historian and controversialist; Mrs Margaret Stafford; Doctor Henry Tichborne and his wife Mary, members of one of the principal Catholic families in Hampshire; and Dame Mary Huddleston, a relative by marriage of the priest who would receive the dying King Charles II into the Roman Catholic faith. The party of refugees also included Mrs Mary Yate, her son Charles and daughter Mary; in exile, Mary senior would be maintained until her death by the Paris Augustinians, while her daughter became a nun in the same order, as did her two sisters.[66]

Any or all of those boarding the *Charlotte* or *Cleveland* yachts would have been potential targets for the rabid anti-Catholic mobs who had virtually free rein in the winter of 1679, but that would have been multiplied many times over in the case of the rotund fifty-year-old figure who boarded the *Portsmouth Yacht* at the beginning of March, bound for exile in Bruges. Henry Howard, sixth Duke of Norfolk, was England's premier Catholic nobleman and the hereditary Earl Marshal of the kingdom. His faith and high status made him an obvious target during the Popish Plot, and he was briefly accused of being party to it; although the charge was never pursued, the execution of his cousin, Viscount Stafford, might have suggested that his time was bound to come.[67] Like all the other Catholic refugees, Norfolk had obtained a pass to leave England from Charles II. But it would have been easy, and politically far more sensible, for the king to have washed his hands of the exiles at that point, and they could have easily arranged their own passage on merchant ships bound for the continent. The fact that Charles put the royal yachts at their disposal suggests that he was determined to take every possible step to ensure the safety of his loyal but widely despised Catholic subjects; and the royal orders were carried out without demur by his trusted captains and crews. This politically risky act of charity had an unintended consequence, too. Word of mouth evidently took its course, and Catholics were soon turning up unannounced at the royal yachts, badgering and bribing the captains to take them overseas – even if they lacked the necessary passes.[68]

In 1685, the yachts were once again the escape routes of choice for refugees fleeing religious persecution, but this time, the flow was going in the opposite direction. In October of that year, King Louis XIV revoked the Edict of Nantes, by which his grandfather had granted a considerable measure of religious freedom to France's Huguenot (Protestant) minority. In fact, an exodus had been under way for some years, as government pressure steadily increased, and many Huguenots sought refuge across the Channel in England. The new King James II's attitude to all this was ambivalent. While he disliked the religious principles of the Huguenots, he also found repugnant the methods of persecution that his cousin Louis had authorised, and made a number of charitable gestures towards the refugees. But these were hedged in with rather more caveats than his brother had provided, and although he recognised the economic benefits that the immigrants brought, James's personal attitude seems to have been essentially hostile to the influx.[69] This ambivalence informed his policy towards those Huguenots who attempted to take passage in the royal yachts as they sailed from their usual French ports of call, Calais and Dieppe. In the autumn of 1685, shortly after the Revocation, James permitted French officers to search outgoing yachts for concealed refugees – an act that one of his yacht captains, William Davies, found 'astonishing'. Davies subsequently used his command, the *Katherine Yacht*, to smuggle Huguenots on a number of occasions, and he was eventually dismissed for this by the king in May 1687. But by then, James was in the middle of a spectacular policy U-turn, having just issued a Declaration of Indulgence which promised toleration to all Protestant dissenters, including the Huguenots. Davies was recommissioned to his command on 12 June, so it is entirely possible that his dismissal was a sham, engineered as a token sop to the French.[70]

Despite their involvement in the two evacuations of religious refugees, it was clear by the mid-1680s that the yachts were markedly underemployed. This was difficult to justify during a time of financial stringency – indeed, the first proposal to lay up some of the yachts to save money was made as early as 1675 – and in December 1686, Pepys undertook a detailed analysis of the activities of the seven principal yachts during the preceding seven years.[71] This revealed that they had undertaken 131 voyages on the king's service, but another 341 on what Pepys described as 'private occasions'; the most marked disparity was in the case of the *Katherine Yacht*, which had undertaken nineteen royal voyages and

seventy-two for private individuals. The total cost of operating the seven yachts (two of which were built only part-way through the period in question) came to £63,450.[72] In typical fashion, Pepys subtly skewed the statistics to prove his point: 'headlining' the crude number of voyages alone omits a vital piece of information, namely the duration of those voyages (a royal voyage to Danzig, for example, would have taken longer than several private, short sea-crossings between England and Calais or Dieppe put together). However, if Pepys actually had judged the yachts on this criterion too, he would have found his thesis confirmed by the logs of the vessels themselves, which show them spending long periods lying idle at moorings off Deptford or Greenwich.[73] As a result of his analysis, four yachts were immediately laid up as a cost-cutting measure, saving £5,000 a year.[74] In the longer term, though, the yachts survived, and they actually obtained a new lease of life after 1689, when foreign monarchs, who needed regular and secure communication with their original homelands in, successively, the Netherlands and Hanover, generated a new demand for their services. Several of Charles II's yachts had astonishingly long lives, albeit with due allowance being made for the eighteenth-century definition of 'rebuilding' as essentially taking a ship to pieces and creating a new one with some of the timbers of the old. The *Fubbs* lasted, in name at least, until 1781, the second *Katherine Yacht* until 1801, and the second *Mary Yacht* until 1816.

Royalty boarding a yacht; a van de Velde drawing which gives a good idea of the size of the entourage the royal family took with them when going to sea.
(© National Maritime Museum, Greenwich, London, PZ7282)

6

Governing the Navy

'THE ADMIRALTY' is one of the most iconic institutional names in British history, and also one of the most iconic addresses. Throughout the Royal Navy's long period of supremacy, and until as relatively recently as 1964, the Admiralty was where the orders to frigates and fireships, dreadnoughts and gunboats, originated; it was to the Admiralty that the captains of far-flung men-of-war reported. During wartime, communications beginning 'The Admiralty regrets ...' were dreaded, not only in the dockyard towns, but in homes the length and breadth of Britain and its empire.

The Admiralty building on Whitehall, the original, front, element of which (the so-called Ripley building) was built in 1726, and the rather larger Admiralty House to the south of it, opened in 1788, witnessed the making of countless crucial decisions, besides a number of great historical events: Nelson's remains lay in the waiting room of the Ripley building overnight prior to their interment in St Paul's, while John F Kennedy and Harold Macmillan met there in 1962 to discuss the global situation. In the late seventeenth century, though, the Admiralty was essentially wherever the Lord High Admiral happened to be, and its establishment was minute: as late as 1687, the entire Admiralty staff consisted of four clerks, a messenger and a doorkeeper, in a kind of inverse corollary of Parkinson's Law.[1] When the Duke of York was Lord High Admiral, from 1660 to 1673, 'the Admiralty' was essentially contained within his apartments at St James's Palace. Between 1673 and 1679, it met most often at the Robes Chamber in Whitehall Palace, while its papers and the Admiralty secretary who presided over them, Samuel Pepys, could usually be found down the road in Derby House on Cannon Row in Westminster. But once or twice a year, elements of the Admiralty, including the most important element of all, could be found in a small town straddling the border of Cambridgeshire and Suffolk, a very long way from the sea. King Charles II saw absolutely no reason at all to let the hard work of running horses at Newmarket interfere with the enjoyment he obtained from running the Royal Navy.

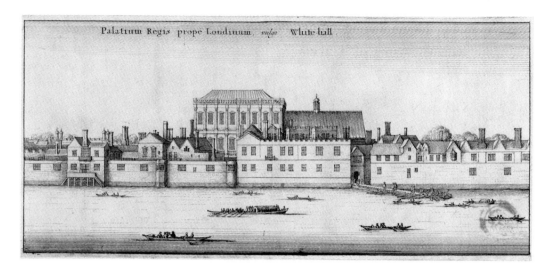

Palatium Regis prope Londinum *vulgo* White-hall

The Palace of Whitehall, as drawn by Wenceslaus Hollar in 1647; for much of the period, the de facto headquarters of the Admiralty. *(Rijksmuseum, Amsterdam)*

In 1660, James, Duke of York, finally entered into the office of Lord High Admiral of England which had been intended for him since his childhood, and to which his brother formally appointed him at the palace of Saint-Germain on 31 August 1649.[2] James issued his first order in his new office on 4 June 1660 and, aptly, it was for the frigate *Sorlings* to sail from Weymouth to Jersey, the island which had figured so largely in the earlier lives of both his brother and himself.[3] From then on, through the summer and into the autumn of 1660, much of the duke's work consisted of confirming office-holders in their places aboard ships, in the dockyards, or in other parts of the naval administration, and appointing new ones to replace those who had been ejected for being too enthusiastic for the previous regime.

What may have been the very last action of the British civil wars had to be smoothed over, by an order of 5 June: Captain Barker of the *Lichfield* was ordered to ensure that his crew did not embezzle the goods aboard the Royalist privateer *Henrietta Maria,* sailing under a commission issued by James before the Restoration, which Barker had fired at and captured in the river at Swansea.[4] Several errors were made. The wrong men were initially given warrants as the chandler and victualler of the navy, so the appointments had to be changed.[5] Such problems were probably inevitable in the confusion and excitement of the Restoration, with an inexperienced new administration attempting to get to grips with a complex organisation and the competing demands of many rival candidates for office. Pepys's own experience amply demonstrates this: he had to buy off the previous holder of his office, Thomas Barlow (appointed in 1639), and reject bids of £500 and later £1,000 from rivals who sought the position.[6] Otherwise, one of the key priorities in the early months of the new regime was ensuring loyalty and stability, and that

meant a succession of purges: captains, lesser officers and dockyard
workers were all removed because they were felt to be politically or religiously unreliable.[7] Another urgent task was to pay off the swollen active
fleet inherited from the Commonwealth, but this was gradually accomplished during the following months.[8] Naval administration then gradually settled down into a routine, with the duke meeting his Navy Board
more or less once a week, as the Lord High Admiral's patent specified.[9]

James was, undoubtedly, fortunate in his subordinates. His secretary
(until 1667), William Coventry, was a formidably talented individual who
swiftly mastered naval business, as his impressive range of papers,
preserved at Longleat House, attests. Below them, the Navy Board was
the traditional subordinate administrative body, dating back to Henry
VIII's reign (and in the case of the office of Clerk of the Acts, over three
hundred years before that). It had been radically remodelled under the
Commonwealth, but in 1660, Charles and James restored it to its
previous model of four 'principal officers', adding three 'extra commissioners' after republican practice. Of the first batch of these, Lord

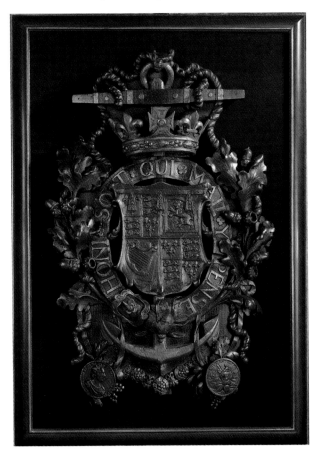

The arms of James,
Duke of York, when
Lord High Admiral,
possibly from the
cabin of the *Anne
Yacht. (© National
Maritime Museum,
Greenwich, London,
F3016)*

Berkeley was an old soldier who had been master of the Duke of York's household in exile, Peter Pett (son of the builder of the *Sovereign of the Seas*) ran Chatham dockyard, while Sir William Penn was a former Commonwealth general-at-sea and a possible originator of the new naval tactic, the 'line of battle'; James came to lean heavily on him for the operational aspects of his job. Three of the principal officers were also veteran officers: Sir George Carteret, the Treasurer, was the man who had paid for the king's first boat; Sir William Batten, the Surveyor, had led the Royalist revolt in the fleet in 1648; while Sir John Mennes, the Controller (after the death of Sir Robert Slyngsbie in October 1661), was one of the few pre-Civil War Royalist officers still active. In this company, the fourth principal officer, the Clerk of the Acts, might have been easily overlooked and overwhelmed, especially as he was young, almost completely ignorant of the navy, and only in post because he was fortuitously related to one of the principal architects of the Restoration, the newly minted Earl of Sandwich. That might very well have been the case, had not the new Clerk been Samuel Pepys.

Between 1660 and the outbreak of the second Anglo-Dutch war, the Duke of York was at least nominally responsible for a number of important sets of instructions and other documents that determined many aspects of the navy's organisation. In 1662, James barred naval officials from trading with the navy on their own accounts, one of the principal causes of the corruption that had been endemic in the navy under the previous republican regimes.[10] In the same year, he promulgated a hugely important set of instructions for the Navy Board, and in the following year, a set of general instructions for captains. In reality, though, these were largely derivative, and borrowed from earlier precedents: the Navy Board instructions were based on those issued by the Earl of Northumberland in 1640, while the captains' instructions were based on previous sets that dated back to the 1630s and probably beyond, as James himself freely admitted.[11] Similarly, the Articles of War of 1661 were based on those issued by the Commonwealth's generals-at-sea in 1652, which in turn were derived largely from earlier examples; the difference was that the Restoration regime gave them the additional force of statute law. Nevertheless, even if many of his measures were derivative and lacked clear means of checking compliance, James implemented them with vigour and determination, and the fact that he issued so many major sets of instructions in such short order (inter alia, there were also new sailing and fighting instructions in 1664/65), demonstrates the passion for order and regulation that he displayed throughout his life. As his friend the Earl of Ailesbury remarked, James's 'heart and soul was set on the flourishing condition of the navy, with this English expression, "our fleet is our bulwark, and therefore each true patriot ought to wish the prosperity of it'".[12] Indeed, James was even prepared to stump up over £9,000 of his own money to pay off crews at a time of serious financial embarrassment for the Crown, while Pepys and others fulsomely praised his attention to detail, his willingness to take advice (in this aspect of his career, if not, fatally for him, in others), and concern for proper regulation.[13]

If James believed that he would be the sole 'ruler of the king's navee', though, he was soon disabused. The Lord High Admiral's patent was notoriously vague, and Charles's royal prerogative, plus the fact that His Majesty's ships really were literally that, alongside his simple fascination with all things maritime, gave the king ample justification for getting involved in his brother's domain. Certain matters could be ordered only by the monarch: at the end of the 1666 campaign, James's secretary, Sir William Coventry, needed the king's order in writing for disposing the fleet.[14] Many matters of naval policy had to go through the Privy Council, over which Charles presided, which dealt with a wide range of matters that seemed to require such additional authority. For instance, it issued orders dealing with the pressing of seamen, the victualling of the fleet, the granting of pensions and gratuities, and authorised embargoes on outward-bound shipping, such as the order it made on 26 October 1664 to put one in place until the fleet was fully manned.[15] The council also had its own committee for Admiralty and naval affairs, and Charles also drew on formal or informal advice on naval matters from a wide range of sources, such as the Privy Council's committee for foreign affairs (widely known as his 'cabinet council', the original precursor of today's Cabinet), the Navy Board, and senior naval officers, such as the informal committee of flag officers which met in 1664/65 to plan the naval campaigns of the second Anglo-Dutch war. Thus the formal relationship between the royal brothers was complex: the king was simultaneously the Lord High Admiral's superior, principal adviser and legal 'enforcer'.

The meticulous attention to detail that Charles and James displayed during their frequent visits to naval facilities is well illustrated by the royal tour of Harwich in October 1668. The brothers went round the coast in three royal yachts, accompanied by the dukes of Monmouth, Buckingham, Richmond and other dignitaries. Silas Taylor, the naval agent at the small royal dockyard which had been established there during the second Anglo-Dutch war, recorded what happened:

> I was then called to show him [the king] the yard, to which he first went, and asked whether the *Resolution* and *Rupert* were built at that launch [ie slipway], and, together with the duke, praised it for a good launch; he viewed the yard, cranes, and situation, and went up the works, and circuiting the greatest part of the town, returned to my house. He asked to whom the house belonged; I said it was his

Majesty's: he then asked if the storehouses in the back yard belonged to it, and what was in them; I told him they were for naval stores; he asked what the house cost; I told him £300, also how big it was, and upon being told it had four rooms on a floor, he replied it was a cheap pennyworth, and the duke entering the parlour, the king said, 'Brother, this house is my house, and it is a pretty one' … He landed alone the next day, Sunday, at 6 o'clock, and was waited upon by Sir Charles Littleton and Sir Bernard de Gomme [royal engineer]; he went on foot out of the town, viewing all the places in relation to fortifications, and examining some drafts offered by Sir Bernard, which he rectified in the field at two or three stations, with his own hand, by a black lead pen and ruler. After a five miles' walk over high stiles and plough grounds, his Royal Highness found him out, and after some discourse and pacing the ground, returned. The king then went to 'his house' (as he called it five or six times that morning) …[16]

The former dockyard bell at Harwich, carrying the monogram of Charles II. *(Author's photograph)*

While the king's constant references to 'his house' might just have been expressions of natural pride in ownership, they might also have been something else – barbed reminders to his younger brother that Charles, not James, was the ultimate authority in the navy, just as in the kingdom as a whole. By the time of their visit to Harwich, the relationship between the siblings was rockier than it had been for years. In the previous year, the Lord Chancellor, the Earl of Clarendon, was removed from office, made the scapegoat for a disastrous war that he had steadfastly opposed. The fall of his father-in-law significantly undermined James's influence, especially as it signalled the concomitant rise of a group of politicians and courtiers who were hostile to the duke's interests.[17] Superficially the most powerful member of this group was George Villiers, second Duke of Buckingham, the son of the royal favourite of an earlier generation. Raised with Charles II, and perhaps the king's oldest and closest friend, Buckingham was brilliant, witty, and arguably even more lecherous than his sovereign. He also had at least a dilettante interest in naval affairs, and perhaps saw himself one day emulating his father by becoming Lord High Admiral. Unfortunately, Buckingham's aspirations were undermined by his arrogance, unreliability and sheer fecklessness. In 1665, he demanded a command in the fleet, and when this was refused, he attempted to secure a place in the council of war by virtue of his social rank and friendship with the king. Although Charles favoured the appointment, James peremptorily rejected the demand, and Buckingham went off in a huff.[18] But the tables were turned following the fall of Clarendon, when Buckingham and his allies, the Earl of Arlington and Sir Thomas Clifford, were politically ascendant.

The king's increasing assertiveness in naval affairs led to a proposal to undermine the Duke of York's independence by joining the Privy Council's naval committee to the Lord High Admiral in order to manage the 'oeconomicall' part of the navy, but with all the officers relating to that part – so presumably the Navy Board, the dockyard officers, and so forth – to be appointed by the king himself.[19] The existing Privy Council committee of the navy was reconstituted and packed with the great men of the day – Rupert, Albemarle, Arlington, the Earls of Anglesey and Craven, and from July 1668, Buckingham, too. This was done without reference to James, who was naturally discontented, and the duke responded by launching his own enquiry into the condition of the navy, with the aim of rooting out abuses.[20] Even so, Charles proceeded to commission the captains of 1668's summer fleet himself, while another sign of the changed balance in the naval administration might have been the removal of the Earl of Anglesey, who had only been installed as Treasurer of the Navy in 1667. He was appointed despite the king's reservations about the accusations of mismanagement made against Anglesey in his previous role as Treasurer of Ireland, but only lasted until the end of 1668, when he was removed from office. Anglesey blamed Charles for his downfall, although it was also undoubtedly connected to his opposition to Buckingham, who was then probably at the height of his influence.[21] Anglesey was replaced by Sir Thomas Osborne and Sir Thomas Littleton, 'creatures' of Buckingham and Arlington, whose initial acts in office were hostile to the Duke of York and his interests.[22] James took all of this personally, and was deeply hurt by his brother's actions – this at a time when, in private, he was going through the throes of his conversion to Roman Catholicism.[23]

Meanwhile, the supposed mismanagement of the second Anglo-Dutch war was under intense scrutiny from the 'Brooke House committee', more formally the Committee of Public Accounts, which had been set up by the king to placate Parliament. Charles was closely involved in the Brooke House discussions, invariably supporting Pepys and his other subordinates. He had little patience with some of the questioning, interrupting the commissioners, and openly expressing his resentment of some of their methods and questions.[24] At the climax of proceedings, the king extracted his Clerk of the Acts from a hole that Pepys had dug for himself. In typical fashion, Pepys confidently asserted that he had never personally benefited from any payment of ticket, only to be immediately confronted by one for £7, marked 'paid to Mr Pepys'. Pepys denied, but did not disprove, any wrongdoing, and Charles remarked that he did not think his man would have stolen such a trifling sum – thus giving the impression that he would not have been surprised if Pepys had purloined a much larger one.[25]

While Charles defended Pepys, his relationship with his brother remained rocky. This was a matter of public knowledge, at least in court

circles: in 1674, for instance, the Venetian ambassador referred to 'the old jealousies between the King and his Highness', and his despatches and those of his predecessors often refer to rumours or first-hand knowledge of tensions between the brothers.[26] During 1668/69, the king became at least briefly interested in the possibility of divorcing his barren queen, and the implications if he remarried a younger, more fertile wife were obvious to all, not least to the heir presumptive. Between 1669 and 1672, though, the relationship between the brothers mended to a considerable extent. According to James, he was one of only four other people present when, on 25 January 1669, the king declared his private intention to become a Roman Catholic; and as the duke was already well on the road to Rome, this shared confidence, and shared enthusiasm for a proscribed faith, might have generated a new bond between the brothers.[27] Both were privy to the greatest secret of the age, the negotiations leading to the secret Treaty of Dover of 1670, by which Charles committed himself to follow James publicly to the Roman Church, taking his entire kingdom with him; but that would occur at some indeterminate point in the future, and more immediately, the treaty committed the king to joining his cousin, Louis XIV, in a declaration of war against the United Provinces of the Netherlands. Preparing for such a colossal conflict would clearly be a huge administrative task (as well as presenting untold opportunities for military and naval glory, which must have appealed to James), and both the king and the duke threw themselves into it.

Above, left: 12 Buckingham Street, London, the home of Samuel Pepys from 1679 to 1689. *(Author's photograph)*

Above, right: St Olave's Church, Hart Street, London. The Navy Board's official church, the blocked-up entrance to their pew being marked by the large plaque on the right. *(Author's photograph)*

But James's private and public personas were now set on entirely irrec-
oncilable paths. At Easter 1672, just as the combined Anglo-French fleet
was preparing to sail under his command, he failed to take communion
in the Chapel Royal, the first clear public sign of his conversion. At the
Battle of Solebay a little over a month later, the seemingly inexplicable
behaviour of the French squadron increased suspicions that the Stuart
brothers were being played for fools by their French cousin.* The war
became increasingly unpopular, and anti-Catholic, anti-French sentiment
grew. During the winter of 1672/73, a Test Act made its way through
Parliament, the principal provision of which was the barring of Catholics
from holding public office. An immediate consequence of this was that
the Duke of York had to resign as Lord High Admiral, which he did on
15 June 1673. The king could easily have carried on as before, simply
bestowing the office on another: Prince Rupert was the obvious candidate. Instead, Charles reverted to his father's precedent of 1628 and
placed the Admiralty in commission. The Privy Council's navy
committee was simply rechristened, its thirteen members becoming
Lords of the Admiralty; Charles seems to have spoken to each member
individually as he appointed them, telling them what his expectations
were. Pepys moved from the Navy Board to become secretary to the new
body and, in practice for much of the time, to the king himself.[28] This
marked a major change, as James's secretaries during the previous thirteen
years had been men of much greater social status. But by this time, Pepys's
professional reputation was unassailable, his mastery in naval affairs a
byword. It was very much a case of 'Cometh the hour, cometh the man.'

Arguably the most important task of the Lord High Admiral and the king
was to decide on the deployment of warships. During the 1660s, this was
part of James's remit, but Charles sometimes meddled, especially when his
brother was at sea in command of the fleet: in 1665, for example, the king
wrote directly to Prince Rupert, then commanding the White Squadron,
to suggest that he should leave some of his Fourth Rate frigates in the
Swale and use their crews to man his larger ships, as well as assigning only
one ketch to each First and Second Rate ship. During the same period,
the king was reported to have ordered ships to go northward to intercept
Dutch ships sailing around the north of Scotland, and although ultimately no such expedition set out, the fact that Pepys believed the king
could order such a deployment on his own initiative is telling.[29] In both
war and peace, the protection of trade was a key imperative for the Stuart
brothers. There was already a system of convoys for the richer overseas
trades, notably those from the Mediterranean, and a small number of

ships were permanently assigned to particular stations, such as Ireland and the Caribbean.* Convoys were sometimes employed in home waters in wartime, but the Stuart brothers also had to dispose their ships there in ways that provided a more flexible response. Consequently, warships were often deployed to cruise at strategic points, such as between Scilly and Cape Clear (West Cork) to meet incoming traders from the Atlantic and Mediterranean, off the east coast to guard the coal fleets from the Tyne, and in and around the Firth of Forth; this was the origin of the term 'cruiser', originally applied to any warship undertaking such duties, and much later, the description of a particular size and type of vessel. In peacetime, warships were not usually assigned to such specific stations, but were deployed as and where necessary from the ships allocated to the Channel and Soundings.[30]

Defending trade has always been one of the most important but least glamorous aspects of naval policy, and both Charles and James fully appreciated this. By the time of the third Anglo-Dutch war (1672–74), several trades were so important that, in many ways, concern over the safe arrival of the merchant fleets assigned to them was not dissimilar to the anxiety that pervaded the Netherlands when the rich 'return fleets' from the East Indies were expected. This was most markedly so in the summer of 1673, when a huge and unusually rich fleet from the Americas, the Caribbean and the East Indies was expected home in England at exactly the same time that the Dutch and Anglo-French fleets were about to engage each other in the North Sea. By early August, concern for the fleet's safe arrival was almost at fever pitch on the London Exchange and at court.[31] But the incoming ships had been provided with a strong convoy of three Fourth Rates and a Fifth, assigned by the Duke of York before he was forced to resign from the Admiralty, and commanded by Sir William Poole, a highly competent and experienced officer (and a cousin of Sir William Penn). The fleet arrived at Cape Clear on 27 July, and was then safely escorted up the Channel. The arrival of these nine East Indiamen, twenty-four ships from Barbados, and two each from Guinea, Jamaica and Virginia, provided a welcome boost to both national morale and the national finances.[32]

During the 1670s and 1680s, with the exception of the years 1679–84, deployment became the exclusive preserve of the king, who decided, for instance, on how many ships to send out to guard the herring fishery, and whether or not a frigate should wait for the tardy Smyrna convoy before sailing on an urgent voyage to Lisbon and Tangier.[33] Both Charles and James gave particular attention to the proper protection of convoys: not only was the prosperity of English trade of natural concern to them, but providing adequate naval cover put them in good stead with the great trading companies, and thus with opinion-makers in the City of London.[34]

* See Chapter 9 and, for the other agendas that drove the royal brothers' deployments of warships during wartime, see Chapter 10.

From early in the restored monarchy, the brothers publicly declared their determination to support and protect trade. They often met delegations of merchants who wished to discuss naval protection for their trades, or responded positively to petitions from them, and took great pains over ensuring the right ships, with the right captains in command of them, were assigned to particular missions.[35] In March 1685, for example, James II intended to set out a number of Fourth Rates for summer service in the Channel, so he got Pepys to order the Surveyor of the Navy to send in a list of those which could be fitted out as quickly and cheaply as possible; James then planned to choose six, eight or ten, depending on his personal knowledge of the ships on the list, possibly substituting one or two Third Rates if he thought the list of Fourths insufficient.[36]

Pepys explained in a nutshell how the navy was run during the years 1673–79: 'the despatch of the general current business ... [of the navy] was wholly performed by the immediate direction of his Majesty (with the advice of his Royal Highness) to Mr Pepys, the meetings of the Commissioners being uncertain, and only in cases admitting delay and requiring the formality of debate'.[37] This was no executive 'Board of Admiralty' in the later sense; Prince Rupert, although named first in the commission's patent, was very far from being a 'First Lord of the Admiralty'. Essentially, the navy was to be governed by a triumvirate, two of whom were the sons of a king, saint and martyr, while the third was the son of a Fleet Street tailor. Therefore, James's resignation in 1673 was by no means the decisive break it could have been, entirely removing the Catholic heir from naval affairs. Although the duke was no longer Lord High Admiral, he remained an influential adviser, and sometimes – or, perhaps, very often – accompanied his brother to Admiralty meetings.* As early as July 1673, the Venetian ambassador claimed that James was still unofficially running the navy, 'but borrows the King's name'.[38] One of the duke's first acts after resigning was to block the appointment of a prominent merchant, James Puckle, as a commissioner of the navy; instead, the position went to Sir Richard Haddock, a long-serving naval officer.[39] Indeed, from 1673 onwards the duke's influence was particularly strong at the Navy Board, which was now an entirely different beast from the body which Pepys had served during his 'diary years'. It included such staunch supporters of James as Sir John Ernle, soon to be Chancellor of the Exchequer; the abrasive old Cavalier quasi-pirate Sir Richard Beach; Sir John Chicheley, a naval officer who had risen under James's patronage; and above all, Sir John Werden, the duke's private secretary.[40]

Pepys therefore had to 'upwardly manage' both the king and the heir

* For a particularly important example of this, see the Appendix, where other instances are cited.

to the throne, usually at the same time. He noted that he sometimes moved both Charles and James on particular issues, such as grants of leaves to officers.[41] Naturally, he knew that Charles could summon him at any moment to deliberate on naval matters, but the same was evidently also true of James. On 22 April 1678, at nine in the evening, Pepys wrote to the duke's secretary, Sir John Werden, to forewarn him just in case James wished to summon Pepys later that night:

> I was driven to my bed by an agueish fit last night at seven of the clock, which was followed by another of the cholic (my old foe) … by bleeding and other helps my pain is pretty well over, but not so much as to put me into a condition of going abroad tonight. Which, as you see it expedient, I pray deliver in my excuse to the duke.[42]

When the court was away, for instance at Newmarket, Pepys and senior naval officers wrote to James about appointments and operational matters.[43] The duke was present at the meetings of 1677/78 which planned the detail of a combined Anglo-Dutch fleet for an anticipated war against France. Although the war never broke out, the plans made, right down to the numbers and sizes of ships to be deployed to specific stations, were identical to, and thus clearly the model for, those implemented at the beginning of the great war of 1689–97 – so in one sense, James was partly responsible for planning the war against himself, and denying himself his earliest and best hope of a restoration.[44]

The Duke of York often had a direct influence in naval affairs, even occasionally issuing orders himself. In March 1676, for example, he informed Captain John Wyborne that he and his men should move from the *Speedwell* to the *Pearl*, and later in the same year he ordered the *Dartmouth* to Sheerness, having decided on his own initiative that she was the fittest ship to be sent to Virginia if his brother decided to send a second warship there, a decision that James was clearly prejudging.[45] In November 1677, it was the Duke of York, not the king, who decided on the gun salutes to be offered by and to the squadron of yachts carrying his new son-in-law, William of Orange, back to the Netherlands, while in January 1678 he decided on the provision of a convoy to Gallipoli.[46] Two months later, Pepys wrote to Sir Thomas Allin, the prospective Admiral of the Fleet, to say that the rules for the proposed Anglo-Dutch fleet had to be finalised before the Dutch admiral Evertsen left on the following day, but to do so, they had to have them agreed by the Duke of York; therefore, he proposed meeting Allin at Derby House at seven that evening, 'where we will agree upon the substance and terms of our articles and then wait upon the duke with it either just before or at his rising from supper'.[47] The duke continued to recommend officers for promotion, among them Thomas Hopson, later to be the hero of the Battle of Vigo in 1702, whose career James rescued from potential oblivion in 1675.[48] Possibly one of his oddest interventions came in September 1674, when he reassured Sir William Wilson that Captain Christopher Mason, who had served as James's lieutenant during the previous war and had just married Wilson's daughter, was, indeed, a perfectly respectable son-in-law: 'I think your daughter hath made a good choice'.[49]

James's resignation under the Test Act applied only to the English Admiralty, so he retained the posts of Lord High Admiral of Ireland and of the Plantations, and thus continued to profit from prizes and wrecks occurring within those jurisdictions. He had also only recently assumed the office of Lord High Admiral of Scotland, which retained an independent Admiralty that issued a host of privateering commissions during the second and third Anglo-Dutch wars.[50] The previous holder of the office, the royal brothers' distant cousin Charles Stuart, Duke of Richmond and Lennox, died in farcical circumstances in December 1672: having enjoyed rather too much Danish hospitality, he slipped when boarding an English warship moored off Copenhagen, and perished in the icy waters. James was granted the post early in 1673, not long before he resigned the English Admiralty. His time as the Scots Lord High Admiral was distinguished principally by attempts to standardise the proceedings of the Admiralty court in Edinburgh, bringing it more into line with English practice, and by blatantly avaricious attempts to usurp the rights of the local vice-admirals of the coast to the profits from wrecks.[51]

Between January 1674 and April 1679, the Admiralty board met 308 times. King Charles attended 195 of these meetings: by far the most impressive attendance rate, well ahead of the nominal 'First Lord', Prince Rupert, on 164.[52] It was also impressive in historical terms. During the 1630s, the Admiralty commission instigated by Charles I met a similar number of times, but the king attended only eight of those meetings. His eldest son, on the other hand, went to great lengths to ensure that he could actively participate in the work of the Admiralty and navy wherever he was, and whatever he was doing. The third ever meeting of the 1673–79 commission was held aboard the *Cleveland Yacht*, moored off Gravesend, because Charles was in transit to the fleet; soon afterwards, another was held aboard Prince Rupert's flagship, the *Sovereign*.[53] From the following year, 1674, onwards the court decamped to Windsor for several months during the summer. In 1678, the king introduced a new system whereby the Navy Board came to Windsor every Sunday; this was clearly not an initiative taken by Pepys, the Admiralty secretary, the tone of whose commiserations with those forced to travel far into the remote wilds of Berkshire once a week, and on a Sunday to boot, suggests that he, too, found the royal commands onerous.[54] Far from falling off, as one might expect if the king really was innately and irredeemably lazy, his attendance record at Admiralty meetings actually improved markedly as time went on. He was present at 16 per cent of meetings in 1674, the first full year of the commission, and at 90 per cent in 1678, the last. He also volunteered for extra work that he did not necessarily need to do. In October 1673, he announced that from then on, he would sign all passes and protections himself, and throughout the period of the board's existence, he also signed all captains' and lieutenants' commissions.[55]

Pepys's Admiralty letters, which fill fourteen magnificent volumes in his library at Magdalene College, Cambridge, together with the complementary Admiralty Journal of the period, contain many other proofs of Charles II's remarkably serious commitment to his naval obligations. When a matter was discussed or decided by the king and Admiralty board jointly, Pepys used the shorthand expression 'His Majesty and Lords'; but when the king alone was responsible, he referred simply to 'His Majesty'. By applying this distinction, it is clear that Charles reserved almost all matters relating to the appointment of commissioned officers and the deployment of warships exclusively to himself. Although he listened to advice from his brother, from Pepys, and from others, the decisions were his alone, and he often acted entirely on his own initiative. In March 1674, for instance, he summoned Pepys and ordered him to send vessels downriver to prevent men leaving the country to go into foreign service; although Pepys informed the Admiralty of this, the signing of the necessary warrant was done by the king alone.[56] Moreover, as Pepys correctly stated, the Admiralty board met relatively infrequently, particularly when Parliament was sitting, so the king and Pepys, often with the Duke of York involved too, were often left largely to their own devices.* There are very few glimpses into exactly how this relationship worked, but an insight can be obtained on 14 April 1678, when, sometime during the night, Pepys went to the king at Whitehall with a letter he had just drafted for immediate despatch to Sir John Narbrough, the admiral commanding in the Mediterranean. Charles made amendments, Pepys had the letter rewritten on the spot (presumably by one of his clerks, as the wording suggests he did not do it himself), the king then signed it, and the letter was immediately sent 'away this night by express to the Downs'. Charles's involvement in the process was clearly much more than a mere rubber stamp on anything Pepys placed in front of him.[57]

Impressive they may be, but the books generated by Pepys, and which survive in his library, were by no means the only ones that existed at the time. The king had his own manuscript volume, recording the decisions

* There were also no meetings at all between 28 September 1678 and 4 January 1679, following the revelation of the Popish Plot.

made and orders given during the time of the Admiralty commission; but the fact that his personal record of that body's proceedings began on 18 June 1673 at folio 67, with that held by the board only beginning on 30 June at folio one, suggests that the king's version was a continuation of a book, now lost, that Charles had possessed for years, and which, if it still existed or was ever found, would probably give a much clearer idea of the king's involvement in naval affairs prior to 1673. Significantly, too, the king's book contained much more information than that held by the board; virtually no appointments of commanders, or sailing orders and instructions, were entered in the latter, confirming the impression given by the Admiralty minutes. During the calendar year 1675, for example, twenty-eight entries were made solely in the king's book, the vast majority being instructions to commanders; only nine were made in the book held by the board, and these were concerned with such routine matters as ensuring that warrant officers slept aboard their ships when in harbour, and preventing dockyard workers carrying 'chips' (spare pieces of wood) out of the yards on a literally industrial scale.[58] The fact that Charles kept the most important decisions and information almost entirely to himself would, in due course, cause a serious rift within the Admiralty, and possibly within his own family, too.

As well as having their own copies of executive decisions, the Stuart brothers also owned a number of pocket books, handwritten and some-times quite elaborately decorated, which provided lists of the names, dimensions, guns, men, and so forth, of their ships. Some provided much more detailed and technical information; for example, one included tables showing the lengths of masts, the scantlings of tops, and weights of sails.[59] In the 1680s, James owned a book containing details of all captains, lieutenants and volunteers, with information about their previous posts and any misdemeanours they had committed; it would have enabled him to look up the candidates for any commissioned post quickly, and to compare them with other potential contenders.[60] The brothers were keen to have up-to-date and comprehensive information. In 1678, Pepys ordered the master shipwrights of all the building yards to send in the exact dimensions of the ships they had built, so that a perfect list could be drawn up 'as soon as may be for his Majesty's own use'.[61]

The availability of much of the key information about the navy in such easily portable formats made it possible for Charles and James to deal authoritatively with naval affairs wherever they were. When the court went to Newmarket for the races, the Admiralty often went with it. Indeed, on 17 October 1676, what was probably a unique occurrence in the annals of naval administrative history took place, when the Admiralty pulled off the not inconsiderable feat of holding simultaneous meetings in two different locations, sixty miles apart. Three commissioners met at

the Navy Office with Pepys and the Duke of York (although his presence was not officially noted among the attendees); meanwhile, the king held a meeting at Newmarket with five others, including his cousin Rupert and his son Monmouth.[62] A year later, Pepys and some of the Admiralty lords went to Newmarket to discuss with the king and Duke of York a number of letters that had been received from Sir John Narbrough, the admiral commanding in the Mediterranean; Charles then wrote orders in his own hand for the sending home of a number of Narbrough's ships. A meeting was held with the Lord Treasurer to discuss the victualling of the navy, with orders being issued for proposals to be brought before a subsequent Admiralty meeting. The king and/or his brother must also have requested that a full list of all surviving captains be sent to them at Newmarket, because Pepys did so immediately on his return to London, sending the list and its covering letter by express to the Duke of York. During the same sojourn, Charles and James dealt with a number of other naval matters, including such similarly mundane ones as the grant of £100 to the widow of an impoverished captain who had recently died.[63]

On other occasions, Pepys had to travel to Newmarket to obtain executive decisions from the king. Charles continued to deal with naval matters during his horse-racing holidays even after he officially ceased to be directly involved in the work of the Admiralty. In September 1680, Pepys, now out of office, went to Newmarket, and almost certainly discussed his proposed book on naval history with the king: it was probably on, or shortly after, this occasion that Charles gave Pepys two of the glorious vellum rolls that had been made for Henry VIII in 1546,

The view from One Tree Hill, Greenwich, 1680, by Johannes Vorsterman. The new royal observatory to the left, the Queen's House, the completed wing of Charles II's unfinished palace, and the remains of the Tudor palace of Placentia to the right. Deptford dockyard in the middle distance, with warships in the river and royal yachts at anchor off there and Greenwich.
(© National Maritime Museum, Greenwich, London, BHC1808)

portraying every one of that monarch's fifty-eight ships (including the famous *Mary Rose*).[64] During the same sojourn at Newmarket, the king also dictated to Pepys the gripping account of his escape after the Battle of Worcester in 1651, and possibly also decided to commission Captain Greenvile Collins's detailed survey of the entire British coast.

Pepys is far and away our most important source for the Admiralty of 1673–79, and historians depend overwhelmingly on the record that he left us, principally the bound volumes at Magdalene. Many of these were published by the splendid Navy Records Society during the first half of the twentieth century: the Admiralty Journal, consisting of the minutes of the commission, was edited by J R Tanner, the Pepys Librarian at Magdalene, and published in 1922. But anyone who has ever attended a meeting of any sort knows full well that the minutes do not necessarily reflect the reality of what happened; and, of course, the writing of the minutes – that is, the creation of the official record that will pass down to posterity – is the task of the secretary, who, consciously or subconsciously, writes up the minutes in a way that reflects his or her recollection and interpretation of it. Moreover, and for the sake of brevity rather than anything more Machiavellian, published minutes usually record only the decisions taken, not the debates that took place, who said what, and the nitty-gritty of who, exactly, persuaded the meeting, perhaps by force of argument, perhaps by simple body language, to take the decisions that it took. This is just as true of, say, any parish council meeting in the twenty-first century as it was of Admiralty meetings during the 1670s. But the published minutes of those meetings, written up by Pepys and then placed in his own library, have the same strengths and weaknesses as the published minutes of every other meeting of every other organisation: namely, they do not give the full picture. That would only be provided by a fuller record of what was actually said in a given meeting, and of who said it. Fortunately, there is one meeting (and, to the best of my knowledge, it is only one) for which an independent record happens

Newmarket in 1668, shortly after Charles II started regularly attending horse races there; the unofficial 'home' of the Admiralty on many occasions during the 1670s. *(Author's collection)*

to survive: the meeting that took place on 22 July 1676. The record was produced by the person perhaps least likely to undermine Samuel Pepys's carefully crafted legacy, even if inadvertently, namely his own brother, John. As it is, the alternative evidence produced by John Pepys suggests that a somewhat different view needs to be taken of what happened in the government of the Royal Navy during the 1670s. Indeed, so compelling is this evidence that all histories of the navy in that decade, including the one presented in this book, may need to be rewritten. But to avoid disrupting the narrative at this point, a detailed analysis of this meeting is provided as an appendix to the book. Those interested in pursuing the matter in detail may find it there, while those who wish to see how the king, his brother, and their navy, responded to one of the greatest crises of the seventeenth century, may read on.

In the autumn of 1678, the Popish Plot completely altered the political landscape. Sensational revelations of a Jesuit conspiracy to kill the king generated a febrile atmosphere and demands to exclude the Catholic Duke of York from the succession. It was against this backdrop that a curious 'attempted coup' took place within the previously pliant Admiralty commission. On 31 January 1679, the commissioners present at that day's meeting suddenly decided to peruse their instructions, and noted that although the only powers officially reserved to the king were those of appointing officers and taking the profits traditionally allowed to the Lord High Admiral, he had also exercised the power to decide on the deployment of warships, which by rights should have belonged to the commission, thus making them 'incapable of rendering the account which may be expected from them as admirals'.[65] They therefore demanded a report on the state of the navy from Pepys. When the king, who was absent from the meeting, learned of this, he was clearly furious, declaring such a report 'inconvenient for his service' as it would trumpet the poor condition of the navy to the world. All of this begs the question of where the sudden 'revolt' could have originated. The timing is clearly critical – after all, the commissioners had worked contentedly within their brief for over five years, and could hardly just have noticed that they had no power to deploy warships, or to issue instructions to captains.[66] The wording of the minutes suggests that someone, at least, was concerned about the prospect of a parliamentary enquiry into the Admiralty, and the possibility that the commissioners might be held to account for matters over which they had actually exercised no control. So who could have instigated the sudden revolt?

Those present at the meeting on 31 January were Prince Rupert; the

Earl of Anglesey, Lord Privy Seal; the Earl of Craven; and Henry
Coventry, Secretary of State. Coventry was very unlikely to take a position contrary to the king's likely (and, in this instance, very obvious)
standpoint, so the other three must have agreed the controversial proposal
effectively to take away from the king the power to give orders to
warships. Charles II's response was immediate and decisive. At the next
meeting, on the very next day, the king attended in person, along with a
formidable phalanx of his loyalists: in addition to the four members who
were present on the previous day, the attendees now included the Duke
of Lauderdale (the de facto viceroy of Scotland), the Lord Chamberlain
and Vice-Chamberlain of the royal household (respectively, the Earl of
Arlington and Sir George Carteret), the Master of the Ordnance (Sir
Thomas Chicheley) and the Chancellor of the Exchequer (Sir John
Ernle).[67] It is perfectly possible that the Duke of York was also there,
although his attendance was not minuted. In these circumstances, it was
hardly surprising that the line taken by the meeting on the previous day
was comprehensively slapped down twenty-four hours later, and it may
be suggestive that Anglesey, the Lord Privy Seal, did not attend another
Admiralty meeting for over two months. But he was very unlikely to have
been the instigator of the revolt on 31 January: the fact that the proposal
was accepted and minuted at all could only have been done with the
wholehearted consent of the man who chaired the meeting in question,
the king's own cousin, Prince Rupert of the Rhine. Rupert was staunchly
anti-Catholic, anti-French, and was connected politically to the Earl of
Shaftesbury, the leader of the campaign to exclude the Duke of York from
the succession; moreover, the other member of the Admiralty board
present on 31 January, the Earl of Craven, was an old friend and former
comrade-in-arms of the prince, and, if popular legend was correct, also
the sometime lover of Rupert's mother.[68] Quite what Rupert hoped to
achieve by embarking on what was certain to be a kamikaze mission, and
which was bound to infuriate his cousins, can only be guessed at.

During the months that followed this curious episode, Charles
dissolved Parliament, and the first general election in eighteen years
brought in a solid majority that favoured exclusion. The king was forced
to send his brother into exile, his chief minister, the Earl of Danby, had
to resign, and a new Privy Council, full of opposition leaders, was sworn
in on 20 April, followed in short order by a new Admiralty commission.
This, too, was packed with long-term critics of the Crown, and especially
of the Duke of York. The new First Lord, Sir Henry Capel, was a relatively innocuous figure, best known for his impressive garden, but he
made a real effort to get on top of naval issues. However, some of his
colleagues were rather less palatable to the Crown, notably the likes of Sir
Thomas Meres and Sir Thomas Lee, who had often been vociferous in

their denunciations of the naval administration. Pepys was forced out of office, and became a prime target for those who saw him as a surrogate through which to attack the king and duke, particularly the latter. James's abiding influence in naval affairs and liking for Irish officers were very obvious, and contributed to the vicious attacks on him in Parliament and opposition pamphlets, which accused him of being complicit in the Popish Plot, of bringing Papist officers into the fleet, and betraying the navy to France: as one poem of 1679 put it,

> T'ensure the plot, France must her legions send
> Rome to restore, and to enthrone Rome's friend.
> 'Tis in return James does our fleet betray
> That fleet whose thunder made the world obey;
> Ships, once our safety & our glorious might,
> Are doom'd with worms & rottenness to fight;
> Whilst France rides sov'reign o'er the British main,
> Our merchants robbed, & our brave seamen ta'en.[69]

James, for his part, reacted to the ensuing crisis by deploying a nautical analogy which amply demonstrates his unwillingness to compromise: 'I have been used all my life to rough weather, and can ply to windward, and you know, do not love to bear up'.[70]

At first, King Charles clearly intended to retain all the important functions of the Admiralty – selecting officers, deploying ships, and so forth – in his own hands, but the new board demanded the full authority of a Lord High Admiral, and the king had no choice but to agree.[71] By May 1679, the new Admiralty was commissioning officers and deciding on the disposition of ships, tasks that had been the exclusive preserve of the king for the previous six years – in other words, doing exactly the things that the breakaway group within the previous board had demanded they be given the power to do back in January.[72] In fact, though, Charles's seeming climbdown was less of a concession than it might have appeared. On 10 May, he approved, and Pepys signed, no fewer than eighty-eight warrants in one day, a completely unprecedented number: most of these were the appointments of gunners, boatswains and so forth to the 'thirty new ships', so it is clear that Charles wanted to ensure that these posts were in safe hands before he relinquished the power to make such appointments.[73] Thereafter, the king simply used the royal prerogative to intervene in naval affairs whenever he wished, just as he had done during his brother's tenure at the Admiralty, while leaving the inexperienced commissioners to implement the draconian austerity agenda demanded by the Treasury. Although the Admiralty board appointed the majority of officers, Charles intervened from time to time to 'request' the appointment of specific individuals. In 1682, he urged that a command be given to Lord Berkeley of Stratton, and that a carpenter's place be granted to the son of Pett the shipbuilder. Charles also regularly talked to, and took advice on naval matters from, sources other than the Admiralty. He met with Pepys a number of times, and continued to listen to the Duke of York, even when he was in exile: James provided recommendations and advice, even to the extent of persuading Charles to accept two nominees for seats on the Admiralty board itself.[74]

Naturally, Pepys had a highly jaundiced view of the Admiralty commission of 1679–84.

> … it is a wonderful thing that under so knowing a king such ignorant admirals [ie Admiralty commissioners] should be chosen, but … their folly was one of good inducement to the king to choose them for the pleasure of teaching them, to show his own mastery over them and to laugh at them.[75]

He subsequently carried out a comprehensive 'hatchet job' on its reputation, accusing it of gross incompetence, of allowing the thirty new ships to rot at their moorings, and of failing to set out a proper number of ships to protect trade. But Pepys's swingeing attack was political in every sense of the word: prompted by a subsequent attack on his own reputation, it brazenly manipulated statistics, and wholly ignored the political and financial contexts of the time, in order to 'prove' how successful Pepys had been. In fact, the board of 1679–84 did its best in almost impossible circumstances, constrained by a king who was openly contemptuous of it, and forced to comply with Treasury-inspired retrenchment, a policy which was simply inescapable if the king was going to avoid going cap in hand for money to obstreperous parliaments which were determined to exclude his brother from the succession.[76] Daniel Finch, First Lord from 1682 and later Earl of Nottingham, summed up the situation rather more accurately than Pepys: '[the king] having great skill and delight in shipping and knowledge of his sea-officers might conclude that he could direct that part of our office, and leave to us the economy, which by our application we might soon learn'.[77]

Charles's independence of the Admiralty in the most important naval matters can best be seen in his treatment of Arthur Herbert, commander-in-chief in the Mediterranean from 1679 to 1683. Herbert was an abrasive, arrogant individual who made enemies easily, and his tactic of relying on convoys, rather than on the large fleets commanded by his predecessors, attracted criticism (although it ultimately proved to be far more effective).[78] The Admiralty requested his dismissal on several occasions, and in this, unusually, they were in agreement with their arch-enemy Samuel Pepys, who also detested Herbert. But Charles and James consistently backed the admiral, who fulfilled many of the criteria that they looked for in their officers. Herbert came from an unimpeachable Royalist background, which had suffered for the Stuarts; his father had been Charles I's attorney-general, and the young Arthur spent the first twelve years of his life in exile. Herbert also had a proven track record as a brave and successful officer. His first commission as a lieutenant was in the *Defiance*, which was in the thick of the action in the great battles of 1666; he earned further credit in the Mediterranean in 1669–72, where he survived a pistol ball lodging in his head, just below his right eye; and he was again in the thick of the battles of the third Anglo-Dutch war. Herbert was, therefore, eminently qualified for the command of the Mediterranean fleet, and Charles II stuck resolutely by his man. His confidence was rewarded by his admiral's achievement, in 1682, of arranging a lasting peace with Algiers, one which would endure until 1816; and although Pepys subsequently collected every piece of salacious gossip and hearsay about Herbert that he could rake up from the admiral's enemies, it served little purpose (other than to reinforce Pepys's conviction that everything had been so much better in his day). The king's favour for Herbert, which was mirrored by that of the Duke of York, culminated in his appointment, on 22 January 1684, to the entirely new office of Rear-Admiral of England, while a year later, the new King James II went even further, making Herbert his Master of the Robes.

By 1682, political circumstances had changed markedly. The exclusionists were decisively defeated by the dissolution of the Oxford Parliament in March 1681, after which no parliament sat for the remainder of Charles II's reign. The Admiralty board itself was increasingly divided, with new Tory appointees like Henry Savile and Sir John Chicheley barely co-operating with Whig colleagues like Meres and Winch, while the Admiralty secretary, the Scottish lawyer John Brisbane, was emphatically no Pepys.[79] All this gave the king even greater independence of action in naval affairs. In 1682, he decided to create a squadron under the command of Sir John Berry, nominally for duties on the coast of Ireland, and funded from the Irish revenue. Charles intended that the commissions for captains in this squadron would be issued by him, rather than by the Admiralty. Two of his chief ministers, Halifax and Hyde, balked at the legality of this, so the king responded simply by using the royal prerogative to order the Admiralty to commission Berry, whose vessels were then to follow Charles's orders, transmitted via the Secretary of State's office rather than the Admiralty.[80] The so-called 'Irish squadron' was actually employed in carrying stores, men and money to the beleaguered outpost at Tangier. It arrived at the North African colony on 25 September 1682, returned to the Downs in November, sailed for Tangier again in February 1683, and finally returned to Plymouth at the end of May. The peculiar status of Berry's force can be gauged by the fact that throughout this time, he corresponded directly with the king and the Secretary of State, Sir Leoline Jenkins, not with the Admiralty, except in matters of routine courtesy; at one point, Jenkins had to write to the Admiralty to inform them where one of their ships actually was.[81]

The strange saga of the 'Irish squadron' is instructive in other ways. It is one of very few episodes during the three decades when Charles and James ruled Britain that one can see the king's direct involvement in naval affairs without the presence of a 'filter', notably an Admiralty secretary whose signature on all correspondence, and responsibility for much of the executive action of the department, has allowed historians to give the secretary in question almost all the credit for what was done. But in the case of the 'Irish squadron', all of the important correspondence was channelled through the Secretary of State, Sir Leoline Jenkins, entirely avoiding the Admiralty (where Pepys was out of office in any case), and Jenkins's own words demonstrate conclusively that he was a mere mouthpiece for the king, not an independent agent in the matter. Perhaps, though, a 'filter' is indeed present during the history of the 'Irish squadron', albeit an invisible one. The first letter on the subject was sent by Jenkins to the king on 3 April 1682, and refers to the commission for Sir John Berry, the commander-designate of the squadron, which had been drafted by Jenkins and was to be signed by Charles. This suggests that the decision to embark on this policy, which brazenly sidelined the Admiralty, was probably taken during March; and James, Duke of York, had been reunited with his brother at Newmarket on the 11th of that month, having been in exile in Edinburgh for two years. The 'Irish squadron' might well be an early proof of James persuading his elder sibling to take more resolute, independent action, and to reassert himself as a literal power behind the throne in naval affairs.[82]

Making due allowance for the Duke of York's likely presence offstage, the king was heavily involved in the detailed administration of the 'Irish squadron'. Although his issuing of commissions had been objected to on legal grounds, there was, significantly, no objection from Halifax, Hyde, or the Admiralty itself, to Charles ordering the deployment of warships that were, after all, his own property.[83] Thereafter, Charles ordered the Admiralty to discipline officers whose conduct offended him; ordered Berry to carry specific individuals and types of provisions to Tangier; ordered the victualling of the warships; issued their sailing orders, just as he had done through the period 1673–79; and commanded Berry to

The Victorian
memorial to Samuel
Pepys, St Olave's, Hart
Street, London.
(Author's photograph)

transport to Tangier four Moors, the wife of one of them, an Algerine
Turk, and two Jews, and 'that all of them be treated with the civility and
humanity becoming the commanders of His Majesty's men of war'.[84] It
is difficult to see how the king could have been more proactive or hands-
on as a naval administrator.

Another proof of Charles II's cavalier attitude to the Admiralty board,
and of his determination to keep the most important royal prerogatives
pertaining to the navy in his own hands, was the peculiar saga of the
appointment to command the fleet sent out to the English colony of
Tangier in 1683, with orders to evacuate and demolish the port (a history
explored in more detail in Chapter 9). The commander-in-chief initially
appointed to this powerful fleet was the king's own son, the Duke of
Grafton, who had succeeded the recently deceased Prince Rupert as
Vice-Admiral of England, a high honorific position which made him
nominally the deputy Lord High Admiral. Grafton must be one of the
few admirals in the history of the Royal Navy to have hoisted his flag
with his mother in attendance: Barbara Palmer, Duchess of Cleveland,
was with him when he boarded the *Grafton*, the flagship named in his
honour, on 23 May 1683, and hoisted his admiral's Union flag at the

Henry, Duke of Grafton, son of King Charles II by Barbara, Countess of Castlemaine and later Duchess of Cleveland. Sent to sea in 1677 at the age of fourteen, Grafton was Vice-Admiral of England six years later. *(Richard Endsor collection)*

* Several sprigs of royalty were given honorary naval ranks at very young ages: Henry VIII's illegitimate son, the Duke of Richmond, was Lord High Admiral at the age of six, the future King Richard III at nine, while Louis XIV's illegitimate sons, the Comtes de Toulouse and Vermandois, were given the equivalent office of Admiral of France at the ages of five and two respectively. But actually commanding a fleet at sea, even in peacetime, was a very different matter. James, Duke of York, had hoisted his flag at the age of fourteen in the fleet that revolted against Parliament in 1648, but did not take it to sea.

maintop.[85] But then, Grafton might have needed maternal support, as he was not yet twenty – quite possibly the youngest admiral ever to hoist a flag and take a fleet, certainly a British fleet, to sea.* If that was peculiar, what happened next was odder still. Grafton took his squadron round from the Downs to Spithead, where further preparations for the Tangier voyage took place. But then, on 27 July, the duke was abruptly summoned to Whitehall by his father, and relieved of his command. Quite why this happened is unknown: the most likely explanation is that on or about the 24th, news arrived at court that the Moors were suddenly attacking Tangier in strength, and it may have been felt that a more experienced commander was needed to cope with the new, and markedly more dangerous, situation.[86] The upshot is clear enough, though. On 2 August, George Legge, Lord Dartmouth, who had significantly more experience both at sea and on land (and was, above all, Master of the Ordnance, and thus reasonably well versed in the requirements for demolishing a fortress) went aboard the *Grafton* at Spithead, and hoisted his own flag as Admiral of the Fleet. The young Duke of Grafton's reaction to being superseded can only be guessed at; that of his notoriously volatile mother is probably rather easier to imagine.

Grafton and his mother were not the only ones to have their noses put out of joint by the king's machinations over the Tangier fleet. When it set sail from Spithead, the Admiralty had no idea who was in command of it, and even less of an idea of where it was going: contemporary rumours of its purpose, all considered equally plausible, included attacking the Spanish plate fleet, escorting a French squadron out of the Baltic, watching the Dutch fleet, establishing a new colony in North Africa, attacking Salé, carrying a lawyer to Cadiz to persuade the local governor to salute British warships, and surveying the Channel Islands.[87] Nor did the Admiralty commissioners know that, at the king's express command, their arch-enemy Samuel Pepys had taken up the post of Dartmouth's secretary at just forty-eight hours' notice. But Pepys, too, had no inkling of the expedition's purpose, 'it being handled by our masters as a secret'.[88] The secrecy surrounding Dartmouth's Tangier expedition gave Charles the best of both worlds: if it succeeded, he would have rid himself of an expensive and politically embarrassing commitment, but if it all went dreadfully wrong, he could simply disown it. Dartmouth and Pepys were well aware of this, and of the fact that their distance from England meant they would be wholly unaware of any political changes and of their opponents' machinations against them.[89]

In the event, and despite many difficulties, the withdrawal from Tangier was accomplished successfully, and as they sailed back to England in the spring of 1684, Pepys and Dartmouth schemed to bring down the existing Admiralty board and restore the Duke of York and Pepys to their former offices. Unknown to them, James was pursuing exactly the same agenda, and had formed an unlikely alliance to that end with his arch-enemies, the 'universally odious' secretary of state, the Earl of Sunderland, and the king's mistress, the Duchess of Portsmouth.[90] But, as usual, King Charles surprised everybody. He appointed Admiral Herbert as a full member of the existing Admiralty Board on 17 April, thus signalling that the body in question would continue exactly as it was; then, on 11 May, he abruptly dissolved it. But instead of restoring the Admiralty to James, he assumed it formally himself. The charitable believed Charles did this because of his respect for the law, in the shape of the Test Act of 1673, which still notionally barred James from office; the cynical suspected that it was a device to save the lord admiral's salary of £8,000 a year.[91] The Tory street ballad-mongers ignored the distinction, with the writer of 'The Royal Admiral' (1684) literally singing the praises of:

Jemmy who quelled the proud foe on the ocean,
And reigned the sole conqueror over the main,
To this brave hero let's all pay devotion,
Since he is England's Admiral again …
York our great Admiral, the Ocean's defender,
The Joy of his friends and the dread of his foes,

The lawful successor, what bastard pretender
Whom heav'n the true heir has ordain'd, dare oppose?[92]

James also knew exactly how things really stood: in September 1684 he
sailed his yacht into Spithead flying the Lord High Admiral's flag, which
he had not been entitled to hoist since his resignation in 1673.[93]
Meanwhile, returning triumphantly alongside 'Jemmy the Valiant, the
Champion Royal', Samuel Pepys was elevated to become a naval equal
of the existing secretaries of state, holding the grand title of Secretary for
the Affairs of the Admiralty. The position had no precedent in the British
Isles, but it did 'in another place': just as Charles II's new palace at
Winchester was, to all intents and purposes, a copy of Versailles, so Pepys's
impressive new job was very much a replica of the French position of
Secrétaire d'État de la Marine, previously held by Jean-Baptiste Colbert.

   Although the king nominally took the Admiralty into his own hands,
in practice he devolved much of its work to the Duke of York, regardless
of the constraints of the Test Act. James met with the Navy Board, just as
he had done when he held the formal title of Lord High Admiral, and
undertook tours of inspection to the dockyards, sometimes taking with
him his new son-in-law, Prince George of Denmark.[94] Although Bishop
Burnet, a critic of the Stuarts, might have been exaggerating, he paints a
vivid picture of the altered balance of power between the brothers during
the last months of Charles's life:

> [James] had got the whole management of affairs … into his hands
> … In England the application and dependence was visibly on the
> Duke. The King had scarce company about him to entertain him,
> when the Duke's *levees* and *couchees* [rising and retiring ceremonies]
> were so crowded that the antechambers were full. The King walked
> about with a small train of the necessary attendants, when the Duke
> had a vast following …[95]

But Charles remained an enigma to the end. One of the principal ministers of the time, the Earl of Halifax, observed that although the king had
raised his brother to such a powerful position, 'he had his jealousies of
him … [and] was not displeased to have him lessened … at the same time
that he [James] reigned in the Cabinet, he was very familiarly used at the
[king's] private supper'.[96]

   Charles II continued to exert an active influence in naval affairs until
the very end of his life. He was particularly occupied by the fraught issue
of salutes to be exchanged between British warships and Spanish forts and
harbours, following the series of clashes in 1683/84, a matter described in
Chapter 8. During the last weeks before he suffered his fatal stroke on

James, Duke of York. Painted by Godfrey Kneller in 1684 to mark the duke's return to the Admiralty, the sitter is portrayed in martial garb, while the ship in the background flies the Lord High Admiral's standard at the main, despite the fact that James had not been formally reappointed to the office. *(National Portrait Gallery, London)*

2 February 1685, Charles presided over several meetings with his senior sea officers to thrash out a new policy, and this was adopted on 25 January. The king then moved on to attempt a resolution of a bitter argument which had been raging for several years among his subordinate naval administrators over whether or not to build a huge new dock at Chatham. On Sunday, 1 February, Pepys ordered the Navy Board to attend the king on the following Tuesday, the 3rd, to discuss the matter.[97] Meanwhile, James, Duke of York, was making ready to return to Scotland, almost certainly by sea, where he was to preside over the state opening of the Scottish Parliament on 10 March.[98] But in the morning of Monday, 2 February, the king suffered a massive stroke. Charles Stuart died between eleven and twelve in the morning on 6 February, and the new king, James II of England and VII of Scots, succeeded peacefully. One incidental effect of his so doing was that he finally, and officially, returned to the office of Lord High Admiral, which he had been forced to vacate in 1673.

7

The Precursors of Hornblower

AT ABOUT TEN IN THE MORNING on 15 September 1668, the captain of the 58-gun, Third Rate man-of-war *Mountagu* chanced to look out through the starboard window of his cabin. It was very foggy, but the squadron of which his ship formed a part had been steering northeast with a westerly breeze since leaving the English colony at Tangier: they should have been well clear of the land, and there ought to have been no danger. Then, just as he was glancing through the window, the mist cleared, just for a moment, and the captain saw 'the beach of the shore within two ships' lengths of me'. He ran out onto the deck, and at once gave orders to put the helm to starboard and for the sails to be trimmed, in order to bring his ship to. His men responded immediately, but even so, the *Mountagu* only missed the rocks by a distance equivalent to its own breadth. The admiral's ship, dead ahead, struck the shore, but managed to get off again; and the captain's firing of a warning gun saved the three frigates sailing in his wake. The captain swiftly realised that the entire English Mediterranean squadron had almost come to grief on the headland called Ape's Hill, the westernmost part of the Bay of Ceuta. When he came to write up the dramatic event in his journal, he reflected on the lesson that should be learned, in the language of a consummate navigator:

> This mistake came by the current that sets here right upon the Barbary shore, therefore he that weighs out of the Bay of Tangier ought to steer away NNE till he be a good distance from the Barbary shore, and then go away ENE which will carry him clear of Gibraltar.

However, the captain in question was not some renowned sailor like Francis Drake or Cloudesley Shovell. He was not a real-life equivalent of the fictitious Horatio Hornblower or Jack Aubrey: officers trained in the ways of the sea since early in childhood. Nor was he like the veteran admiral who had ploughed onto Ape's Hill, Sir Thomas Allin, one of the oldest and most experienced officers in the navy, who hailed from an age-old dynasty of Lowestoft mariners: in other words, a 'tarpaulin', the kind of officer who rose to command in the navy after serving for years in merchant ships, or in such lesser naval posts as masters, boatswains or gunners. The captain who saved the Mediterranean squadron was Francis Digby. Twenty-seven-year-old Francis was the second son of the second Earl of Bristol, one of the most important – if disastrously inept – politicians of the seventeenth century. Francis's sister would be an ancestor of both Diana, Princess of Wales, and Sir Winston Churchill. His childhood home, Sherborne Castle, was one of the grandest houses in the southwest, but it was a good twenty-five miles from the sea. As far as can be ascertained, Francis had hardly been to sea at all until perhaps just three years before his quick thinking saved the squadron; he received his first naval commission, as a lieutenant, only in March 1666.[1] Yet his journal reveals a confident command of navigation, is full of astronomical and mathematical symbols, and contains various technical memoranda clearly designed for his own future reference: for instance, notes on the best ways of steering into and through the Downs. Digby was not some vacuous aristocrat, given command by virtue of his social rank alone, and leaving the actual sailing of the ship to the professionals. A 'gentleman captain' he may have been, but he was a true seaman, and his actions on 15 September 1668 comprehensively give the lie to Lord Macaulay's famous but completely inaccurate quip about the captains of the Restoration navy: 'There were gentlemen and there were seamen in the navy of Charles the Second. But the seamen were not gentlemen; and the gentlemen were not seamen'.

The entry into the navy of Francis Digby, and others like him, stemmed directly from one of the most vital and urgent issues that confronted Charles and James Stuart when they returned from exile at the Restoration. In a nutshell, the republican regime of the Commonwealth and Protectorate was sustained for so long by its huge and formidable armed forces, both of which gained a Europe-wide reputation for efficiency and success. The New Model Army had triumphed in campaign after campaign, as had the navy, which defeated first the Dutch and then the Spanish under the command of the 'generals at sea', men like Robert Blake, Richard Deane, George Monck and William Penn. In 1660, those of them who survived, and the captains and lesser officers who had served during the interregnum, provided the Stuart brothers with a ready-made officer corps, composed of battle-hardened veterans with a proven track record of victory. But there was a catch. Many of the Commonwealth's officers were also religious and political radicals, who either refused to serve or were too extreme to be considered for employment under a restored monarchy; and the loyalty of many of the others was questionable. From the beginning, there were suspicions that an indeterminate number of officers who swore loyalty to the crown in 1660 would defect back to the 'Good Old Cause' at the first opportunity. Dealing with the formidable New Model Army, which had been so famous and so dreaded for so very long, actually proved remarkably easy: it was simply disbanded en masse, the old soldiers drifted off to their homes to grumble, and a new, very small, and overwhelmingly Royalist army was formed instead.

Charles and James did not have that option with the navy. From the beginning, they aimed to maintain a fleet that, in wartime, would be proportionately much larger and more important than the army, the reverse of the situation in the 1640s and 1650s. But there were very few Cavaliers qualified to command at sea, and several of the most experienced were too old to give much service: Sir John Mennes, who first went to sea before 1620, served as an admiral in 1661/62 and helped bring over Queen Catherine of Braganza, but he then moved ashore as Controller of the Navy, a much-loved but increasingly ancient and ineffectual colleague of Pepys. But a few became stalwarts of the Restoration navy. Thomas Allin and Robert Holmes were both veterans of Prince Rupert's fleet: both held a succession of important commands after the Restoration, and were knighted, before finding comfortable billets ashore, Allin as Mennes's successor in the post of Controller, Holmes as Governor of the Isle of Wight. John Kempthorne, whose father had been an officer in Rupert's army, came into the navy in 1664, was a flag officer within two years, and died as Commissioner of the Navy at, and Member of Parliament for, Portsmouth.[2]

Even if the Stuart brothers had enough Cavalier officers available to them to fill every post in the fleet, it would have been politically crass for them to do so. Charles and James were keen to emphasise the need for reconciliation, and creating an exclusively Royalist officer corps would have been disastrously counter-productive. Moreover, the fighting record of the Commonwealth's officers simply could not be ignored. Nor could the expectations of their patrons, the great men who, by deciding that the return of the king was the only realistic political option, essentially handed Charles his throne on a plate: above all, George Monck, Duke of Albemarle, and Edward Mountagu, Earl of Sandwich. The former brought in men like Jeremiah Smith, who became a vice-admiral and a commissioner of the navy, while the latter promoted, inter alia, Roger Cuttance, a Weymouth man who also became a flag officer. Other senior officers of the Commonwealth navy, like Sir John Lawson and Sir William Penn, had to be given posts, and they, in turn, recommended their own followers. In the years immediately after the Restoration, therefore, Charles and James were appointing

many men on trust, and inevitably, some did not measure up: Edward Nixon, who was praised to the heights by Albemarle, was sentenced to death for cowardice in 1665.[3]

From the very beginning, the brothers had an eye to the longer term. In theory, it might have been possible, especially in peacetime, to draw their officer corps entirely from the 'tarpaulins' – experienced merchant captains, or warrant officers of royal warships. But naval captains were expected to be much more than competent ship-handlers: they had to be diplomats, fighters and leaders in battle. In a nutshell, they were the king's representatives afloat, and had to have the qualities to be able to sustain such a responsibility. Moreover, Charles and James wanted their aristocracy and gentry to become more connected to the sea, and getting them to send younger sons into the navy was an obvious means to this end.[4] Older candidates could be commissioned at once, even if they had little or no seagoing experience: in May 1661, Hugh Hyde, a kinsman of Lord Chancellor Clarendon, became captain of the powerful Fourth Rate *Antelope*, and William Finch, a son of the Earl of Winchilsea, was appointed to the *Forrester*.[5] For younger men, a new system was put in place, meant to ensure that they received at least a modicum of training before moving on to lieutenancies and commands. In 1661, James instituted the post of 'volunteers per order', by which well-born young men were given places aboard men-of-war with the expectation that they would learn the ways of the sea before qualifying for commissions.[6]

One anonymous author, writing exactly twenty years after Charles II's death, described the effects of these royal policies:

Above, left: George Monck, Duke of Albemarle, architect of the Restoration and a general-at-sea during both the first and second Anglo-Dutch wars. Sir Peter Lely. *(Rijksmuseum, Amsterdam)*

Above, right: Sir Thomas Allin. Of a Royalist shipowning family from Lowestoft, Allin became a prominent admiral of the Restoration period. Sir Peter Lely. *(© National Maritime Museum, Greenwich, London, BHC2511)*

… that [the king] might give a spirit to the sea-service, he very
much countenanced not only his officers, but all such as went to sea,
there to acquire qualifications fit for commands in the fleet, allowing
them free access to his presence and ear; which procured them a
general respect at Court, and prompted men of the best quality and
estates to send their sons to sea, knowing that to be the way for
obtaining the king's favour, who himself frequently went aboard his
men of war and yachts, and sometimes cruised in the Channel; by
that means bringing the whole Court to sea, not only for a passage,
but a kind of sejour; so that in his days it was become a mode at
Court to discourse of naval affairs, the captains of men of war
meeting there many of their acquaintance, scarce any of the courtiers
not having been at sea, either with the king or the Duke of York.[7]

Of course, it was easy to turn this on its head. For those who assumed
that the Stuarts, especially James, wished to subjugate Parliament and the
laws of the land, the introduction of the so-called 'gentlemen captains'
could be seen as a cunning plan to transform the fleet from the bulwark
of liberty it supposedly had been in the 1650s into a harbinger of royal
absolutism.[8] But this was always a gross over-simplification of a complex
situation. As in the case of Digby, 'gentlemen' often made remarkable
efforts to master seamanship; conversely, some 'tarpaulins' proved to be
hopelessly incompetent. Over time, too, the supposed divisions between
the different types of officer diminished, and there were many instances
where 'tarpaulins' were actually of higher social status than some of the
so-called 'gentlemen'. Pepys formed a powerful prejudice against
'gentlemen captains' during his early years at the Navy Board, much of it
absorbed from his mentor Sir William Coventry, and then retained it for
life, proving unable or unwilling to accept that the situation in the late
1670s and 1680s was very different from that which had shaped his attitudes twenty years earlier.[9] A similarly 'black and white' view of the types
of Restoration naval officer passed into pamphlet literature and even
appeared on the stage, perpetuating stereotypes which bore less and less
resemblance to reality, but which were ultimately accepted uncritically by
historians like Macaulay, and so passed into popular consciousness.[10]

The first generation of 'gentlemen captains' consisted of men born in the
1630s and 1640s, exact contemporaries of the king and the Duke of York.
In other words, they grew up during the civil wars, but were, generally
speaking, too young to have fought in them. Thus there was a powerful
imperative to prove themselves in battle; and, perhaps subconsciously, to

outdo the previous generation of Cavaliers, who, from a Royalist perspective at least, had suffered ignominious defeat. One of Francis Digby's exact contemporaries was Hugh Seymour, a member of one of England's most illustrious dynasties, sometime of Wolf Hall in Wiltshire; young Hugh's great-great-great-aunt had been King Henry VIII's third queen, and his direct ancestor, her brother, was the first Protector of King Edward VI. Hugh's own brother would serve twice as Speaker of the House of Commons. When Seymour was killed in the St James's day battle of 1666, aged twenty-nine, he obtained the accolade of a memorial ode, just like a knight of the age of chivalry:

> Let fame with silver trump sound high
> Thy loss, and may a doleful lyre
> Be tuned by better muse whilst I
> Sing thy victorious elegy.[11]

Another 'gentleman captain' of the same vintage was Thomas Darcy, from an ancient Yorkshire noble house whose title dated back to 1344 and who could trace their descent back to the Domesday Book. More immediately, Thomas's elder brother had been a Royalist commander during the Civil Wars, and the family was heavily fined for its loyalty to the Crown.[12] Francis Courtenay, who obtained his first command in 1666, was a younger brother of the Cavalier owner of Powderham Castle, Devon, and belonged to a family line that had come over with Eleanor of Aquitaine in 1152. Like his cousin Hugh Seymour, and so many other young aristocratic officers of the age, he gave his life to the Stuart navy, taking over four months to die of the wounds he sustained in the Battle of the Texel in August 1673.[13]

The motives driving these 'gentlemen captains' were complex. The elusive concept of 'honour' was certainly present, as was the desire of young men to prove themselves in battle; the army was reduced to a rump, and confined principally to tedious garrison duty. 'Seeing the world' was undoubtedly a motivator for some, as it always has been in naval recruitment (even if 'the world' in question was, more often than not, the North Sea and the English Channel). As the anonymous author suggested, joining a service which the king and the heir to the throne were known to love and patronise was an obvious way of currying royal favour. But many of this first generation came from families which had been punished heavily for their Royalism after the civil wars: fines and confiscations had ruined, or seriously diminished, many a proud Cavalier dynasty. Potentially, therefore, the navy provided an opportunity to repair shattered family fortunes, and if that also personally enriched the officer himself, then all well and good. This can hardly be condemned as avarice:

indeed, in many respects it was astonishingly altruistic, with young men being prepared to put themselves in harm's way in a completely alien environment if it provided the means of improving the lots of their parents, siblings and family estates. Francis Digby's career is a case in point. In 1667, he presented an extraordinary proposal to the king:

> There being due to Francis Digby, youngest son to the earl of Bristol, the sum of ten thousand pounds out of His Majesty's privy purse, in lieu of the like sum of the said Earl his father's money received by the Keeper of His Majesty's privy purse during his troubles, as hath been made particularly to appear to His Majesty in such manner as the said Francis Digby cannot doubt of his justice in the repayment thereof. But he being also very sensible how unlikely it is that His Majesty should spare at this time such a sum as that from his great occasions, and he being not more desirous to secure the only provision which his father has been able to make for him, than to be engaged in some honourable way of doing His Majesty service, the said Francis Digby doth humbly offer unto His Majesty:
>
> That if he be pleased to lend him three of his royal frigates and a fireship, to wit, one of the Fourth rate and two of the Fifth rate, manned and victualled and set out, from the first of February to the fifth of March next ensuing, and after that to be employed as His Majesty shall think fit with the rest of his royal fleet, he will by the credit of his friends join unto them by that time five other frigates of war at least, and employing the same in a well laid design for His Majesty's service, be content to take for all reimbursement he shall ever expect of the said ten thousand pounds by His Majesty's assignation upon the first profits of what shall be gained in the said expedition and the rest to be accounted for to His Majesty according to the course held in other prizes.
>
> Now the said Francis Digby being far from the presumption of thinking that a proposition of this nature shall be proceeded in upon a bare overture made from one of his years, and little experience, he humbly beseeches His Majesty that with his gracious approbation and that of His Royal Highness the Duke of York it may be recommended to my Lord Duke of Albemarle to hear in particular his proposals and to reject them or give orders for putting them in execution as he shall find them well grounded for His Majesty's service.
>
> And he humbly beseeches His Majesty not to believe him by this proposition capable of such a vanity (how much so ever he hath been applied to sea affairs) as to think himself fit to conduct a fleet,

his only aim in this business if it shall be entertained being to offer
unto His Majesty for that charge, such an experienced commander
as His Highness the Duke of York and the Duke of Albemarle shall
approve of, and who at the same time will not envy him the
honour and encouragement in His Majesty's service of having his
name joined with his in the commission for the command of the
said fleet.

Digby never got his squadron, and probably never got the £10,000
before he died in battle five years later. But his proposal gives a fascinating
glimpse into the mental world of the young naval officer of the
Restoration, for whom personal, family and royal honour merged seam-
lessly with patriotism and financial acquisitiveness.[14]

Charles and James saw their sea-officers as their knights errant, and
encouraged their captains in a number of ways. Perhaps the simplest was
that the captains of even relatively small warships going on routine
voyages were permitted to kiss the king's and Duke of York's hands before
setting out.[15] Those going on more important expeditions had frequent
and direct access to the royal brothers. In 1669, Captain John Narbrough
saw Charles and James several times before setting off on his voyage to
the South Seas; on his return in 1671, the king ordered him to Whitehall
on the very day that Narbrough arrived in the Thames, subsequently
spending several hours discussing the captain's voyage with him.[16] When
Narbrough went out to the Mediterranean as admiral in 1677, he met
the king alone on three occasions between 6 June and 13 July, the Duke
of York once, the brothers together once, and the king and his Privy
Council seven times. The royal brothers' relationship with many of their
sea-officers was informal and intimate. In December 1670, the Duke of
York was on his way into dinner when he spotted Captain Thomas Guy,
called him over, told him he had talked to the king, and that Guy would
shortly obtain the royal yacht command that he had been soliciting for.[17]
In August 1674, the relatively junior captain Henry Carverth went to
Windsor and talked to the king about the depredations of French privateers around the Channel Islands: Carverth and the Earl of Ossory, who
was also present in the conversation, persuaded the king to order a larger
ship to the station.[18] In November 1682, Charles took to one side the
young Captain Francis Wheeler, a protégé of Arthur Herbert, the admiral
commanding in the Mediterranean, and told Wheeler of his support for
Herbert: 'His Majesty bid me tell you that you are highly in his favour,
that he is most extremely well satisfied that you have served him very
well, and that he will constantly support you'. Charles also told Wheeler
of his determination that the admiral should join the Admiralty board
when he returned from sea; Wheeler suggested that Herbert should be a

supernumerary commissioner first, a notion which Charles accepted, so it appears that this significant political change, which took place when Herbert returned to England in the following year, was determined during a private conversation between the king and one of the most junior captains in the navy.[19]

King Charles seems to have had the good manager's knack of knowing when and how to praise and encourage. Pepys experienced this relatively early in his career, in January 1666, when 'the king came to me himself and told me: "Mr Pepys," says he, "I do give you thanks for your good service all this year, and I do assure you I am very sensible of it."' The royal praise sent the diarist into 'a great delirium'.[20] Even the socially more awkward James interacted relatively easily with his officers in private. In October 1682, he brought together in his own closet Christopher Gunman, captain of his yacht, and Sir Richard Haddock, who had presided over the court martial which dismissed Gunman from the service four months earlier, because of his alleged partial responsibility for the sinking of the *Gloucester*, with the duke on board. According to Gunman, James 'commanded Sir Richard Haddock and myself to become good friends as we had been formerly, and would not let us part until it was so agreed on of all sides and shook hands together'.[21]

Naval officers were often seen at court – sometimes, indeed, when they were meant to be at sea. Throughout the period, Pepys struggled to get the royal brothers to restrict captains' applications for shore leave, the granting of which was exclusively the domain of the king or Lord High Admiral; but the court was an irresistible magnet. Indeed, many 'gentlemen captains' had close relations in the royal household, providing a network of tightly knit connections that ultimately proved to be hugely important during the Glorious Revolution of 1688: Captain Richard Trevanion's brother John was a gentleman usher to the Duke of York; Robert Werden, who commanded six warships between 1665 and 1673, was a brother of John, who became the duke's secretary in 1672; while Compton Felton, who held two lieutenants' and one captain's commission in the 1670s, was a brother of the Controller of the Queen's household. The Stuart brothers' accessibility, and the attractions of their court, drove Pepys to despair, although there may have been an element of vaguely paranoid sour grapes here – after all, if young captains could talk privately to the king and Duke of York, they might take the opportunity to complain of the unjust strictures of the Secretary of the Admiralty. In 1683, Pepys observed:

The king's familiarity with commanders and under-officers makes them insolent, presuming upon their access to the king, and frights poor commanders or others their superiors from using their just authority (especially poor tarpaulins) considering what they say of the king's familiarity with those that offend.[22]

But for all his undoubted efficiency and perceptiveness, Pepys was missing a simple truth. The presence of naval men at court, so often and in such numbers, demonstrated the perfectly natural importance for such men of access to the royal brothers; but it also demonstrated the importance of the navy to those brothers, and the simple fact that they liked having naval men around them.

As well as being permitted such generous access, sea-officers benefited from royal patronage in a number of other ways. During the second Anglo-Dutch war in particular, successful officers were often granted prize ships, which could either be sold or set out as privateers or merchantmen. During peacetime, favoured captains were granted 'good voyages', usually within or from the Mediterranean, which enabled them to carry merchants' bullion and charge a commission for so doing.[23] Above all, sea-officers were often honoured with knighthoods, sometimes as a sort of 'lifetime achievement award', more often as a reward for notable service in action. The honour was bestowed on men from relatively humble backgrounds, at once catapulting them into the ranks of the armigerous gentry. Richard Munden, knighted in 1673 for capturing St Helena from the Dutch, was a son of the ferryman at Chelsea; John Wetwang, a veteran captain who was knighted in 1680, came from Northumberland freeholder stock.[24] Moreover, the profits from prize money and 'good voyages' enabled a number of naval officers to set themselves up as landed gentlemen. Sir John Narbrough, whose father had been a small tenant in Norfolk, did so well out of his naval service that he could acquire the Knowlton estate in Kent; his son was made a baronet by James II at the age of four, in recognition of the father's services, and the estate remained the property of Narbrough's descendants until 1904. In these senses, then, the navy of the Stuart kings provided one of the relatively few pathways to significant social mobility during the latter part of the seventeenth century. So although 'gentlemen captains' increasingly dominated the commissioned officer corps, it was still perfectly possible for a former cabin boy from Norfolk to hold command over a lineal descendant of the Earls of Huntingdon, the Dukes of Buckingham, and the royal house of York.[*]

*This was in 1683/84, when Cloudesley Shovell commanded the 'Sallee squadron' and one of his subordinate captains was Anthony Hastings, whose four times great-grandmother, Margaret Pole, Countess of Salisbury, was executed by Henry VIII because of her proximity to the throne; an uncle of Hastings's grandfather was, for a time, one of the principal candidates to succeed Queen Elizabeth I.

Charles II's thinking on the subject of 'gentlemen captains' was set out explicitly in a rare letter of his, written to Daniel Finch, then First Lord of the Admiralty. Charles wanted Finch to give Charles, Lord Berkeley of

Stratton, command of the Fourth Rate *Tyger*. Berkeley, a son of the Royalist soldier who had served as a colleague of Pepys on the Navy Board in the 1660s, was a relative rarity, as very few peers or their eldest sons went into the navy. The king stated that

> … tho' I am not for employing of men merely for quality, yet when men of quality are fit for the trade they desire to enter into, I think 'tis reasonable they should be encouraged at least equally with others, and I assure you, this young man has been so industrious to improve himself and so successful in it, as he deserves some partiality in his case, to encourage others to do the like …[25]

Charles got his way, and in August 1681, he demonstrated his personal interest in Berkeley's career by dining with him aboard the *Tyger*, bound for the Mediterranean.[26] Berkeley died in post seven months later, aged only twenty; the king provided two troops of his Horse Guards to escort the coffin from Berkeley House in Piccadilly to Twickenham church. Both Charles and James then promoted the career of his next brother, John, third Lord Berkeley of Stratton, who was a captain by 1686 and a rear-admiral by the end of 1688 (despite having murdered a pub landlord in the interim).[27]

In the fullness of time, Charles II even sent one of his own sons into the navy. Henry Fitzroy, Duke of Grafton, born in 1663, was his son by Barbara Palmer, Countess of Castlemaine, and later Duchess of Cleveland. The king initially refused to admit paternity, but finally did so when young Henry's bushy black eyebrows, large nose and dark, languid eyes put his paternity beyond any doubt whatsoever. In September 1678, at his father's request, Grafton was entered on the ship's books of the Fourth Rate frigate *Happy Return*, commanded by Sir William Poole, a veteran who had commanded men-of-war since before the Restoration.[28] In her, the young duke went out to the Mediterranean, returned to England in 1679 for long enough to get married, and then went back out again in the *Leopard*, commanded by Sir John Berry, another long-serving senior officer. The *Leopard* convoyed English trade to and from the Levant, but the duke was also able to visit the supposed ruins of Troy and the more recent ruins of Malaga, which had just been devastated by an earthquake. Importantly, the voyage also brought him into contact with the ship's master, Greenvile Collins, soon to be appointed hydrographer to the king. Grafton served as Master of Trinity House in 1682/83, and on 13 January 1683 was appointed Vice-Admiral of England, nominally deputy to the Lord High Admiral, in succession to the recently deceased Prince Rupert. Grafton's naval career further strengthened the close bond between his father, King Charles, and the navy that served him; unsurprisingly, several believed that Grafton would inevitably become Lord High Admiral in the fullness of time. Pepys, for one, thought this a dangerous development:

> The king having his own son Grafton in the place that he cannot be put by, being the top of all, by anybody else in time of action, and it maybe has a young favourite under him as the captain, and then what can come of it? ... the king ... is so fond of him upon the score of the sea ...[29]

Officers generally gained appointments and promotion through a system based on the workings of patronage. Courtiers, aristocrats, politicians, royal mistresses, senior naval officers, and many others, all competed to ensure that their recommendations came to the notice of those responsible for naval appointments. In the case of commissioned officers, but also to an extent of warrant officers too, that meant Charles or James Stuart. The formal system was for the names of candidates and those recommending them, along with the certificates testifying to their previous good service, to be entered in list books, which were then laid before the king or Lord High Admiral by the Admiralty secretary. Although unrecorded 'words in the ear' no doubt played a part as well – and the secretary, namely Pepys for much of the period, was ideally placed to promote his own agenda – the system was clearly understood and, by the standards of the time, reasonably transparent. Knowing this, candidates for office sometimes went to extraordinary lengths to 'play the system', although few were as blatant as a Mr Lacey, who in 1679 attempted to hoodwink Pepys and Charles II into believing that he had once served as lieutenant of the Second Rate *St Andrew*. Lacey even amended his captain's certificate to his previous good service to insert the word 'lieutenant', brought, as Pepys wryly noted, 'blotted to my hand with an ink different to the body of the certificate'. Lacey had also reckoned without the exemplary record-keeping of the king's navy, and the diligence of the man he was trying to hoodwink; Pepys was able to use the ship's books of *St Andrew* to prove that Lacey had never served as her lieutenant.[30]

There were many instances of Charles and James appointing men on their own initiative, without recourse to the recommendations of others. These were often cases where the individuals concerned, or their families, had rendered some special service to the royal brothers, were known to them personally, or were from families that had suffered for the Crown during the civil wars. Richard Le Neve was a page to the Duke of York, but was commissioned a lieutenant at the age of twenty and fell in battle at the Texel in 1673, earning the posthumous accolade of a memorial in

Westminster Abbey; Edward Pinn served as temporary captain of the *Cleveland Yacht* in 1675/76, and so impressed the king with his 'sobriety, seamanship, diligence, approved valour, and measure of civility … above what is ordinarily met with in a seaman', that Charles promised to promote him at the first opportunity.[31] The brothers' knowledge of their officers was encyclopaedic. In 1678, the king gave a guard-boat command to Dominic Nugent, even though Pepys knew nothing at all about him; but 'His Majesty was pleased to pitch upon him as an old officer, and poor, and one that he judged qualified for it.'[32] Edward Furlong became second lieutenant of the *Newcastle* 'by the king's particular direction, being wounded in the mouth'; James Dunbar became first lieutenant of the same ship 'by the king & duke's particular direction'; while Charles rejected his Admiralty board's recommendation of Lieutenant Temple for the *Norwich*, 'upon recollection of some former failures of his'.[33] Charles and James even appointed such relatively lowly individuals as boatswains and carpenters on their own initiative. In 1677, Pepys was clearly miffed when the king granted the carpenter's place on the *Charles* to someone who was 'entirely a stranger to me', ignoring Pepys's solicitations for William Bagwell, whom Pepys had brazenly cuckolded years before.[34]

The royal brothers were generous to officers and men who suffered or died in their service, and to their families. In 1680, Charles intervened personally to recommend support for Robert Cook, a seaman who had served 'three score years' in his and his father's navy, and to have had 'great sufferings for loyalty in the late times' (the civil wars).[35] Highly regarded old officers were not forgotten. Peter Bonamy, a fireship captain in both Dutch Wars of Charles II's reign, received £100 of royal bounty in 1677, exactly fifty years after he had gone to sea during the Duke of Buckingham's expedition to the Ile de Ré. In January of the following year, Charles and James enquired whether Captain Charles Wylde was well enough to return to sea, 'both His Majesty and Highness having a just esteem of and kindness towards you'.[36] Nor did recollections of the sacrifices made by Cavalier families during the civil wars fade with the passage of time. In 1683, the king recommended a Mister Dabridgecourt for a naval post if he was found to be fit for it, 'His Majesty remembering the sufferings of the father, and the ancientness of the descent'.[37] Indeed, the royal brothers' compassion and decency were bywords: Count Gramont, the gossipmonger-general of the early Restoration court, said of Charles that he was 'compassionate to the unhappy … and tender even to excess'.[38] These traits were sometimes exercised to the detriment of the service. In 1678, Lieutenant Mansell of the *Oxford* was kept in post despite being seriously ill for months on end, 'his Majesty being unwilling out of respect to himself and Sir Edward Mansell his kinsman, to put him out of his employment'.[39]

Charles and James were directly responsible for some notable naval careers. Sir William Berkeley, a knight and vice-admiral by the age of twenty-five, owed his stellar rise to the Stuart brothers, who, in turn, were being swayed by Berkeley's father and brother (respectively, the treasurer of the royal household and the king's favourite, the Earl of Falmouth), and by Admiral Sir John Lawson, who took the young man under his wing as a way of strengthening his own credit at court.[40] The naval career of Arthur Herbert, the future Earl of Torrington and nominal commander of the successful Dutch invasion in 1688, was launched by the Duke of York in 1663–66, and Charles II subsequently elevated this son of his former attorney general in exile to command in the Mediterranean.[41] Edward Russell, later the victor of Barfleur, Earl of Orford, and effectively joint 'prime minister' of England, was given his first commissions by the Duke of York in 1671, aged eighteen, and was subsequently promoted several times at James's behest. George Rooke, who would capture Gibraltar in 1704, obtained his first lieutenant's commission from James in 1672, and was first appointed a captain by Charles at the end of the following year.

However, royal patronage could also backfire, and sometimes, the failure of a naval career that seemed to have everything going for it seems to have been down to simple personal disinclination. In 1668, Charles O'Brian, captain of the *Leopard*, was described as one of the most influential officers in the navy by the Italian envoy Magalotti; a son of the powerful Irish politician, the Earl of Inchiquin, his astonishing dancing skills brought him to the attention of both the Duke of Monmouth and the king's mistress, the Countess of Castlemaine. But despite such advantages, O'Brian abandoned his naval career, and was eventually killed while soldiering at the Siege of Maastricht in 1673.[42] In 1672, the twenty-three-year-old Earl of Mulgrave went to sea as a volunteer, and so impressed the king by his conduct that he was given command of the Second Rate *Royal Katherine*, thus emulating his grandfather, who had commanded a ship against the Spanish Armada. But Mulgrave never returned to the sea, embarking instead on a lengthy career as a soldier, politician and author.[43] Another stillborn naval career was that of Sir John Anthony van Valkenbergh, second baronet, who was commissioned lieutenant of the powerful Third Rate *Fairfax* in 1666. Van Valkenbergh's distinctly un-English name came from his father, one of the Dutch engineers who had come over with Vermuyden to drain the Fens. But John Anthony seems to have decided that a naval life was not for him, and he went back to managing his estates on the Yorkshire–Lincolnshire border. Other unsuccessful naval appointments were simply quixotic. In 1682, Charles gave a command to Bartholomew Sharpe, a notorious 'pirate of the Caribbean', although

* For the
circumstances,
see Chapter 9.

Sharpe absconded from it almost immediately.* This was by no means the most eccentric of the king's naval appointments: he also gave pursers' posts on his warships to two of the sons of Colonel Blood, who had attempted to steal his Crown jewels.[44]

Above all, the appointment of naval officers provides ample evidence of one of the relatively few personality traits that Charles and James shared, and one that they both shared with their martyred father: a tendency stubbornly to persist with men whose inadequacies were glaringly obvious to virtually everyone else. This trait was particularly marked in James, who invariably displayed blind loyalty towards members of his favoured inner circle.[45] The man himself put it differently: for James, in cases of poor performance of duty or in battle, 'he was sure it did not arise from want of ability or good will, but from some other fault or misfortune'.[46] In some ways, of course, this was highly creditable: it sometimes made him fight ferociously for subordinates who had been wronged, as in 1682, when he swiftly overturned a sentence of dismissal from the navy and a year's imprisonment on his yacht captain, Christopher Gunman, who had unjustly taken some of the blame for the wreck of the *Gloucester*.[47] But James took exactly the same stubborn line even when more dispassionate observers reckoned that some of the individuals in question were irredeemably incompetent. Charles Talbot was dismissed the service in 1666 for bringing his ship into port, relatively undamaged, while the Four Days' Battle was still raging, and with the captain 'walking the deck in his silk morning gown and powdered hair'. But Talbot had very influential friends, notably the Duke of Ormonde, de facto viceroy of Ireland.[48] Consequently, he was given a new command in 1678, and then a further one by King James in 1685.

Perhaps the worst case, though, was that of Sir Jean-Baptiste Bardou du Teil. Probably a brother of the most notoriously ugly lady-in-waiting at the Restoration court, du Teil, who was unable to speak English, served in the Cavalier army in the civil war, seems to have assisted the royal cause in Jersey in 1649, had served in the French galley fleet, the Corps des Galères, and became a gentleman-waiter in the Queen Mother's household.[49] Despite his obvious linguistic deficiencies, du Teil was made captain of the *Fountain* by James in February 1665 and was promoted to the larger *Jersey* for the 1666 campaign. But Prince Rupert and the Duke of Albemarle, who commanded at sea that year, considered his lack of English a disqualification from command and turned him out, although the fact that he supposedly fired on his flagship might also have had something to do with it.[50] Instead, du Teil became the Duke of York's cupbearer, prompting a typically acid barb from Marvell:

> Cashier the memory of Du Tell, rais'd up
> To taste, instead of death's, his Highness' cup …[51]

The Frenchman was soon given even greater naval responsibility, and in 1671 was sent out to Tuscany to take command of the galley under construction there.* His appointment to such a responsible position might have been due in part to the fact that his brother was a prominent merchant at Malta, where he helped du Teil to buy slaves to man the galley's oars.[52] But the Frenchman's command of the *Margaret Galley* became an unmitigated fiasco: he quarrelled with the Grand Duke of Tuscany, in whose dockyard the galley was being built, experienced great difficulty in manning the vessel, and then saw relatively little service, with Charles and James swiftly realising that the galley was far too expensive to operate.[53] When du Teil died at Tangier in 1675, he described himself as 'belonging to His Royal Highness the Duke of York'. But James was not the only one to see a positive side to the much-derided Frenchman that eluded everybody else: the crew of the galley praised him for 'his merits of well governing them, and everyone hath been sensible of his sudden departure as if it had been their own father'.[54]

The leniency and inconsistency of the royal brothers was clearly apparent to their subordinates. Lord Dartmouth, one of the Duke of York's closest friends, told Pepys something that Sir Edward Spragge, his old patron in the navy, had once said to him:

* For the history of the galley, see Chapter 4.

... our masters the king and the Duke of York were very good at giving good orders and encouragement to their servants in office to be strict in keeping of good order, but were never yet found stable enough to support their officers in the performance of those their orders when they had done. By which no man was safe in doing them service as he should do.[55]

Many cases prove Spragge's point. One particularly blatant example occurred in 1672, when Sir William Coventry discovered 'a very notorious knavery' – unspecified – of Captain Richard Sadlington, and informed the Duke of York. He 'out of compassion ... absolutely forbade' Coventry to inform the Treasury commissioners, spoke privately to Sadlington, got his agreement 'to restore all that is embezzled', and then effectively lied to Lord Clifford, the head of the Treasury commission, by dictating a letter which claimed Sadlington's affairs could not be investigated properly because of bad weather. The duke was 'very desirous the Lords Commissioners should not have the particulars for fear of utter ruin to Sadlington'.[56] James's brother was equally reluctant to act too harshly against a trusted officer with an impressive service record. In July 1682, the king ordered the Admiralty board to suspend the court martial of Captain Sir Robert Robinson, who had controversially dispersed a convoy under his command. The board protested, arguing that complaints had been received from English merchants at Cadiz, and that the discipline of the navy would suffer if he was not tried. The Admiralty ordered the court martial to proceed, but the king again overruled them, ordering Robinson's release.[57]

Charles and James also turned a blind eye to the 'good voyage', the practice by which captains of warships were able to charge commission for carrying precious goods on merchant accounts from A to B. Pepys regularly fulminated against the ills of the practice, notably warships lingering in port in the hope a lucrative cargo would show up, and although the king and Duke of York occasionally made gestures against it (with James, as king, abolishing it in 1686, on paper at least), their reprimands were weakened by the fact that they often benefited personally from such voyages. In 1674, for instance, one warship brought from the Mediterranean four chests of Florence wine and one butt of sherry each for the king and the Duke of York (together with two more chests of Florence for Pepys), while another brought yet more sherry and wine for the royal brothers and their Admiralty secretary.[58] The collusion of Charles and James in such voyages went well beyond the contents of their own drinks cellars: they knew that officers' pay alone was insufficient to attract well-born young men into the navy, and that only by tolerating such perquisites – what some might call abuses –

would they be able to form the sort of officer corps they wished to see.

The leniency of the royal brothers had limits. In January 1667, a large number of seamen marched down the Strand towards Whitehall Palace, to protest about the tardiness of their payment. The mob was locked up in Scotland Yard, but the king went in person to reassure them that every effort was being made to pay them as quickly as possible. There was a rider, though: 'if ever [again] they should assemble in such numbers to demand payment, they should be paid with the gallows'.[59] When Captain Thomas Booth of the *Falcon* killed a night watchman in a brawl at Yarmouth in 1677, the king's only leniency was to change his sentence from hanging to beheading; Pepys considered this justified, because Booth had effectively murdered 'a magistrate (for so a watchman is at night) in the exercise of his duty, [so] His Majesty's clemency would have been subject to much censure, should he have been prevailed with to have pardoned him'.[60] The clear implication of Pepys's words is that Charles often *was* prevailed upon to exercise clemency in instances where it was unwarranted. Five years later, James Ayres, the pilot held responsible for the loss of the *Gloucester* – and thus for gravely endangering the life of the heir to the throne – was sentenced to perpetual imprisonment, despite 'his deep and hearty sorrow and repentance for that evil which is not now to be remedied, and that he was fatally instrumental therein'.[61]

The introduction of a qualifying examination for the post of lieutenant, in 1677, is traditionally regarded as Samuel Pepys's defining achievement, and as a milestone in the history of the Royal Navy. 'Passing for lieutenant' became one of the two critical stages in the career of every commissioned officer, from that time until well into the nineteenth century – the other being his advancement to the rank of post captain, which guaranteed that, if he remained alive long enough, he would eventually die an admiral, regardless of merit. But, in many respects, the genesis of the examination remains shrouded in mystery: the sequence of events is clear enough, but exactly why it was proposed when it was, why it took the final form that it did, and, above all, who originally conceived the idea, are all unclear.

The proposition was first raised publicly at a meeting of the Admiralty commission on 1 September 1677. Pepys reminded the board that since 1674, all masters and commanders of Sixth Rate frigates had been examined at Trinity House, and proposed that this should be extended to those who were previously captains of larger ships, but had been forced to take Sixth Rate commands due to the small number of posts available in peacetime. This was actually a minuscule issue: on the exact day when

Pepys raised it, there were precisely two Sixth Rates in commission, and the scenario described by Pepys applied to only one of the two commanders, Richard Trevanion of the *Saudadoes*, who had been a captain almost continuously since 1666 and thus, quite naturally, might have resented being forced to sit an examination before Trinity House, rather as a Formula One driver might object to being compelled to undertake a driving theory test.[62] The Admiralty agreed to Pepys's proposal, but then, according to the formal minutes of the meeting, the Duke of York intervened, enthusiastically seconding the change to the system for Sixth Rate commanders, before going to suggest that 'towards the making of able captains … a thorough scrutiny be had in the proficiencies and qualifications of every person pretending to be a lieutenant, before he be admitted thereto'. According to James, the establishment of May 1676, which provided for set numbers of young volunteers to serve aboard ships of each rate, had led many to demand lieutenancies, without any method existing to test their ability and fitness for the post. He suggested that 'Trinity House, the Officers of the Navy, or both' should carry out an examination of candidates. Pepys seconded the duke, proposing that a detailed list of instructions for lieutenants should be drawn up for the first time, enabling candidates to be assessed on their ability to meet each point of the instructions. Pepys was commanded to go away and prepare drafts of both a set of instructions and a scheme for an examination.[63]

Although James's remark about candidates clamouring for lieutenancies is perfectly plausible, it is distinctly curious, given the circumstances of the time. On one level, the competence of lieutenants was a virtual non-issue in September 1677. There were hardly any posts available: during the three and a half years between the end of the third Anglo-Dutch war in February 1674 and the end of August 1677, only fifty-four lieutenants' commissions were granted, to fewer than four dozen men (several had more than one commission). But in 1674/75, twenty of the commissions were granted to men who were first promoted by the Duke of York before he resigned as Lord High Admiral, while only seven were new appointments; in 1676/77, though, fourteen commissions went to officers originally commissioned by James, thirteen to new men. Perhaps the duke felt that the officer corps was no longer that which he had shaped, and that his influence over it was slowly slipping away: certainly, he might have had misgivings about a man like George Aylmer, a former page to James's old adversary, the Earl of Arlington.[64] Similarly, one of the arguments that Pepys used to reinforce the case for the introduction of a lieutenants' examination was a complaint that had been received from Sir John Narbrough, the admiral commanding in the Mediterranean, who was dissatisfied with the competence of the lieutenants under his command. In particular, Narbrough took umbrage at one specific failing of the lieutenant of the *Sapphire*; although the wording is unclear, it seems as though the officer in question had allowed a hammock to be made out of some of the ship's rigging.[65]

On closer analysis, though, there is rather more to the story than this. In the summer of 1677, Sir John Narbrough's fleet contained sixteen lieutenants. Of these, all but two had held posts in the rank before; indeed, two of the sixteen had previously served as captains of small ships. Six had held between two and four previous commissions, while no fewer than ten had fought right through one or both of the previous Dutch wars. Three would eventually become highly successful admirals – indeed, one of them, Cloudesley Shovell, would become one of Britain's most famous seamen of all – and another ultimately became governor of Greenwich Hospital. Of the two lieutenants who had never served in the rank before, one, Robert Reynolds, was Narbrough's own second lieutenant aboard his flagship, *Plymouth*, a man whom he had personally selected. Finally, the errant lieutenant who particularly offended the admiral was John Nevill, who had held a commission previously, during the 1673 campaign, and who had served in the *Sapphire* for two years before this incident; he would eventually die on active service as a vice-admiral. Clearly, then, the lieutenants of the Mediterranean fleet were not some coterie of wet-behind-the-ears incompetents; almost all of them had some years' experience at sea, in a couple of cases up to fifteen or more years' worth, and most of them were veterans of battle. Therefore, it is very difficult to see why Narbrough should have been so angered by their performance that he reacted in the way he did; they were exactly the same sort of men he had always known, and whom he had once been.

Pepys himself hinted at what may have been the real reason for Narbrough's displeasure in a letter he wrote to the admiral on 19 November 1677, where, immediately after informing Narbrough of the establishment of the new examination, he gently chided him for recommending Robert Reynolds: 'we are all frail', Pepys observed, and the new system 'will in a good measure prevent us in the exercise of our frailty in this particular'.[66] Thus Narbrough's complaint might have had more to do with his lack of control over the appointment of his officers than concern over the actual competence of his lieutenants, and the fact that Lieutenant Nevill, whose alleged shortcomings so offended the admiral, was a 'gentleman officer', a scion of the Barons Bergavenny, who might have rubbed up the 'tarpaulin' Narbrough in the wrong way. This, in turn, might have impacted on the Duke of York's attitude: Narbrough was very much James's man. Therefore, the proposal to introduce a lieutenants' examination might have had as much to do with court faction and the composition of the navy's officer corps as it was with actually improving the competence of the profession. Pepys's own opinion on the matter makes clear that the establishment of the lieutenants' examination was not only a case of improving technical competence, but also of reducing the role of the court in their appointment. According to him, the perceived 'ignorance and idleness' of lieutenants was due to their having spent too little time at sea before obtaining their commissions through their relationship to 'families of interest at court'; Pepys dreaded to think what sort of captains the navy would have to rely upon when 'the few commanders (for God knows there are but few) that are now surviving of the true breed shall be worn out'.[67] As far as the secretary was concerned, then, ending the distinction between 'gentlemen' and 'tarpaulins' was one of the principal objectives of the new dispensation.[68]

Having been tasked with drawing up both instructions for lieutenants and the scheme for an examination, Pepys duly reported back to the Admiralty board on 1 December, exactly three months after the original proposal was mooted. The board approved his proposals after 'a large debate', but changed two crucial elements. The idea that the examination should be conducted by Trinity House and the Navy Board was rejected, and replaced by a panel of flag officers and former or current captains of First and Second Rate ships. Pepys's formal minutes barely conceal his anger: Trinity House, in his opinion, contained 'the only proper judges' of 'the art and practice of navigation and the duty of a mariner'. But the commissioners considered it 'a diminution to the honour of lieutenants to be submitted to the examination of any but the king's own commanders', and the secretary had to concede – although as he knew full well, for the short to medium term, at least, the list of flag officers and captains of great ships contained several men whose own seagoing qualifications and experience were debatable, so in theory, a lucky young prospective lieutenant might end up being examined by men who knew less than he did. The slight amendment made at the following meeting, to add one Navy Board officer to two senior commanders, did not greatly ameliorate this flaw: after all, in 1677 the Navy Board included the likes of Pepys's brother John and the Duke of York's secretary Sir John Werden, whose seamanship was sketchy at best. Nevertheless, this system held sway for centuries, and the examination before three senior officers became a rite of passage for every young officer, even though it did not entirely eliminate the influence of connections and even downright nepotism: this was demonstrated on 9 April 1777, when the young Horatio Nelson was examined for lieutenant by a panel chaired by the

Above, left: George St Lo in later years, when he served as a commissioner of the navy; but in his younger days, he was the first man to sit and pass the examination for lieutenant introduced in 1677. *(Wikimedia Commons)*

Above, right: The elaborate memorial to Sir John Narbrough and his two sons, Knowlton Church, Kent. *(Author's photograph)*

Left: Detail of relief depicting HMS *Association* wrecked on the Isles of Scilly, 1707. *(Julian Mannering)*

Controller of the Navy, who happened to be his uncle.[69] The second of Pepys's proposals to be queried by the board was that for prospective lieutenants to serve at least a year as a midshipman, then regarded as a relatively lowly post held by 'tarpaulins'. This, again, was thought to be 'beneath the quality of a gentleman', and was referred to the Navy Board and 'some of the principal commanders of the fleet now in town'.[70]

The conference on the question of 'gentlemen' doing a midshipman's duty took place within the following week, attended by five officers of the navy and nine senior captains. A similar panel then attended the Admiralty board meeting on 8 December, at which the king was present, where the question was put to the captains attending – who, as Pepys noted, included 'gentlemen' and 'tarpaulins' alike. The crucial intervention came from George Legge, the future Lord Dartmouth, a captain during the Dutch Wars, who had never served in any lesser capacity beforehand. When asked if he had spent any time as a midshipman, he answered '*No*, but that it had cost him many an aching head and heart since to make up the want of it'; Legge believed that compelling gentlemen volunteers to serve in the rank would 'unite the officers and destroy the distinction between gentlemen and tarpaulins'. The year's qualifying service as a midshipman was duly adopted.[71] On 24 January 1678, Pepys was able to report that the first batch of examinations had taken place, with four passes and one fail, 'to the great satisfaction of His Majesty and My Lords in the prospect it gives them of the good breed of lieutenants, and consequently of commanders, which may hereafter be expected in the navy'.[72] The first officer to pass was George St Lo, who went on to a distinguished career culminating in service as Commissioner of the Navy at Chatham. But the old ways were a long time dying: St Lo obtained a commission almost at once, which might not have been unrelated to the fact that his wife was a granddaughter of William Chiffinch, Charles II's 'pimpmaster-general'.[73]

The fact that Pepys clearly wanted Trinity House, of which he had recently been master (and whose special interests he might, therefore, have had in mind) to be central to the examination process is one of several indications that the proposed reform was probably not his brainchild. As the debates of December 1677 suggest, too, imposing any sort of examination on the likes of two of the first officers affected by it, a brother of the Earl of Manchester and a son of the Lord Privy Seal, simply could not have been done solely on the initiative of a tailor's son: after all, 'middle ranking civil servants do not start great projects'.[74] The Duke of York's suggestion that an examination might be carried out by 'Trinity House, the Officers of the Navy, or both', smacks of something thought up on the spur of the moment, rather than of a scheme which had been carefully planned in advance, be it by James or Pepys. Moreover, the Admiralty meeting where the idea was first proposed, that of 1 September 1677, was very small: the only attendees were the king, Lord Chancellor Finch, the Earl of Craven, and Secretary of State Henry Coventry, along with the Duke of York, whose presence Pepys did not formally record. If Pepys had devised a project and persuaded the Duke of York to present it, as has been suggested, he would surely have waited until he had the largest possible audience, always very much a Pepysian trait.[75] Nor was the king's presence exceptional, suggesting that he might have attended in order to add weight to a proposal he knew was coming: quite apart from Charles's usually excellent attendance record, he was also present at the five meetings immediately preceding that on 1 September (unlike modern executives, the king generally worked hard during the summer, and took a lengthy break in the autumn).[76] Moreover, the new evidence of how Admiralty meetings actually worked during the 1670s, presented in the Appendix, suggests that Pepys's minutes invariably downplay, if anything, the influence of the Duke of York: so it is likely that his intervention on 1 September 1677 was accurately recorded in the published record, was both spontaneous and decisive, and that, therefore, James, not Pepys, was the original instigator of the lieutenants' examination.

Circumstantial evidence to support this suggestion can, perhaps, be traced in the genesis of the establishment for volunteers and midshipmen extraordinary, the effects of which James criticised at the meeting on 1 September 1677. This suggests that he had probably played no part in devising the measure in question, and the chronology seems to support this. The establishment appeared in an order issued by the king on 8 May 1676, which was then promulgated in a further order signed by Pepys on 1 July.[77] At that time, relations between James and his brother were distinctly rocky: at Easter, the duke finally abandoned the token gesture of attending Anglican services, a move which drove the king to despair, while James had also rowed ferociously with Charles's trusted chief minister, the Earl of Danby, at Newmarket in April.[78] Therefore, it seems very unlikely that James was behind the volunteers' establishment, and more likely that in September 1677 he proposed a radical response to the perceived unintended ill-consequences of a measure instigated by his brother and/or Pepys. Further circumstantial evidence to support James's responsibility for the lieutenants' examination might be found in the list of those brought into the meeting on 8 December 1677 to support the case for reform. James's secretary, Sir John Werden, turned up, although he had not been directly consulted on the subject, and the experienced naval captains who were called upon to provide expert opinion were overwhelmingly the duke's own followers, including his friend Legge, his protégés Herbert, Strickland and Berry, and Christopher Gunman, the captain of his personal yacht.[79] True, it was Pepys's energy and efficiency that had the scheme up and running within four months, but in its final form, it was clearly not the method of examination that the Admiralty secretary would have chosen if he had free rein; and the fact that thereafter he took credit both for the results and for the original proposal was entirely characteristic, as he also did in the case of the Mathematical School at Christ's Hospital.

Pepys undoubtedly played a significant role in establishing the lieutenants' examination, for rooting out what he called 'the bastard breed' of
unqualified, incompetent aristocratic lieutenants was a long-held ambition.[80] But the exact extent of his role is more problematic. Biographers
and historians have invariably given Pepys all the credit for this pivotal
reform – in other words, for both its conception and its execution. But
to do so, they have had to ignore, or somehow explain away, the inconvenient evidence of Pepys's own words in the Admiralty journal, where
he states categorically that the idea came from the Duke of York.[81] The
most extreme version of the tortuous reasoning that has resulted came
from Richard Ollard, who started from the assumption that the idea for
the lieutenants' examination can only have come from the fertile mind
of his infallible hero Pepys, ergo the duke's suggestions must have been
'planted' by the Admiralty secretary, no matter how ludicrous the idea of
the future King James II and VII being such a pliant stooge.[82] In reality,
the introduction of a lieutenants' examination was the culmination of a
long process of reform to the method of entry and promotion within the
commissioned officers corps, and in this sense, it was merely the last of a
number of measures introduced between 1661 and 1677, and was an
entirely logical extension of the system of volunteers per order that
Charles and James introduced just after the Restoration. Half pay for officers was introduced in 1668 and extended in 1674/75; superannuation
in 1672; gratuities for officers wounded at sea in 1673, building on the
existing provision to the relatives of those slain at sea (1665) and to those
who had done good service.[83]

None of the measures introduced before 1673 were Pepys's work in
any shape or form, as he simply had no responsibility for the commissioned officers before that date – their appointment and promotion was
exclusively the remit of the Admiralty, and Pepys's then position as Clerk
of the Acts meant his responsibilities were confined exclusively to the
subordinate Navy Board. In November 1674, though, Pepys got the
Admiralty's agreement to stricter enforcement of the rule that
'midshipmen extraordinary' should be former commissioned officers and
no other, placed on warships to give them some employment when there
were otherwise too few posts available for them. As already noted, the
regularisation in 1676 of the number of volunteers and midshipmen
extraordinary on each rate of ship may well have been his work; and
Pepys also instigated hugely important reforms to the system of
appointing naval chaplains.[84] But the fact that Pepys effectively wrote the
Duke of York out of the records of the Admiralty commission of
1673–79, as the evidence presented in the Appendix demonstrates,
muddies the waters. Since his first days as Lord High Admiral in 1660,
James had proved to be a man who liked order, and who sought to

enshrine that order in written establishments. It seems inconceivable that James Stuart, one of the least changeable royals in British history, dramatically changed his spots when he resigned as Lord High Admiral in 1673. Indeed, this is demonstrated by James's actions both when he was exile during the Exclusion Crisis, and after he became king. When he was in Edinburgh, James requested that various documents relating to the management of the navy be sent to him, perhaps with a view to making amendments to them when he was once again in a position to do so; one of the documents he asked for related to the management of the Chatham Chest, and after his accession, James did, indeed, make a number of changes to the provision for it, suggesting perhaps that he first contemplated these during his time in Scotland, when he had the relative leisure to think upon such matters.[85] On coming to the throne, he returned with a vengeance to the devising of new establishments and systems, such as that of 1686 which nominally abolished plate carriage. In April 1688, James proposed to Pepys and the Lord Treasurer, Lord Godolphin, that there should be 'one entire scheme or plan of the government of the navy',[86] and in July 1688, he implemented an establishment to regulate the circumstances and number of gun salutes.[87] It is certainly true that in this desire for order and standardisation, the prince and Mr Pepys were as one; but while Pepys was certainly primarily responsible for many of the reforms of the period, it is both churlish and inaccurate to deny James responsibility for many elements of naval reform after 1673, particularly the lieutenants' examination.

During the final months of 1677, the principal naval priority of Charles II and the Duke of York was not the reform of the officer corps and the introduction of an examination for lieutenants, but the huge new construction programme for thirty ships. One incidental effect of this was a sudden explosion in the number of naval offices available to be filled, for even if the new vessels were not sent to sea at once, they would still each require five standing officers (a boatswain, a carpenter, a gunner, a purser and a cook) while they were laid up in harbour. Consequently, the king was subjected to 'great solicitations' from courtiers and naval men pushing their own favoured candidates, and at the same time that the lieutenants' examination was being introduced, he decided to pursue a policy of filling the new posts in the first instance with men who had demonstrated their competence in older ships.[88] If promotion by proven merit and previously demonstrated competence was to be the rule for warrant officers, it was clearly only logical for it to apply to commissioned officers too. The fact that the lieutenants'

examination was actually part of a wider agenda to drive up professional standards in *all* naval offices was alluded to by Pepys in January 1678: 'high time it is, and so His Majesty is pleased (blessed be God) to declare it, that his service at sea ... be committed and placed upon such as by their experience and virtues are best qualified for it'.[89] One consequence of this was that Charles also began to prefer lieutenants with previous experience to those who had none – the policy that drove the desperate Mr Lacey to forge the word 'lieutenant' on his certificate. Ironically, but perhaps rather obviously, the principal side-effect of this policy was effectively to close the door on the great majority of those who passed the much-vaunted new examination: in the first eleven years of the system's existence, fewer than 14 per cent of those who qualified under it actually managed to obtain commissions.[90] War, and only war, ultimately satisfied the pent-up demand.

Indeed, until at least 1688, the results of the introduction of the examination were rather more mixed than Pepys ever stated in any of his writings. He had no doubt of the importance of the new system, and of the role that he had to play in implementing it:

> For as much as if this regulation be well observed into the admitting of none to lieutenancies but such as are fully qualified for it ... I doubt not but one seven years [*sic*] will furnish his Majesty with a race of commanders much better qualified for his service than for want thereof his Majesty has for a great while been forced sometimes to content himself with ... I do and shall make it my business to see this matter executed ... with all the care and integrity that may be.[91]

* These were principally aristocrats, demonstrating that the old notion of the peerage's innate ability to command in war died hard: those given ships in this way by Charles II and James II in the 1680s included the second and third Lord Berkeleys of Stratton and William Constable (later Viscount Dunbar).

But as with the appointment of lieutenants who had qualified through the examination, and despite the 'care and integrity' that he undoubtedly displayed, Pepys's optimism proved unfounded. During the 1680s, several men were still commissioned as captains without having served as lieutenants at all, let alone having passed an examination;* and in 1685, at the end of the seven-year period in which Pepys placed such hopes, two of the captains in active commission were Henry Priestman, whom both Charles II and James II continued to promote (and who eventually merited a lavish memorial in Westminster Abbey), despite Pepys and the Navy Board regarding him as a feckless, arrogant nightmare; and the perennially incompetent Charles Talbot, he of the silk morning gown.[92]

8

—⟶⟵—

The Sovereignty of the Sea

O N ANY GIVEN SUMMER'S DAY from the mid-1670s onwards, when the court decamped to Windsor Castle for several months at a time, King Charles II and his 'significant other' *de jour* might have woken in the king's bedchamber, and looked sleepily upward at a ceiling adorned with a painting of Charles wearing the robes of the Garter, seated on a throne, under a canopy supported by Time, Jupiter and Neptune, with a subservient France at his feet. After the king stirred, and moved out into his drawing room, he could look up at another ceiling to see Britannia and Neptune paying homage to him as he passed in a triumphal car. Going still further out into the state rooms, Charles might have paused to examine some new paintings by the finest marine artists of the age, the Willem van de Veldes, father and son, whom he had 'poached' from the Netherlands in 1672/73, installed in a studio in the Queen's House at Greenwich, and commissioned 'for taking and making draughts of sea fights' (in the case of the father) and 'putting the said draughts into colours for our particular use' (the son).[1] At some point during the day, the king might have listened to some music: say, one of the welcome odes to mark Charles's return to Whitehall in the autumn, penned by the prodigy Henry Purcell from 1680 onwards, such as 'The summer's absence unconcerned we bear', written to mark the king's return from Newmarket in October 1682:

> Britannia shall now her large empire bestride
> And over the seas she unrivalled shall ride,
> Sole Empress she the vast flood shall command
> And awe the great blustering Hectors at land.

When he finally went back to Whitehall in the autumn, with or without the significant other, Charles would immediately have become reacquainted with the astonishing painting that dominated the second privy lodging room, arguably the most politically important space in the royal apartments. Antonio Verrio, who painted the ceilings at Windsor, was also responsible for *The Sea Triumph of Charles II*, in which Charles, attired as a Roman emperor and attended by his fleet, is driven through the waters by Neptune and four sea horses. Victory presents the king with a plumed

helmet, while Envy (the Dutch or French, perhaps?) is struck by light-
ning. A fleet of British warships lies at anchor, while Minerva and Juno
look on approvingly. The whole is adorned with the legend '*imperium
oceano famam qui terminet astris*' ('whose empire ocean, and whose fame
the skies alone shall bound'). In short, *The Sea Triumph* was emphatically
not a modest and understated piece of domestic art.[2]

When Charles died and James succeeded to the throne, the message
remained exactly the same. 'Sound the trumpet, beat the drum', set to
music by Purcell for the king's birthday in 1687, referred to James as
'monarch of Britain and Lord of the Ocean'. Over the years, the new
king had issued many medals proclaiming his naval victories and
connecting himself explicitly with the image of Britannia; the most
famous painting of him as an admiral, painted by Henri Gascar in
1672/73, portrayed him as the god Mars, his fleet lying behind him,
symbolising a new British Empire, the true successor to Rome.[3]

Heady stuff indeed: but all of this would have been mere bluster, art for
art's sake, without some sort of historical and legal justification. Above all,
it would have been irrelevant, pompous daubing and caterwauling, but
for royal warships running out their guns time and time again to give
very real meaning to the ideology that permeated the culture of the
court, and which even spilled over into popular culture, too: an ideology
founded on the belief that the King of England was also sovereign over
the 'British Seas' which surrounded his islands, and that all foreign ships
should strike their flags and take in their topsails to acknowledge that
sovereignty, even right up to their own high water marks, Charles II's
quite literal definition of 'British borders'. The aggressive enforcement by
royal warships of what seems an inexplicable, utterly arcane and almost
insanely arrogant pretension could only be justified if there was a genuine
belief in the ideology that united the art of Verrio and the music of
Purcell with the very specific set of aspirations that underpinned the
naming of the greatest British warship of the seventeenth century, the
Sovereign of the Seas.

Moreover, both the art of Verrio, which depicted Charles II triumphant
over France, and the fact that Stuart warships most often ran out their
guns against French vessels, casts some doubt on the traditional picture of
Charles as a submissive client of Louis XIV. Charles might have been
willing to take his cousin's money, but deep down, he dreamed of
supplanting him: after all, the royal titles, announced at every state event
Charles attended, proclaimed him to be King of England, Scotland,
Ireland *and France*. What appears to modern mentalities to be arcane anti-
quarianism and legalistic mumbo jumbo could have very real meaning,
and very real power, in the seventeenth century. Not only did the King
of England still retain the claim, left over from the Hundred Years War, to

be the rightful King of France (a claim dropped only in 1801), but he also continued, at least in name, to assert his right to the duchies of Normandy, lost in 1204, and Aquitaine, lost in 1453.

It is often assumed that these claims were anachronistic curiosities with no real substance, but this is not necessarily the case. Two individuals attired 'in fantastique habits' represented the two duchies during Charles II's coronation procession, much to the fury of Louis XIV's representatives; French attempts to get Charles to drop the title 'King of France' were dismissed out of hand; and when war was declared against France in February 1666, the official form of words styled Louis XIV dismissively as 'the French King', and Charles II as 'King of France'.[4] The Duke of York's patent appointed him not only Lord High Admiral of England and Ireland, but also that of Normandy, Calais, Gascony and Aquitaine. This seems to have been the legal justification for the granting of several privateering commissions to captains from Honfleur and Dunkirk during the second Anglo-Dutch war; while George Monck, the man who had restored the monarchy (and was joint commander-in-chief of the fleet in both the first and second Anglo-Dutch wars) took his ducal title of Albemarle from a region of Normandy.[5] There are still echoes of this today: British monarchs' rights to sovereignty over the Channel Islands are still explicitly derived from their 'being anciently part of the Duchy of Normandy, in right of Her [Majesty's] illustrious and royal predecessor, William, Duke of Normandy and King of England'.[6]

Of course, King Louis XIV was very unlikely ever to enter the King of England's bedchamber at Windsor Castle, where he would have seen the ceiling painting that showed his proud France humbled, prostrate at Charles Stuart's feet. Far from being a supine puppet of the French king, then, Charles II literally dreamed of being his master.

The special, apart, literally insular, nature of England and its appendages was a recurrent theme in medieval and early modern English writings, long before it found its finest expressions in the speech Shakespeare gave to John of Gaunt, and in John Dryden's lyrics for 'Fairest Isle', as set to music by Henry Purcell. During the fifteenth and sixteenth centuries, writers like William Caxton, William Harrison, William Camden and John Speed all took very similar lines.[7] In the middle of Elizabeth I's reign, the Welsh polymath and reputed conjuror John Dee took a spat over herring – or, more precisely, the rights or otherwise of foreigners to fish freely in English waters – and built upon it an extraordinary vision of the queen's 'petty naval royal' enforcing her right over the entire Narrow Sea, even up to the French coast itself.[8] Dee and others looked

back to the alleged history of Edgar, King of England from 959 to 975,
who was supposed to have maintained a thousand ships to control his
'four seas', and who, it was said, was rowed on the River Dee by six or
eight subordinate kings, who thus acknowledged his maritime
supremacy. John Dee described Edgar as 'one of the perfect Imperial
Monarchs of the British Empire' – a term that he was the first to coin, at
least in its maritime sense, and which he gradually developed into an
extraordinary vision of imperial hegemony which was at least a century
ahead of its time.[9] Elizabeth was sceptical, partly because she knew how
much making good Dee's grand designs would cost, but her successors
had no such reservations. As noted earlier, Charles I subsequently used
Edgar as the centrepiece of the figurehead of the *Sovereign of the Seas* –
indeed, for a time there was a strong rumour that the ship was actually
going to be named *Edgar* – and his son James, Duke of York, gave the
name to his own son, born in September 1667, an infant who seemed set
fair to become King of England if he lived beyond childhood (which,
ultimately, he did not).[10] In reality, many of the claims advanced on
Edgar's behalf were fictions, the origins of which can be found in a series
of blatant forgeries produced by some monks of Worcester in the twelfth
century to further the interests of their abbey in local property disputes.[11]
But seventeenth-century monarchs, statesmen, lawyers and naval captains
did not know that, and can hardly be blamed for adopting Edgar as the
'creation myth' of their navy.

Similarly, they did not know that some of the other original legal
precedents for English 'sovereignty of the sea' were equally dubious. In

1201, King John issued the Ordinance of Hastings, which commanded foreign ships to lower their sails; but there was no mention of this being an acknowledgement of sovereignty. The ordinance was concerned more with allowing the goods of such ships to be searched (and, no doubt, ransacked), and was issued at a time when John still controlled both sides of the Channel, thus making 'the English Sea' a very different, and much more literal, construct.[12] In 1293, King Edward I's Gascon fleet launched a surprise attack on a French fleet in the Channel. This could have been embarrassing, or worse, as Edward held Gascony as a feudal vassal of the King of France, so English lawyers swiftly produced a claim that their kings had 'time out of mind ... been in peaceable possession of the sovereign lordship of the English seas and the islands therein'.[13] This, like the 'striking' to King John's ships, gradually became gospel, 'proving' a legal right that had existed 'since time immemorial'.[14] But it also became very much a double-edged sword: if the kings of England were sovereigns of the sea, it could be argued all too easily by the likes of dispossessed shipmasters and the inhabitants of devastated coastal communities, why did the king not demonstrate the fact by protecting them properly? The undoubted logic of this argument appeared many times in complaints lodged with the Crown throughout the Middle Ages, and emerged again during the Stuart era.[15] As Thomas Corbett, an eighteenth-century Secretary of the Admiralty, put it:

> it is not wise in a state to take to itself great titles and pretensions, beyond what it can maintain, and may one day prove fatal to it ... if the Narrow Seas are part of the territory of the crown of England, our ancestors were great fools to permit the Dutch and other foreigners to run away with the profits of our fish for so many ages ...[16]

The claim to English dominion over the 'British seas' lay largely dormant until the accession of James I in 1603. A king trained originally in Scots law, founded more closely on the precepts of Roman law than the English common law, had a somewhat different understanding of the concepts involved than his English predecessors, ministers and lawyers alike, and this became clear as his reign progressed. Moreover, Scotland had its own tradition of quasi-historical imperial pretensions, expressed in the works of the likes of Hector Boece, John Major, Andrew Melville and George Buchanan, all of which would have been very familiar to James.[17] Scottish monarchs and lawyers had invariably favoured a policy of 'closed seas', and developed the concept of 'the King's Chambers' – essentially another name for territorial waters, over which the King of Scots held unchallenged sway.[18] In 1613 and 1615, the Scottish lawyer

William Welwood produced two counterblasts to the Dutchman Hugo Grotius, whose *Mare Liberum* argued that the seas were free to all; Welwood's work was carried out partly at the instigation of James I's queen, Anna of Denmark, who had just been granted a monopoly over certain fisheries and wished to strengthen her legal claim to them.[19] Charles I took an even more proactive, aggressively expansionist, line over the 'sovereignty of the sea', partly as a result of the discovery by John Burough, the keeper of the records at the Tower of London, of the original thirteenth-century roll containing the Law of Oléron, which seemed to prove the jurisdiction of the kings of England over the Narrow Seas at least. Charles directly commissioned Burough to produce an essay proving England's maritime pretensions, while the first medal asserting England's dominion over the seas was struck in 1630.[20] The propaganda campaign culminated in 1635 with the publication of John Selden's *Mare Clausum*, originally written in James's reign, which both produced a theoretical justification for rejecting 'the freedom of the seas', and also duly recycled the so-called 'evidence' from King Edgar onwards to prove the specific case of Charles I's sovereignty in the 'British Seas'.[21]

The ship-money fleets, built and set out during the same period, were clear evidence of Charles I attempting to turn these somewhat vague and abstract legal claims into a visible reality on the seas, at a time when those seas were threatened not only by Dutch fishermen, but also by Barbary corsair raids and, potentially, by the fleets of the combatants in the Thirty Years War as they transited the Channel. Indeed, while responding to these threats provided the immediate, practical justification for levying ship money, the legal justification was underpinned by 'the ancient and undoubted right' of the Crown to dominion over the 'British seas'.[22] The king's ambition was epitomised most clearly in the name and figurehead of the vast *Sovereign of the Seas*, but also in a series of clashes at sea between the English and the increasingly assertive French, who had maritime pretensions of their own. Cardinal Richelieu was determined to end the 'insolence' of English demands for the salute, and in 1635 proposed a system of reciprocity to Charles I, who rejected it out of hand.[23]

The claim to sovereignty over the sea was not abandoned when the civil war broke out, nor when the monarchy was replaced by a republic: quite the opposite. In 1647, three Swedish warships refused to strike their flags to two Parliamentarian ones, and the resulting battle and pursuit led to the Swedish commander's ship being escorted ignominiously into the Downs. The immediate catalyst for the first Anglo-Dutch war, in 1652, was the refusal of a Dutch convoy to salute a small English squadron off Start Point; this triggered a full-scale battle between the fleets of Blake and Tromp, which began the war.[24] An English edition of *Mare Clausum*, produced by Marchmont Nedham, also came out in 1652, close on the heels of the first publication of Burough's tract, based on the documents he had discovered in the Tower. In this way, the republican regime brazenly appropriated and, indeed, extended, the fallen House of Stuart's grand maritime pretensions.[25] The Nedham edition was reprinted at the Restoration, and, not long afterwards, Pepys surreptitiously had his older copy re-covered with the royal arms, because he was ashamed to be caught out with a copy bearing the politically incorrect Commonwealth insignia (Pepys usually only employed such covert tactics with French porn).[26] The Selden/Nedham book in particular was remarkably influential. For example, the legend *Quatuor Maria Vindico*, an invention by Nedham which claimed that Edgar ruled over the 'four seas' around Britain, subsequently appeared on Restoration farthings.[27] In 1672, both the same denomination and the next largest, the copper halfpenny, received an even more iconic symbol of the aspiration to sovereignty over the seas: the first appearance on British coinage of Britannia ruling the waves, just as she did in the frontispiece of the Nedham edition. Many years later, the poem that Nedham provided as a preface was set to music by Joseph Haydn, no less, almost certainly the only part of any work of maritime law ever to receive such a distinction.[28]

At first, though, despite this apparent weight of precedent, the restored brothers Charles and James were somewhat unsure of their positions. In

Below, left: Frontispiece to the 1652 Marchmont Nedham edition of John Selden's *Mare Clausum. (Author's collection)*

Below, right: The extent of the 'four British seas'; from *Mare Clausum. (Author's collection)*

1661, the duke asked his advisers 'what hath been the common practice about making of foreign ships to strike sail to us', and received a report in January 1662 which defined the 'British Seas' – the 'four seas' of King Edgar – as 'the North, Narrow, and Irish seas, and St George's Channel'.[29] During these discussions, Pepys, the new Clerk of the Acts at the Navy Board, was so desperate to impress the Duke of York that he invented an outrageous lie: namely, that he had heard Selden (whom the young Pepys presumably knew) say that Henry VII ordered his captains to make the King of Denmark's ships strike the flag in the Baltic. It is a sure proof of the inexperienced naval administration's uncertainty about the entire subject that Pepys could even think of successfully fobbing off such a whopper on James's remarkably astute secretary, William Coventry – although the duke, never a quick or original thinker, and who probably had only a 'vague understanding' of Selden, might well have fallen for it.[30] The irony, of course, was that Charles II and his brother could only aspire to such sovereignty of the 'British seas' at all because of the achievements of Oliver Cromwell and the Commonwealth's navy. Until new construction started to come on stream in the later 1660s, the king's ships were overwhelmingly the Lord Protector's ships too, while the victories of Blake, Monck and the rest provided Charles and James with a victorious inheritance that they had done nothing whatsoever to earn. Nevertheless, the brothers soon demonstrated the vision they had for an even greater navy than that which Cromwell had left them. In January 1662, £18,766 was allocated to build a wet dock at Chatham and wharf the islands in the Medway to make them capable of taking twenty-four Second Rate ships – this at a time when the Stuart brothers had only ten of that type.[31]

There were several subsequent attempts to collect as many precedents as possible to reinforce the Crown's pretensions to maritime sovereignty. In 1671, for instance, Trinity House was canvassed to provide examples of Dutch ships striking their flags to English ones; its 'institutional memory' went back to examples from the 1620s, and based on these, it concluded that

> As to the extent of the British Seas, it hath been commonly reckoned by us and our predecessors that it doth extend to Cape Finisterre … and that the sea which washes the coasts of the Low Countries and France hath been always reputed part of the British seas.[32]

More collections of precedents about this subject were assembled, and subsequently retained within the Admiralty offices, than on virtually any other theme. These books duly recorded the precedents of Edgar, King John, the Laws of Oléron (the medieval code that formed the basis of much maritime law), and many others, too. Even the hoary old tale of King Cnut ordering the tide to turn back was produced as evidence, despite the fact that if it proved anything, it surely demonstrated that the King of England was anything but lord over the oceans.[33] Sir Leoline Jenkins, head of the Admiralty court during both the second and third Anglo-Dutch wars, was categorical, though: the sheer number of precedents, even if some of them were a little dubious, established 'the sovereignty of the Kings of England in the British ocean, and … the judgment of the English in sea affairs'.[34] Others outside the government chipped in. The lawyer Charles Molloy claimed, somewhat optimistically, that

> After the writings of the illustrious Selden, certainly it's impossible to find any prince or republic, or single person imbued with reason or sense, that doubts the dominion of the British Sea to be entirely subject to that imperial diadem [of Charles II] … the importance of the dominion of the sea unto this nation is very great, for alone on that depends our security, our wealth and our glory.[35]

Emboldened by such advice, the royal brothers adopted a firm line on the issue. As the Venetian ambassador observed, early in 1662, 'such a dominion is set over the sea and the English will not abandon it upon any consideration, more particularly as they always find themselves with naval forces so enormously superior to the French'.[36] When the first formal set of general instructions was issued to naval captains in 1663, the twenty-second article specified that foreign vessels should strike their topsails and take in their flags when meeting an English warship in the 'British seas', defined as extending from Stadtland, half way up the coast of Norway, to Cape Finisterre in Spain. If they failed to do so, captains were to use their 'utmost endeavour to compel them thereunto and in no wise to suffer any dishonour to be done to His Majesty'. Even outside those seas, English warships were never to strike their colours first.

This unequivocal position was bound to cause trouble with other powers, especially with France, but Charles was perfectly prepared to stand up to his powerful cousin Louis. One of his earliest letters to his sister Henrietta after her marriage to Louis's brother, the Duc d'Orléans, complained of the refusal of some French ships to strike their flags when meeting British ones: 'this is a right so well known and never disputed by any king before, that if I should have it questioned now, I must conclude it to be a *querrelle d'Alman* [a trumped-up quarrel] … I should be very unworthy if I quit a right and go lower than ever any of my predecessors did'.[37] Discussions about a compromise dragged on half-heartedly through the 1660s, but Charles remained intransigent, as the French ambassador reported in 1667: 'they say that this custom [the striking of the flag to British ships] is ancient and has always been observed. They claim that the British seas stretch as far as the Pyrenees'.[38] Although Charles made concessions with regard to his and Louis's ships meeting each other in the Mediterranean and elsewhere, the supposedly pragmatic and unprincipled king was not prepared to budge an inch over the Channel, the North Sea and other 'home waters'.[39] Similarly, peace talks with the Dutch in both 1667 and 1674 saw Charles's diplomats insist rigidly upon recognition of the claim to the 'salute to the flag'; and although the Dutch, in the latter treaty, finally got the British to concede that this was simply a mark of respect, not an acknowledgement of sovereignty over the sea, Charles II's lawyers and pamphleteers swiftly reasserted the old line.[40]

Despite all the public bluster, many in positions of influence were always privately sceptical of the pretensions to the dominion of the seas. Sir William Coventry, Pepys's early mentor, found the claims vain and unconvincing, and characteristically cut straight to the heart of the matter: enforcing the claim was bound to lead to strife with other nations, while not enforcing it would be dishonourable.[41] In private, Pepys, too, was one of the sceptics. He wrote himself memoranda to enquire into the truth of the examples quoted by Selden, and of the oft-quoted 'evidence' about Kings Edgar and John.[42] Sir William Petty complained that 'he could never yet hear our doctrine of Sea Dominion justified with as much as common sense'; but Petty jumped on the bandwagon nonetheless, proposing a quite literal 'mare clausum' which would have seen guard-boats spaced out every league across the routes into the 'British seas', 'manned by convicts who also busily knitted stockings and manufactured fishing-nets'.[43] During the 1670s, Sir Philip Meadowes wrote a tract called 'Observations Concerning the Dominion and Sovereignty of the Seas'; he presented it to James II in 1687, and eventually published it in 1689. In it, he made the obvious point that the claim to the salute would lead England into constant conflict with other nations, while a failure to enforce it would destroy the king's reputation at home; nevertheless, Meadowes pressed on to reassert a grand vision of mare clausum.[44] Even Charles II, who was so unequivocal about the matter in his early dealings with France, seems to have developed doubts. In October 1678, the king summoned a meeting of former admirals and other senior naval figures to debate the whole principle of the 'salute to the flag', while it is possible that some in the naval administration were aware of the 'urban legend' that John Selden himself had come to mock his own thesis, having 'afterwards turned it into ridicule in his common conversation'.[45] The fundamental problem, as Meadowes had rightly recognised, was that claiming the sovereignty of the sea sounded splendid, at once distinguishing the King of England from those monarchs who held sway principally over the land, and it seemed to be an inalienable part of the patrimony that had been handed down to Charles and James by their predecessors; but in practice, upholding it, and exercising its supposed prerogatives, was bound to be an unmitigated nightmare.

So it proved. There was barely a year during the Restoration era that did not witness at least one serious clash over the 'salute to the flag' with at least one foreign state; and in this context, a 'serious clash' usually involved the firing of loaded cannon, and often meant casualties, too. In April 1668, the frigate *Constant Warwick* fired at a Dutch squadron that refused to salute in the Channel; in October 1670, the Earl of Ossory complained that he was not saluted properly when he arrived at Hellevoetsluis to collect William of Orange, and in February 1671, a passing Dutch fleet failed to give the appropriate salute to Dover Castle.[46] The immediate catalyst for the outbreak of the third Anglo-Dutch war was a deliberate provocation: Captain Crow of the tiny *Merlin Yacht*, bringing back Lady Temple, the wife of the English ambassador to the Netherlands, was ordered to sail through the Dutch fleet in its own harbour and attempt to exact a salute from it, thereby demonstrating that Charles II's sovereignty of the sea extended right up to the continental shoreline. But the plan foundered on the reasonableness of the Dutch, who pointed out to Crow the absurdity of an entire fleet striking its flags to a tiny yacht, especially in its own waters, and proposed the referral of the matter to negotiation. Uncertain of his position, Crow backed down. The king was furious and had his captain imprisoned in the Tower, essentially for refusing to commit virtually certain suicide, not to mention the slaughter of Lady Temple and her children; although he was eventually released, Crow was never employed as a captain again.[47] In truth, Charles had chosen the wrong man to start a war. Belying the exemplary reputation of royal yacht captains, Crow was subsequently dismissed for incompetence from two other, much lowlier, capacities – firstly as a pilot, and later as porter of Portsmouth dockyard. Lady Temple was probably lucky: the likes of Christopher Gunman might well have opened fire, sending her to a watery grave twenty-five years before the former Dorothy Osborne, one half of one of English history's most famous love stories, was laid to rest in Westminster Abbey.[48]

Although the Peace of Breda (1667) provided for the continuation of the 'salute to the flag' by the Dutch (and all other nations), it did not resolve many of the ambiguities which infuriated foreign states. From their viewpoint, there was no clarity about the boundaries of the seas where the salute should be rendered, whether or not it should be

rendered by ships or fleets (no matter how large) to any single one of
Charles II's ships (no matter how small), or whether British warships
should return the salute in any shape or form.[49] The attitude of the Stuarts
was unequivocal. In the 'British Seas' every individual warship was to
compel a foreign ship, or ships, to strike to it, and was not to strike in
return. In other seas, it was only to strike if the foreign ship struck first or
simultaneously. This was logical in terms of the Stuarts' own pretensions,
but it was bound to cause offence; ultimately, it implied that in the crucial
areas of conflict, the North Sea and the English Channel, any British ship,
even the very smallest (say, the *Merlin Yacht*), should be saluted by a foreign
ship – or even an entire fleet – without returning that salute.[50]
Meanwhile, the subsidiary but related question of how many guns should
be fired as a mark of respect, and how many should be expected in return,
when a British warship encountered a warship of any other nation, or
entered a foreign port, frequently consumed Restoration naval officers;
indeed, some of them, like the old Cavalier Sir Thomas Allin, were
obsessed by it.[51] The extravagance of British salutes was notorious. In
1671, the Portuguese ambassador complained to Charles II that the latter's
warships were firing lengthy salutes in the River Tagus after sunset: the
British were, quite literally, Western Europe's noisy neighbours.[52]

Inevitably, all of these 'grey areas' created tensions throughout
European waters. Between 1668 and 1670, for instance, the regulations
relating to the giving and receiving of salutes at Leghorn, the main
entrepôt for British merchant shipping in the Mediterranean, were tight-
ened following a series of disputes with the Tuscan authorities, and there
were similar tensions with Genoa. In 1673, Captain Charles Wylde
refused to salute at Malta on the grounds that it was 'a den of thieves',
and subsequently threatened to bombard Messina for what would now
be termed 'disrespect'.[53] But other captains adopted a more pragmatic

approach, born of the realisation that in the Mediterranean, unlike in the Channel or the North Sea, British ships were always going to be seriously outnumbered, and that trade might suffer if captains were too inflexible. In 1680, the *Leopard* and the *Foresight* saw a fleet of thirty-one galleys 'under the shore of Mettelena' (Mitilini, or Lesbos). The galleys began to pursue the English vessels, which cleared their decks and kept on a northerly course, but the lack of wind permitted the galley fleet to catch them by ten o'clock. The flagship made a signal to speak with the English commander, and Sir John Berry, the veteran captain of the *Leopard*, sent his lieutenant over to her. The 'Admiral Pasha' of the Turkish fleet demanded to know why the English ships did not salute him, and requested to speak directly to their captains. Berry refused, stating that 'it was not the custom of the King of England's captains to go out of their ships', but he then conferred with Killigrew, captain of the *Foresight*, on the advisability of saluting the admiral, 'for fear they might offer some abuse on our merchants or their ships', and an 11-gun salute was fired. No reply was received, and the galleys went away satisfied.[54] While Berry and Killigrew claimed to be thinking of the best interests of British trade, they might have had another agenda in mind: the Duke of Grafton was aboard the *Leopard*, learning the ways of the sea, and the two captains' career prospects might have been diminished somewhat if, on their watch, the king's son was decapitated by an Ottoman cannonball.

Particular difficulties were created when the pretensions of the kings of England came up against the equally cherished pretensions of their continental equals. The kings of Denmark claimed sovereignty over the Sound and the other waterways leading to and from the Baltic, and there were a number of clashes with British vessels that were determined not to acknowledge this. When Captain Christopher Gunman took the *Anne Yacht* through the Sound in September 1670, after landing Charles II's new ambassador in Stockholm, he refused to strike his flag to Kronborg Castle, which promptly opened fire. Warning shots over his masts failed to shake Gunman's resolve, at which the gunners of Kronborg adjusted their aim and opened fire on the yacht itself. One man was killed, one of the main shrouds was shot to pieces, and several shot tore through the sails, but Gunman kept his course, and after an hour was out of range. At that point, with considerable sangfroid, the yacht captain 'gave them three guns [in mock salute] to thank them for their civility, and to let them know they had not killed us all'.[55] So proud was Gunman of his perform-ance during this episode that he had an anonymous artist paint a large canvas of it, which now hangs at Doddington Hall in Lincolnshire, the home of Gunman's descendants. But his resistance led to a full-scale diplomatic spat with Denmark over the winter of 1670, and a similar quarrel with Portugal developed in the summer of 1671.[56]

The Spanish Habsburgs were as obsessed as their British counterparts with exacting the honours they considered due to their flag, with new orders to this effect being issued by the Queen Regent Mariana in 1671.[57] The worst clash of the age took place in July 1683, when two captains who would later go on to much greater things, Matthew Aylmer and Cloudesley Shovell, tangled with the Spanish. In the first incident, at Cadiz, Shovell of the *James Galley* received a demand to salute the flag-ship of the Conde de Aguilar, and when he refused to comply, the much larger Spanish ship opened fire. Hemmed in by Spanish ships and thus unable to escape, Shovell was forced to comply. The local English consul was unsympathetic, saying of Shovell that 'if he and all had been lost by maintaining our king's honour, he had done his duty and left a famous behind him'.[58] A few days later, Matthew Aylmer of the *Tiger Prize* encountered a Spanish fleet at sea. He attempted to escape, but his ship's hull was too foul, and Aylmer, too, was forced to fire his guns in salute.[59] Charles II was enough of a realist not to impose any punishment on either captain, perhaps judging that the dishonour they would undoubtedly have felt was already punishment enough. However, he took a tougher line with Joseph Harris, captain of the *Quaker Ketch*, who in 1675 struck his topsail in the Bay of Biscay when a much larger Spanish warship demanded he salute her. A court martial sentenced him to be shot to death aboard the *Anne Yacht*, and the king insisted that the entire ritual be played out, right up to the order to fire – at which point a royal reprieve would be read, 'upon consideration of his former good services and known proofs of his courage, and his having by fits his judgment greatly impaired by wounds heretofore received in his head'.[60]

The King of England's pretensions caused particular difficulties with the French. Both Charles and James Stuart have often been perceived as mere puppets of Louis XIV, but at sea, nothing was further from the truth. Inevitably, then, there were frequent clashes between British and French warships over the former's attempts to enforce the king's pretensions. In the Mediterranean on 11 April 1669, a dispute over the salute between the 28-gun Fifth Rate frigate *Milford* and a French man-of-war of between seventy and eighty guns turned into a shooting match and a chase, with the British ship eventually getting away; special rules were subsequently adopted for the Mediterranean in order to prevent such clashes over precedence.[61] Disputes about the salute seem to have increased markedly in frequency in the years of peace after 1674. The more 'absolutist' mentality evident in court culture, epitomised by Verrio's ceiling depictions of Charles metaphorically trampling Louis underfoot, may have encouraged a new assertiveness on the part of the king and his captains; conversely, an impatience with British pretensions, and a new-found confidence in their own strength at sea, may be apparent in the increasingly belligerent response of French ships in particular. In May 1675, the powerful 70-gun Third Rate *Cambridge* was returning from the Mediterranean when she encountered four French men-of-war and two fireships off Dungeness. The *Cambridge's* captain, the forthright Arthur Herbert, demanded that the French lower their topsails in salute. The French ships not only refused but opened fire, the 'admiral' giving the *Cambridge* a whole broadside. Herbert tried to pursue them, but his ship was foul after its long voyage, and the French got away during the night. Charles II immediately protested to the French ambassador, and sent an indignant note to the French court.[62] In 1677, the *Newcastle* and the *Saudadoes*, sailing on the coast of France, encountered two French men-of-war which refused to strike, and forced them to sail to Sheerness.[63] In May of the following year, Captain Charles Skelton of the *Stavoreen* forced a French man-of-war to strike its colours to him.[64] Soon afterwards, the French frigate *Pearle* refused to strike to the *Dover.* The offending officers were detained, and the king ordered his ambassador in Paris to demand satisfaction for the affront to his dignity.[65] In September 1681, the frigate *Pearl* (the English version, this time), cruising in the Western Approaches, encountered a French privateer which refused to strike, even after warning shots were fired. The quarrel swiftly escalated to the firing of full broadsides, and three of the *Pearl's* men were killed, with another three wounded. The Frenchman finally surrendered, and was taken into Plymouth.[66]

Individual clashes with French ships were given greater significance by a wider and, from the Stuart brothers' point of view, much more threatening development.[67] In 1661, the French navy consisted of nine rated warships, none of which was larger than a Third Rate. Ten years later it comprised 119 ships, over a fifth of which were First and Second rates.[68] In 1668/69 alone, six First Rates were launched, the largest of which, the *Royal Louis* and *Soleil Royal*, could carry up to 120 guns each, twenty more than the greatest of Charles II's ships, and were the largest ships in the world. This astonishing rate of expansion was bound to raise eyebrows across *La Manche*, especially as between 1668 and 1671, Charles and his ministers received countless intelligence reports about Louis XIV's building programme. Even if Charles retained his confidence in Louis XIV's friendship, and even if he convinced himself that the new French navy was directed only against the Dutch and the Spanish and thus presented no immediate threat, its existence was not something that the King of Great Britain could simply ignore. Consequently, in the late summer of 1668, a spy, a Portsmouth shipwright named Thomas Castle, was despatched to reconnoitre the French Atlantic dockyards. Castle produced detailed reports on the ships and works at La Rochelle and Brest, and on the entirely new yard at Rochefort. Seventeenth-century naval espionage was a long way removed from the world of James Bond: Castle spent a month at Brest, moved around perfectly openly, talked to ships' captains and dockyard workers, and even went into the hull of a colossal new First Rate under construction.[69] Castle's reports probably contributed to the significant change of attitude towards France's naval ambitions that began to appear from the autumn of 1668 onwards in the king's correspondence with his sister Henrietta. Even before Castle's first despatch arrived from La Rochelle, Charles informed 'Madame', as she was known, that

> the first [obstacle to an Anglo-French treaty] is the great application there is at this time in France to establish trade and to be very considerable at sea, which is so jealous a point to us here who can be only considerable by our trade and power at sea, as any steps that France makes that way must continue a jealousy between the two nations which will upon all occasions be a great hindrance to an entire friendship, and you cannot choose but believe that it must be dangerous to me at home to make an entire league till first the great and principal interest of this nation be secured which is trade.[70]

The king returned to this theme in January 1669, when he informed Henrietta that the only obstacle to an alliance with Louis was 'the matter of the sea', a point so important to Charles that he could not be 'answerable to my kingdoms if I should enter into an alliance wherein their present and future security were not fully provided for'; consequently, he demanded that Louis should suspend all naval construction, a point that France conceded (albeit only for one year).[71]

Despite these concerns, in May 1670, Charles joined with Louis in a secret alliance, the principal aim of which was the wiping from the map of the Dutch republic. The other central plank of the Treaty of Dover, which created the alliance, appears to be the king's statement of intent to convert to Catholicism and lead his kingdoms back to the Church of Rome, funded by French subsidies. Much less attention has been paid to the second half of the treaty, by which Charles was to gain 'Walcheren, the mouth of the Scheldt, and the isle of Cadzand'. These territorial gains have often been dismissed as insignificant, or ignored altogether; the most thorough modern account of the Treaty of Dover notes in passing that Charles II was to receive 'two Dutch islands and a port', but does not even name them, let alone analyse their strategic significance.[72] However, these towns were not merely token prizes selected at random. Den Briel and particularly Vlissingen were important centres for the Dutch navy's Zeeland admiralty; taking control of them would hand to Charles II's England the power to open and close the rivers Maas and Scheldt, cripple the finances of the Dutch navy, close down the port of Rotterdam, and, most importantly, open or close the port of Antwerp, which had effectively been blockaded by the Dutch since 1585. The Dutch made a healthy profit out of the situation, charging for 'convoys' and 'licences' which granted the privilege of shipping to and from Antwerp; these two sources of income essentially paid for the Dutch navy, at least in peacetime.[73]

Louis XIV's foreign policy between 1667 and 1672 was directed above all at gaining control of Spanish Flanders, including Antwerp, so he might legitimately have expected that, once the port came under his control, he would restore it to the dominance in European maritime trade that it had once possessed, driving down Amsterdam in the process. There is some evidence to suggest that Louis's much-vaunted diplomats simply had no idea of the importance of the concessions they were making to Charles II. When this was pointed out to him, Hugues de Lionne, Louis's veteran Secretary of State, merely laughed, perhaps a little nervously: 'To be perfectly frank, when we made the treaty it didn't occur to us that Middelburg and Flushing [Vlissingen] were on the island of Walcheren'.[74] Of course, one could also take the cynical view that Louis could give away as much of somebody else's territory as he wished, especially if he had no actual intention of keeping his word; or else, perhaps he believed that his cousin's forces would, in any case, be too feeble or incompetent to take the promised territories.[75]

Below, left: Sir Cloudesley Shovell, who as a young captain was involved in one of the most contentious disputes over saluting in the Restoration era. *(Rijksmuseum, Amsterdam)*

Below, right: The isle of Walcheren: map by Nicholas Sanson, published in Paris in 1681. *(Wikimedia Commons)*

As Charles II's short-lived enthusiasm to convert his realms to Rome cooled (if it had ever really existed at all), so the prospect of gaining the Dutch towns, and transforming them into a strategically and economically lucrative fortress-colony, grew in significance. The king's sister Henrietta encouraged this train of thought. As early as September 1669, she wrote to Charles, stressing how the acquisition of these territories would be at once glorious, lucrative, and politically revolutionary:

> Indeed what is there more glorious and more profitable than to extend the confines of your kingdom beyond the sea and to become supreme in commerce, which is what your people most passionately desire and what will probably never occur so long as the Republic of Holland exists? ... [You should reserve] for yourself, in the division you will make, the most important maritime towns, whose commerce will depend entirely on the laws which you choose to impose upon them for the benefit of your kingdom and yourself ... it is easy to see that the execution of the design which is being proposed to you would be the veritable foundation for your own greatness, because, having a pretext for keeping up troops outside your kingdom to protect your conquests, the thought alone of those troops, which for greater safety could be composed of foreigners and would be practically in sight of England, could keep it in check and render Parliament more amenable than it has been accustomed to be.[76]

Simultaneously destroying Dutch economic dominance and his reliance on Parliament: could there possibly have been a more attractive win–win scenario for Charles II?

Conversely, of course, there was a very real risk that once the war against the Dutch was won, possession of the Dutch ports might lead swiftly to conflict between Great Britain and France. Charles seems to have realised this, and to have backed away from the prospect at the last, as the progress of the abortive peace negotiations with the Dutch during the summer of 1672 suggests. The king was initially prepared to forego his claim to Cadzand and Sluis 'to gratify the French with yielding them to them, not to retard the making of the peace', but his ambassadors (Buckingham and Arlington) used their own initiative to insist on retaining the demand for the two towns, along with the inviolable demands for Vlissingen, Den Briel and a war indemnity of £500,000. As they argued:

> what he is like to have besides [Cadzand and Sluis] will be of little value without them for the opening of the river to Antwerp, and consequently lessening the trade and value of Amsterdam, and this

made us heretofore fight this battle so warmly with the ministers [of France], that perhaps they thought it fit to avoid the coming again to us in the same argument.[77]

Buckingham and Arlington clearly envisaged the reopening of the Scheldt as an outcome of the proposed treaty, and if that happened, following a successful French conquest of Spanish Flanders, Louis XIV would have had much to lose by handing over the mouth of the river to the British. In any event, the dispute over Cadzand and Sluis hardly suggests two allies who implicitly trusted each other.[78] Although Charles might still have wished to reassure Louis of his good intentions by offering to abandon the claim to the two towns, Arlington and even the Francophile Buckingham were clearly looking beyond the immediate outcome of the war against the Dutch to a future that seemed to suggest at least potential grounds for Anglo-French hostility. Charles's comment to his council at much the same time, 'the French will have us or Holland always with them, and if we take them not, Holland will have them', was hardly the sentiment of a monarch passionately committed to a French alliance and convinced of a 'special relationship' between himself and Louis XIV.[79] On the contrary: the treaty proposals for the Dutch territories were an almost guaranteed recipe for a future war between the British kingdoms and France.

That the king had this possibility at least at the back of his mind during the period 1668–72 is also suggested by the almost unknown story of a vast project which has been wholly ignored in histories of the reign of Charles II. In about July 1670, shortly after the conclusion of the Dover treaty, construction of an entirely new royal dockyard commenced at Greenhithe, with the proximity of the timing strongly suggesting that the one was very much a consequence of the other. Charles himself visited the site, but the ground at Greenhithe seems to have proved unsatisfactory, and nothing more is heard of digging work at that site after the end of September 1670.[80] In November, though, John Tippetts, a commissioner of the navy, produced a report on potential dockyard sites along the Thames. He condemned the site at Greenhithe as too narrow and the ground there as too loose, soft and sandy to accommodate docks. By contrast, a site at Erith had firm, deep clay and ample space for the proposed facilities.[81] During the spring and summer of 1671, the dockyard project was focused exclusively on Erith, the site of an old Tudor dockyard.

The new yard was to be vast, far outdoing even Chatham – the largest industrial site in the British Isles, if not Western Europe – in the scale and capabilities of its facilities. Chatham had one single and one double dry dock; Erith would have two double docks, each 350ft long. Erith was to have both a wet dock, a facility that permitted enclosed above-water repair and laying-up facilities for the ships within it, and a mast dock. At the time, only Deptford possessed similar docks. Erith was to have 900ft of wharfage; Chatham had significantly more, at about 1,300ft, but that was due to and offset by its lack of a wet dock. Erith was to be equipped with several storehouses, the largest of which would be 1,000ft long – more than twice the size of the 'great storehouse' at Deptford and the similar facility at Portsmouth. The whole was to be surrounded by a brick wall, 12ft high, protected by six watchtowers. The yard was to cost £63,014; the site at Chatham, often regarded by contemporaries as one of the most prodigious spectacles in the kingdom, was worth only £45,000, and Erith dockyard would have cost about the same as the huge new palace at Winchester, commenced in 1682 as virtually a copy of Versailles.[82]

Why did Charles embark on such a colossal, and colossally expensive, project at that precise moment? True, there were problems with the existing dockyards in the Thames and Medway, notably silting in the latter which was threatening the viability of Chatham yard. However, Erith yard was not even begun by the time that war broke out in March 1672; realistically, it could never have been ready in time for any war against the Dutch fought in the early 1670s. The vast new royal dockyard at Erith would be a consequence, not a cause, of a final victory over the United Provinces, and it would be ready to accommodate the much larger 'navy royal' that would be funded by such a victory; a navy that would have to defend the Stuarts' new territories in Zeeland, the Caribbean and the East Indies against the only European power capable of threatening them, and of disputing the control of the Scheldt and Maas estuaries. After all, the explicit logic of the Treaty of Dover was that the Dutch republic would cease to exist as a significant political and economic entity, and that Spain would cease to hold any sway in Flanders, where its territories – including the coastline that was always a key imperative in British foreign policy, up to and beyond the point where the colour of the flag flying over it took the United Kingdom into the First World War – were to be taken over by France. That being the case, the only strategic rationale for Erith dockyard was anticipation of a future war between Britain and France: and although the project perished amid the failures of the third Anglo-Dutch war, it would only be a very few years before Verrio adorned the ceiling of the royal bedchamber at Windsor, with its image of France subservient beneath the triumphant figure of the King of England. Charles II's secret dreams died hard.

Ultimately, of course, the king's ambitions for naval and imperial glory foundered, but the problems caused by clashes between his warships and those of virtually every other maritime nation over his pretension to the 'sovereignty of the sea' continued to the very end of his reign: indeed, literally to the very end of it. During the last fortnight before he suffered his fatal stroke on 2 February 1685, Charles presided over several meetings with his senior sea officers to thrash out a new policy over the fraught issue of salutes to be exchanged between British warships and Spanish forts and harbours, following the series of clashes in 1683/84; this was adopted on 25 January. In the years that followed, the 'salute to the flag', founded upon a set of medieval forgeries, became something of a diplomatic joke, albeit one that could still become very bloody indeed. In August 1694, the Danish warship *Gyldenløve* and the *Stirling Castle* fought a ferocious battle over the salute in the Downs, which led to the death of the Danish captain. In July 1704, off the East Anglian coast, the Swedish captain Gustaf Psilander encountered eight British ships of the line which demanded that he strike to them, in contravention of explicit orders Psilander had received from King Karl XII. Following an engagement that lasted more than four hours, Psilander's ship was captured, but three of his opponents were put out of action, and some seventy fatalities were reported on the British side. The irony of this action is that the ships under Psilander's escort were carrying supplies intended for the Royal Navy.[83]

By 1714, the French thought it best just to humour *les rosbifs* over demands for the salute: as one of their admirals wrote in that year, 'it is not appropriate to give any concern thereon to the English, who have claims, albeit fanciful and ill-founded, to have all nations salute them in the Channel of La Manche and even as far as the Cape Finisterre, [as] this could provoke arguments'. The last incident with the French seems to have occurred in 1787, when a frigate from Morlaix was forced to strike off Portland.[84] But difficulties with the Swedes and Danes persisted, despite attempts by those and other states to get round the problem by simply not flying their ensigns at all in the 'British seas'; the battle fought by the Danish frigate *Freya* against four British frigates in 1800 was very much a throwback to the era of the Stuarts.[85] In a practical sense, the claim to the salute was quietly dropped by Britain in 1805, when the order to enforce it was removed from the book of naval instructions; but because of fears of a public outcry, it was never formally annulled, despite the claim being regarded as 'mischievous and ridiculous' by the naval officers of Nelson's time.[86] Thus, in theory at least, Her Britannic Majesty still silently claims the sovereignty of the seas from the Stadlandet peninsula in Norway to Cape Finisterre in Galicia, right up to the high water mark of the entire French coast.

The Dominion of the Oceans

SOME MIGHT HAVE DOUBTED the Stuart kings' aspirations to sovereignty over the seas, but others took an entirely opposite line. Sir Henry Sheres was a military engineer whom Pepys once suspected of having designs on his wife, but he was also an author who fancied himself as both a poet and a policy guru. One of his writings was a collection of naval essays, and this culminated in what he called 'a scheme for a maritime monarchy':

> I conceive this nation has by nature all the materials necessary to lay the foundation of such a power by sea, as to entitle us not only to a dominion of the narrow seas, but to the wide oceans. That having nature so much in our favour, nothing but want of genius, art and application can be thought to frustrate so vast a design; which giving us a paramount incontestable power by sea ... ensures our safety and liberty at home, to a demonstration against all foreign attempts whatsoever.[1]

Curiously, the views of Sheres, and those who thought like him, were not that far removed from those espoused two or three decades later by Daniel Defoe in *Robinson Crusoe* and several of his other works.[2] A great trading empire founded upon colonies, navies and navigation, existing in a virtuous circle where trade led to an increase in shipping, which increased the number of seamen, which increased employment and general well-being, which drove down rebellion and dissent: it was truly a vision of Arcadia afloat, a new Carthage rather than a new Rome. Unfortunately, it was also a pipe dream, as the circumstances of Sheres's composition of the book indicate. He wrote it in 1691, when the two brothers who would probably have agreed with his thesis were no longer on the throne, and when he was in prison in the Gatehouse, suspected of Jacobitism.[3]

Even some foreign observers noted the vaunting aspirations of the Stuarts and their kingdoms. In 1671, a report on England presented to the Venetian Senate – which knew a thing or two about maritime dominion – suggested that the country 'has the ocean for its territory where by the practice of navigation it carries on trade with the world, or establishes its trade by the mobile fortresses of its ships'.[4] The primarily terrestrial powers, like France and Spain, might aim at 'universal monarchy', the part-paranoid, part-envious barb invariably aimed by seventeenth-century Englishmen at any state which seemed to be more powerful than they were. But, building upon their sovereignty over the 'four seas' around the British Isles, Charles II and James II could aspire to much more: to the sort of 'maritime monarchy' that Sheres and others envisaged, in which their navy was at the heart of an elaborate world of terrestrial empire, trading hegemony, and constant improvement in science, navigation and exploration, all directed at the same end.[5] The obvious fact that this sort of regime might be regarded by foreigners as precisely the same sort of universal monarchy that the English feared was recognised explicitly by some Stuart polemicists and others, both then and afterwards. A few decades later, Thomas Corbett, the secretary to the Admiralty, remarked that 'France was hated for the imputation of affecting an universal monarchy at land; the Dutch insinuate to other nations the same of us at sea, and we too unwarily contribute to it' by enforcing the 'salute to the flag'.[6] But such unpatriotic quibbles were swiftly slapped down. After all, any system run by the English was bound to be benevolent and beneficial, unlike any governed by the Papist tyrannies of France and Spain, or the unprincipled avarice of the Dutch. It is unlikely that everyone – especially, perhaps, the slaves of the West African coast and the Americas – entirely appreciated this distinction.

The later Stuart period has often been seen as an important epoch in the supposedly 'inevitable' development of the British Empire. According to this line of argument, Cromwell's conquest of Jamaica (1655) gave Britain a substantial foothold in the Caribbean, while after the Restoration, the British presence in North America was greatly enhanced by the acquisition of New Amsterdam (1664, when it was renamed New York) and the development of new colonies in New Jersey and Pennsylvania; the acorns from which 'manifest destiny' and 'American exceptionalism' grew. A similar analysis can be applied to the acquisition of Bombay/Mumbai in 1662, often seen as the foundation stone for subsequent expansion in what ultimately became the 'jewel in the crown' of the British Empire. Such territorial aggrandisement was promoted by the Navigation Acts of 1660 and 1663, which explicitly visualised a great commercial empire sustained by the largest merchant fleet in Europe (all of which, of course, would have required a great navy to protect and sustain it).[7]

   In fact, this view of the 'inevitable' development of the British Empire is flawed on many levels. For one thing, the 'colonies' that existed during the reigns of Charles and James were fragile, marginal, desperately diverse affairs, a simple truth well conveyed by the London diarist Thomas Rugg when he listed the overseas territories that Charles ruled in 1660 – here given in his original spelling, which suggests something of the sheer unfamiliarity and downright strangeness of these places to the average 'man in the street': 'Vergina [*sic*], New England, Barebadus, St Christopher, Antegio, Meveus [Nevis], and al the rest of Crebeine islands, withe the conquest of Jemecao'.[8] They had widely differing forms of government, and were overseen by the central authorities in England in a distinctly haphazard way.

This diversity was increased in 1664 when New Amsterdam was captured and transformed into New York, where James had a considerable amount of free rein and developed yet another different form of rule; virtually simultaneously, another new colony was developed in New Jersey, followed in the 1670s by yet another, Pennyslvania, established under the auspices of the Quakers.[9] But there were strong naval influences in all of these new colonies. New York was captured by a naval expedition commanded by Colonel Richard Nicholls, a member of James's house-hold who would be killed serving with him in the Battle of Solebay in 1672. New Jersey was established by John, Lord Berkeley, a commissioner of the navy, and Sir George Carteret, the navy treasurer; named after Carteret's home island, the choice of name might also have pandered to

New Amsterdam, subsequently New York, in 1660. (*Rijksmuseum, Amsterdam*)

NIEUW AMSTERDAM OFTE NUE NIEUW IORX OPT T. EYLANT MAN

the king's fond memories of the place where he learned to sail. Finally, William Penn's ability to obtain royal authority for the foundation of his new colony was undoubtedly due to the doors that were opened for him by the reputation of his father, Sir William, who had served as 'great captain commander' of the fleet in 1665, standing alongside and providing tactical advice to the Duke of York during the Battle of Lowestoft.

Similarly, the acquisition of Bombay appears significant only in the light of what it subsequently became: at the time, it was overshadowed by the more substantial Portuguese trading post at nearby Caranja, which might have been why the Braganza Queen Regent was so willing to part with it. In this respect, the English takeover of Bombay is less important in its own right than because it marked the first occasion when a major squadron of the Royal Navy ever ventured so far. Control of such an unprecedentedly ambitious operation was vested in a new committee of the Privy Council, headed by the Lord High Admiral, the Duke of York.[10] At first, it seems that this body intended to send to India the Second Rates *Unicorn* and *Victory*, which would have represented an astonishing statement of intent by the restored monarchy; but nothing came of this,

Two views of the English fort at Bombay, *c*1665, from a plate published in the Netherlands in 1672. *(Wikimedia Commons)*

presumably for financial reasons.[11] Even so, the squadron that was eventually despatched was powerful by any standards. It consisted of a Third Rate, the *Dunkirk*, along with three Fourths, the *Leopard*, *Mary Rose* and *Convertine*, along with a transport, the *Chestnut*. Significantly, Charles and James did not give the command of this force to one of the many experienced and amply qualified veterans that they inherited from the Commonwealth's navy. Instead, they gave it to one of their own, the Cavalier James Ley, third Earl of Marlborough, whose previous time at sea was comparatively limited.[12] But Marlborough had a long-standing interest in colonial expansion and had been very active in Caribbean ventures, at least partly because he saw at as a way of acquiring a new fortune to replace that which his family had lost. Marlborough's expedition eventually got bogged down in a quagmire of fraught diplomatic negotiations with the Portuguese, but the precedent was established: the Royal Navy had gone to India for the first time.[13]

At first, it seemed as if this willingness to deploy royal warships on far distant seas was a short-lived aberration. Bombay was transferred from direct royal control to that of the East India Company (EIC) in 1668, and it was the company's marine forces alone that operated in Indian waters for most of the period. However, an exception occurred in 1684, when the king ordered the frigate *Phoenix*, commanded by John Tyrell, to sail to the subcontinent. Tyrell's mission was to put down a rebellion in Bombay led by Richard Keigwin, a Cornish former naval officer; under pressure from the EIC, Charles II decided to send the *Phoenix* as it was nearly ready for sea, having been fitted out for a voyage to Newfoundland. In fact, the rebellion was already over before Tyrell sailed, and all was quiet in Bombay when he arrived there on 10 June 1685. On 24 October, the *Phoenix* was lying at Swally, the port for the EIC headquarters at Surat, when Tyrell received confirmation of the death of King Charles, eight months earlier. Forty guns were fired to mourn the old king, and thirty-nine to salute the accession of the new. The *Phoenix* remained in Indian waters, supporting the activities of the EIC, until January 1687, when she sailed for home.[14] Although her voyage was futile in most respects (apart from running up a colossal wage bill for her crew at a time of deep austerity), it was the precursor of the lengthy deployments 'east of Suez' which, ever since, the Royal Navy has never entirely managed to shake off, despite several supposedly definitive 'permanent withdrawals' from the theatre.

The naval presence in India might have been temporary and occasional, but the same was certainly not true of the Americas. Given their direct responsibility for the deployment of warships, Charles and James must be credited with the establishment of permanent 'station ships' in foreign waters, building on the long-standing precedent of having at least one ship, and sometimes three or four, on the coast of Ireland. From the beginning of the restored monarchy, ships were stationed at Jamaica: the *Diamond*, a Fourth Rate frigate, and the *Rosebush*, were there in October 1661, the *Centurion* and *Great Gift* in May 1663.[15] A warship was on permanent station in New England by 1668, when the *Portsmouth Ketch* was fulfilling the role. A permanent or semi-permanent naval presence was established at Barbados and St Kitts in 1677, and at Virginia in 1684/85. Thus when Charles II died in February 1685, the *Diamond* was at Barbados, *Guernsey* in the Leeward Islands, the *Ruby* and *Bonetta Sloop* at Jamaica, and the *Quaker Ketch* in Virginia; before the end of the year, the *Oxford* and the *Rose* were on their way to New England.[16] Newfoundland was a special case. Not only did the warships assigned to the station escort the fishing craft to the Grand Banks, and then on to their primarily Mediterranean markets in Catholic countries, they also remained on station to protect them while they fished, especially against their French competitors.[17] So close was the relationship between the naval, diplomatic and political elements of the convoy commanders' functions that, in the following century, the senior officer on the station also served as governor of Newfoundland.

If India, and even the Americas, were initially somewhat peripheral to the imperial ambitions of the Stuarts, the same was certainly not true of the Mediterranean. During the 1660s, the Mediterranean accounted for almost half of all English overseas trade; indeed, until 1669 the value of trade with the Levant (the eastern Mediterranean), was greater than that with the East Indies.[18] But since the sixteenth century, this trade had been threatened intermittently by the Barbary corsairs, based in Algiers, Tripoli and Tunis, nominally Ottoman territories on the north African coast, and by the Sallee rovers based at Salé in Morocco, to all intents and purposes a self-governing pirate republic. It was partly because of their depredations that the elaborate system of convoy protection in the Mediterranean had been put in place.

In 1662, though, Charles II was presented with what seemed like a heaven-sent opportunity to both extend England's trading empire in the Mediterranean and deal once and for all with the corsairs. His marriage dowry from Catherine of Braganza's father, King João IV, included not only Bombay, but also Tangier on the Moroccan coast. This meant that both new colonies were not really possessions of the English state at all, nor even of the Crown: they were the personal property of Charles Stuart, the man, as part of his wife's dowry, and subsequent attempts by Parliament to formally annexe Tangier to the 'Crown Imperial' never succeeded.[19] Unlike distant Bombay, though, Charles kept direct control of Tangier.

While simple geography undoubtedly played a part in this, it may also be the case that at the time, Charles saw the Moroccan town as the more valuable acquisition, at least in terms of its potential future development.

Only hindsight – the knowledge of what British India subsequently became, and of what ultimately happened to British Tangier – can make Bombay appear the more important prize. During the 1660s and 1670s, most informed commentators believed quite the opposite. Tangier, not India, would be the jewel in the crown of the British Empire: the key to making a reality of all the abstract claims to sovereignty over the seas. Several writers expressed the ambition of making Tangier a great choke-point, both strategically and economically, which could open or close the Mediterranean and control the trade in and out of that sea, much as the Danes controlled the Sound and the passage of shipping into and out of the Baltic, which had to pay significant tolls for the privilege to Charles II's cousin, the King of Denmark. From Tangier, Britain could reach out into the Mediterranean, outdo all its European rivals, and establish a true maritime empire.[20]

Charles spent far more on Tangier than on any of his colonies in America (or, come to that, on all of his garrisons in Britain put together), made it a free port – in direct contradiction of *mare clausum* principles – and sent out both settlers and a succession of distinguished noble governors. One of his sons even died in its defence.[21] But the reality proved

View of Salé, Morocco, by Reiner Nooms, 1662–68. (Rijksmuseum, Amsterdam)

1. The Upper Castle,   2. Yorke Castle,
3. The Mould,   4. Coast of Spaine.   *The South–East Corner of Tangier. etc.*   5. Point of Gibraltar,
6. The Bar of Tangier.

very different from the dream. Tangier became a byword for immorality and royal absolutism – a warning to Charles's subjects of what the future might be like if the king ever had free rein within his own realms. It was also widely perceived as a den of popery, and became a focus for opponents of Charles and James during the great political crisis of 1678–81.[22]

Tangier in 1673, showing the mole under construction. Wenceslaus Hollar. *(Rijksmuseum, Amsterdam)*

Above all, though, Tangier failed to fulfil the high hopes that it could become a major naval base. It was too far away to be of any use during the wars against Tripoli and Tunis in the 1660s and 1670s; Charles II's admirals had to use Port Mahon, Leghorn and Malta instead, making ad hoc arrangements with the local authorities. But Tangier also proved of limited value during the longest wars of all, those against Algiers and Salé. Despite the vast amount spent on the mole, or breakwater, the harbour remained wholly inadequate for warships and merchant ships alike. After nearly twenty years of construction, the mole remained incomplete, and was in any case desperately vulnerable to Moorish attacks; so, during the war with Algiers that he conducted between 1679 and 1682, Admiral Arthur Herbert preferred to take his ships to Gibraltar to use hired Spanish facilities.[23] This proved to be one of the final nails in the coffin of Tangier as an English colony. According to Pepys, the abandonment of the city was first proposed by the Earl of Sunderland in about 1680, but in January 1683 the king, on his own initiative, finally decided to embark on the controversial policy.[24] The last great mine was blown on 5 February 1684, as a band played the tune 'Tangier's Lamentation', and Lord Dartmouth's fleet sailed for home.[25]

Although the most obvious symbol of the Stuart brothers' imperial ambitions had been literally blown to pieces, their involvement with Africa extended far beyond the beleaguered boundaries of Tangier. The various incarnations of the Royal African Company, which 'shipped more enslaved African women, men and children to the Americas than any other single institution during the entire period of the transatlantic slave trade', remain highly controversial for precisely that reason. But in its original creation and constitution, first as the Company of Royal Adventurers Trading to Africa (chartered in 1660), it was very much a manifestation of the king's royal prerogative, and the dividing lines between it and the Royal Navy, and the government as a whole, were distinctly blurred. Charles himself, his brother and their two most senior admirals, Prince Rupert and the Duke of Albemarle, were all active participants, while other subscribers to the company also served on the government's committees of Trade and Foreign Plantations.[26] In 1664, the Duke of York, as Lord High Admiral, put the frigate *Jersey* at the disposal of the company, of which he was governor, and her captain Robert Holmes subsequently captured Dutch forts, took Dutch prizes, and generally wreaked havoc, along the coasts of Gambia, Sierra Leone and Guinea.[27]

The Company of Adventurers folded in 1672, but was immediately relaunched as the Royal African Company. This was, in many respects, a very different beast from its predecessor: for instance, its directors were primarily merchants, not courtiers, and it was focused much more heavily on the slave trade.[28] But it could still call on naval resources, enthusiastically provided by the king and the Duke of York. In 1676, the frigate *Hunter* was put at the service of the company; she was commanded by Richard Dickinson, an officer much liked by the royal brothers, who had served in 1673 as second captain of the *Charles*. This mission proved highly controversial, and was raked up several times in later years by opponents of the Stuarts.[*] They had good reason to do so: James was particularly deeply involved in the company's work and active on its behalf, at least partly because of the personal financial benefit he expected to obtain from its expansion.[29]

Therefore, the lines between the royal, state and private manifestations of imperial expansion were remarkably blurred, and perhaps this was most obviously the case with the warship deployed to support the Royal African Company in 1684/85. The *Mordaunt*, a Fourth Rate capable of carrying up to forty-six guns, was originally built as a private venture by a consortium headed by the hot-headed twenty-three-year-old Charles Mordaunt, Lord Mordaunt (later the third Earl of Peterborough), with the likely intention of operating against the Dutch and/or the Spanish in the Mediterranean while sailing under the colours of Brandenburg. Mordaunt entertained Charles II to dinner aboard the ship in November

[*] See Appendix.

1681.[30] The *Mordaunt* was bought for the navy in the following year, only to be loaned out to the Royal African Company in 1684/85 to defend the company's profits against the unauthorised interlopers who were trying to break into the lucrative slave trade. Like the *Hunter*, the captain chosen for the mission was a firm favourite of the royal brothers, in this case Henry Killigrew, son of the Duke of York's almoner, and a sometime bedmate of the king's former mistress, Barbara, Duchess of Cleveland.

If a great Stuart 'maritime monarchy' was to be established, it would need to be at the cutting edge of advances in applied science and navigation. Thus it was no coincidence that from its very beginning in 1660, the Royal Society was intimately concerned with promoting the naval and imperial ambitions of its founder, Charles II. Naval officers and administrators like Sandwich, Coventry, Brouncker and Pepys were members, with the latter serving as president in 1684–86. Many were also involved with the Africa companies or other government bodies: the government's Tangier committee, established in 1662, originally included Sandwich, Coventry and Pepys once again. For these men, then, just as for their masters, the king and Duke of York, the Royal Society was one element in a greater vision of a more prosperous and powerful kingdom. In this context, experimental philosophy was not some esoteric, ivory-tower discipline; it contributed directly to enhancing the power of the state. Greater knowledge would lead inevitably to greater wealth, both for individuals and for the kingdom: success in trade would at once demand a stronger navy to protect it, and provide the funds that could pay for such a force.[31] These connections were grasped by the poet who saluted the Royal Society and its original meeting place, Gresham College:

> This college will the whole world measure
> Which most impossible conclude,
> And navigation make a pleasure,
> By finding out the longitude;
> Every Tarpaulin shall then with ease
> Sail any ship to the Antipodes.[32]

Virtually the first topic to be discussed by the Royal Society, following its formal establishment in 1660, was 'the philosophy of shipping', and it often discussed naval subjects.[33] From very early in its existence, it got seamen bound on 'far voyages', such as to the East Indies, to submit journals recording natural curiosities and phenomena. It also immediately began to work on ways of obtaining more accurate tide tables, with the likes of Boyle, Newton and Flamsteed all tackling the subject.[34] In September 1662, the society heard a paper about the planting of timber, submitted by the Navy Board, and another about the feasibility of building warships in North America.[35] Not long afterwards, it considered the double-hulled vessel designed by society member Sir William Petty, who in 1671 produced a 'Treatise of Naval Philosophy'.[36] Hooke, Wren and others examined ways of improving ship design, with Hooke being tasked to study different types of wood to discover which would provide the toughest ships' timbers.[37] As already noted, in 1664, the society provided the lines for the new *Royal Katherine*, in the hope that they would prove a theory about water resistance; indeed, a meeting of the society was cancelled so that its members could attend the launch. Regrettably, though, the significant deficiencies of the new ship discouraged the society from providing such direct and practical advice on future occasions.[38] The Royal Society also had ties to the Board of Ordnance, which supplied both the navy and the army with artillery: in 1674, a series of ballistics trials was attended by the likes of Brouncker and Hooke.[39] Gunnery was the particular passion of Charles II's cousin Prince Rupert, a member of the society from its beginning, who invented an entirely new type of cannon, the Rupertino. Some of the earliest operational examples of this were mounted on the king's new and then favourite yacht, the *Cleveland*, before being adopted more widely in the arming of large ships during the 1670s.[40]

As the poet predicted, the society was also deeply involved in attempts to resolve the age-old problem of accurately establishing longitude at sea, with the likes of Hooke, Newton and Huygens all touching on the issue at various times. Early in its life, for example, the society assessed the performance of pendulum clocks designed by Christian Huygens and installed about Robert Holmes's ship, the royal frigate *Jersey*, during its expedition in West Africa in 1664; the supposed results of the trial were reported in the first issue of the society's journal, *The Philosophical Transactions*. Holmes's claims for the success of the clocks were greatly exaggerated, but even so, erroneous accounts of the voyage enhanced Huygens's fame, and a fair copy of the *Jersey*'s log was made for the Duke of York.[41] All of these investigations contributed, explicitly or implicitly, to the advancement of the Crown's claim to maritime dominion. In 1675, Sir Robert Southwell addressed the Royal Society on the subject of the oceans, dealing with such scientific questions as their nature and size, but also stressing that the English were the rightful controllers of the seas: 'the English Empire, besides their ancient rights by custom, conquest, and concessions, are the best qualified, even in nature, to receive and administer this power', and that there were 'natural reasons for our sovereignty of the seas', as a result of which 'a *mare clausum* we intend'.[42] The king, though, was not entirely impressed by the society's efforts. Charles always wanted scientific research to have practical applications, and in 1664 he 'mightily laughed at [the Royal Society] for spending time only in weighing air, and doing nothing else since they sat'.[43]

The membership of the Royal Society did not only overlap with that of the royal family, the court and the naval administration. Many of the same people were involved with the Company of Royal Adventurers Trading into Africa and its successor, the Royal African Company.[44] The Duke of York also headed the ill-fated Royal Fishery Society, established in 1661 with the intention of boosting the English fishing industry against foreign competition; other members of its council included courtiers, noblemen, naval officers, London merchants, and the ever-ubiquitous Samuel Pepys.[45] In addition to the members already named who were also members of the Royal Society, the government's Tangier committee also included the likes of the Duke of York, Prince Rupert, the Duke of Albemarle, Pepys's Navy Board colleague Sir John Mennes, and Sandwich's closest naval ally, Roger Cuttance; its 1673 incarnation included seven members who were also in the Admiralty commission, plus Pepys.[46]

There were similar overlaps in personnel with Trinity House, the body responsible for navigation, pilotage, lighthouses, the qualifications of shipmasters, and a number of other maritime activities: its masters between 1660 and 1688 were almost all prominent naval officers and administrators, including Albemarle, Sandwich, Sir George Carteret, Sir William Penn, the king's son, the Duke of Grafton, and, inevitably, Samuel Pepys, the latter on two occasions, the second of which overlapped with his presidency of the Royal Society.* The Duke of York profited from Trinity House's perquisite of selling ballast.[47] And so on. Therefore, these seemingly very different institutions were actually all mutually connected elements within a much broader, holistic vision based upon the belief in British 'sovereignty of the sea', sustained by the Royal Navy. But if the vision was a reasonably consistent one, the Stuart brothers' attempts to make it a reality were patchy, as suggested, for example, by Charles's loss of interest in the Royal Society, and by James's failure to support the Royal Fishery Company, or to develop a sustained approach to developing England's colonies, particularly his own in New York.[48]

If the Stuarts wanted a maritime empire, unchallengeable at sea, then they would have to take steps to ensure a future supply of highly trained mariners. The notion of establishing a mathematical school, to train boys who, it was hoped, would develop into proficient navigators, originated with Richard Aldworth, a governor of Christ's Hospital, whose will of

* Perhaps unsurprisingly, Pepys once complained (in his diary on 14 February 1668) that his life was rendered 'troublesome' by the sheer number of committees he had to attend.

1654 left a legacy to provide for the education of forty needy boys. Political changes and procrastination meant that Aldworth's bequest was still in limbo in the mid–1660s, when the wealthy financier Sir Robert Clayton read about the navigation schools that Louis XIV was establishing in France. In 1673, Clayton became involved in discussions with Christ's Hospital about how to implement Aldworth's legacy, and used his connections to approach Lord Clifford, the Lord High Treasurer. Both agreed that the king might be interested in a proposal to establish a mathematical school with Aldworth's money. Charles was, indeed, enthusiastic about the proposal, couched by Clifford as a means of training 'such whose genius and constitution are proper fit for Sea Service and who have arrived to a proportionable degree of learning to be placed out as apprentices to captains and masters of ships'. The letters patent establishing the Royal Mathematical School were fixed with the Great Seal on 19 August 1673.[49] Thus the establishment of the school had nothing to do with Samuel Pepys, despite his subsequent attempt in his own writings to claim the credit for the original idea: as the present historian of the school remarks, in his definitive new history of the institution, 'there is no evidence that Pepys was the original promoter of the Royal Mathematical School'.[50] That honour must go to Clayton and Clifford, and, indeed, to King Charles, who acted so decisively and rapidly on their proposal. Nevertheless, Pepys soon became heavily involved with the new establishment. The early history of the mathematical school was troubled, and after being appointed a governor in the winter of 1675/76, Pepys attempted to reform the system in order to bring it more into line with the king's original intentions. He continued to play an active role in its affairs during the 1690s, well after his enforced retirement from his official position in the navy.[51]

Fittingly for a monarch whose entire life, from his birth beneath a brilliant and unexplained daytime star, had been bound up with astronomical symbolism, Charles was deeply interested in the heavens, with the installation of a telescope in the Privy Garden at Whitehall being one of his first priorities after his Restoration. His passions for astronomy, ships and the sea dovetailed naturally, and inevitably led him to develop an interest in solving the problems of celestial navigation.[52] The king's establishment in 1675 of a Royal Observatory at Greenwich may have been inspired in part by the establishment of such an institution in Paris four years earlier, but the immediate impetus came from the ongoing drive to discover an accurate method for establishing a ship's longitude. A Frenchman, the Sieur de Saint-Pierre, approached Charles II with a supposedly infallible method of his discovering, based on the use of astronomical tables. The king appointed a commission to investigate; the composition of this body was suitably stellar, containing as it did the likes of Christopher Wren and Robert Hooke. Saint-Pierre's claims were exposed as entirely false, but the process revealed serious shortcomings in the tables then in use, and the king responded almost at once by commissioning his own observatory. John Flamsteed, the commission's secretary, became the first Astronomer Royal. From the very beginning, the observatory – like the Royal Society and the Mathematical School – was closely associated with both the monarch and the navy. Its very location was proof of this, high on the hill that overlooked the royal palace of Greenwich, a few hundreds to the north, and the royal dockyard at Deptford, not much more than a mile to the west.

The royal brothers acquired large numbers of maps and sea charts. In 1665, Pepys went on a shopping expedition to John Burston's shop in Ratcliffe to acquire charts for the king, the Duke of York, and himself, while when John Evelyn, the other great diarist of the age, visited Whitehall twenty years apart, in 1660 and 1680, one of the things that he found had not changed in the interim was the prodigious quantities of charts (and, indeed, other naval materials) to be found in the royal apartments.[53] In April 1688, James II personally selected a large number of

Chart showing the environs of Harwich, from Great Britain's Coasting Pilot. (© National Maritime Museum, Greenwich, London, L7515)

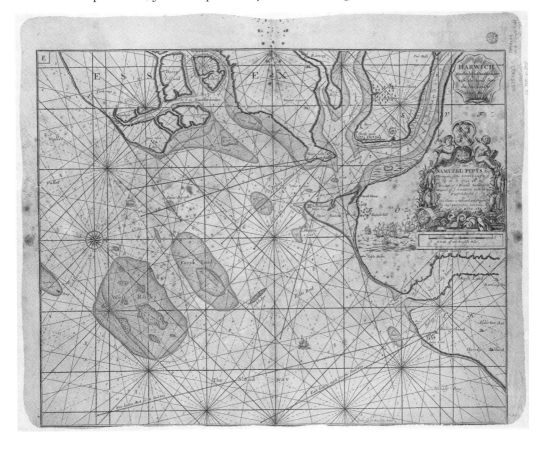

maps and other documents for transfer to the Admiralty. These included maps of virtually every part of the world, including Spanish and Portuguese specimens that were clearly of a considerable vintage. The geographical coverage ranged from 'the isles of Orkney' to 'Philippina, Java, Japan, and several other islands in the East Indies', while the transfer also included part of the 'Anthony Roll' of Henry VIII's navy, a print of the Earl of Essex's attack on Cadiz in 1596, and plans of fortresses and harbours throughout the British Isles.[54] The office of royal hydrographer was instituted in 1671, and was initially held jointly by the globe-maker Joseph Moxon and the map-seller and compass-maker John Seller, whose work both Charles and James personally promoted.[55] The king also advanced £500 (with another £500 from his wife) to fund the atlas *Britannia*, produced by John Ogilby, whom Charles appointed as royal cosmographer, also in 1671.[56]

The Royal Observatory at Greenwich, established under Charles II's personal auspices in 1675. *(Author's photograph)*

The royal brothers were keen to promote voyages of exploration. In 1669, Captain John Narbrough was commissioned to command an expedition to South America, and set sail on 26 September. Narbrough, a firm favourite of the Duke of York who had distinguished himself during the recent Dutch war, had two royal warships, the frigate *Sweepstakes* and the

Bachelor Pink, and was carrying 'knives, scissors, glasses, beads … hoes, nails, needles, pins, pipes, bells, boxes … linen cloth … tobacco … etc, to trade with the natives at His Majesty's charge' – the king had paid for the cargo, hoping that such prime examples of English manufacturing skill would awe the natives of Patagonia.[57] But Narbrough also had an eye to other outcomes, as he demonstrated when his ships arrived at Port Desire (Porto Deseado) and he claimed 'all the land in this country on both shores for the use of His Majesty King Charles the Second of Great Britain and his heirs'.[58]

As he passed through the Straits of Magellan, Narbrough named the islands after those whom he wished to impress: Charles Island, James Island, Monmouth Island, Lord Arlington's Island, the Earl of Sandwich's Island, and Secretary Wren's Island (Matthew Wren, the Duke of York's secretary at the time, was Sir Christopher's cousin).[59] Narbrough's ships pressed on into the Pacific, but the expedition encountered more and more difficulties. The natives were unimpressed by the English trinkets, seemed irritatingly unaware of the location of any gold mines, and behaved in ways that Narbrough thought 'very brutish'.[60] At Valdivia, they quarrelled with the Spanish authorities, who took prisoner Narbrough's lieutenant, Thomas Armiger, and three other men, one of whom, his interpreter Thomas Highway, was a Moor who had converted to Christianity. Narbrough had to sail and leave them behind; Armiger lived on at Valdivia for another sixteen years.[61] Despite its limited outcomes, and Narbrough's controversial decision to abandon his men without a fight, the expedition proved to be the making of his career. Within a little over two years, he was a knight of the realm and a flag officer; within another two, he was commander-in-chief in the Mediterranean.[62]

The likes of Prince Rupert, the Duke of Albemarle and Sir George Carteret, Treasurer of the Navy, were among the financial backers of an expedition to the north of Canada in 1668/69 by the French adventurers Radisson and des Groseillers. Although the king and Duke of York were not as directly involved with this expedition as they were with Narbrough's, Charles II provided them with two of his own warships, initially the *Eaglet Ketch* and, after she was badly damaged in a storm, the *Wivenhoe*, while the expedition also acquired the *Nonsuch Ketch* after it was sold out of the navy at the end of 1667. The French explorers, who had been to the area before, promoted the idea that lucrative trades could be established there, but at least some at court believed that the expedition might yet reveal the fabled Northwest Passage to the East Indies: even nearly two hundred years after his voyage, Christopher Columbus still had a lot to answer for.[63] The expedition's main achievement was that it led directly to the establishment of the Hudson's Bay Company, which received its royal charter on 2 May 1670, with Prince Rupert as its governor.[64] In its early days, the company was far and away the largest landowner in the world, and, like the Royal African Company, it could call on the resources of the Royal Navy: in 1674, the frigate *Francis* was loaned to it.[65]

Early in 1676, Charles and James heard a proposal from Captain John Wood for a voyage to China and Japan via the diametrically opposite route, the Northeast Passage. This, too, had long and respectable antecedents: English explorers had first set off in search of such a sea route in 1553. Wood was closely connected with both the Stuarts and voyages of exploration. As with so many of those whom Charles and James favoured, he had strong Cavalier credentials, and had 'approved his fidelity to His Majesty by his services in the late troubles'. He was made a midshipman in 1661 by the Duke of York's express command.[66] Wood was on the Narbrough expedition of 1669–71, and gained a place in the fleet in 1672, again on James's direct order. He became a lieutenant for the first time in November 1672, and only nine months later, he was captain of the powerful frigate *Bonaventure*.[67] The royal warship *Speedwell* was provided for his Arctic voyage, and James and Pepys were among the eight sponsors funding the other ship intended for the expedition, the *Prosperous Pink*, which was to carry a range of English commodities intended to impress the Chinese and Japanese. On 1 May 1676, Charles and James went to Sheerness to inspect the ships commanded by Wood, 'who is a very ingenious man'.[68] Unfortunately, Wood's ingenuity was unable to prevent the expedition ending in disaster. The *Speedwell* and the *Prosperous* sailed from the Nore on 28 May, but the former ran aground on the island of Novaya Zemlya on 29 June 1676 and broke up on the following day. Wood escaped with his life (albeit only after nine days ashore, prior to rescue by the *Prosperous*), but not with his papers, which perished with the *Speedwell*. Despite this, the king insisted on seeing a journal of the expedition as quickly as possible, and both Wood and Pepys must have had sleepless nights complying with his demand.[69]

Charles and James ordered a number of hydrographic expeditions in home waters, either informally or more officially. In 1670, James ordered Christopher Gunman, captain of the *Anne Yacht*, to carry out a survey in the Downs, while in 1684 Charles ordered a survey of the Thames from London Bridge to Limehouse.[70] Moreover, the potential scientific value of ships' logbooks was clearly recognised. The first-ever volume of transactions of the Royal Society, for 1665/66, included directions for seamen aboard merchant ships going far afield to keep journals, which were to be delivered upon their return to James, as Lord High Admiral, to the

Society and to Trinity House.[71] Naval captains already submitted their journals, albeit for administrative rather than scientific reasons, due to an injunction laid down in the General Instructions to Commanders of 1663; although it is sometimes assumed that this policy was only enforced when Pepys went to the Admiralty in 1673, it is clear that such journals were being submitted as a matter of course to the Duke of York's secretary, and later to the Controller of the Navy, throughout the 1660s.[72] Masters' and lieutenants' journals were submitted as a matter of course from the 1670s. Although the runs of all three types of journal at the National Archives and the National Maritime Museum are by no means comprehensive – and, indeed, the lieutenants' logs, now at Greenwich, were very nearly destroyed during a brutal Admiralty 'weeding' at the end of the nineteenth century – they continue to form a remarkable resource for scientists in the twenty-first century, following the belated discovery of their value as evidence of historical climate change.

By far the most important hydrographic development of the later Stuart age was the commissioning of the first comprehensive survey of the British coasts, and this was very much the direct initiative of King Charles, who was concerned that almost all the charts of his kingdoms were originally produced by the Dutch. His chosen agent was relatively unlikely in some respects. Greenvile Collins, a Devonian, was distinctly inexperienced, and he was not drawn from the closed ranks of the junior or elder Brethren of Trinity House, who might have been expected to provide the commander for such an important mission. However, Collins had voyaged widely, including (allegedly) to the East Indies, and he served under Narbrough during the South Seas voyage in 1669–71; Narbrough continued to advance his career throughout the 1670s.[73] Collins first came to the attention of the king in 1676. He served as master of the ill-fated *Speedwell* in Wood's expedition to navigate the Northeast Passage, and his journal of the voyage greatly impressed Charles, who swiftly appointed him master of the new *Charles Galley*. In 1680, Collins was hand-picked for the same post on the *Leopard*, which carried the king's son, the Duke of Grafton, on a cruise in the Mediterranean. His journals for both of these latter voyages reveal him to have been a navigator of considerable skill and perception, as well as one who possessed talent as a draughtsman and hydrographer.[74]

On 18 June 1681, Collins was commissioned captain of the *Merlin Yacht* and began the survey, which eventually took seven years. Collins undertook his work by virtue of a warrant directly from the king; as with the 'Irish squadron' of 1682, the Admiralty was effectively bypassed. Charles even specified which yacht Collins should use for the survey.[75] Pepys was somewhat disgruntled at first, believing that the task should have been entrusted to a man of greater experience, ideally drawn from Trinity

House; but 'it fell into Collins' hands by virtue of his having served the king and being thereby known to him, His Royal Highness, the Navy Officers, myself, etc'.[76] In 1683, Collins was appointed hydrographer to Trinity House, as well as to the king, and Pepys noted that this was due primarily to the instigation of the Duke of Grafton, then master of that body, who was evidently keen to advance the career of his old shipmate. Although Collins's completed work was not published as *Great Britain's Coasting Pilot* until 1694, Charles II was greatly impressed by its progress in the early stages, declaring that the coasts had never been so well charted, and announced his intention of personally supporting the work as much as he could. Charles hoped that such advances would drive out the sort of ignorance that he witnessed at first hand in a veteran captain who had commanded several East Indies voyages, but who could not distinguish east from west on a map, despite the king's best efforts to enlighten him.[77]

However, it would be wrong to suggest that Charles's and James's sponsorship of navigational excellence and voyages of exploration stemmed solely from disinterested scientific curiosity. They were integral elements of their ambition to achieve supremacy at sea; not just an absolute, military supremacy, but an intellectual supremacy too. In that respect, they had considerable success, with the reputation of English navigators and mapmakers (and the actual number of the latter) rising markedly between 1660 and 1690.[78] But as with the frequently avaricious 'strategies' they pursued in wartime (described in the next chapter), a number of the distant voyages were undertaken either principally or partly to increase the wealth of the nation, and by extension that of the monarch. Narbrough's South Seas voyage of 1669–71 was, more or less overtly, a reconnaissance to try and establish direct English access to South American bullion, and Spanish authorities, local and imperial, certainly perceived it as a threat in those terms.[79]

Similar considerations undoubtedly underpinned Charles's extraordinary decision in 1682 to pardon the notorious buccaneer Bartholomew Sharpe, who had mounted a series of attacks on Spanish territory and shipping in Panama and Chile. During one such raid, he captured a book of charts detailing all the anchorages from Cape Horn to California. Arrested on his return to England, he showed the book to the king, who immediately ordered an English translation to be made, which was presented to him in October 1682. By that time Sharpe, had both been released and commissioned as captain of a royal warship, the *Bonetta Sloop*, much to the fury of the Spanish ambassador.[80] The fact that he absconded almost at once from his new command might cast some doubt on Charles II's judgement of men, but the important point is that the king had the book, and annoying the Spanish was a small price to pay for such priceless information.

An early twentieth-century photograph taken on, and of, the remains of the 'English mole' at Tangier. *(Author's collection)*

Ultimately, the Stuart brothers' dreams of a great maritime empire came to nothing; £400,000 a year, all that the state could often afford to spend on its navy in peacetime, was barely enough to secure the coasts of Cornwall, Kerry and Caithness, let alone the trades of the Levant, Indies and Americas. By 1685, even the staunchly royalist John Evelyn believed that Charles II's weaknesses and inconsistencies had squandered his chance of attaining greatness by bringing a great British maritime empire into being, a couple of centuries before its time. Moreover, the French alliance to which the king adhered during the last years of his reign seemed to his critics to be inimical to national interests.[81] When he succeeded to the throne, James pursued the imperial dream with renewed vigour, but crucially, and unlike many of his subjects, he saw no contradiction between doing so and adhering closely to France: in a curious echo of the peace proposals mooted by both the Nazis and British defeatists in 1940, James seems genuinely to have believed that unrestrained French hegemony in continental Europe and the Mediterranean could co-exist with a British maritime empire elsewhere around the world.[82] Meanwhile, though, Tangier, the great hope of the royal brothers' imperial dream, lay in ruins. But two reminders of the days when Charles II's flag flew over the North African city had been left behind. The huge remains of the base of the mole survived well into the twentieth century; and:

> by the king's direction there were buried among the ruins a considerable number of milled crown pieces of His Majesty's coin, which haply, many centuries hence, when other memory of it shall be lost, may declare to succeeding ages that that place was once a member of the British Empire.[83]

10

Warlords

AWHILE AFTER NOON on 3 June 1665, the entire course of British history changed. In that moment, the heads of three men, standing upon the quarterdeck of the flagship *Royal Charles*, were ripped from their shoulders by a chain shot fired from the Dutch flagship *Eendracht*. The three men were Charles, Viscount Muskerry, heir to the Earl of Clancarty; the Honourable Richard Boyle, younger son of the Earl of Burlington and nephew of the great scientist Robert Boyle; and Charles Berkeley, newly minted Earl of Falmouth, the rapidly rising favourite of King Charles II. Their blood and brains spattered the man standing immediately next to them, who survived. But if the aim of the gun captain aboard the *Eendracht* had been just fractionally different – the smallest, almost incalculable, fraction, affected by the minutest change in the wind or the swell – then, perhaps, Falmouth might have lived, and gone on to reshape Charles II's reign in who knows what ways, while the man covered in his gore might have died. That man was James, Duke of York, Lord High Admiral and the heir to the throne: the future King James II and VII. And if James Stuart had died in the Battle of Lowestoft on 3 June 1665, instead of at the palace of Saint-Germain on 5 September 1701, there would certainly have been no event called the Glorious Revolution; no King William of Orange; no Battle of the Boyne; and no Battle of Culloden, assuming there had ever been a union between England and Scotland at all. Whether the Dutch gun captain should be thanked or cursed must, therefore, remain a matter of personal opinion or personal prejudice.

The years between 1660 and 1688 saw two major wars against the Dutch, in 1664–67 and 1672–74 respectively, following on from the war the Commonwealth had fought against the same enemy in 1652–54. The so-called second Anglo-Dutch war also included relatively half-hearted wars against France and Denmark–Norway (1666/67), while the third war was fought in alliance with the French. In addition to these two titanic conflicts, there was also a mobilisation in 1678 for a war against France, which was settled by diplomatic means before serious fighting

broke out; and for much of the period, there were wars against one or more of the north African city states of Algiers, Tripoli, Tunis and Salé. Finally, 1688 saw an invasion of Great Britain by the Dutch, an invasion so entirely successful in achieving its objectives that, to this day, many people do not even realise or accept that any such thing as an 'invasion' took place at all. For Charles and James Stuart, therefore, there were plenty of opportunities to fulfil the traditional role of their ancestors, both English and Scottish: that of the warrior prince. But there was one crucial difference. Unlike their predecessors, the nature of their opponents, and of the wars they fought against them, meant that the Stuart brothers had to fight wars that were overwhelmingly, and in most cases exclusively, naval.

Historians have spilled much ink in trying to establish the causes of the Anglo-Dutch wars, particularly the second, which broke out informally in 1664 and was formally declared in 1665. But regardless of whether this was a war over trade, or the product of factional politics at court, it is clear that the war only began because the Stuart brothers very much wanted it to. James, in particular:

... having been bred in arms was willing to have an occasion to show his courage on the sea as well as on land ... the vigour of his Royal Highness broke the measure of those ministers who would otherwise have preserved the peace at any rate.[1]

The destruction of the Dutch flagship at the Battle of Lowestoft, 3 June 1665, the Duke of York's greatest victory as an admiral. (Rijksmuseum, Amsterdam)

Sir John Narbrough's
fleet burning four
corsair vessels at
Tripoli, January 1676,
an episode during the
Restoration regime's
nearly constant wars
against the Barbary
regencies.
Narbrough's boats
were commanded by
the young Lieutenant
Cloudesley Shovell.
Willem van de Velde.
*(© National Maritime
Museum, Greenwich,
London)*

Both James and his brother were heavily involved in war planning, both
for this and subsequent conflicts. The detailed planning for the opening
naval campaign of the second Anglo-Dutch war took place in a series of
meetings held between October and December 1664, attended by the
likes of the Duke of York, Prince Rupert, the Duke of Albemarle and the
principal admirals. But in many cases, this body only made recommendations which were placed before the king, who took the final decisions.[2]
A similar pattern can be seen before the outbreak of the third war, with
Charles and James holding meetings with all their key naval advisers and
subordinate bodies from the spring of 1670 onwards, even before the
signing of the secret Treaty of Dover.[3] Above all, the king, and no one
else, decided on the size of the wartime fleet. While he was Lord High
Admiral, James then chose the individual ships to make up the number
laid down by his brother, but after his resignation, Charles decided on
these specifics, too. During the 'French war' of 1678 (which never actually began), Charles decided on a larger deployment to the
Mediterranean than was originally planned, then personally selected the
flagships for the admirals of this new fleet.[4]

There was no such thing as 'strategy' in the Stuart age; or at least, the
word was still more than a century shy of acquiring its modern meaning.[5]
But, for all its anachronistic aspects, the word provides a convenient
shorthand for the diverse and often muddled agglomeration of policies,
aspirations and knee-jerk responses that characterised the Stuart brothers'
use of their navy in war and peace. Whatever one calls it, though, the king
was the ultimate arbiter of it. In August 1664, James had to ask his brother

what the Earl of Sandwich should do if his fleet encountered a larger
Dutch force coming up the Channel 'in a bravado'.[6] In February 1665,
the duke's secretary William Coventry wrote to the Secretary of State, Sir
Henry Bennet, to ask Bennet to obtain the king's command for a course
of action for the fleet to take; Coventry hoped that Charles would be
well advised, for it would be 'of ill consequences' if the wrong decisions
were taken. Coventry's remark demonstrates that the king alone, not the
Lord High Admiral, decided what the fleet actually did. Two months
later, Coventry was pressing for more detailed instructions, fearing otherwise that the duke would be blamed for any and all reverses, especially
by those who sought to undermine his father-in-law, Clarendon.
Coventry even claimed that James's instructions were so general 'because
others were unwilling to burn their fingers with it'.[7] However, even if
Charles received the sort of advice that Coventry desired, he did not
need to accept it: by April 1665, at least some of his advisers were telling
him not to divide the fleet by sending a squadron westward to monitor
Dutch and French moves, but Charles remained convinced that 'if the
Dutch fleet be divided, ours ought to be'.[8]

Above all, the Stuart brothers advocated an aggressive, forward 'strategy'.
They favoured bold strokes, such as attempts to intercept Dutch convoys
and deploying the fleet within sight of the Dutch coast so as to terrorise
the Dutch population, perhaps thereby provoking an uprising against their
rulers. In April 1665, the fleet's council of war decided to stand off the
Dutch shore because its members knew the king would be pleased with
such a move.[9] At the end of the year, realising that war with France was
imminent, Charles ordered a pre-emptive attack on French trade, but was
persuaded by Clarendon and others to rescind this command on the
grounds that it would be 'unfit to hasten the breach with the French'.[10]

During the third war, Charles's personal interventions reveal a sound
command of navigation and tactics, as well as an openness to advice. On
2 May 1672, for example, he and Prince Rupert disagreed about the
effects of wind direction in the North Sea on the stationing of the fleet;
on 16 June, Charles proposed that James should make a feint to the north
in an attempt to induce the Dutch to follow him out, a proposal with
which several ministers disagreed. Several initiatives came directly from
the king, such as his scheme of September 1672 (albeit never implemented) to send a squadron to Guinea and the East Indies, which seems
to have been imposed on his ministers without prior consultation.[11]
Although his admirals must have been aware of their monarch's strategic
preferences, Charles directly imposed his favoured course of action on
them only rarely. Several of the 1672 debates at the committee of foreign
affairs ended with a decision to defer to the judgement of the admiral,
the Duke of York. Even when Charles did issue explicit orders, he qual-

ified them to allow his admirals freedom of action. In July 1672, he ordered James to attack the Dutch East Indies fleet, but added the rider, 'although I send you these directions by way of an order, yet if you see a notorious inconvenience likely to follow upon it, I allow you to suspend the execution, and to represent to me your opinion'.[12] In 1673, Charles was rather freer with his advice to Prince Rupert, suggesting attacks on particular targets in a way which led the prince to believe that his freedom of action was being restricted, but the king was careful to back up his admiral both by explicit assurances of support and by acceding to Rupert's requests.[13] In other ways, too, Charles did his utmost to ensure the success of the fleet. When a letter arrived from Rupert, complaining that ordnance stores had not arrived, the king immediately sent for the Master of the Ordnance, listened to his explanation, and then ordered him to expedite the despatch of the stores in question.[14]

Given the outcomes of the second and third Anglo–Dutch wars, it is easy to condemn Charles and James as incompetent naval strategists. It is certainly true that they embarked on, and then abandoned, objectives too quickly, and were often wildly over-optimistic about what their navy could realistically achieve. But this was not entirely their fault. During 1664 and the first half of 1665, the overwhelming feeling of confidence at court that the Dutch could be rapidly and comprehensively defeated at sea did not originate with Charles or James, but with the professionals whose advice they took – veterans like the Duke of Albemarle and Admiral Sir John Lawson, who believed they had beaten the Dutch before, only to be deprived of total victory by Cromwell's sudden making of peace, and were overwhelmingly confident of completing their unfinished business. The second greatest strategic blunder of Charles's reign, the division of the fleet in 1666, was born out of catastrophic intelligence failures which misled the king and his ministers to believe that a French fleet was on its way to join the Dutch and might mount a disruptive invasion of Ireland in the process. This led to a considerable squadron under Prince Rupert being sent west to deal with this illusory threat, leaving Albemarle's weakened fleet to face a greatly superior Dutch force. The resulting Four Days' Battle was a calamity for the British, with the deaths of more captains than in any other naval engagement in national history, the only ever case of a British admiral surrendering in action, and the loss of the *Royal Prince*, the huge ship and national icon which had originally been built for Henry, Prince of Wales, in 1610.[15]

However, the greatest strategic blunder of the reign, and one of the most humiliating defeats in the whole of British history, must be laid largely at Charles II's door. The decision to lay up the main fleet in 1667 was opposed by the Duke of York, but Charles believed (or was persuaded to believe) that he could not afford to set out a fleet and that peace was

imminent in any case, so he took up a plan for a commerce-raiding war which he had rejected three years before, and began strengthening the fortifications of Sheerness as a defensive precaution. The Dutch saw matters rather differently, and were determined above all to avenge Holmes's Bonfire (August 1666), a devastating attack on merchant shipping in the Vlie anchorage, during which the town of Westerschelling was burned to the ground. Work on the new fortifications for the Thames and Medway proceeded too slowly, and they proved unable to prevent the Dutch sailing up the latter, burning three of Charles's greatest ships – the *Royal James*, *Royal Oak* and *Loyal London* – and towing back to Holland the *Royal Charles*, the vessel which he had renamed after himself when he first stepped aboard her at Scheveningen in May 1660. The king's many critics had a field day, exploiting the Chatham catastrophe to make a connection between Charles's known proclivities and the humiliating defeat: naval and national failure was linked to sexual impotence, as in the vicious satire, *Last Instructions to a Painter*. For others, the shocking defeat was God's righteous judgement for the immorality of the court, just as the Great Fire of London had been.[16]

'Sir Robert Holmes, his bonfire': the destruction of 150 Dutch merchant ships in the Vlie anchorage, August 1666. Willem van de Velde the Elder. *(Rijksmuseum, Amsterdam)*

Overleaf: The burning of the English fleet at Chatham, with the surrendered *Royal Charles* flying the Dutch colours. *(Rijksmuseum, Amsterdam)*

Immoral or not, the king and Duke of York benefited personally from naval warfare. Between the beginning of December 1664 and March 1665, eighty-six foreign ships were taken as prizes, even though the second Anglo-Dutch war did not officially begin until the latter month. At least ten of those condemned as legitimate seizures (about seventy-two of the ships captured) were appropriated personally by the king: they included by far the richest of the ships in question, the *Crown Malaga* of Amsterdam, carrying beams and tar, and valued at £813.[17] Meanwhile James, as Lord High Admiral of England, was entitled to one-tenth of the value of all prizes taken at sea and all foreign ships taken in English, Welsh and Irish ports. The Italian visitor, Lorenzo Magalotti, reckoned that the duke's income from this during the second Anglo-Dutch war came to some £40,000 a year, but this phenomenal amount (five times the Lord High Admiral's annual salary) must have been a 'guesstimate' that was being bandied around the court at the time.[18] On the other hand, the total value of prizes taken in the war came to £676,248, so Magalotti might not have been too far off the mark.[19] It might be possible to unpick this figure to calculate how much Charles and James were individually entitled to, but it would be a huge task; the king was entitled to the ships taken by his warships, the duke to those taken by privateers, so each individual capture would need to be analysed, and the amounts totalled up.[20] The profits from war of the royal brothers and their ministers were not only financial. In May 1666, Charles ordered 15 tons of wine from the captured *Vrede* of Vlissingen to be taken to his cellar, with James getting another six and others going to members of the prize commission, which, significantly, was identical in personnel to the Privy Council's navy committee.[21] Therefore, simple personal avarice gave Charles and James obvious motive to advocate bold attacks on the enemy.

But the belief that naval war could be lucrative extended far beyond the windfall acquisition of a few barrels of wine. One of the great myths about the Elizabethan navy with which Charles and James grew up was that it was possible for naval warfare to be self-financing, and the message seemed to have been reinforced by the experience of the hated Interregnum regimes, which captured perhaps 1,500 Dutch prizes in the war of 1652–54, and subsequently intercepted Spanish plate convoys on two occasions. If regicidal usurpers could gain such windfalls, who knew what riches awaited a righteous, divinely ordained monarch? Reflecting this mindset, Charles II's favourite, Lord Falmouth, was probably only echoing his master's own thoughts when, in 1665, he asked Sir William Coventry how much money the king might save out of the £2.5 million that Parliament had voted to fund the second Anglo-Dutch war. Coventry replied that far from saving money, the war was likely to cost far more, and that if Parliament thought 'the quarrel raised only to get money, and then a peace huddled up for private profit', it would rightly never trust the king again.[22] In the end, Charles ended up with the worst of both worlds, losing the trust of Parliament and finding himself hugely out of pocket: even the king's critics on the Brooke House Committee of 1668–70, which investigated the naval failures of the war, acknowledged that he had spent over half a million pounds of his own money on naval preparations for the second Anglo-Dutch war.[23]

For a time, negative voices, such as William Coventry's, were drowned out. In 1666, the Duke of Albemarle even advocated immediate declarations of war against France and Denmark, on the grounds that waiting for them to declare war on England would lose several weeks' opportunities for capturing many valuable prizes. When the fleet moved north to intercept the Dutch East Indies fleet in 1665, it was in the belief that the escorting flagship was carrying two chests of gold and the vice-admiral three more, and when it was learned that they had taken refuge in the neutral harbour of Bergen, the Duke of York ordered that 'if a fair opportunity offer itself of doing any service upon them, I desire you would not neglect it out of any scrupulous consideration of that port in which they lie', regardless of the fact that sending the fleet to Norway effectively left the English coast defenceless.[24] After the attack on Bergen was ignominiously repulsed by the Dutch and Danes, James justified it on the grounds that 'the value of the ships to be seized was considerable enough to make it fit to run some hazard'.[25] Whether his comment was motivated principally by the prospect of the glory that victory would bring to his brother's kingdoms, by the tremendous boost to the state's finances that such a capture would provide, or by the vast windfall that would accrue to the Duke of York's finances, must remain a matter of speculation.*

Reputation – of the king, and of the nation as a whole – was a vital imperative driving what the navy did during the Restoration era. In 1664, Admiral Sir John Lawson and the navy treasurer, Sir George Carteret, suggested that the planned war against the Dutch should be fought as a *guerre de course*, with raiding squadrons picking off the rich Dutch convoys and blockading their harbours. Despite the likely financial advantages of such a strategy, Charles rejected it in favour of a 'grand fleet', arguing that it would be dishonourable for him not to be seen as 'the most potent Prince in the world at sea'.[26] In October 1665, despite the huge success the fleet had won at Lowestoft four months earlier, Dutch ships were thronging British coasts. The Duke of York demanded

* Similar considerations impelled the attack on the Dutch Smyrna fleet in March 1672, before war had been declared: although international treaties protected shipping in such circumstances, Charles coveted the fabulously wealthy cargoes in the fleet and ordered an attack, the pretext being the refusal of the Dutch ships to strike their flags in salute.

immediate remedial action, 'being very unwilling that it should appear either at home or abroad, that after the success that it hath pleased God to give the king, it should yet remain in the choice of the Dutch how long they will continue to ride upon our coast'.[27] In July 1672, Charles warned that if there was no attack on the Dutch fleet, or else a landing on the Dutch coast, 'we shall lose the reputation and advantage of this summer'.[28] As a lawyer put it a few years later:

> since we know how much it imports a state that it be reverenced abroad, and that repute is the principal support of any government, it equally influences the subjects at home and foreign allies abroad; and as there is no nation in the world more tender of their honour than the English, so none more impatiently tolerate the diminution thereof.[29]

Despite such evidence, it is curious that historians invariably treat seriously King Louis XIV's concerns for his reputation and quest for *la gloire*, but disallow the possibility that his English cousin could have had precisely the same concerns and ambitions. Charles II's reputation per se has undoubtedly been shaped by his activities in the bedroom, but dismissing his public protestations about his and his kingdoms' broader 'reputation' as the empty bluster of a duplicitous libertine is seriously to misjudge some of the king's most important policies. In reality, such statements, along with the 'salute to the flag', were simply manifestations of the almost obsessive concern of all European monarchs of the age with rank, privilege, honour and reputation, and which also contributed, for example, to many vicious quarrels over precedence between diplomats. Nor were Charles II and the polemicists who gave public voice to his attitude alone in stressing the importance of preserving a king's reputation. Louis XIV's much-trumpeted craving for *gloire* was accepted both by that monarch himself and by almost all subsequent historians of his reign as one of the most important motivations driving French foreign policy. Yet *gloire* was not simply a quest for military glory: contemporaries often translated the word as 'reputation', and Louis's own writings make clear that this was often what he had in mind.[30] In other words, the Sun King's stated priorities, and those of his English cousin, were identical: the degrees of consistency in pursuing them, and of their success, were rather different.

Nothing demonstrated this point more conclusively than the success of the Dutch attack on the Medway in 1667. This was about as serious a blow to national prestige, and to Charles II's personal reputation, as can be imagined, but he immediately set out to mend the damage. Only a month after the disaster, one of his ministers reported that 'His

Majesty resolves though we have peace to have a strong fleet next year [as] it will be but what is necessary after the affronts we have received to show we resolve still to be masters of the sea'.[31] Charles was as good as his word, setting out some fifty large ships in the summer of 1668, an act that was clearly intended to send a powerful signal to all of the king's potential allies and enemies. Even though Charles was allied to the Dutch by this time, in a Triple Alliance which also included Sweden and which was intended to restrain French expansion, he was increasingly preoccupied with a succession of gestures which seemed deliberately to cause offence and to undermine his reputation. Medals glorifying the attack on Chatham had been struck in the United Provinces, while the *Royal Charles*, captured in the Medway, was on display as a tourist attraction at Hellevoetsluis. A number of Dutch paintings showed the *Royal Charles* being towed away; in one she was flying the royal standard from the mainmast, a permanent record of personal humiliation that was bound to enrage Charles. Offence was also caused by Jan de Baen's picture, *The Apotheosis of Cornelis de Witt*, which by June 1670 was hanging in the town hall of Dordrecht. In the foreground, Sheerness

The sternpiece of the *Royal Charles*. *(Rijksmuseum, Amsterdam)*

Fort was shown, occupied by Dutch troops and with the Dutch flag flying over it – a clear proof of a successful Dutch invasion, and a deliberate attempt to impugn the territorial integrity and national sovereignty of Charles II's kingdoms.[32]

English writers were unequivocal: 'the provocations of the Dutch by their pictures, medals and monuments ... were such as would have justified a more early war'.[33] The quack medic and royal propagandist John Stubbe considered the effect of 'exposing him [the king] to scorn and derision by ridiculous pictures and odious medals':

> The reputation of a prince is all in all ... when a prince is wounded in his reputation, and his forces are cried down, when his prosperities are lessened, and his disgraces increased, when endeavours are used to obscure the lustre of his greatness and puissance ... this is the subject of a just war ...[34]

The king's reputation had also been diminished by the behaviour of the Dutch in foreign ports. During a visit to Genoa, Jan van Brakel, who had led the successful attack on the Medway chain in 1667, hoisted beneath his Dutch ensign the colours that he had captured during the battle – the traditional sign of surrender and humiliation.[35] William de Britaine made the crucial point that such Dutch affronts diminished Charles II in the eyes of both his subjects and his equals:

> The reputation of a prince ought to be as sacred as his person ... contumely to a private person is but a private injury; but to a king, it's an affront to a whole nation; for the honour of the king is wound up with the safety and reputation of the people. It's not enough for a prince to be great among his own subjects, but he must carry a *grandezza* amongst kings ...[36]

But the Dutch had employed an even more humiliating tactic against the Stuart king: according to the Earl of Arlington, one of Charles's principal ministers, the Dutch were guilty of 'giving way to a malicious disrespect towards a great king and descending to satire, a manner of revenge unworthy even of private individuals'.[37]

All of this has usually been dismissed as mere window dressing, or else the propaganda put out by the Stuart regime to justify a war which was actually driven by much more important imperatives, those contained within the secret terms of the Treaty of Dover. There was certainly an element of that, but the two were not necessarily mutually exclusive, and there is ample evidence to indicate that Charles II's fury over perceived Dutch disrespect was genuine. Above all, the reaction of the

Dutch to the Stuart king's protests suggests that they, at least, took his public expressions seriously, even if many historians do not. Charles took particular exception to the medal produced by Christopher Adolfszoon to commemorate the end of the second Anglo–Dutch war, and which seemed to identify the king as '*mala bestia*', an evil beast; when he protested, the states of Holland and West Friesland, which had commissioned the medal, ordered the dies to be broken and the surviving copies melted down.[38] Protests over van Brakel's humiliating treatment of Charles's naval colours led to their return to him. In November 1670, the king further protested about the fact that the Stuart royal arms still adorned the stern of the captured *Royal Charles*, which was effectively a floating pub at Hellevoetsluis. The arms were duly taken down, which is why they still hang to this day in Amsterdam's Rijksmuseum. Finally, the inhabitants of Dordrecht certainly accepted the notion that the painting hanging in their town hall had caused fatal offence to the King of Great Britain: following the nearly catastrophic invasion of their country by Charles's French allies in the spring of 1672, they stormed the building and tore the painting to pieces, subsequently bestowing exactly the same fate on its subject, Cornelis de Witt.

Charles II was thus acutely aware of the need to uphold the reputations of his nation, his navy and himself. This was not simply a matter of operatic symbolism, or of wounded pride; it also stemmed from a very real concern for domestic security. As a paper drawn up as part of the negotiations leading to the Dover treaty put it, 'the affront to the nation of the Dutch laying upon our unfortified coasts and blocking up our open rivers would not be borne without a danger of mutinies and universal disorders', not to mention the prospect of the Dutch cutting off trade and thus eliminating the Crown's lucrative and indispensable income from customs.[39] A similar concern for reputation and security can be seen in a letter that Charles wrote to his brother on 4 September 1672. It was normal practice to start bringing the fleet back into port at the beginning of September, when the weather began to deteriorate and threatened the safety of the larger ships. Charles's opinion on the subject was clearly shaped by the bitter memory of 1667, by his concern for his reputation in the world, and by optimism that there might still be a chance to deliver a decisive blow against the Dutch:

> … if we should let it be known now, that there is no more to be done this year, and draw in our great ships, I am confident De Ruyter would come vapouring upon our coast, *which would make a very ill noise here and everywhere else* [my emphasis], and though I am as wary as anybody of venturing our great ships upon their coasts at

The Apotheosis of Cornelis de Witt, ... by Jan de Baen, a copy of the destroyed painting that supposedly enraged King Charles II; the Dutch flag flies over Sheerness fort as the ships in the Medway burn. (Rijksmuseum, Amsterdam)

this time of the year, yet there may happen such an opportunity as we should be sorry not to have it in our power to lay hold of ...[40]

Charles II might no longer have been able to take a fleet to war, as he had done as Prince of Wales in 1648, but he compensated by spending as much time as possible aboard it before it actually set sail, and returning to it as soon as he could after it came in from sea. In 1664, for example, he inspected the ships being fitted out at Chatham on 23 May, and after they had moved out into the Thames, he went down to the Hope anchorage with the queen on 4 July.[41] In March 1665, the Venetian ambassador reported that 'King Charles frequently amuses himself at Portsmouth in viewing his ships'.[42] In June of both 1665 and 1666, he went to the fleet almost as soon as it came in following the Battle of Lowestoft and the Four Days' Fight.[43] In 1672, with even higher stakes in play – a possible British invasion of the Netherlands, one element of the strategy specified in the secret Treaty of Dover – Charles visited the fleet often. In March, he went to Sheerness to view the damage to Sir Robert Holmes's ships following their engagement with the Dutch Smyrna fleet.[44] He went aboard the flagship *Prince* on St George's Day, was still aboard her when she sailed to Sheerness on 26 April, and only returned to London the following day. He was back on 6 June, following the Battle of Solebay, and stayed aboard for two nights; he returned on 18 June with the queen 'and all the court', this time breakfasting aboard the French flagship. Further visits followed between 24 and 27 August, and between 9 and 13 September, during which time he even held a meeting of the Privy Council aboard the *Prince*.[45] Charles made another five visits to the fleet during the 1673 campaign: court insiders could always predict how long these excursions were going to be by counting the number of meals the king took with him.[46] Charles usually took some of his ministers along – for instance, Buckingham, Arlington, Ashley Cooper and Clifford went with him during the August and September 1672 visits to the fleet – and there was some disquiet among the officers at the extent of their influence.[47] But Charles knew that, quite apart from allowing him to exercise direct authority over what the fleet did, his presence raised morale, and encouraged courtiers and ministers alike to become knowledgeable about, and actively involved in, naval affairs. Above all, it demonstrated conclusively his concern for his and his nation's reputation, and his understanding that this reputation depended above all on the performance of his royal navy.

A royal visit to the fleet, 1672. King Charles II has just transferred from the *Cleveland Yacht* to the *Prince*, which has just hoisted the royal standard at the main; the second royal standard in the mizzen shrouds is summoning a council of war. Willem van de Velde the Younger. (© *National Maritime Museum, Greenwich, London, BHC0299*)

The king's most significant act as a war leader during both the second and third wars was to remove his brother from command after the first campaign of each. Quite why Charles did this has always generated hypotheses and conspiracy theories, mainly because the king told no one of his reasons, refusing to give a straight answer even to James.[48] But if he really was jealous of his younger brother's dynamic, heroic role as the commander of fleets in battle, as has been suggested, why did he appoint him in the first place, only to apparently change his mind several months later? The same question could be asked of the theory that Charles might have removed James because he feared for the safety of the heir to his throne. Charles knew full well what battle was like, having witnessed his first at the age of twelve and having escaped narrowly with his life at the Battle of Worcester; and although James's lucky escape at the Battle of Lowestoft might have brought home the dangers, Charles would hardly have been ignorant of them when he first agreed to James going to sea. Moreover, if the threat to the heir's life justified the duke's removal from command in June 1665, what changed to permit the appointment of James to command once again at the start of the 1672 campaign?

The answers to these questions probably lie somewhere within both the brothers' complex relationship, and the pressures of politics and history. For one thing, it would have been virtually impossible for Charles to deny James's right to command at the beginning of the 1665 campaign: it was, after all, what Lord High Admirals traditionally did, and for Charles to display an apparent lack of confidence in his younger sibling by overlooking his claim could well have seriously damaged the heir's credibility. But the close shave at Lowestoft would have allowed both brothers to claim that honour was satisfied. James could retire with his reputation for bravery greatly enhanced, while Charles could claim, rightly, that precedent had been followed and the Lord High Admiral's right preserved. Moreover, Charles must have known that his brother's presence constrained his other commanders: in April 1665, a bold project to attack the Dutch within their Texel anchorage was abandoned because 'the circumstance of the duke's person commanding the fleet make it of very great weight to determine'.[49] There were probably other considerations specific to the moment. When the king recalled the duke at the beginning of July 1665, plague was sweeping through London, which had not been the case when James went to sea in March. Although the court swiftly moved to Oxford, and then to Salisbury, there was clearly a risk of the king succumbing to the pestilence, so it made no sort of sense for his heir to be running an equal, if not greater, risk from Dutch cannonades at exactly the same time; and it is perfectly possible that some sort of argument to this effect was used to persuade James to come ashore. This interpretation might be strengthened by the fact that James immediately went about as far away from his brother as he possibly could, paying an extended visit to the city from which he derived his ducal title, York. Finally, there was a strong rumour to the effect that the Queen Mother, Henrietta Maria, who had already lost six of her nine children, was determined to protect her younger surviving son from the terrible risks he was running, and lobbied the elder furiously to that end.[50]

In 1672, the political and dynastic considerations were rather different. Above all, Henrietta Maria was dead; and whereas in 1665, the next heirs after James had been babies and toddlers, by 1672 his elder daughter, Mary, was a healthy ten, so the risk of James being carried off by a Dutch cannonball might have seemed a little less significant. More immediately, though, only James had the status to ensure that the huge Anglo-French combined fleet could be commanded without the danger of national jealousies and personal spites handicapping its prospects in battle: as the duke was both the heir to the throne and a former general in the French army, Louis XIV and his admirals could hardly quibble with James's credentials. As it was, though, the naval campaign of 1672, especially the Battle of Solebay on 28 May, exposed one of the most critical flaws in the duke's personality and make-up as a military commander.

James hoisted his flag aboard the new *Prince* on 2 April 1672. Superficially, the combined fleet under his command was remarkably impressive: fifty-one British men-of-war and thirty-four French, the latter under the command of the Comte d'Estrées. King Charles himself went aboard the French fleet for some three hours on 5 May. This now sounds like an innocuous, even insignificant, gesture, but at the time it was heavily laden with significance. By going aboard d'Estrées' ships, Charles was literally going into French territory, an act that was 'an open testimony of sincere friendship and simple faith by going on board and entrusting his royal person to the good faith of the French'.[51] But despite the impressive appearance of Louis XIV's men-of-war, and the king's public expression of confidence in them, the French simply had no experience of operating in such a large fleet in wartime, certainly not in the waters of the North Sea. In private, the king took a rather different line. Even before d'Estrées arrived at Spithead, Charles II himself, at a meeting of the Committee for Foreign Affairs, expressed the view that James should 'ripen the Fr[ench] in passage and rules of sailing and fighting etc before they fall in with the Dutch', adding that it would be better if the French were not committed to battle too soon.[52]

After the juncture of the fleets, the French were regularly found guilty of manoeuvring and sailing errors by experienced British officers, whose comments ranged from the sympathetic to the caustic.[53] Only time could have righted these problems, and the Dutch were well aware of this. The

Dutch commander, Michiel de Ruyter, had already made an abortive attempt to engage before the juncture of the two allied fleets, and when he learned on 27 May that the combined fleet was moored in Sole, or Southwold, Bay to take on provisions, he immediately ordered his fleet to attack, taking the allies by surprise in the early hours of the 28th. The combined fleet was moored parallel to the shore in its squadrons and divisions: the French squadron, forming the van, was the most southerly, while the Earl of Sandwich's Blue squadron lay to the north of James's Red. The wind was from the east–southeast, the Dutch approaching from the northeast. What happened next was to be the most controversial aspect of the battle, and the cause of both contemporary and later criticism of the conduct of the French. While both the Blue and Red squadrons got underway to the north on the starboard tack, thereby reversing the order of the fleet, d'Estrées got underway to the south on the port tack. The spectacle of the French fleet going in the opposite direction to its British allies was the origin of the charge that the French had deliberately deserted the rest of the combined fleet. In fact, the

French put up a good fight against Adriaen Banckert's Zeeland squadron, which was detached to engage them: up to 450 French mariners were killed, among them the Huguenot admiral, des Rabesnières, who was subsequently honoured with a spectacular funeral at Rochester Cathedral at Charles II's expense (perhaps a tribute as much to his Protestant faith as to his gallantry).[54]

Meanwhile, the British fleet was hotly engaged to the north, with the main force of de Ruyter's attack concentrating on Sandwich's flagship, the *Royal James*, which was burned to the waterline by fireships, and on whichever ship the Duke of York was aboard. Seeing his first flagship, the *Prince*, lose her topmast, standard, flagstaff and jackstaff, with men falling 'wonderful fast about' him, James realised he had to change ships, and moved to the *St Michael* and later to the *London*; but yet again the heir to the throne led a charmed life, escaping even the slightest wound, and displayed throughout the undoubted personal courage that he possessed. Around him, though, all was carnage. Richard Nicholls, the conqueror of New Amsterdam, was 'shot in the breast with a six pounder which stuck

The Battle of Solebay, 28 May 1672: the Duke of York's flagship, the *Prince*, with her maintopmast shot away following a fierce engagement with de Ruyter. Willem van de Velde the Younger. *(Rijksmuseum, Amsterdam)*

in the back of his buff coat' – which is how the ball in question came to adorn his monument in Ampthill church, Bedfordshire. One Vaughan, a volunteer, was struck 'by a great shot that took off his left hand and went through his belly, and left him in a power of saying no more but presenting his duty to the duke and expressing his concern that he had not the honour to die by his side'. Captain Digby of the *Henry*, he who had saved the Mediterranean fleet from catastrophe in 1668, 'kept his station with honour and lost 300 men, at last his hand was shot off upon the quarterdeck and his best lieutenant killed: the poor gentleman, least that should discourage the remainder of his men, instead of going to a surgeon went all along the waist to encourage his men, where another bullet came and killed him'.[55]

Solebay did little to foster greater unity within the combined fleet. Indeed, in the immediate aftermath of the battle the most bitter recriminations were not those between the British and the French, but those between individual officers in the two fleets – Sir Joseph Jordan and Sir John Kempthorne, Sandwich's two subordinate flag officers in the Blue squadron, were both accused of not supporting their commander, while d'Estrées launched a vitriolic attack against his own second-in-command, Duquesne.[56] Meanwhile, Francophobe hysteria was rampant at court, in the navy, and in the coffee houses of London, during the early days of June. Undoubtedly, there were agendas: tales of French misconduct were inevitable at a time when many Englishmen were opposed to the French alliance and the Dutch war. Many had expected the French to betray the British since before the war began, so in that sense, Solebay provided almost reassuring wish-fulfilment.

In fact, there were few, if any, grounds on which to criticise the conduct of the French fleet at Solebay. The French were the van squadron, and would therefore expect to lead the combined fleet's line of battle to sea – unless they received contradictory orders from the commander-in-chief.[57] Both British and French sources indicate that the only order of any sort which d'Estrées received was a verbal one to keep as close to the wind as he could, an order which did not imply a preference for one tack or the other. If d'Estrées had followed the Blue and Red squadrons to the north he would almost certainly have fallen to leeward of the Dutch, and would thus have been at a grave disadvantage; similarly, the direction taken by the British ships was born of pragmatism, rather than design, because in the flood tide between five and seven on the morning of 28 May the ships would already have had their heads to the north.[58]

Why, then, were no clearer orders given by the admiral command of the combined fleet, the Duke of York? In the first place, the Dutch attack was an almost complete surprise, with the allies having placed too much store on intelligence reports which indicated the Dutch were in their own anchorages; consequently, all parts of the combined fleet, including the French, were in considerable confusion for some time.[59] Crucially, the confusion seems to have been particularly great aboard the fleet flagship, the *Prince*, which had begun to careen at two in the morning of the 28th. When the approach of the Dutch was reported at about three, her master noted '[we] cleared ship in God's name', but even so, the ship was only ready for action by seven, half an hour before she engaged and some time after she had got under sail.[60] The ship had been heeled over for the careen and her yards had been topped. Therefore, for an indeterminate amount of time after three it is doubtful whether the flagship could have made many signals at all, and there is no evidence that James ever attempted to communicate with individual ships or squadrons; the only signal recorded in all the contemporary accounts is the general one for the fleet to weigh, namely a gun firing and the *Prince*'s foretopsail being let loose.[61]

At about six, d'Estrées sent one of his officers, Hérouard, to request specific orders, but received in reply only the verbal command to keep close to the wind. The comment of the great naval historian Sir Julian Corbett, that 'it apparently never entered the duke's head to tell [the French] the rear was to lead', makes more sense if it is set in the context of a flagship aboard which confusion reigned, making James forget a simple but essential part of an order whose verbal nature, again, suggests an element of haste. Significantly, James never seems to have suggested, even in private, that the French had disobeyed his orders.[62] But there is, perhaps, rather more to it than that. After all, the making ready of the *Prince* for battle was the responsibility of Captain Sir John Cox and his warrant officers, not of the admiral. James should have been focused entirely on the wider situation, and, given the previous concerns over the competence of the French, he should surely have been especially careful to explain exactly what he wanted to Hérouard. But rather like Lord Raglan and Captain Nolan in the Charge of the Light Brigade, when James issued an order, he expected its meaning to be perfectly clear to all within earshot; he saw no need to explain himself further, perhaps because he felt his intent was obvious, perhaps because he expected nothing but blind obedience from them. It is very likely that this flaw also explains the failure to follow up his greatest victory, the Battle of Lowestoft on 3 June 1665, when James retired to bed after giving an ambiguous order which a timorous courtier was able to twist into a command to shorten sail, allowing the Dutch fleet to escape.[63] The same lack of clarity in issuing orders would be apparent once again, this time fatally for his throne, during William of Orange's invasion in 1688.* If the young Duke of York learned nothing else during his time as a trusted staff

* See Chapter 11.

officer to the great Marshal Turenne, it should surely have been the importance of giving unambiguous orders; but James seems never to have grasped this, perhaps the most vital attribute of any competent officer of any rank, in any age.

If James's conduct during the Battle of Solebay exposed a number of his principal flaws, the campaign of 1673, notably its final battle, demonstrated some of his brother's. There were no further major naval actions in 1672, and, contrary to expectations, the French army failed to completely conquer the United Provinces. In extremis, the Dutch turned to their republic's traditional war leader, the head of the House of Orange: in this case, the twenty-two-year-old William III, the nephew of Charles and James. His uncles' war strategy for 1673 focused above all on a British invasion of the Netherlands, which, it was hoped, would bring them the territorial acquisitions agreed in the Treaty of Dover. But the invasion army of eight to ten thousand men, originally assembled at Blackheath, was shipped only as far as Harwich and then Great Yarmouth, there to await what was hoped to be a successful campaign at sea by the combined fleet, no longer under James but commanded instead by Prince Rupert, now in his fifties, ever more cantankerous, and a notorious Francophobe. Two indecisive battles took place off the Schooneveld in May and June, but early in August, de Ruyter and the Dutch came out once again, at the behest of the republic's new ruler, William of Orange, and Amsterdam merchant interests, vociferous in their demands that rich incoming convoys should be protected.

The battle that occurred off the Dutch coast on 11 August 1673 was known to the British as the Texel, and to the Dutch as Kijkduin. Neither description was geographically correct, although the Dutch name was marginally more so. The action quickly broke up into three separate engagements, with Sir Edward Spragge and the Blue Squadron falling behind to engage the ships of his old rival Cornelis Tromp, while the French in the van moved a considerable distance away, and were relatively little engaged. Prince Rupert, with the Red Squadron in the centre, fought a ferocious battle against de Ruyter, but then sailed to join the Blue, where Spragge had been killed while changing ship; his former flagship, the *Prince*, put up an astonishing defence against successive Dutch attacks. Rupert hoisted a blue flag at his mizzen peak, signalling the French to return to the main action and commit themselves fully, but even though they saw the flag, the Comte d'Estreés and his captains stayed where they were. By nightfall, when the fleets separated, both sides were able to claim the victory, but the Dutch claims were rather more plausible: simply by avoiding defeat, de Ruyter ensured there could be no seaborne invasion, and arguably, saved the Dutch republic in the process.*

The unsatisfactory outcome of the battle immediately generated a storm of suspicion and furious finger-pointing. Even journals and accounts which were clearly written up in the fleet almost at once, several of them probably on the evening of the 11th itself, contained the essential ingredients of the story which swept through London for the following two or three months – and the most essential ingredient of all was the belief that, through one or more of incompetence, cowardice or duplicity, the French had betrayed the British. Aboard the *Royal Katherine*, one of the servants of Captain George Legge (a close ally of the Duke of York) saw the French at about six in the evening 'above a league to windward of us all, and all the time of this our latter engagement the French never bore up a foot but looked one'.[64] In the log of the *Crown*, which had lain just ahead of Rupert's flagship in the Red Squadron, Captain Richard Carter noted that the French 'made so little use of so great an advantage, they kept the wind as near as possible they could, and to the best of my knowledge fired but very few guns after they had so great an advantage of doing considerable service'.[65] Such reports swiftly reached London, leading to an immediate explosion of anti-French xenophobia. On the 12th, Rupert wrote to Charles II to claim that his failure to obtain a decisive victory was due chiefly to the failure of the French squadron, and his report was swiftly embellished in the coffee houses. One story had one of the prince's officers, standing next to him on the quarterdeck, asking '"Does your Highness see the French yonder?" and that the prince replied in a great passion, "Yes, God zounds, do I."'[66]

These early rumours were quickly supported by other evidence from the fleet, as damaged ships returned to the Thames and injured officers and seamen returned to land. The reaction in the coffee houses and alehouses of the capital was predictable. By the 17th, 'the din [was] so great against the French squadron for not bearing in when they had the full advantage of the wind, and might have destroyed all, that the prince will never forgive them ... This is like to breed ill blood ... the whole town has been strangely enraged against the French'.[67] Official narratives of the battle were hurried out on that day, but these only appeared under the (justified) suspicion that they had been doctored to appear more favourable to the French.[68] By the end of August, the popular clamour against the French was already at fever-pitch – 'every seaman's wife having an account from her husband of their having been betrayed, as they call it, by the French' – when two developments served only to

* That was certainly the line taken in the 2015 Dutch film about de Ruyter, released in the English-speaking world as *Admiral: Command and Conquer*, although this played fast and loose with historical accuracy – to the extent of having the French squadron come to grief by running ashore on the beaches of north Holland.

exacerbate the frenzy.[69] First, Rupert himself came to London from the fleet on the 27th 'and complains much of the behaviour of the French in the late engagement ... they did not, he thinks, absolutely run away, but 'twas so like it, that he knows not how else to call it.'[70] Rupert followed up his verbal complaints by publishing his own narrative of the battle at the beginning of September. Secondly, the English attempt to scapegoat their allies, which a few more dispassionate commentators had suggested might have originated in 'the little inclination the English generally have for the French',[71] suddenly received what seemed to be conclusive support from an unexpected quarter. Before the end of August, a relation by the vice-admiral of the French squadron, the Marquis de Martel, was circulating in London. This supported Rupert's position by claiming that Martel had attempted to engage as actively as he could, but that he had not been seconded by d'Estrées and the rest of the squadron, whose inactivity he described as 'shameful'. Martel even hinted that his admiral had given many of the captains secret orders to stay out of the battle as much as possible.[72]

These new revelations gave fresh impetus to the popular disgust against the French squadron, especially when it was learned that Martel's punishment for producing his version of events was to be a spell in the Bastille. It was said that 'every apple-woman makes it a proverb, Will you fight like the French?', while at Claydon House in Buckinghamshire, Sir Ralph Verney was informed that 'the Monsieurs played the pultroons'.[73] The barrage of criticism was sustained throughout September, with an increasing awareness of the impact it was likely to have on the imminent meeting of Parliament. Graphic accounts of the popular hostility to the French fleet and the French alliance continued to fill letters from London until well into October, when Ball wrote 'the hate and malice against the French continues as high as ever ... the French treachery daily appears more palpable'.[74] True, there were also heated arguments and recriminations among the officers of the British fleet, notably between the followers of Prince Rupert and those of the Duke of York. On 16 August 1673, for example, a seaman calling himself 'Tom Tell Truth', serving on the St Andrew, wrote a short note to the secretary of state, Henry Coventry: 'This is to let you understand that Prince Rupert ran away from the Dutch fleet, and that if you do not acquaint his Majesty with it you do the nation a great wrong'.[75] 'Tom' was not the only authority to blame Rupert for the failure to achieve victory: many of his subordinates, and the French, took the same line, accusing the prince of executing perverse tactics during the battle and, above all, of not engaging on the 10th, when he had a greater advantage, or resuming the action on the 12th. But ultimately, these factional battles and 'blame games' paled into insignificance alongside the pervasive and unstoppable 'urban myth' that

Louis XIV had given d'Estreés secret orders not to engage, thus allowing the British and Dutch to shatter each other and hand supremacy at sea to France.

As it was, though, Charles II displayed a remarkably complacent, even dangerous, disregard of such strongly expressed popular opinion. In November 1673, he granted three large diamonds worth £2,200 to d'Estrées and individual jewels worth between £400 and £600 to three other French officers including, astonishingly, even the disgraced Martel.[76] By then, Parliament had met, and there was a torrent of criticism both of the French and of the regime's policies. Charles's actions, so directly contrary to public and parliamentary sentiment, could only weaken his position; indeed, in short order his ministry collapsed, and he was forced to make a humiliating withdrawal from the war in February 1674. The legend of French treachery at the Battle of the Texel proved remarkably durable, and was, indeed an important factor in the growth of anti-French sentiment in Britain during the latter part of Charles II's reign, and into that of his successor. If it is possible to identify one single day when British public opinion shifted from regarding the Dutch, and previously the Spanish, as the principal national enemy, to casting France in that role, then that day would have to be 11 August 1673.

11

Inglorious Revolution

KING CHARLES II DIED on 6 February 1685, just as the roof was going onto his new palace at Winchester and the final stages of planking were under way on the last of his 'thirty new ships', a Second Rate, as yet unnamed, on the stocks at Portsmouth dockyard. His funeral was a curiously understated affair, with little ceremonial of any sort, let alone the kinds of naval references that had abounded in his coronation procession.[1] But eulogists, including several who had known him very well, commended his deep and genuine love of the sea and the navy. Halifax, one of his ministers, remarked that Charles 'had a mechanical head, which appeared in his inclination to shipping and fortifications, etc'.[2] The Earl of Mulgrave, who had commanded a warship during the third Anglo-Dutch war, said of the dead king, 'besides the great and almost only pleasure of mind he appeared addicted to, was shipping and sea affairs; which seemed to be so much his talent both for knowledge, as well as inclination, that a war of that kind was rather an entertainment, than any disturbance to his thoughts'.[3] John Evelyn called him 'the most knowing in naval affairs, and vigilant to improve and maintain the safety and glory of these kingdoms in its highest and chiefest concern, which is certainly its strength at sea … a lover of the sea, and skilful in shipping'.[4] In the navy, as in most other aspects of his rule, he would be a hard act to follow.

Charles II's private quarters had been full of naval mementoes and maritime symbolism, ranging from ship models to paintings and tapestries. Curiously, though, the private quarters of his brother, the new King James II and VII, sometime Lord High Admiral and commander-in-chief of the fleet in battle, contained very little evidence of a similarly profound personal love of the sea and ships. In 1674, the great gallery of the then Duke of York's rooms at St James's Palace displayed Sir Peter Lely's glorious Flagmen of Lowestoft series, now on display in the Queen's House at Greenwich, which immortalises James's brothers-in-arms in his greatest victory. Otherwise, the ducal apartments (at least at that time) seem to have contained not one representation of a ship, nor of the sea.[5] True, James had collections of ship models, charts and maritime books, and Godfrey Kneller's great painting, commissioned to mark his de facto return to the Admiralty in the previous year, showed an anchor and a fleet behind him, but it also displayed James in virtually complete armour, an ensemble that would not have been out of place in a joust two centuries earlier. Newly elevated to the throne, James told his sea-officers of his pride in having been their admiral before their king, but the Kneller portrait and the symbolism of the new reign told a rather different story.[6] There was no coronation procession, perhaps because of fears of unrest, so we will never know whether, in an ideal world, James would have repeated his brother's 'Naval Arch' and chorus of sailors; but the coronation medal bore the legend *A Militari ad Regiam*, 'from the camp to the throne', not 'from the fleet to the throne', and the portraiture and other imagery of the new reign was uncompromisingly military.[7] James II was, first and foremost, a soldier who found himself having to be an admiral; whereas his dead brother had been, first and foremost, a sailor who found himself having to be a king.

Like his father and his long-dead uncle Henry, James set out with an agenda of naval reform. Once the coronation was over, James turned at once to naval matters, ordering the Navy Board to meet him at the Treasury on 29 April.[8] He also inherited a detailed report which Pepys (retained in post as Secretary for the Affairs of the Admiralty) had prepared for King Charles, detailing the need for urgent and expensive remedial work to repair the larger ships of the navy after the austerity-driven cuts to maintenance work during the preceding five years. James encouraged Pepys to investigate options, and early in 1686, he presented a plan for an extensive programme of repairs and new building, overseen by an entirely new body that would replace the existing Navy Board.[9] Pepys justified this suspension of the usual model of naval administration, and its replacement by a special commission, by referring to Jacobean precedent, but the fact that he packed the new body with his own friends, shamelessly libelling potential alternative candidates in order to do so, suggests that his motives were not entirely dispassionate.[10] Even so, the ends justified the means. With the king's unwavering support, the Special Commission successfully repaired the 'great ships' within its specified timescale, namely, by the end of 1688; indeed, it completed work rather sooner than this, in October.[11] When the time came, it was James, rather than Pepys, who proposed a return to the previous structure of the Navy Board, albeit with a new innovation – inspectors who would scrutinise the work of the board members, a system 'borrowed, as His Majesty is pleased to tell me, from the present practice of France'.[12] James II did not benefit from the improvements for which he was ultimately responsible; ironically, William of Orange, the man who overthrew him, would benefit in spades from his predecessor's successful refurbishment of the men-of-war of the Stuart navy.

In the short term, though, the concentration of resources on repairing the 'great ships' meant that the day-to-day operations of the navy suffered. In July 1686, there were only twenty-four warships in commission, along with ten yachts: of these, only four were patrolling the Channel, exactly the same number as had served on the station eighty years earlier, under Great Britain's first King James.[13] Nearly a year later, in May 1687, the numbers were exactly the same, although an impressive squadron, led by the Third Rate *Anne*, was being fitted out to take the new Queen of Portugal to her adopted homeland before making a foray into the Mediterranean. By contrast, in July 1681, the Admiralty commission whose reputation Pepys denigrated at every opportunity had forty-one ships at sea, nine of them operating in the Channel, with nine yachts and another five warships fitting out; in May 1683, despite retrenchment, there were still thirty-three ships at sea. The 'Sallee squadron' set out by the commissioners in 1684 consisted of three Fourth Rates, two Fifths and two Sixths; that maintained by James and Pepys in 1687 was smaller, with two Fourths and three Fifths.[14] Thus, far from being strengthened under a monarch who had more direct experience of the navy than any other in British history, including even his own brother, and an Admiralty secretary of remarkable gifts and dedication to duty, the operational navy during most of the reign of King James II and VII was reduced to levels of weakness not seen for three-quarters of a century.

Despite this, James and Pepys pressed on with other reforms. There were significant improvements in the dockyards. At Portsmouth, for example, a large new storehouse was built in 1686, the double dock was repaired, and the victualling storehouses updated.[15] In 1686, captains were banned from carrying bullion and plate in their warships, and their wages were greatly increased to compensate; but the financial constraints ensured that it was simply impossible to carry through the proposal.[16] In 1687, the king sought to clarify the practice of flags flown by naval and merchant ships, and got Pepys to consult Captain Anthony Young, an Elder Brother of Trinity House who had first gone to sea in a warship during the Ile de Ré expedition of 1627; and, as mentioned previously, he laid down new regulations for the firing of salutes.[17]

James was notably generous to the Chatham Chest, the Elizabethan institution that provided charitable funds for wounded and superannuated seamen. As well as reinforcing the decree that all fines imposed on members of the Royal Navy should go to the Chest, he added a new regulation by which a charge of one shilling per ton per voyage would be imposed on all foreign ships engaged in coastal trade around the British Isles, the proceeds being divided equally between the Chest and

Trinity House, which also provided support to seafarers.[18] He supported the project to complete his brother's unfinished palace at Greenwich by adding another wing to it, joined to the existing one by a hall and chapel, to form a hospital for wounded seamen – the project that would come to fruition under his daughter and son-in-law, forming what is now the Old Royal Naval College, Greenwich.[19] James was more ruthless than his brother when it came to disposing of old warships, another indication of his long-standing concerns for efficiency and economy. Charles had changed his mind several times over whether to dispose of the Second Rate *Old James*, originally built in 1634, and in the late 1670s, he was on the point several times of ordering her expensive reconstruction; but he finally parted with her in 1682. Apart from this, during the whole of the rest of his twenty-five year reign, and excluding captured enemy vessels, Charles disposed of one Third Rate and one Fourth. In the three years and ten months of his reign, though, James sold off the *Unicorn*, *Triumph* and *St George* of the Second Rate, along with the *Adventure* of the Fourth, and several vessels of lesser rates.[20]

King James's religious policy has caused endless debate among historians. Was he a fanatical, proselytising Catholic, whose overtures towards Nonconformists were merely lip service designed to undermine the Church of England? Or was he genuinely committed to religious toleration for all? Whatever the answers, the fact that the king was a committed 'papist', in the derogatory language of the time, impacted on the navy in a number of ways. For instance, it was only natural that he should seek to appoint fellow Catholics to commands in the fleet, but at first, he was stymied by the fact that there were very few suitable candidates. The first appointment of an avowed Catholic was made only in July 1686, when John Tyrwhitt was given command of a guard-ship. But leaving his religion to one side, Tyrwhitt's qualifications for such a position were impeccable: he had held nine commands, all of them substantial warships, and fought all the way through two Anglo-Dutch wars, before being forced out of the navy by the 1673 Test Act, which James now effectively tore up by appointing him. A member of an old and prominent Lincolnshire recusant dynasty, members of which had fought and died for Charles I in the civil wars, this 'true old English cavalier' had been reduced to poverty by his dismissal from the navy, so the king's reappointment of him was as much an act of charity as of religious solidarity – an act entirely consistent with the Stuart brothers' long-standing policy of rewarding those who suffered for their loyalty to the Crown.[21]

During the winter of 1686/87, though, Sir Roger Strickland's 'conversion' became public knowledge. In some respects, Strickland's religion had long fallen into the category of 'worst-kept secrets': the Stricklands, whose senior seat was at Sizergh Castle, Westmorland, were and always had been a staunchly Catholic family, with a few exceptions like Roger who conformed at least nominally to the Church of England in order to hold public office. Strickland was accused of Catholicism several times during his naval career, but always managed to survive. Even so, Pepys consistently opposed his advancement,[22] but as with Tyrwhitt, there were actually no real professional grounds on which to do so. In most respects, Strickland was undoubtedly senior to Arthur Herbert, the Rear-Admiral of England: he was first commissioned as a captain several months before Herbert, and had held many more commissions in total. But Herbert had been promoted over his head in 1678, and never looked back. Strickland effectively retired from the sea in September 1679, and used the profits of his naval service and an inheritance from an aunt to become a wealthy landowner in north Yorkshire; but four days after succeeding to the throne, in one of his first executive acts as sovereign, King James invited Strickland to return to sea, with a prestigious appointment to convey the new English ambassador to Constantinople.[23]

Strickland's return, and subsequent public conversion, dramatically altered the internal politics of the Royal Navy. Sir Roger was a close friend of Lord Dartmouth, who, in turn, was probably the closest thing to a real friend that King James had, while his brother Robert was the vice-chamberlain of the king's household. By the beginning of 1688, Strickland was said to be 'a man now in much request', and part of the inner circle around the king and queen.[24] Several of Strickland's naval followers followed him to the Church of Rome, and were rewarded with commissions or promotions in the ships set out in the summer of 1687, by which time the proportion of Catholic commissioned officers in the fleet stood at some 10 to 12 per cent of the total (roughly the same percentage as in the much larger army).[25]

Arthur Herbert probably saw the writing on the wall, both in terms of the direction naval patronage was taking and the broader policies the king was pursuing in the country at large. He had much to lose: as well as the honorific position of Rear-Admiral of England, which had been created specifically for him in 1684, he also held the lucrative court position of Master of the Robes. He was the obvious first choice to command a fleet in an emergency, as he had been in 1685 when he took charge of the ships mobilised at the time of the Duke of Monmouth's rebellion. 'Some thought if any subject had made his station necessary it had been this man', wrote Bishop Burnet, a well-informed contemporary.[26] Despite all this, in March 1687 Herbert refused outright to agree to the king's pet project, the repeal of the Test Acts that banned Catholics (and Protestant dissenters) from holding public office. Such a move would only have strengthened the hand of Strickland and the other Catholic officers; and, in turn, Strickland's advancement was bound to benefit his friend Dartmouth, Herbert's bitter rival. Herbert's sudden stand on a point of conscience shocked all those who were astonished to discover that he actually possessed such a thing. The king, though, was furious, and dismissed Herbert from all his offices.[27]

In some respects, James's mindset was a throwback to a lost past: the medieval past, when Christendom was united under the Pope, and Crusade was still regarded as a cause worth fighting for. A particularly remarkable proof of this is that the king and queen revived the pre-Reformation practice of royal pilgrimage, in their case to the shrine at Holywell, north Wales, in August 1686, where they prayed for the birth of a male, Catholic heir – a 'miracle' which took place just under two years later. In 1687, the king re-established the long-defunct High Court of Chivalry and 'revived' (or rather, created) the Order of the Thistle. Above all, he had a genuine interest in the progress of the ongoing war against the Ottoman Turks. As early as 1668, for instance, James had informed the Venetian ambassador that 'it was shameful for the Christian princes to leave [Venice] in the lurch' against the Ottoman assault on its fortress of Candia (Crete): 'you [the Doge and Senate] were making such a bold, prolonged and steadfast resistance that assuredly aroused the admiration and astonishment of the world'.[28] In 1683, the Ottomans famously reached the gates of Vienna, and placed the Habsburg capital under siege. That year saw James recommend three officers who wanted to serve in the emperor's army, joining a number who were already serving in it – notably Viscount Taaffe, who had distinguished himself during the siege of the imperial capital.[29] Up to another twenty British officers went out to fight with the imperial forces at the siege of Buda in 1686, among them the king's elder illegitimate son, the soon-to-be-created Duke of Berwick, who stayed on to campaign in Hungary in 1687.[30] In May 1688, James wrote to his son-in-law William of Orange that 'I continue still of the mind I was, and will endeavour to support the peace of Christendom that the Emperor and Venetian[s] may prosecute the war against the Turk'.[31] And it was as a consequence of this quasi-medieval mentality, and his belief in a united Christendom fighting a common enemy, that James embarked on what would have been one of his most provocative and controversial policies, had the full implications of it been realised at the time: the use of naval diplomacy to enhance relations between James's kingdoms and the Order of St John of

Jerusalem, better known as the Knights of Malta, leading, perhaps, in the fullness of time, to the re-establishment of the order in the British Isles.

There had been a number of contacts between the Order of Malta and British rulers during the reigns of Charles I, Charles II, and even during the Commonwealth, with the order seeking the restoration of the lands that had been taken from it during the Reformation. For their parts, Charles and, more especially, James respected the order for its frontline role in the defence of Christendom.[32] In 1675/76, royal warships of Sir John Narbrough's fleet used Malta as a base during the war against Tripoli.[33] During 1687, though, there were no fewer than three British naval visits to Malta: a level of contact unprecedented in the seventeenth century, and which occurred at the same time as negotiations (ultimately unsuccessful) for the restoration of the British properties that the order had lost at the Reformation.[34] The frigate *Crown* called en route to Constantinople with yet another new English ambassador to the Sublime Porte of the Ottoman Sultans, while three ships of the Sallee squadron, the small force which maintained the war against the Moroccan pirate republic of Salé,* visited in March. It remained in the Grand Harbour for the best part of a fortnight, and its commander, Henry Killigrew, was received honourably and entertained lavishly by the Grand Master. Killigrew was accompanied by John, Lord Berkeley, captain of the *Charles Galley*, and Lord William Murray, a son of the Marquess of Atholl, who was serving as a volunteer in the squadron. On 19 November 1687, though, an even more impressive British naval force arrived at Malta. Flying his admiral's flag in the *Anne*, a new 70-gun Third Rate, was the twenty-four-year-old Henry Fitzroy, Duke of Grafton. The eldest surviving illegitimate son of King Charles II, Grafton also held the honorific office of Vice-Admiral of England, and as such was notionally the deputy to the Lord High Admiral – namely his uncle, King James.

The Mediterranean cruise of Grafton's fleet had already been of some diplomatic significance. In addition to renewing the treaties with the Barbary regencies, Grafton had transported from Den Brielle to Lisbon the new Queen of Portugal, Maria Sophia of Neuburg (her husband, King Pedro II, was the brother of Catherine of Braganza, Charles II's widow).[35] This visit to Malta was turned into a particularly spectacular set-piece, calculated to impress, for Grafton's small force, comprising the *Anne*, *Sedgemoor* and *Pearl*, had been substantially reinforced for the occasion. The *Crown*, *Hampshire* and *Mermaid* from the Sallee squadron had arrived in Malta a few days earlier, as had the *Isabella Yacht,* the duke's personal despatch and pleasure boat. There was no obvious strategic or operational reason for any of this, other than to assemble the largest possible force in the Grand Harbour at the same time: in other words, to 'show the flag' in unmistakeable terms. Grafton's original written instruc-

* Between 1686 and 1688, this squadron was based at Gibraltar, with the permission of, and using facilities leased from, the local Spanish authorities: the first sustained use of the port as a British naval base, nearly twenty years before its capture by Sir George Rooke and his fleet.

tions from the king made no mention of a visit to Malta, but this does not preclude the possibility of verbal orders being given by James. The *Anne* needed time in harbour to repair storm damage, but the simultaneous presence of the Sallee squadron suggests that there might have been an element of predetermined co-ordination behind the visit.

In any event, the Knights of St John were suitably impressed. Grafton's arrival in the Grand Harbour was greeted by a salute of at least sixty-one guns, a remarkably generous gesture and one which reflected Grafton's quasi-royal status.[36] The fleet remained at Malta for ten days, and like all the earlier visits by British warships, the visit was taken up by a hectic social round and diplomacy. Grafton's audience with Grand Master Carafa was a great success, primarily because of the presence alongside the duke of his first cousin Henry Fitzjames, the fourteen-year-old younger illegitimate son of King James by Arabella Churchill, the sister of the future Duke of Marlborough. Just as Charles II designed a naval career for Grafton, so James II did for Fitzjames, delighting in reports of 'the early progress he has made in the Trade [seamanship], wherein he doubts not of his arriving at length at a mastership'.[37] Unlike the staunchly Protestant Grafton, though, Fitzjames, the younger brother of the Duke of Berwick, had been brought up as a Catholic, and apparently at once displayed a clear vocation for the Knights of St John; indeed, to flatter him the Grand Master sent four knights of the order to welcome him to the island in person.[38] Fitzjames was given the most honourable form of reception the Grand Masters bestowed, and received a cross of diamonds from Carafa. After the Glorious Revolution, he was received into the order at his father's request, with the nominal title of Grand Prior of England.[39] Whether James intended to give him this title in 1687, which, of course, would imply that he intended at that time to readmit the Order of Malta to Britain and restore its lost lands, is a moot point: but as James spent most of the last thirteen years of his life fully expecting to be restored to his rightful throne at any moment, it is surely inconceivable that he would have awarded titles in exile that he would not have confirmed as soon as he was ensconced in Whitehall once again.

The birth of James's son, James Edward, Prince of Wales, on 10 June 1688, swiftly led to the political crisis that precipitated the so-called Glorious Revolution. At first, though, the navy's response was conventional and time-honoured: 'the fleet express[ed] their joy by firing of guns' when news of the prince's birth was received on 11 June, and did the same on the official day of thanksgiving, 1 July.[40] But the king's policies, both in the navy and the country at large, had alienated a significant number of members of the fleet's officer corps, alarmed by such developments as James's attempts to prevent Huguenots coming over in the royal yachts, and his employment of Catholic officers. And then there was France.

Charles II's attitude towards Louis XIV's realm, like so many of his other attitudes, had always been ambiguous. But James, once the eager pupil of the great French military hero Marshal Turenne, was much more of an unalloyed Francophile: he even happily revealed what can only be described as state secrets about the condition of the Royal Navy to a French envoy. As it happened, the diplomat in question, Bonrepaus, had little need of the king's astonishing indiscretions. He was soon bribing one of the clerks in Pepys's own office, whom he met every Sunday and who provided him with a stream of confidential material, including precise lists of the ships and dispositions of the Royal Navy, and detailed plans of ports and harbours.[41] Meanwhile, in 1686, construction began on a new French royal dockyard at Cherbourg. Although the project was abandoned on grounds of cost after only a couple of years, it could easily have been interpreted as a threat to the south coast of England and, in particular, to the dockyard at Portsmouth (as, indeed, it was when Cherbourg was finally developed into a naval arsenal in the nineteenth century).[42] Despite this, James's attitude seemed complacent, if not complicit: in April 1688, the operational navy still consisted of only twenty-six ships. But as spring turned to summer, naval preparations in the Netherlands looked increasingly ominous, and a larger fleet was ordered to be fitted out. By the beginning of July, one Third Rate, fifteen Fourths and nine other ships were massing in the Thames and the Downs. An admiral's Union flag flew from the maintopmast head of the *Mary*; but the admiral in question was the Catholic Sir Roger Strickland.[43]

Despite what was bound to be the controversial presence of Strickland, the rapid expansion of the fleet actually made it much less Catholic, not more. The king had already appointed all his eligible co-religionists; there were simply no others in warrant posts or merchant ships who could be promoted. Moreover, the growth of the fleet brought thousands of new men onto the lower decks, many of whom were virulently anti-Catholic. Sir Roger Strickland's crass attempt to permit Catholic priests to say mass aboard his ships caused a near-mutiny, so the king had to spent 18 and 19 July 1688 aboard the fleet, placating the men, promising liberty of conscience, and ordering the priests to withdraw.[44] And then, yet again, there was France.

In June, Louis XIV offered James fifteen or sixteen warships to bolster his fleet against William's preparations. This was no secret: indeed, the French wanted to broadcast it as widely as possible, to act as a deterrent to the Dutch. By the time that James decided to investigate the offer, France was rather less convinced of the British king's prospects, and James was soon convinced of the damage French support might do to his reputation; but even so, desultory negotiations for a naval alliance took place at Windsor in early September. Yet again, the king managed to have the worst of both worlds.[45] He ended up with no French naval assistance, but the very fact that it had been contemplated with such apparent seriousness damaged him to an incalculable degree. Many naval men had fought in, and undoubtedly still had memories of, the battles of Solebay and the Texel, fifteen and sixteen years before, so the prospect of serving once again in a combined fleet alongside the supposedly incompetent, duplicitous, and generally hated French, was hardly likely to make them want to fight to the death for King James.

A few days before the king's visit to the fleet, Arthur Herbert surreptitiously left the country and fled to the Netherlands. He had been corresponding with William of Orange for some time, and knew that the prince planned to invade England later in the year. Therefore, he found himself sharing uncomfortable common ground with Captain Edward Russell, Herbert's bitter rival during the latter's command of the fleet in the Mediterranean, from 1681 to 1683. Russell was significantly junior to Herbert, but much better connected; he was a son of the Earl of Bedford, and brother of Lord William Russell, executed in 1683 for alleged conspiracy against Charles and James, and a revered martyr among those who detested the king's policies. Russell had been going back and forth to Holland for the past year, and was deeply involved in the secret discussions of those who opposed James. Thus it was as a representative of his family and name that Edward Russell signed the famous letter of 30 June, inviting William of Orange to come to England to defend the Protestant religion and becoming, in the process, one of the so-called 'immortal seven' signatories. The letter was carried to the Netherlands by Herbert, disguised as a common seaman.[46]

The existence of these 'admirals over the water' strained loyalties within the fleet. Many of James's officers had been promoted by Herbert, or were connected to him or Russell by other ties of loyalty, many of them dating back to their shared service at Tangier in the early 1680s. Many of these so-called 'Tangerines' held parallel commissions in the army, where plotting was rife. Many were uneasy about the king's pro-Catholic policies, and the perception that he was also following too slavish a pro-French line. James ignored all this. It is possible to claim that he did so out of the blinkered wilfulness and rigidity that characterised so many aspects of his rule, but James knew the navy better than almost any other part of the kingdoms that he ruled, and in that respect, there was a not unreasonable logic to his position. True, many officers in the

To the Right Honble GEORGE Lord Dartmouth Master of his Maties Horse Master Gen^ll of all his Maties Ordnance &c. Armory Constable of the Tower & one of his Maties most hon^ble Privy Councell's

Above, left: King James II and VII; statue by Grinling Gibbons, now located in front of the National Gallery, London. *(Author's photograph)*

Above, right: George Legge, Lord Dartmouth, commander of the fleet ordered to repel William of Orange's invasion in 1688. *(Wikimedia Commons)*

Opposite: William of Orange's fleet in unrealistically precise formation. *(Rijksmuseum, Amsterdam)*

fleet owed much to Herbert or Russell; but surely they owed much more to him, the man who had originally commissioned many of them, quite apart from the natural, unthinking obedience that James would undoubtedly have believed all true subjects owed to their anointed monarch.[47] The king, his ministers, and their hired propagandists, all emphasised the message that the prospect facing the nation in the summer and autumn of 1688 was a fourth Dutch war, and a Dutch invasion to outdo the humiliation at Chatham. Pepys's erstwhile brother-in-law Balty St Michel was in no doubt of what was going on, referring gloomily in October 1688 to 'the prospect we have of a Dutch war'.[48] Many of the older captains had fought the Dutch, and could remember the events of 1667; the younger officers would have been brought up on such stories. The king might reasonably have expected them all to support him against the old enemy. What James could not comprehend was that times had changed, and that many had come to regard him as a greater threat to England than a Dutch invasion.

The king also had one powerful advantage that none of his, or his opponent's, admirals possessed: he had personally commanded fleets in action, in exactly the same waters where the issue of the 1688 crisis would be decided. Arguably no one, on either side, knew the potential battleground so well – certainly not William of Orange. James knew the anchorages intimately, he knew the distances, he knew the tides, he knew the sandbanks. If he had been able to appoint an admiral with only

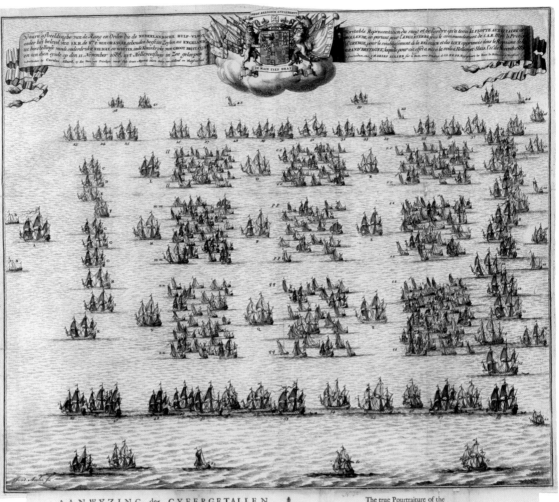

a modicum of his knowledge and experience, he might well have saved his throne. But although the third Anglo-Dutch war had ended only fifteen years before, all bar one of those who had held flag rank during it, and during the second war, were dead.* Consequently, the king had only a very limited number of candidates from whom he could choose. The Duke of Grafton expected the command by virtue of his honorary rank as Vice-Admiral of England and his successful command of the 1687 expedition to the Mediterranean; but Grafton was still only twenty-five, and had never seen action, let alone commanded a ship or a fleet during it. James dealt with his nephew's expectations in his characteristically tactless way, by simply abolishing the office of Vice-Admiral of England and thus removing Grafton's claim at a stroke. It was the second time in five years that the young duke had been passed over for an important command, and this latest slight drove him firmly into the Orangist camp.[49]

Sir Roger Strickland was impossible as a potential commander-in-chief, as even James recognised, although he was retained as vice-admiral: logical in terms of Strickland's seniority and undoubted experience of battle, entirely consistent with James's lifelong favour toward those who had displayed unstinting loyalty toward the House of Stuart, but counter-productive, even downright crass, in the circumstances of the time, thanks to the deep resentment against Strickland in large parts of the fleet. Sir John Berry, nominated as rear-admiral, was undoubtedly a sensible choice, though. A hugely respected veteran who had started out as the boatswain of a ketch in the West Indies twenty-five years earlier, the Devonian Berry had held no fewer than fifteen commands, and should have been unimpeachably loyal. But he was vehemently anti-Catholic, and had bought some former monastic lands in Kent; he seems to have been concerned that these might be reclaimed if the king's policies led inexorably to the restoration of monasteries in England. It was a sign of the times, for if James II and VII could not rely on the loyalty of Sir John Berry, of all men, then he was in serious trouble.

In the circumstances, there was only one realistic candidate for the command of the fleet. (It never seems to have occurred to James to take command himself; whether he was contemplating the likely eventuality of ultimately having to command a land campaign as a general, or was of the mind that kings simply did not command at sea, is impossible to tell.[50]) George Legge, Lord Dartmouth, was the king's personal friend, the man who had probably saved James's life during the wreck of the *Gloucester* in 1682, and who had bravely defended him in the hostile environment of the Exclusion Parliaments.[51] Not only should James have been assured of his loyalty, it was obvious that Dartmouth would lose everything if William won, which should have ensured that he did his

*The one exception, who fitted the bill perfectly in terms of experience and fighting record, was Sir Robert Holmes, but he was now sixty-six, regarded as too old to go to sea (although de Ruyter had died in action at sixty-nine), and indispensable in his post as governor of the strategically important Isle of Wight. Besides, even in his pomp, it is doubtful whether anyone would have seriously contemplated giving the abrasive, unpredictable Holmes the command of a major fleet. But what a counterfactual history of 1688 it might have been if James had!

utmost to fight and repel the invaders. Dartmouth had commanded a
fleet, albeit only a very small one, and not in wartime. Otherwise,
though, his experience was distinctly limited, especially when compared
with the likes of Herbert, Russell, Strickland and Berry. Unlike them, he
had not held a commission during the second Dutch war; unlike them,
he had managed to wreck his first ship after barely a month in command
of her. He was even prepared to confess that his early training as a seaman
was wholly inadequate, although he had subsequently served with
distinction in command of large ships during the campaigns of 1672/73.
His principal services, though, were as a land officer (he was Master of
the Ordnance), a politician (he was an MP before gaining his peerage),
and a courtier (he was Master of the Horse). Above all, Dartmouth's
entire career up to that point demonstrated that he was prone to inde-
cision and self-doubt. He was hardly a Nelson, or even a Beatty; if
anything, he was more of a John Byng.

Nevertheless, Dartmouth hoisted the Union flag at the main of the
Resolution on 3 October 1688, and took command of the fleet tasked
with defeating the Dutch invasion – or, alternatively, the Protestant
crusade to secure English liberties, depending on one's point of view. The
fleet, now consisting of eleven Third Rates, nineteen Fourths, four Sixths
and fourteen fireships, moved to the Gunfleet anchorage off Harwich to
await the invasion fleet that William of Orange was known to be massing
at Hellevoetsluis, under the nominal command of Arthur Herbert.
William was believed to be heading for Yorkshire, where he had considerable support, so the Gunfleet made sense as a base from which to cover
such a move; it made rather less sense if the Dutch headed southwest,
down the Channel. On 30 October, Dartmouth, who had intelligence
that William was about to set out, attempted to sail, but the strong east-
erly wind that brought the Dutch out two days later kept the British fleet
trapped behind the sandbanks. Dartmouth finally managed to get out on
3 November, but by then his ships were too far behind the Dutch to
prevent the landing they made in Torbay on the 5th. King James's fleet
eventually withdrew to Spithead, where it surrendered to the authority
of William of Orange on 13 December.[52]

Much ink has been spilled in attempting to establish how far, if at all,
the outcome of the naval campaign in 1688 can be attributed to a
conspiracy by Orangist, anti-Catholic elements in Dartmouth's fleet, or
else to the weather – the strong east wind that blew William's fleet
down the Channel and kept Dartmouth's behind the Gunfleet, which
gleeful sermonisers proclaimed to be the second 'Protestant wind' to
save England in a hundred years. There certainly was a conspiracy in the
fleet, closely allied to that in the army. Naval men were, as a rule, vehemently anti-Catholic, and were offended by many royal policies; there

were close-knit connections between those who had served under
Herbert in the Mediterranean in the early 1680s; and many personal
and factional concerns were at play.[53]

King James's fifty-fifth birthday was on 14 October 1688, and the
occasion was marked appropriately in the fleet. John, Lord Berkeley,
captain of the *Charles Galley*, invited all the captains to dine with him to
celebrate the auspicious day. The king's health was toasted, and a 21-gun
salute fired.[54] Ironically, though, the dinner might well have provided an
ideal cover and opportunity for talk of treason: Berkeley, who had been
given his first naval commission only three years earlier at the king's
specific direction, would soon be revealed as one of the leading Orangists
in the fleet, and was described by his admiral, Lord Dartmouth, as 'very
pert', an euphemism for downright treacherous. James subsequently
described him as one of the 'most factious and disaffected officers of the
navy'.[55] The young man (he was only twenty-five), was the son of one of
the then Duke of York's oldest adherents, a devoted Cavalier who had
attempted to engineer the escape of King Charles I from Hampton
Court in 1647, and who subsequently served alongside the duke
throughout his campaigns in exile. As in the case of Sir John Berry, if
King James could not count on someone like John, Lord Berkeley, then
his throne had come to rest on very shaky foundations indeed. But
despite Dartmouth's suspicions of the likes of Berkeley, and the evidence
presented to him about the activities of other conspirators, James still
refused to act.[56] The leniency, and willingness to give men a second
chance, which he had displayed throughout his time as Duke of York, still
shaped James's outlook: ironically, a king whom contemporaries and
many later historians damned as an autocrat, ultimately lost his throne
because he was simply not autocratic enough.

Even so, the failure to intercept William's fleet shook James's faith in
Dartmouth; the king considered the failure 'a mystery', and later became
convinced that Dartmouth's 'loyalty was worsted' by 'religion, faction or
interest'.[57] But rather than blame his admiral, the king should have
looked in the mirror. Throughout the time at the Gunfleet, James had
sent Dartmouth orders and 'advice' that made his task more difficult,
forgetting the fact that, during the second and third Anglo-Dutch wars,
the then Duke of York had complained about exactly such interference
from his elder brother and his ministers. For instance, the king told
Dartmouth that he had complete freedom to choose his anchorage,
before adding a rider advising him not to go to the Gunfleet; on
27 October, James advised Dartmouth to sail to the Dutch coast to
attack William as he sailed, before telling his admiral that he left the
matter entirely to his judgement.[58] The king's old fault as a commander,
the giving of unclear and ambiguous orders, had evidently not deserted

him with age. Even so, James was still confident of ultimate victory in a land battle. After all, he was a pupil of the great Marshal Turenne, and a triumph in battle over his ungrateful nephew and son-in-law William, while leading the new army that he had personally built up from just under 9,000 men in 1685 to 21,000 in 1688,[59] would have been proof positive that God really was on the side of the Catholic king. But his best generals defected (notably the best of all, John Churchill, the future Duke of Marlborough), his troops deserted, and James was laid low by a severe psychosomatic nose bleed. He lost his nerve, returned to Whitehall, and could do nothing to prevent the conquering Dutch army entering London on 18 December 1688, cheered by crowds waving oranges on sticks.[60]

James had failed in the two areas where he was undoubtedly experienced, competent and successful: as a general, and as an admiral. But in the latter capacity, he could still draw on extensive reserves of residual loyalty in the navy, and he drew on them now in order to devise and order his last naval operation as de facto King of England. James actually had a remarkable pedigree when it came to elaborate, deeply laid escape plans, having devised his flight from Parliamentarian custody at Hampton Court Palace with extraordinary perspicacity at the age of just fourteen. Now, over forty years later, he masterminded a hastily improvised, audacious, and barely known, Jacobite naval conspiracy to smuggle himself and his family out of the country.

The confusion of loyalties in the navy – and, indeed, the sheer confusion of the entire Glorious Revolution – is epitomised by the 15-gun salute fired by the Third Rate *Cambridge* as she came into Spithead on 24 November 1688, to honour the infant Prince of Wales, who was then in Portsmouth.[61] For one thing, the new regime in London, headed by William of Orange, was already denouncing the prince as a changeling, an infant smuggled into the queen's bedchamber to replace the royal couple's real, dead, child. The prince had arrived in Portsmouth on 17 November, and would remain there until 8 December, when he was taken back to the capital. But he was in Portsmouth for one very specific reason. When the *Cambridge* saluted him, perhaps the very last occasion when a British warship saluted the senior line of the House of Stuart, those closest to James Edward Stuart were scheming frantically to get him out of the country, and Portsmouth, which James had garrisoned with large numbers of Irish troops, had been their first choice as an escape route.[62]

The sending away of the prince, the future and hope of his bloodline, was perhaps the most vital ingredient of all in James's strategy following

William's successful invasion. His unbending personality made it impossible for him to contemplate the notion of working with his treacherous nephew and a free Parliament, so the only honourable course open to him was to get his family, and finally himself, to safety. When all was said and done, after all, James had experience on his side: he had been in exile before, no fewer than three times, and he had returned each time, so who was to say there would not be an identical outcome now? His first priority was to get the queen and Prince of Wales out of the country via a royal yacht sailing from Portsmouth, 'that with as much secrecy as may be, and so that trusty men may be put in the yachts, that he [the prince] may be exposed to no other danger but that of the sea'. Dartmouth's refusal to co-operate stymied this plan.[63] James already had an alternative strategy in place, though. On 30 November, the king wrote an order in his own hand for the *Isabella* and *Anne* yachts to sail down to Erith on the following day.[64] On the following day, he sent orders to Randall MacDonnell, the Irish Catholic captain of the frigate *Assurance*, lying at Sheerness, to have her ready for sea at short notice. The *Assurance* was soon joined by the *Henrietta*, an elderly Third Rate, which James ordered to Sheerness on or about the 8th; the Sixth Rate *Sallee Rose*, which had been captured from the eponymous pirate republic in north Africa; and the two guard-ships on the station, the *Eagle* and *Samson*.[65] On the 4th, the king ordered William Sanderson, captain of the *Isabella Yacht* (son of Ralph, still the captain of the *Fubbs Yacht* at this time), to carry the Comte de Lauzun to the continent before returning to Margate to await further orders. The royal yachts usually returned to their anchorages off Deptford or Greenwich, or, if employed in cross-Channel operations, to Dover, so James clearly wished to have her available away from her usual (and thus expected) moorings.[66] Lauzun, an old comrade-in-arms of James from his time in the French army thirty years earlier, was a close confidante, and the man most responsible for arranging the escape of the queen and the infant Prince of Wales; in 1689–90, he would command the king's army in Ireland.*

However, James's plans for the *Isabella* were stymied by an astonishing sequence of events at Margate.[67] Sanderson brought her to an anchor there on the 8th, but there was no sign of his passenger, and within forty-eight hours, he found the entire area 'up in arms'. He sent a boat toward the shore to try and find out what was going on, but some two hundred 'horse and foot' lined the beach and forced the boat to retire, lest it be seized by this ad hoc militia. Sanderson consulted his officers and resolved to return to the Thames, but before they could do so, just after midday on 13 December and when the captain and his officers were at dinner, a ship suddenly rammed the yacht on the starboard quarter. Sanderson ran up onto the deck, assuming an accidental collision had

* His imprisonment by Louis XIV in the early 1670s led some later writers to suggest him as a candidate for 'the Man in the Iron Mask'.

taken place, but was immediately accosted by two men, 'one making a thrust at me and the other clapping a pistol to my breast' and saying '"Yield you dog, your king is taken"'. By now there were about eighty boarders on the deck of the yacht, all armed with swords and pistols, who were making prisoners of Sanderson's crewmen. The yacht's cable was cut and she was brought alongside Margate pier, where the boarders tried to persuade Sanderson to go ashore. He refused, but at about four o'clock they told him he had to go ashore 'by fair means or by foul'. He called his officers and men together to witness the fact that he was being taken out of the yacht by force, and went to the White Hart inn with the leaders of 'the rabble'. He demanded to know their authority, saying he wanted a magistrate summoned, but they responded that 'their authority was sufficient, setting defiance to all authority and government'. Sanderson's papers were taken from him, after which he was allowed to return to the yacht.

The next day, Sanderson was taken again to the White Hart. The intervention of a 'deputy' briefly freed the captain, but confusion seems to have reigned among the rebels, and he was swiftly made a prisoner again. On the 15th, he was taken to Canterbury, where the Marquess of Winchester freed him on condition that he did not move the yacht until further orders were received. He got back to the *Isabella* on the 16th, but found 'the rabble keeping possession of the yacht, committing several riots and disorders aboard, [such] as drunkenness and keeping women aboard all night'. When Sanderson's officers objected, the rebels 'abused them, beat the boatswain, and [turned] him ashore at two o'clock in the morning'. The captain protested to the leaders, but 'they taking no notice of it continued their rudeness'. An uneasy truce then reigned for the rest of the month, through the storms, snow and great frosts of a hard December. Sanderson and the crew of the *Isabella* spent Christmas and New Year under effective arrest at Margate, only receiving official orders to return to Greenwich on 2 January.

While Sanderson was dealing with the state of virtual anarchy in Margate, events had moved to a climax in London, the Thames and the Medway. On 10 December, the king wrote to Dartmouth, ordering any ships that remained loyal to sail for Ireland: 'never any prince took more care of his sea and land men, as I have done, and been so very ill repaid by them', James reflected, bitterly.[68] Dartmouth later recorded that he 'received [this letter] the 14th by the common post, Mr Pepys or whom this was committed to should be answerable for the delay, for this letter came not till after the Council of War [on 13 December] that sent to the Prince [of Orange] upon the letter from the Lords at Guildhall [ordering him to place the fleet under William's command], and the quitting of the Roman Catholic officers'.[69] Of course, it suited Dartmouth to claim that the king's letter was 'lost in the post', as it covered his back if James regained power; but it was probably academic, as it seems highly unlikely that any entire crews would have been willing to take their ships to Ireland, even if they could have managed to get out of Spithead under the guns of other warships loyal to William of Orange. Meanwhile, the king had made his first attempt to escape on 11 December, taking a rowing boat from Whitehall to Vauxhall and dropping the Great Seal over the side during the crossing, in a (successful) attempt to ensure that no lawful Parliament could be summoned by his enemies. He took a coach down the Kent Road and reached Faversham, intending to take ship from there to France, but he was identified and detained.[70] Early on the 13th, the *Assurance* set sail from Sheerness, bound for Margate, perhaps to escort the king's vessel to France, 'but at 9 (hearing the news of the king's being taken) came back into the Swale'. The *Crown* was starting to unload her lower tier of guns, but 'upon a sudden private information [of the king being captured?] we took them in again'.[71]

On the following day, the 14th, the captains at Sheerness agreed to surrender their ships to William, and Captain Richard Trevanion of the *Henrietta*, the commander-in-chief in the anchorage, went up to London. Trevanion was very much a Cavalier of the 'old school'. His father, Colonel Jack Trevanion of Caerhays, Cornwall, had been killed at the siege of Bristol in 1643, aged only thirty, and his brother John was a gentleman usher to King James. Richard had received his first commission as a lieutenant, and four subsequent captain's commissions, from James when the latter was Duke of York and Lord High Admiral; his dependability and competence can be gauged by the fact that unlike the vast majority of his colleagues, he was almost never unemployed during over two decades as a commissioned officer. He was an obvious man for the king to turn to in his hour of extremity, and was in London when James returned there from Faversham, under escort, on the 15th. It would have been perfectly possible for the king and Trevanion to have met some time on the 16th or 17th, particularly if his brother John ensured a private audience for him. James certainly had a Medway escape route in mind when, having been told that William wanted him to withdraw to Ham House at Richmond, he said he would prefer to go to Rochester – only a short boat journey from Trevanion's and MacDonnell's ships. The king went down river by barge, arrived at Rochester on the 19th, and, with imminent escape at the forefront of his thinking, attempted to settle as many of his affairs as he could, for instance by giving instructions to sell his £3,000 of Royal Africa Company stock and his £10,000 of East India Company stock.[72]

Once again, the immediate preliminary to his escape plan was an attempt to contact Dartmouth, who had been ordered by William (as

James presumably knew) to take his fleet round to the buoy of the Nore. On the 21st, the king wrote to ask him whether he planned to obey this order or to remain where he was. James's message was so secret that it could not be committed to paper, but was conveyed verbally by another captain of a warship at Sheerness, Edmund Elliott of the *Sallee Rose*. Although it seems likely that he was a fellow Cornishman, Elliott was much younger than Trevanion, having received his first commission only in 1685. But he was highly regarded by the king and had been promoted by Dartmouth and Strickland, the admirals whose fall from power was now obvious to all. Quite what the king wanted Elliott to say to

The escape of James II by boat from Rochester. *(Rijksmuseum, Amsterdam)*

De Koning van Engelant, Iacobus d'II, vlugt bij naght uijt Rochester, na Vranckrijck.

Dartmouth is a mystery. Perhaps it was a plan for the royal family's escape to the fleet, or an attempt to obtain a guarantee that Dartmouth's ships did not obstruct that escape. Given James's disenchantment with the fleet's performance in the preceding campaign, the second of these interpretations is more plausible, but the exact content of the message must remain open to debate. Dartmouth claimed that he sailed immediately in response to James's message: this was probably just an invention to cover his back, for there is no record of Dartmouth, his ship, or any other vessel, leaving the main fleet at this time.

As it was, Elliott never delivered the message, which was delivered instead by Captain David Lloyd, an old friend of Dartmouth's, who had acted as his agent in the early 1680s. Lloyd was a Welshman, from Ffos-y-Bleiddiad in Ceredigion; moreover, he was also a groom of the bedchamber to the king, and the only naval captain of the age who had been able to maintain a parallel career in the royal household.[73] As such, he might have been in contact with other members of that household, several of whom were related to officers in the navy, and who were heavily involved in facilitating the king's escape from England.[74] However, Lloyd's ship, the brand-new and provocatively named *Sedgemoor*, only returned to Plymouth from the Mediterranean on 17 December; according to one report, she was carrying a Knight of Malta and twelve priests, but 'it is thought they have come to a bad market'.[75] Despite the fact that his ship had only just returned home, Lloyd must somehow have met Elliott and then got to Dartmouth's flagship in the Downs within five days, bearing the king's cryptic message.[76] Meanwhile, the *Sedgemoor* herself also seems to have been moving into position to take part in the royal family's escape, which suggests that Lloyd must have had the connivance at least of his first lieutenant and acting successor, Thomas Bulkeley, a fellow Welshman (a native of Anglesey), whose uncle was master of the king's household.[77] The ship's movements are unclear, as her log was lost when she was wrecked on the Kent coast in a snowstorm, barely a fortnight later; but on Christmas Eve she put in to Boulogne Bay to land Henry Fitzjames, the king's illegitimate son, who had been serving aboard her as a volunteer, and there was a rumour that she was meant to embark the king at Deal on Christmas Day, in order to convey him to France. If so, the *Sedgemoor*'s potential role in history had already been overtaken by the fast-moving events in London and at Rochester.

For William of Orange, his father-in-law's continued presence in England was an embarrassment and a huge political problem. Admittedly, allowing him to go into exile opened up the possibility of ongoing conflict and French efforts to restore him; but all of that would be in the medium to long term, and William's most pressing need was to resolve the short-term political crisis presented by the divided loyalties of many in the political, military and naval elites. Whether William knew of James's conversations with Richard Trevanion, and gave the latter explicit orders to expedite an escape, or hinted that no serious effort would be made to obstruct what he and the king proposed to do, will almost certainly never be known. But Trevanion returned to his ship at Sheerness on the 21st, and must have immediately procured a local fishing boat for transporting the king to France. On the following day, William withdrew the guards from the river side of James's lodging (since named Abdication House, on Rochester High Street). During the night of the 22nd, MacDonnell guided the king through the secluded, heavily wooded garden, down to the river, where Trevanion was waiting in a rowing-boat.

They set off downstream, accompanied by several attendants and by the Duke of Berwick, Henry Fitzjames's brother. But wind and tide made it impossible to reach the fishing smack awaiting them at Sheerness. They were forced to divert instead into the Swale and to make for Trevanion's ship, the *Henrietta*, but the Cornish captain was doubtful how his men would react to the embarkation of the king, although he believed his officers would stand by him. The fugitives therefore went aboard another unit of the Sheerness squadron, the guard-ship *Eagle* commanded by Robert Wilford, whose loyalty to James was known to be firm.[78] When daylight broke on the 23rd, Trevanion was able to get the king and his party aboard the fishing smack, where MacDonnell joined them. A tense, rough crossing was enlivened by Trevanion's farcical attempt to fry bacon, only to discover there was a hole in the bottom of the pan; with typical naval ingenuity, he plugged it with a rag soaked in pitch, and James duly declared that he had never eaten or drunk 'more heartily in his life'.[79] The royal party landed safely at Ambleteuse on Christmas Day.

A daring, hastily improvised enterprise, seemingly rooted in the close family connections between individual naval officers (most of them Celtic) and members of the king's household, had achieved its one objective in spectacular fashion. By doing so, it ensured that for the next seventy years, British politics would be sometimes dominated, sometimes subverted, and always challenged, by nothing less than an alternative royal dynasty, and an alternative model of what Britain could be: a Jacobite Britain.

12

—→←—

The Stuarts and the Sea, II:
The 'Jacobite Navy'

THERE IS A STORY which goes something like this. In the winter of 1798, an elderly, scarlet-clad cardinal of the Roman Catholic Church stepped on board the British warship *Agamemnon* in the Bay of Naples. Like many others, he was fleeing before the advancing armies of revolutionary France. Unlike the others, he might, perhaps, have had conflicting thoughts as he was welcomed aboard the vessel that would carry him to safety; for if circumstances had been different, the ship might have been his, and he the 'HM'. He was Henry Benedict Stuart, Cardinal Duke of York, the titular Jacobite 'King Henry IX' of England. He was the grandson of the prince and admiral who had commanded the Royal Navy in the battles of Lowestoft and Solebay, and done so much to create the fighting force that now offered him sanctuary.

The story claims that Henry, the younger brother and nominal successor of Bonnie Prince Charlie, was given charity by the captain commanding the British ship. 'He was accommodated with a part of the Captain's cabin and proper apparel, suitable to his dignity, furnished him. He remained on board seven weeks, during which period the ship was thrice engaged in action.' The captain then 'landed him in the Austrian territories, forcing upon him £100 to defray his expenses to Vienna. The old man shed tears when he left his benefactor, and was regretted by all on board, to whom he was endeared by his mild and unassuming manners.' The captain is said have spoken of the cardinal 'with admiration, and said "that man's example would almost make me a convert to the Catholic faith"'.

A few months later, after his fortunes had been restored, the cardinal returned aboard the *Agamemnon* in Genoa. 'His delight at seeing his deliverer was sincere. In the fullness of his gratitude, he embraced all the Officers and ran about the ship shaking hands with the crew.' He repaid what he owed, and offered the captain three times the sum, which the latter refused. According to the story, when the Cardinal Duke finally parted from the captain he gave him 'a sword and a cane, which the "Pretender" had used all his life; they were plainly mounted in silver, and highly valued' by their recipient.

The captain in question was Horatio Nelson.

Unfortunately, this wonderful tale is probably wholly apocryphal.[1] The Cardinal Duke did not leave Naples on a British warship; he set sail in a small vessel that he had hired. Moreover, Nelson had not been in command of the *Agamemnon* since 1796: at the time of Henry's flight, he was Rear-Admiral of the Blue, flying his flag in the *Vanguard*. Even so, it is a remarkable quirk of history that Henry Benedict Stuart, grandson of King James II and VII, the last Lord High Admiral to command a fleet in battle, lived long enough to hear of the death of Nelson at Trafalgar.[*] One of the cardinal's few remaining Jacobite adherents was even moved to poetry by the battle: the titular Duke of Melfort penned the unremittingly awful 'In Nelsonis mortem et victoriam carmen'. Tellingly, though, he dedicated it, not to Cardinal York, 'King Henry IX', but to the Hanoverian Prince of Wales, the future King George IV.[2]

King James II expected to regain his crowns in very short order, and to regain them by way of an invasion of Ireland. To facilitate this, a large French expedition set out from Brest on 17 March 1689: a fleet of over twenty warships, thirteen of which were ships of the line, carrying 4,500 men. Although they were, of course, French, James acted as though they were his own: he hoisted his own standard aboard the flagship *St Michel*, and insisted that the rest of the fleet should fly British colours.[3] This force landed the king at Kinsale, setting him on the course that would eventually lead him to defeat at the Battle of the Boyne in June 1690 and to his subsequent ignominious flight back to France, an act of desertion that destroyed much of his credibility among his Irish subjects. But the voyage back to France was significant in another respect: it was the last time that the sometime Lord High Admiral went to sea. Nevertheless, the deposed king continued to demonstrate his interest in, and knowledge of, naval matters. In 1690, for example, he visited the Paris observatory, the original model on which his brother's foundation at Greenwich had been based.[4] More importantly, he was closely involved in the planning of all the various French invasion attempts on his behalf. In April and May 1692, he was at Caen, planning the invasion that was intended to be launched from the Cotentin Peninsula before the British and Dutch fleets could unite to wage the summer's campaign. But this scheme had depended on the French Mediterranean fleet arriving at Brest to join with the Comte de Tourville's force that already lay there, and the former was severely delayed by adverse weather. Tourville, though, had been given orders by Louis XIV to attack the enemy *whatever their strength*, and that is precisely what he did on 19 May 1692, when his fleet of forty-four ships engaged the combined Anglo-Dutch fleet of eighty-two under Admiral Edward

[*] Another quirk of history had occurred in December 1796, when Nelson, temporarily flying his commodore's pennant in the *Minerve*, captured the Spanish frigate *Santa Sabina* near Elba: her captain was Don Jacobo Stuart, a great-grandson of King James II. There was also a strong naval element to the stories of the two brothers who turned up in Scotland in the 1820s, claiming to be the legitimate grandsons of Bonnie Prince Charlie – their father, an otherwise obscure lieutenant RN, supposedly having been entrusted to the naval officer and future admiral John Carter Allen for 'safe keeping'. Despite the inherent implaus-ibilities of their story, the Sobieski Stuarts gained a following, and became responsible for the invention or embellishment of many elements of the 'traditions' of clans and tartans which continue to pervade (or blight, depending on your point of view) Scottish culture to the present day.

Russell. The English admiral had been involved in covert negotiations with the Jacobites for some time, but now he held true to his allegiance to William of Orange. Although the heavily outnumbered French fleet did heroically well in the open sea, it was forced to retreat, splitting into several smaller forces as it did so. Three ships, including Tourville's huge flagship, *Soleil Royal*, went to Cherbourg, where they were destroyed on 3 June; on the same day and the next, Russell burned the twelve ships that had sought refuge at La Hogue, further around the Cotentin Peninsula.[5]

Although the burning of the ships at La Hogue decisively ended any chance of a French invasion of Britain in 1692, James could not help but cheer as he watched from the clifftops: 'none but my brave English could do so brave an action!' Quite what the senior French officers standing around him made of this is not recorded.[6] In the aftermath of Barfleur/La Hogue, the king was also said to have sent his congratulations to Admiral Edward Russell.[7] He must have done so through gritted teeth: after all, it was he who had granted Russell his first captain's commission, in June 1672, during his last campaign at sea, and he who insisted on Russell's promotion in 1677.[8] Similarly, James had promoted the careers of many of Russell's captains, young 'gentlemen' like Basil Beaumont, Ralph Delaval and Anthony Hastings, who had benefited from Charles's and James's encouragement of their kind, and who were commanding ships that Charles and James had built: twenty-five of their 'thirty new ships' made up nearly half the British force in the battle. Consequently, when the king spoke proudly of 'my brave English', he was being literally correct. In the longer term, though, and once he had time to reflect, the defeat of Barfleur/La Hogue shattered James's increasingly fragile self-confidence. He blamed himself for the disaster, convincing himself that his very presence had blighted the French preparations: God had rejected his cause, so he could only be a Jonah.[9] By 1696, though, James was again optimistic enough to become actively involved in formulating plans for a French invasion intended to capitalise on the hoped-for success of a plot to assassinate William III. He went to Calais with his soldier son, the Duke of Berwick, to take charge of twenty warships and 150 transports, but the plot was betrayed by an informer, and the old king went ashore for the last time.[10]

While the exiled James and his followers waited for the inevitable miracle that would restore them to their patrimonies, daily life settled down into a humdrum routine at the palace of Saint-Germain. A number of the naval Jacobites played prominent parts at the court-in-exile: Richard Trevanion and Randal MacDonnell, architects of James II's escape from England, were rewarded with posts as grooms of the bedchamber, while Sir William Jennens and Sir Roger Strickland were also prominent figures at court.[11] MacDonnell was appointed to James's war council in 1692, and was behind a scheme for a landing at the mouth of the Shannon to take place simultaneously with the invasion of England that was ultimately thwarted at La Hogue.[12] David Lloyd was the go-between in negotiations between the Jacobites and the likes of Edward Russell, commander of William III's fleet, and John Churchill, the future Duke of Marlborough, even carrying a letter from King James's daughter, Princess Anne, back to her father.[13]

The Jacobite naval officers were hardly a band of brothers. Old jealousies quickly resurfaced: by 1691, for instance, Sir William Jennens and Sir Roger Strickland were at loggerheads, with the former complaining bitterly that the king undervalued him. 'I could heartily wish His Majesty had the same esteem for me as the French have ... I am [branded] a traitor if I take one false step in what relates to the sea', grumbled the ever-cantankerous Jennens.[14] His disillusionment increased in the years that followed, and in 1698 he suddenly returned to England, hoping to obtain a pardon. His abrupt departure stunned the court in exile at Saint-Germain, but Jennens's pathetic fate soon provided a terrible example: rebuffed by William III's ministers, the old captain drifted off into obscurity, hawking his services to whoever might accept them, eventually dying, alone and friendless, in Lisbon.[15]

While James II's naval 'old guard' squabbled among themselves in the crowded corridors and rooms of Saint-Germain, a Jacobite presence still fought a war at sea in the name of the Catholic king. From 1689 onwards, James issued commissions to significant numbers of privateers: around forty in 1692 and 1693 alone. Unsurprisingly, the king, deprived of the income he had been accustomed to in England and dependent on a pension from Louis XIV, was keen to enforce his right to one-tenth of the proceeds of the prize goods captured by the ships that acted in his name.[16] The Jacobite men-of-war operated primarily out of Breton and Norman ports, such as St Malo and Morlaix, and were often commanded by Irishmen, such as the Walshes and the Geraldines, who commanded several ships in the 1690s.[17] These privateers were manned to a considerable extent by their fellow countrymen, especially after the capitulation of Limerick in October 1691 and the subsequent 'flight of the wild geese', and they often returned to hunt in familiar waters. Right up to the end of the great war between Britain and France in 1713, many such ships thronged the coast of Munster in particular, preying on British or Dutch shipping, and providing an important point of contact between local Jacobites and the exiles in France.[18] The *Prince de Galles*, captured in 1693, was commanded by Thomas Tully, and manned almost entirely by Irishmen. Her crew included the likes of Francis Keagher, a Galway lad who claimed he was pressed by some of Tully's men and made to sweep the decks for nothing more than his victuals, and Morris Dessett, who

Above, left: Henry Benedict Stuart, Cardinal Duke of York. *(National Library of Scotland)*

Above, right: Edward Russell, Earl of Orford. Initially promoted by James, Duke of York, he actively conspired against his old master in 1688 and defeated his invasion fleet at Barfleur/La Hogue in 1692. Godfrey Kneller. *(© National Maritime Museum, Greenwich, London, BHC2993)*

said some of the crew had got him drunk in a Nantes tavern and pressed him aboard the ship; but as they were being interrogated by English captors, there may well have been an element of 'they would say that, wouldn't they?' about their stories.[19]

Other Jacobite privateers were based at Dunkirk, and were more involved in operations off the Scottish coast. From 1691 to 1694 they provided supplies to the Bass Rock, the only part of the British Isles to remain under Jacobite control during that period, and their number included the Scot Robert Dunbar, who terrorised the coastal shipping along the coast between the Firths of Forth and Moray.[20] The Jacobite privateers often sailed in company with men-of-war of the regular French navy, and from 1693 they had to have French commissions alongside those of the exiled king (although this policy was swiftly reversed, for reasons that are unclear). Indeed, the lines between the Jacobite and French 'navies' was often distinctly blurred: royal warships were loaned to the privateers on several occasions, such as in 1693/94 when Dunbar successively commanded *Le Sauvage* and *La Railleuse,* and in 1695 when Peter Nagle commanded *Le Marin.*[21] These vessels, and their French counterparts, wreaked havoc on British coastal shipping. In the middle of June 1693 alone, for example, they captured nearly a third of an entire collier fleet from the Tyne, over thirty merchantmen off North Wales, several more ships on the Irish coast, and two Sixth Rate frigates that were convoying mackerel boats off the North Foreland.[22]

A number of Jacobites were granted commands in the French navy itself. Peter Nagle commanded a French frigate in 1689, while the incorrigible Sir William Jennens described himself as 'captain under the Admiral of France' aboard the flagship *Soleil Royal* in 1690, but this was probably a typical Jennens exaggeration.[23] He also interrogated English prisoners, flying into 'a great rage' when informed that the British admiral, the Earl of Torrington, had more than thirty ships, and sent letters ashore, promising pardon to any naval officers who came over to serve James II while also claiming that he, as a Protestant, was proof that James would allow freedom of worship to any who took such a step. Jennens also played a prominent part planning of the proposed Franco-Jacobite invasion of 1692.[24] Thomas Smith, a former cavalry officer who held two naval commands before the Glorious Revolution, also served the French: in 1708 he piloted a squadron of six galleys into the mouth of the Thames, intending to attack Harwich, and was awarded the command of the frigate *Nightingale*, which was captured by the galleys and taken into the French navy as a prize. But he, in turn, was captured in the following year, and executed as a traitor. A French Protestant galley slave, who took part in the action, observed:

> he was condemned to be hanged, drawn and quartered, which was duly carried out in the way that they deal with traitors in England. He was struck in the face by his still living heart. I saw in 1713, when I was in London, pieces of his body exposed all along the Thames-side. A good lesson to those who like him, give way to their feelings to such an extent that they betray their own country.[25]

The most prestigious, but also most nominal, command in the French navy to be bestowed on a Jacobite went to King James's illegitimate son, Henry Fitzjames, created Duke of Albemarle by his father in 1696 – perhaps significantly, the title borne by the man who had engineered the previous restoration of the legitimate monarchy, in 1660. Fitzjames's experiences on the Duke of Grafton's Mediterranean voyage in 1687 seem to have turned his inclinations toward the sea. He served with the French at the Battle of Lagos Bay in 1693, was given the command of the (inactive) Toulon squadron in 1696, and was apparently intended by his father for high rank in the navy if James was restored.[26] In a sense, both his actual and hypothetical careers hark back to a much earlier time, when Grand Priors of England had commanded at sea as admirals of the king's navy; but at the end of the seventeenth century, this was merely proof of just how out of touch with contemporary British politics and popular concerns King James Stuart had become.

James II and VII died at Saint-Germain on 5 September 1701. His thirteen-year-old son was immediately proclaimed king by the Jacobite exiles, and recognised as such by Louis XIV of France, who had made a promise to do so to the dying James. The young monarch in exile, known in Britain as the Pretender, inherited a number of his father's old officers, who might have given him advice about the Royal Navy and how to govern it: Sir Roger Strickland lived on at Saint-Germain until 1717, while Richard Trevanion continued to serve as a groom of the bedchamber until the following year. By then, though, the upheaval that followed the death of 'James III's' half-sister Queen Anne in 1714, leading to the accession of the distantly related (but Protestant) Georg Ludwig of Hanover as King George I, had brought much needed new blood to the 'Jacobite navy'. In 1715, George Camocke, an Irish Protestant who had held a number of commands since 1695, went over to the Jacobites.[27] His defection might have been inspired in part by the fact that he had just been dismissed from the Royal Navy for misconduct, but he was also a protégé of the Duke of Ormonde, who had just declared his allegiance to the 'Old Pretender'. In October 1715, James Edward appointed Camocke Admiral of the White – a non-existent squadron of a non-existent navy. In 1718, though, he hoisted a real flag as a rear-admiral in the Spanish fleet. Camocke attempted to buy the defection of Admiral George Byng, who commanded the Mediterranean fleet, with 100,000 pieces of eight and the promise of a dukedom, with a reward of £10,000 going to every naval captain who pledged loyalty to King James.[28] Such schemes came to nothing, as did all the other negotiations for support from foreign powers that 'Admiral' Camocke subsequently embarked upon. Disillusioned and bankrupt, by the early 1720s he was secretly feeding information to the Hanoverians. When this was discovered, the Jacobites banished him; Camocke eventually died in great poverty.

Equally unsuccessful were the grand naval projects of Peregrine Osborne, second Duke of Leeds, who, as Marquess of Carmarthen, had been a prominent admiral in the 1690s, a successful yacht designer, and an unlikely friend of Tsar Peter the Great, whom he introduced to his favourite drink, brandy with peppers.[29] Leeds went over to the Jacobites in 1714, and subsequently attempted to suborn Admiral John Baker, then commanding George I's fleet in the Mediterranean, by offering him

£200,000 and an earldom; Baker's fleet would then be used to transport Irish troops from Corunna for an invasion of the British Isles. Like so many Jacobite schemes, this, not to put too fine a point on it, was pure fantasy. Leeds, of all people, should have known that even if an admiral changed sides, the likelihood of him carrying the several thousand men under his command with him were distinctly slim. Even so, Leeds was appointed admiral and commander-in-chief of the 'Jacobite navy' in April 1716.[30] At much the same time, attempts were made to win over John Norris, the admiral commanding in the Baltic, but these, too, fell on deaf ears, as had an earlier attempt to win over the Scots-born Admiral Sir James Wishart by granting him the honorific post of Vice-Admiral of England, second in precedence only to the Lord High Admiral.[31]

Elsewhere, the Jacobites had rather more success in acquiring 'naval' forces, albeit ones with a distinctly dubious provenance. Lord Archibald Hamilton, seventh son of the third Duke of Hamilton, was a career naval officer whose victory over a large French privateer in 1695, when in command of the frigate *Lichfield*, was immortalised in a fine painting by Willem van de Velde the younger. Hamilton commanded the *Eagle* during the capture of Gibraltar and the subsequent Battle of Malaga, but developed a political career after the Anglo-Scottish union and was appointed governor of Jamaica in 1711. He used the position to turn a blind eye to, and share in the proceeds of, a number of pirates and privateers, and there were strong rumours to the effect that he was a covert Jacobite; his commissioning of a substantial armed fleet in 1715, at exactly the same time that his brother was a general in the Earl of Mar's army fighting for 'James VIII' in Scotland, attracted considerable suspicion.[32] The enormous upsurge in piracy in the West Indies from 1716/17, so soon after the accession of the Hanoverian George I and the failed Jacobite attempt to overthrow him in 1715, witnessed several 'pirates' and their crews, many of them originally sanctioned by Hamilton, expressing support for the Old Pretender. The name of Blackbeard's ship, *Queen Anne's Revenge*, might well be a coded Jacobite message, while Stede Bonnet, who had sailed with Blackbeard, subsequently set out his own ship, naming it the *Royal James*. He and his crew 'made Bowls of Punch, and went to Drinking of the Pretender's Health, and hoped to see him King of the English Nation.' Other pirates operating on the African coast declared their allegiance to the Jacobite cause, and gave their ships names like *King James*.[33]

Of course, none of this is necessarily proof of intense political conviction among the 'pirates of the Caribbean': more likely, it was an attempt to give a fig leaf of respectability to the activities of gangs of rogues who were determined to break the law anyway. Alternatively, Jacobitism was a very useful extra charge for those who captured pirates to bring against their prisoners; it was 'the classic frame-up of the early eighteenth century'.[34] Nevertheless, the Jacobite leadership took these professions of support seriously. By the end of 1718, the pirates who still remained at New Providence in the Bahamas 'did with one heart and voice proclaim King James for their king', and they made contact with 'Admiral' George Camocke, who proposed going out in a 50-gun ship to take command of them in order to seize Bermuda.[35] Like so many Jacobite schemes, this came to nothing, but it was not the end of the somewhat surreal idea of a pirate-Jacobite alliance. In 1722, two vessels, together with a sympathetic Swedish frigate commanded by an Irishman and former Royal Navy officer, Jaspar Ó Morugh, sailed for Madagascar, hoping to recruit the pirate crews based on the island. This was part of a larger scheme, known to history as the Atterbury plot, which called upon substantial Spanish and Swedish naval resources, and would have seen 'James III' carried from Genoa to England in the Swedish warship *Revolution*. In the event, the Ó Morugh expedition got no further than Spain, thus finally putting paid to the delicious fantasy of a pirate army storming ashore on a British beach in the name of the House of Stuart.[36]

The failure of the 'Fifteen', the Jacobite uprising that followed the accession of George I, had many consequences, not just an upsurge in Jacobite support among pirates. In addition to Camocke, a number of other experienced naval officers, many of them Scots, refused to serve the Hanoverian regime, declared for 'James III and VIII', and then joined the fledgling navy of Tsar Peter the Great of Russia. Thomas Gordon, who had risen from master of an Aberdeen merchantman to a captain in first the Scots and then the British navies, followed this path in 1716, followed in 1718 by Thomas Saunders and in 1722 by Kenneth, Lord Duffus, who had distinguished himself when captain of the *Advice* in 1711 in a losing fight against a squadron of Dunkirk privateers.[37] Despite having never commanded anything larger than that small Fourth Rate frigate during his relatively brief service in the Royal Navy, Duffus became a Russian rear-admiral in short order. Meanwhile, Gordon had an illustrious career, rising to admiral of the fleet in 1727, thanks partly to active lobbying on his behalf by influential Jacobites.[38] Others who went into the tsar's naval service included Captains Robert Little and William Hay, along with Lieutenant Adam Urquhart.[39] In effect, these men served two masters, retaining their allegiance to the Jacobite cause while holding commands for Peter the Great and his successors. Gordon in particular regularly acted as an intermediary between the exiled Stuart court and the tsar, proposing a number of schemes for Russian military and naval assistance.[40] These early incomers into the Russian navy paved the way for others, and promoted their careers. The Welshman Thomas Lewis went into the tsar's service in 1725, the Irishman Christopher O'Brian in 1737; while there is no firm evidence that the former was a Jacobite, the latter definitely was.[41]

The Jacobite risings of the early eighteenth century are always remembered as land campaigns, but in reality, there was a substantial naval element to all of them. In 1708, a powerful French fleet of over thirty ships sailed for Scotland, carrying the titular King James aboard the flagship, *Le Mars*. The fleet sailed into the Firth of Forth and dropped anchor off Crail in Fife, but the arrival of a strong British squadron under Admiral George Byng, combined with poor weather, led to the loss of several opportunities to land the Jacobite king and his troops; the expedition eventually skulked back to Dunkirk, and James returned to his phantom court at Saint-Germain.[42] Byng again played a prominent part

HM ships *Lion* and *Elizabeth* engaging the French ship *Du Teillay*, carrying Bonnie Prince Charlie to Scotland in July 1745. Dominic Serres. (© *National Maritime Museum, Greenwich, London, BHC0364*)

in the much more serious Jacobite attempt in 1715, using his fleet in home waters to prevent supplies and reinforcements getting to the rebels. The next attempt, in 1719, was originally meant to consist of two Spanish naval expeditions, with a large *armada* sailing from Cadiz and Corunna under the command of James and the Duke of Ormonde, while a diversionary force of two frigates and 307 Spanish infantry under the command of the Earl Marischal was to sail to the Western Isles. In the end, storms scattered the main force, leaving Marischal's little fleet and army on their own. Their prospects were dented by the rapid deployment of a Royal Navy squadron, which blocked their escape route and bombarded into surrender the Spanish garrison in Eilean Donan Castle.[43]

In May 1745, the twenty-year-old Lord Lewis Gordon suddenly deserted his lowly post as third lieutenant of the 60-gun *Dunkirk* in the Mediterranean fleet. This was arguably the first act of the 'Forty-Five', which formally began a couple of months later when Charles Edward Stuart, the Jacobite Prince of Wales, sailed for Scotland. Making due allowance for the 'parallel universe' nature of Jacobitism, Gordon must surely rank as the most rapidly promoted junior naval officer in history, as he was swiftly appointed to the Bonnie Prince's military council and commanded a small Jacobite army to victory at Inverurie in December 1745.[44] Meanwhile, Charles Edward was actually transported to Scotland in *Du Teillay*, a privateer owned by Antoine Walsh, a Franco-Irishman who had served in the French navy before making a fortune in the Nantes slave trade. After landing the prince, Walsh returned to France and played a leading part in the preparations for a French invasion. When this was abandoned, he sent two more of his own ships to the west coast of Scotland to land arms and money, and to pick up Charles Edward if necessary; but after landing the supplies, the ships were engaged by three British warships in Loch-nan-Uamh, and had to leave without retrieving the prince. Walsh continued to be involved in projects for Jacobite invasions, and was given an earldom by King James III.[45]

From January 1746 onwards, British seapower, and specifically its ability to blockade the Scottish coast, was a significant factor contributing to the ultimate defeat of the Jacobite cause.[46] Even so, its success has often been overstated: of thirty-four French ships sent to assist the rebels in Scotland between October 1745 and August 1746, twenty-four got through safely. The Royal Navy's relative success was actually down to luck, in that several of the ships which were captured or destroyed were the really important ones, such as the 60-gun *Elizabeth*, carrying the arms intended to support Charles's uprising, but taken by HMS *Lion* off the Lizard before the prince even reached Scotland; and the *Prince Charles*, taken on 4 April 1746 when carrying 252,000 livres to her namesake.[47] And, of course, the Royal Navy failed entirely in its attempts to prevent the flight of the Bonnie Prince after Culloden.[48] Hunting in vain for Charles Stuart around Mingulay in the Hebrides constituted the first serious naval service for the fifteen-year-old Midshipman Adam Duncan of HMS *Trial*. Half a century later, Duncan would lead the British fleet to victory over the Dutch at the Battle of Camperdown; and at the time of writing this book, he is the only fighting admiral to have an operational warship of the Royal Navy named after him.[49]

The Jacobite presence at sea lingered on, sometimes in unexpected ways and places. In 1749, the outwardly Protestant and law-abiding baronet Sir Thomas Stepney of Llanelli, an almost uniquely entrepreneurial example of his class, christened one of his trading ships *Prince Charles*, apparently with no regard at all for potential consequences (of which there were, in fact, none).[50] Seven years later, the launch of what was surely one of the last Jacobite privateers, the *York*, inspired the commissioning of a celebratory punchbowl, adorned with the Jacobite symbols of a six-petalled rose and a closed rosebud.[51] Ships often featured on Jacobite coins and medals: they represented both the ship of state and the physical act of restoration, as had been the case in 1660.[52] In Ireland, Jacobites penned poems in Gaelic deriding the string of British naval failures at the start of the Seven Years War (1756–63), notably the disgrace and execution of Admiral John Byng, son of one of the naval heroes of the Glorious Revolution.[53]

In due course, the tide of that war turned; and a good case can be made for stating that Jacobite hopes of a restoration finally perished for good as a result of the naval Battle of Quiberon Bay in 1759, not the much vaunted and much more widely feted Battle of Culloden.[54] On 20 November 1759, off the coast of Brittany, a fleet of twenty-nine ships commanded by Admiral Edward Hawke engaged the French under the Comte de Conflans. The latter's force was intended to shepherd across the Channel the troops and transport ships assembled in the Bay of Morbihan, destined for a landing in Scotland in support of the elderly King James, the Old Pretender, along with his sons, the depressive drunk formerly known as Bonnie Prince Charlie, and the Cardinal Duke of York. The hard-fought engagement led to the destruction or capture of seven French ships and the scattering of the rest, putting paid to the last lingering hopes of the House of Stuart. At the heart of the battle was the 74-gun *Torbay*, commanded by Augustus Keppel, one of the most distinguished predecessors of Nelson; Keppel was both a great-grandson of King Charles II, and grandson of one of the favourites of King William of Orange.[55] During the action, the *Torbay* applied the *coup de grâce* to *Le Formidable*, flagship of the French rear-admiral, du Verger, and then

Overleaf: The Battle of Quiberon Bay, 1759, the end of the last attempt to invade Britain on behalf of the Jacobites. Nicholas Pocock. (© National Maritime Museum, Greenwich, London, BHC0399)

The memorial at St Peter's Basilica, Rome, to James Francis Edward, 'King James III and VIII', the Old Pretender, and his sons Charles and Henry.
(Photograph by Michael Berliner)

attacked the 74-gun *Thesée*, which foundered after succumbing to both the *Torbay*'s broadsides and the squally weather, which sent water pouring into her leeward gun ports.[56]

The victorious *Torbay* once had another incarnation, though. She had been 'rebuilt' three times, and renamed once, but in theory, at least, she was the former *Neptune*, named and launched by King Charles II at Deptford dockyard on 17 April 1683. John Evelyn, who was present that day, described her as 'one of the goodliest vessels of the whole navy, and of the world'. Evelyn could not have known it then, but the *Neptune*, subsequently the *Torbay*, would be the last ship ever to be named by the king, became one of the last survivors of his navy, and played a significant part in destroying the lingering hopes of his dynasty.

Appendix

The Admiralty Meeting of
22 July 1676

ACCORDING TO THE MINUTES in the Admiralty journal, written up by Pepys, kept in his library in Cambridge, and published by the Navy Records Society,[1] this meeting was attended by King Charles, the Lord Privy Seal (Anglesey), the Earls of Ossory and Craven, Secretaries of State Henry Coventry and Sir Joseph Williamson, and Edward Seymour, the Speaker of the House of Commons, who was also the Treasurer of the Navy. Members of the Navy Board are also recorded as attending, although their identities are not specified. The minutes are relatively brief, occupying little more than a page in the published version. They suggest that there were four brief items of business, and two more substantial ones. The king raised a request from the Governor of Dover to wear the Union Flag on his private yacht; but 'the practice and rule of the navy being opened by the Secretary of the Admiralty therein', the proposal was rejected. A Mister Gaudy's invention 'for blowing up of ships' was 'found vain, and rejected'. The master of the *Henrietta* was ordered to be committed to a court martial for running the ship aground, and the king granted a Quaker merchant skipper exemption from swearing an oath prior to receiving a pass for his ship. The published minutes devote significantly more space, but still no more than a paragraph each, to the other two items. The king confirmed the substantial rewards he had promised to the men who had served under Sir John Narbrough during an attack on the corsair base at Tripoli, together with a medal to the man who actually led the attack, Narbrough's lieutenant and protégé, Cloudesley Shovell. Finally (although actually the second item in the minutes as published), there was a debate on the instructions issued to the commander of the royal warship *Hunter*, loaned to the Royal African Company, 'in case any acts of violence should be committed upon any of His Majesty's subjects by virtue of the said instructions'. Pepys gives no indication of what was said in the debate, only the conclusion:

His Majesty was pleased to conclude that the said instructions were indispensably necessary to be given, unless the present Royal Company and their trade by virtue of his charter were to be delivered up, and that therefore the same should be engrossed fair for his signature, giving the Secretary of the Admiralty express order to see the same forthwith done accordingly.

In this item, as in the minutes of the meeting as a whole, only two individuals are specifically named as actors: the king and Secretary Pepys. The impression is given, as it so often is throughout the Admiralty journal, that all business was guided by the latter, and the fact that interventions by other members of the board are noted very rarely indeed (not at all in this particular meeting, as in so many others) creates an impression of a wholly compliant, subordinate body.

However, what are clearly rough minutes of part of this meeting are preserved in the other, much less systematic, collection of Pepys naval papers, in the Rawlinson manuscripts at the Bodleian Library in Oxford.[2] They are in a volume principally containing papers of Pepys's brother John, his successor as Clerk of the Acts to the Navy Board, who was present at the meeting and must therefore have kept his own record of it for his own purposes.[3] The catalogue of the Rawlinson manuscripts does not make any reference to this as being a meeting of the Admiralty, so this document has never previously been connected to the published minutes. John Pepys immediately provides us with two pieces of factual information that his brother omitted: the venue of the meeting (the Robes Chamber at Whitehall), and a more complete list of those who attended. The Navy Board members present were himself, Sir John Werden (the Duke of York's secretary), Sir Anthony Deane, Sir Richard Haddock and Sir John Kempthorne. Crucially, too, after writing 'His Majesty' at the top of the page, John Pepys then noted the name of 'His Royal Highness the Duke of York', whose attendance is not noted at all in the elder brother's minutes. This confirms what has long has been suspected, namely that James was present at more Admiralty meetings in the 1670s than those he was recorded at, and that his influence on naval business during that period was, therefore, probably significantly greater than has been assumed.[4]

John Pepys minuted only the debate about the *Hunter*, clearly the most important item of business in the meeting. (A pity: it would have been intriguing to find out more about Mister Gaudy's 'vain' invention for blowing up ships.) However, he records that the Earl of Ossory left before the debate began, which suggests that this item of business might not have come second in the agenda, as Samuel's minutes suggest it did; Ossory would hardly have left after attending only a brief item of business about the Governor of Dover (assuming it really was as brief as Samuel makes it out to be), and would almost certainly have wanted to be present for what Samuel gives as the fourth item, the rewards to

Narbrough's men and the medal to Cloudesley Shovell, as both Narbrough and Shovell had served under him. John also gives the impression that there was very nearly no debate at all. According to the rough minutes, Pepys asked the king's directions about the instructions to Richard Dickinson, captain of the *Hunter*, as they had been read at the board at a previous meeting.[5] Charles signified his consent, and 'Mister Secretary put them in his book (as a paper read and agreed to)', seemingly concluding the item of business. From this point onwards, none of what John Pepys records appears in the minutes produced by his brother.

Edward Seymour, the Speaker of the Commons and Treasurer of the Navy (who had been absent from the meeting where the instructions were previously discussed) 'beckoned to Sir John Werden for them, who took them and [delivered] them to him'. Seymour read them, then informed the king that 'some of those instructions (if sent) might prove of ill consequence'. He pointed out that some gentlemen in the West Country, his political power base, had a charter from Charles I to trade in the same area, and the validity of this in law, vis-à-vis that of the much newer Royal African Company, had not been settled. Therefore, Seymour envisaged a situation where Dickinson and the *Hunter* might attack and capture West Country ships, who believed themselves to be acting lawfully, and who might, indeed, ultimately be vindicated in that belief. The Duke of York answered that the claim of the West Countrymen had been heard before the king, and found not to be valid; that the Royal African Company (in which, of course, James had an important interest) had purchased the rights to the trades in question from the East India Company; that it had traded undisturbed for fifteen years before the West Countrymen suddenly brought forward their claim; and that the king had granted the Royal African Company a monopoly in those parts. If Dickinson 'should do any injury,' James suggested, 'satisfaction should be required of him at his return'; but otherwise, the two ships going out from the West Country should be treated as interlopers.

Astonishingly, the king then cast doubt on the validity of an act apparently carried out by his and James's father, the sacred saint and martyr. Charles remarked that although the first patent to the West Country adventurers was certainly under the Great Seal, it still might not be legally valid; at the time, '(when the King was at Oxford), the Great Seal was abused, specifying My Lord of Worcester's having a trunkful of patents to make dukes, earls, etc', and to issue patents aimed primarily at attacking Parliamentarian trade.[6] Anglesey then intervened, saying it would be a hard thing for an English ship to be seized and tried as an interloper in Guinea. Secretary Williamson replied that they would have recourse under English law, but Anglesey was still not happy, proposing that the instructions should be debated at the Privy Council. The Duke of York now intervened once again, protesting that 'if these instructions were not sent out, the whole African Company would be ruined'. The Earl of Craven spoke up, claiming that the company had invested some £80,000 in the trade, which would ultimately bring a return to the king in customs revenue. The king in question remarked that the *Hunter* was ready to sail, and his brother stated baldly 'that these things had already been long since considered'. The two secretaries of state then raised some broader legal issues about patents, with Henry Coventry urging that 'a man's ship is like a man's house, that none can enter into it legally without power by the law'. James objected that 'if a man have stolen any goods, his house may be broke by force, and the law will justify it', extending the analogy to those he called 'the interlopers'.

Anglesey and Seymour now joined forces to ask what would happen if Dickinson's guns killed any men on the West Country ships. Secretary Williamson replied, somewhat unconvincingly, along the lines that nobody had been killed yet, although ships had been seized after being shot at. Anglesey, clearly uneasy about potential future implications for himself, now complained that 'they, being only commissioners for the Admiralty of England, he did not know how they could give any instructions in this case'. The Duke of York replied bluntly that 'if His Majesty would give him order as Lord Admiral of the coast of Guinea, he would then give the captain the same instructions'. This extraordinary comment seems to have abruptly terminated the discussion. John Pepys recorded what happened next:

> After the whole debate, Mister Secretary Pepys, *who was silent all the time* [my emphasis], acquainting His Majesty, that His Majesty himself being to sign the said instructions, he prayed His Majesty's pleasure concerning them, to whom His Majesty replied, that they should be sent.

This remarkable record changes our understanding of the relationship between the key players in naval affairs during the 1670s, and casts doubt on the reliability of the record presented by Samuel Pepys in his Admiralty journal. As his own brother noted, the elder Pepys said nothing at all during the debate; his role was the classic one of most secretaries at most meetings, namely raising the agenda item and then recording the conclusion of the discussion upon it, nothing more. By far the most important interventions during the debate on 22 July 1676 came from a man who, according to Samuel, was not actually there at all: James, Duke of York, whose comments confirm his autocratic mindset, his near-contempt of legal process, and his protective attitude towards his own personal interest, in this case the monopoly position of the Royal African Company. One wonders how many other meetings he attended where his presence was never recorded by Samuel Pepys, but where James's rigid arguments either won the day or reinforced his elder brother's stance. As for the king, his cavalier dismissal of a patent granted by his own father, and determination to ride roughshod over the objections of several of his principal advisers, shows Charles at his most decisive, but also his most cynical. Above all, John Pepys's minutes show that there was lively debate at Admiralty meetings, with strong differences of opinion being aired: something that does not emerge at all from the sanitised versions presented by his brother, but which provides a much clearer context for the 'attempted coup' in the Admiralty in January 1679. Commissioners like Anglesey, Coventry, Craven, Seymour and Williamson, virtually written out of the record in Samuel Pepys's Admiralty journal, were evidently active members with independent mindsets, not afraid to state their opinions. It is now clear that as it stands, the journal, one of the most important and extensively cited primary sources for the later Stuart navy, presents a flawed and incomplete picture of what went on in the government of the navy in the 1670s. It slightly underplays the role of the king in naval administration, does a grave disservice to the other members of the Admiralty Board, and significantly exaggerates the importance of the Secretary of the Admiralty; but then, Pepys would not be the last secretary to write up sets of minutes in ways that presented himself in the best possible light.

Above all, Pepys's Admiralty journal wholly underestimates the abiding importance of the Duke of York in naval affairs, even after his resignation as Lord High Admiral in 1673. Because the elder Pepys simply excised most references to James's presence from the minutes he wrote up, we will probably never know how many meetings the duke attended in tandem with his brother; and we cannot rule out the possibility that he attended at least a number of others on his own, in which case he is even more likely to have dominated debates, and, by definition, decisions, than he did in the meeting of 22 July 1676. If it is ever possible for a member of the royal family to be an elephant in a room, then that is what James Stuart was when he attended meetings of the Admiralty commission of 1673–79.

Select Bibliography and Suggestions for Further Reading

Place of publication is London unless stated otherwise.

Aubrey, P, *The Defeat of James Stuart's Armada* (Leicester, 1979)

Callow, J, *The Making of King James II: The Formative Years of a Fallen King* (Stroud, 2000)

——, *King in Exile: James II, Warrior, King and Saint* (Stroud, 2004)

Canny, N, ed, *The Origins of Empire: British Overseas Enterprise to the Close of the Seventeenth Century* (Oxford, 1998)

Capp, B, *Cromwell's Navy: The Fleet and the English Revolution, 1648-60* (Oxford, 1989)

Davies, J D, 'Pepys and the Admiralty Commission of 1679–84', *Historical Research*, 62 (1989)

——, *Gentlemen and Tarpaulins: The Officers and Men of the Restoration Navy* (Oxford, 1991)

——, *Pepys's Navy: Ships, Men and Warfare 1649–89* (Barnsley, 2008)

Endsor, R, *The Restoration Warship: the Design, Construction and Career of a Third Rate of Charles II's Navy* (2009),

Fox, F, *The Four Days Battle of 1666: The Greatest Sea Fight in the Age of Sail* (Barnsley, 2009)

Fraser, A, *King Charles II* (2002 edn)

Fulton, T W, *The Sovereignty of the Seas* (1911)

Glickman, G, 'Conflicting Visions: Foreign Affairs in Domestic Debate 1660–89', in *The Primacy of Foreign Policy in British History, 1660–2000: How Strategic Concerns Shaped Modern Britain*, ed W Mulligan, B Simms (Basingstoke, 2010)

Hornstein, S, *The Restoration Navy and English Foreign Trade, 1674–88* (Aldershot, 1991)

Jones, J R, *The Anglo-Dutch Wars of the Seventeenth Century* (1996)

Keay, A, *The Magnificent Monarch: Charles II and the Ceremonies of Power* (2008)

Knighton, C S, *Pepys and the Navy* (Stroud, 2003)

Latham, R, and Matthews, W, eds, *The Diary of Samuel Pepys* (11 vols, 1970–83)

Levillain, C-E, *Vaincre Louis XIV: Angleterre, Hollande, France, Histoire d'une relation triangulaire* (Paris, 2010)

Murdoch, S, *The Terror of the Seas? Scottish Maritime Warfare 1513–1713* (Leiden, 2010)

Rodger, N A M, *The Command of the Ocean: A Naval History of Britain 1649–1815* (2006)

Tomalin, C, *Samuel Pepys: The Unequalled Self* (2002)

Winfield, R, *British Warships in the Age of Sail, 1603–1714: Design, Construction, Careers and Fates* (Barnsley, 2010)

Notes

Abbreviations used in references
Throughout the references, the place of publication is London unless stated otherwise.

BL – The British Library (Add MS – Additional Manuscripts)

Bod – The Bodleian Library, Oxford (Rawl MS – Rawlinson Manuscripts)

Burnet – *Burnet's History of my own time*, ed O Airy, 2 vols (1897–1900)

Callow – J Callow, *The Making of King James II: The Formative Years of a Fallen King* (Stroud, 2000)

Catalogue – J R Tanner, ed, *A Descriptive Catalogue of the Naval Manuscripts in the Pepysian Library at Magdalene College, Cambridge* (Navy Records Society, 4 vols, 1903, 1904, 1922)

Clarke – *The life of James the Second, king of England*, ed J S Clarke, 2 vols (1816)

CSPD – Various editors, *Calendar of State Papers, Domestic Series, James I, Charles I, Commonwealth, Charles II, James II* (1856–1972)

CSPVen – Various editors, *Calendar of State Papers Relating to English Affairs in the Archives of Venice* (1900–47)

Coventry MS – Papers of the Coventry family, Longleat House, consulted on microfilm at the Institute of Historical Research

Evelyn, Diary – E S De Beer, ed, *The Diary of John Evelyn*, 6 vols (Oxford, 1955); but references are given by date, rather than the page numbers in this edition, to accommodate those using other editions

Gentlemen and Tarpaulins – J D Davies, *Gentlemen and Tarpaulins: The Officers and Men of the Restoration Navy* (Oxford, 1991)

HMC – reports of the Historical Manuscripts Commission

HoP – The History of Parliament: all volumes now fully searchable online at www.historyof parliamentonline.org, with the exception of R Paley, ed, *The House of Lords 1660–1715*, 5 vols (Cambridge, 2016).

Knighton – C S Knighton, *Pepys and the Navy* (Stroud, 2003)

Lincs AO – Lincolnshire Archives

Luttrell – N Luttrell, *A Brief Historical Relation of State Affairs from September 1678 to April 1714* (1857)

MM – *The Mariner's Mirror*, journal of the Society for Nautical Research, 1914 to date

TNA – The National Archives, Kew ('ADM' – Admiralty papers)

NMM – The National Maritime Museum, Greenwich

NRS – Publications of the Navy Records Society, 1893 to date

Naval Minutes – J R Tanner, ed, *Samuel Pepys's Naval Minutes*, NRS (1925)

ODNB – Various editors, *The Oxford Dictionary of National Biography* (Oxford, 2004 to date), accessible online at www.oxforddnb.com

Pepys Diary – R Latham and W Matthews, eds, *The Diary of Samuel Pepys* (11 vols, 1970–83), but to accommodate those using other editions (including the online version at www.pepysdiary. com), references are given by date, rather than the page numbers in this edition

Pepys MS – Pepys manuscripts at the Pepys Library, Magdalene College, Cambridge

Tangier Papers – E Chappell, ed, *The Tangier Papers of Samuel Pepys*, NRS (1935)

Winfield – R Winfield, *British Warships in the Age of Sail, 1603–1714: Design, Construction, Careers and Fates* (Barnsley, 2010)

Introduction

1 *CSPVen 1673–5, 431.*

2 *CSPD 1675–6*, pp183–95, quotation from p195. Another detailed account of the voyage can be found in Lincs AO, Jarvis MS 9/1/A4, Christopher Gunman's journal aboard the *Anne Yacht*.

3 Accounts of 1671 voyage: HMC, *The Manuscripts of S H Le Fleming, Esq, of Rydal Hall* (1890), 81; B Weiser, *Charles II and the Politics of Access* (Woodbridge, 2003), 99–101.

4 *The Right Honourable the Earl of Arlington's letters to Sir W Temple, Bart* (1701), II.341.

5 TNA ADM106/325/188; ADM51/3876; Lincs AO, Jarvis MS 9/1/A/4.

6 K Sharpe, *Rebranding Rule: The Restoration and Revolution Monarchy* (2013), 192.

7 Evelyn Diary, 1 Oct 1661.

8 A Keay, *The Last Royal Rebel: The Life and Death of James, Duke of Monmouth* (2016), 95.

9 Anon, *To His Royal Highness the Duke of York, upon his Return to the Care and Management of the Navy of England* (1684).

10 *CSPVen 1661–4*, 168–9.

11 Lincs AO, Jarvis MS 9/1/A/5; BL Add MS 15892, fos130–35; Callow, 234–6.

12 Some may have followed this reference expecting me to 'name and shame' the miscreant. But I prefer to employ the old armed forces adage, 'no names, no pack drill'.

13 J S Wheeler, *The Making of a World Power: War and the Military Revolution in Seventeenth Century England* (Stroud, 1999), 203–5.

14 Ironically, the modern study by a non-naval historian which best integrates the Royal Navy into national history is by a Frenchman: C-E Levillain, *Vaincre Louis XIV: Angleterre, Hollande, France, Histoire d'une relation triangulaire* (Paris, 2010), a brilliant study of relations between Britain, France and the Netherlands, giving equal weight to all three countries.

15 C Jackson, *Charles II: The Star King* (2016), 92–3.

16 W E K Middleton, ed, *Lorenzo Magalotti at the court of Charles II : his Relazione d'Inghilterra of 1668* (1980), 28. Cf J Miller, *Charles II* (1991), 32.

17 O Airy, ed, *Burnet's History of My Own Time* (Oxford, 1897), I.168; R Hutton, *Charles II, King of England, Scotland and Ireland* (Oxford, 1989), 232.

18 Cited by Jackson, *Charles II*, 104; R Hutton, 'Why Don't the Stuarts Get Filmed?', in S Doran and T S Freeman, eds, *Tudors and Stuarts on Film: Historical Perspectives* (Basingstoke, 2009), 256.

19 In reality, Hutton's analysis of Charles's role in the navy is so brief as to be nearly invisible; but his assertions that Charles 'intervened little in the running of the navy', and that his interest was principally in 'the gilding of [his ships'] gilded sterns', are simply wrong. Hutton, *Charles II*, 221. Cf J R Jones, *Charles II: Royal Politician* (1987), 99.

20 Notably Sir Arthur Bryant: R Griffiths, 'Bryant, Sir Arthur Wynne Morgan (1899–1985), historian', *ODNB*. Another popular Stuart historian of the same vintage, Sir Charles Petrie, also flirted with Fascism.

21 Professor David Taylor has suggested that Britain now takes the person and aura of the monarch much more seriously than it ever has done, and that such reverence is both unwarranted and stultifying: https://theconversation.com/when-did-the-british-become-so-uptight-about-mocking-the-monarch-66658, accessed 9 October 2016.

22 Jackson, *Charles II*, 2–4 and passim.

23 Burnet, I.168.

24 Pepys Diary, 7 July, 31 Oct, 8 Dec 1666 (quotation).

25 A Keay, *The Magnificent Monarch: Charles II and the Ceremonies of Power* (2008), 186–90; Jackson, *Charles II*, 85.

26 A Hamilton, *Memoirs of the Count of Grammont* (1890 edn), 114; Sharpe, *Rebranding Rule*, 190–1.

27 BL Add MS 38141; quotation from Pepys Diary, 4 June 1664.

28 R Latham, ed, *Samuel Pepys and the Second Dutch War: Pepys's Navy White Book and Brooke House Papers* (NRS, 1995), 162; *Naval Minutes*, 197.

29 BL Add MS 40860, fo51v. The one truly substantial and revealing personal correspondence of Charles's life, that with his younger sister Henrietta, ended abruptly with her sudden death in 1670.

30 Callow, 22–7. As Callow notes, James's *Life* is concerned above all with presenting its subject as a gracious and chivalric warrior in pursuit of glory, qualities that modern historians (including Callow himself) tend to find anachronistic.

31 Quoted by N A M Rodger, *The Command of the Ocean: A Naval History of Britain 1649–1815* (2006), 98.

32 M Knights, 'Samuel Pepys and Corruption', *Parliamentary History*, 33 (2014), 19–35; D C Magliocco, 'Samuel Pepys, the Restoration Public, and the Politics of Publicity', University of London PhD thesis (2013), 177. Pepys was also Treasurer of the Tangier Committee, but the proceeds of that office – or at least, the official proceeds – come nowhere near making up the shortfall.

33 Knights, 'Pepys and Corruption', 21–2, and 19–35 passim; Knighton, 53.

34 As in the cases of the Admiralty commission of

1679-84 and his bête noire, Arthur Herbert, commander-in-chief in the Mediterranean from 1679 to 1682. See respectively J D Davies, 'Pepys and the Admiralty Commission of 1679–84', *Historical Research*, 34–53; P J Le Fevre, 'Arthur Herbert, Earl of Torrington, 1648–1716', *Precursors of Nelson: British Admirals of the Eighteenth Century*, ed Le Fevre and R Harding (2000), 23–6, 40.

35 See the judicious assessment of Pepys by Rodger, *Command of the Ocean*, 97–8.

Chapter 1

1 Admittedly, this can be a very short one, across the Kyles of Bute; but it is likely that, then as now, the great majority of visitors to Rothesay took the longer passage from the mouth of the Clyde or the Ayrshire coast.

2 E M Spiers, J A Craig and M J Strickland, eds, *A Military History of Scotland* (Edinburgh, 2014 edn), 151–2, 171–2, 212–14.

3 Notably in the establishment of maritime jurisdictions and boundaries: I P Grohse, 'Medieval Maritime Diplomacy: the case of Norwegian-Scottish Relations, *c*1266–1468/9', *International Journal of Maritime History*, 26 (2014), 512–28.

4 D M Hall, 'The Navy of James IV of Scotland', Pennsylvania State University PhD thesis (1998), 94–102 and passim; N MacDougall, *James IV* (2006), 223–46.

5 Hall, 'Navy', 165–6.

6 Hall, 'Navy', 8, 169–71, 174–7; http://www.gardenhistorysociety.org/post/agenda/tracking-down-%E2%80%98the-great-michael%E2%80%99/, accessed 29 June 2016.

7 A Thomas, *Princelie Majestie: The Court of James V of Scotland, 1528–42* (Edinburgh, 2005), 157–8.

8 S Murdoch, *The Terror of the Seas? Scottish Maritime Warfare, 1513–1713* (Leiden, 2010), 40–1.

9 Thomas, *Princelie Majestie*, 158–62.

10 Thomas, *Princelie Majestie*, 162–4 and 162–81 passim.

11 Murdoch, *Terror*, 69.

12 R Macpherson, 'Stewart, Francis, first earl of Bothwell (1562–1612), courtier and politician', *ODNB*.

13 D Armitage, 'Making the Empire British: Scotland in the Atlantic World, 1542–1707', *Past and Present*, 155 (1997), 42.

14 R Appelbaum, 'War and Peace in *The Lepanto* of James VI and I', *Modern Philology*, 97 (2000), 333–63.

15 S Murdoch, 'James VI and the Formation of a Scottish-British Military Identity', *Fighting for Identity: Scottish Military Experience, c1550–1900* (2002), 5–11. I am grateful to Professor Murdoch for

drawing my attention to this essay.

16 A Coats, 'English Naval Administration under Charles I – Top Down and Bottom Up – Tracing Continuities', *Transactions of the Naval Dockyards Society*, 8 (Portsmouth, 2012), 14–15. James personally presided over the meetings held to implement the commissions' proposals.

17 A P McGowan, ed, *The Jacobean Commissions of Enquiry*, NRS (1971), xv–xvi.

18 E Milford, 'The Navy at Peace: the Activities of the Early Jacobean Navy, 1603–18', *MM*, 76 (1990), 24.

19 Milford, 23–36.

20 W G Perrin, ed, *The Autobiography of Phineas Pett*, NRS (1917), 21–2; R Strong, *Henry Prince of Wales and England's Lost Renaissance* (1986), 57.

21 Pett, *Autobiography*, 81–4.

22 Strong, *Henry Prince of Wales*, 58.

23 Pett, *Autobiography*, 34–6, 89–91; T Marshall, *Theatre and Empire: Great Britain on the London Stages under James VI and I* (Manchester UP, 2000), 92–4.

24 Strong, *Henry Prince of Wales*, 155–8.

25 www.royalcollection.org.uk/collection/72830/armour-of-henry-future-prince-of-wales-for-the-tilt, accessed 15 September 2016.

26 Strong, *Henry Prince of Wales*, 59–61.

27 Pett, *Autobiography*, 75–6.

28 Murdoch, *Terror of the Seas*, 128–40. A summary of the navy's operations during the reign is provided by Milford, 'The Navy at Peace'.

29 *Jacobean Commissions*, xxvi; Coats, *Transactions*, 15–16.

30 Quoted by A Thrush, 'In Pursuit of the Frigate, 1603–40', *Historical Research*, 64 (1991), 29.

31 A P McGowan, 'The Royal Navy under the First Duke of Buckingham, Lord High Admiral 1618–28', University of London PhD thesis (1967), 187–90.

32 McGowan, 'Buckingham', 208–11.

33 BL Add MS 9302, fo5; Coats, *Transactions*, 16.

Chapter 2

1 J Sephton, *Sovereign of the Seas: the Seventeenth Century Warship* (Stroud, 2011), 197, 201, 203–5.

2 A D Thrush, 'The Navy under Charles I, 1625–40', University of London PhD thesis (1990), 38.

3 The original contemporary account of the ship and its decoration is T Heywood, *His Majesty's Royal Ship: A Critical Edition of Thomas Heywood's 'A True Description of His Majesties Royall Ship'*, ed A Young (2006). A remarkably detailed description and analysis of the decoration is provided by H Busmann, *Sovereign of the Seas: die Skulpturen des Britischen Königsschiffes von 1637* (Hamburg, 2002).

4 Pepys Diary, 17 Jan 1661.

5 J D Davies, *Pepys's Navy: Ships, Men and Warfare*

1649–89 (Barnsley, 2008), 47.

6   *CSPD 1637*, 212.

7   Pett, *Autobiography*, 164–7.

8   Pett, *Autobiography*, 128–9.

9   Pett, *Autobiography*, 130–1.

10 Pett, *Autobiography*, 135; C D Penn, *The Navy under the Early Stuarts* (facsimile reprint, 1970), 110.

11 C D Penn, 173.

12 National Archives of Scotland, MS 5741, log of Sir John Pennington.

13 Thrush, 26–7.

14 Thrush, 34–7; K Sharpe, *The Personal Rule of Charles I* (1992), 98–100.

15 B W Quintrell, 'Charles I and His Navy in the 1630s', *The Seventeenth Century*, 3 (1988), 161–2.

16 Pett, *Autobiography*, 147, 149, 154–5.

17 S Rodgers, 'The Symbolism of Ship Launching in the Royal Navy', University of Oxford DPhil thesis (1983), 221.

18 Thrush, 27–31.

19 Thrush, 31–3.

20 TNA SP16/260/86.

21 C Knighton, 'A Century On: Pepys and the Elizabethan Navy', *Transactions of the Royal Historical Society*, 14 (2004), 142.

22 S E Hoskins, *Charles the Second in the Channel Islands, a Contribution to his Biography and to the History of his Age* (1854), I, 357–8; G G Harris, 'Mainwaring, Sir Henry (1586/7–1653), pirate and naval officer', *ODNB*.

23 J Moshenska, *A Stain in the Blood: The Remarkable Voyage of Sir Kenelm Digby* (2016).

24 Pett, *Autobiography*, 156; R Morton Nance, 'The Little Ship of the Ashmolean', *MM*, 24 (1939), 95–100.

25 *Naval Minutes*, 132, 302.

26 F W Fairholt, 'Ancient Ships', *The Art Journal* (1849), 347.

27 Hoskins, *Charles the Second in the Channel Islands*, I, 367–8, 413–14; A Fraser, *King Charles II* (2011 edn), 42–3.

28 Hoskins, *Charles the Second in the Channel Islands*, II, 309–10; A Hopper, *Turncoats and Renegadoes: Changing Sides During the English Civil Wars* (Oxford, 2012), 65.

29 Callow, 53–4.

30 Hutton, *Charles II*, 29.

31 R C Anderson, 'The Royalists at Sea in 1648', *MM*, 9 (1923), 41–4.

32 S Kelsey, 'King of the Sea: the Prince of Wales and the Stuart Monarchy, 1648–9', *History*, 92 (1997), 428–48. Another example was the honours bestowed on Carteret and Wake in Jersey.

33 I owe this point to Dr Peter Le Fevre. The fading away of the practice of commemorating Charles I's execution as a matter of state policy through sermons and other forms of 'media' effectively died out at about that time: A Lacey, *The Cult of King Charles the Martyr* (2003).

34 B Capp, *Cromwell's Navy: the Fleet and the English Revolution 1648–60* (Oxford, 1989), 4–5.

35 C G 't Hooft, 'The First English Yachts', *MM*, 5 (1919), 108.

36 Hoskins, *Charles the Second in the Channel Islands*, II, 309–10.

37 R C Anderson, 'The Royalists at Sea in 1649', *MM*, 14 (1928), 320–38; Anderson, 'The Royalists at Sea in 1650', *MM*, 17 (1931), 135–68; Anderson, 'The Royalists at Sea in 1651–3', *MM*, 21 (1935), 61–90.

38 Hutton, *Charles II*, 76.

39 *Naval Minutes*, 233, 382.

40 Callow, 58.

41 Callow, 63–83.

42 Callow, 85–6. James resigned the position in Jan 1661: *CSPVen 1659–61*, 239.

43 *Gentlemen and Tarpaulins*, 119–21.

44 Knighton, 8.

45 C A Edie, 'The Public Face of Royal Ritual: Sermons, Medals and Civic Ceremony in Later Stuart Coronations', *Huntington Library Quarterly*, 53 (1990), 314–15.

46 Ogilby, John, *The Entertainment of His Most Excellent Majestie Charles II* (London, 1662). A facsimile of the first edition with introduction by Ronald Knowles (Center for Medieval and Early Renaissance Studies: State University of New York at Binghamton, NY, 1988); L M Madway, 'Majesty and Mockery: Representations of Royal Power in the Reign of Charles II, 1660–85', Yale University PhD thesis (1999), 107–13.

47 https://pepyssmallchange.wordpress.com/2014/02/02/a-ticket-to-attend-the-royal-touching-ceremonies-of-charles-ii/, accessed 27 January 2016.

Chapter 3

1   For the highly politicised naming of warships during the Interregnum, 1649–60, see M Seymour, 'Warships' Names of the English Republic 1649–59', *MM*, 76 (1990), 317–24.

2   R Simek, 'Old Norse Ship Names and Ship Terms', *Northern Studies*, 13 (1979), 27.

3   I Friel, *Henry V's Navy: The Sea Road to Agincourt and Conquest, 1413–22* (Stroud, 2015).

4   Rodgers, 'Ship Naming', 192, 318–22.

5   Rodgers, 'Ship Naming', 204–6; S W May, *Queen Elizabeth I: Selected Works* (2005), 223.

6 Evelyn Diary, 15 Feb 1652; Seymour, 'Warships' Names of the English Republic', 319–20.

7 Rodgers, 'Ship Naming', p147A

8 TNA ADM116/1113; ADM116/4629.

9 Personal knowledge, gleaned from a source who was in a position to know.

10 BL Add MS 34,335, fo29v.

11 http://www.churchillarchive.com/explore/page?id=CHAR%2013%2F62%2F6#image=0, accessed 20 April 2016; Catalogue, IV.19, 51, 458, 482. For the origins of explicitly personal royal ownership of the navy, see T J Runyan, 'The Organisation of Royal Fleets in Medieval England', in Runyan, ed, Ships, Seafaring and Society: Essays in Maritime History (1987), 44.

12 B Lubbock, ed, Barlow's Journal of His Life at Sea (1934), I.44.

13 Ogilby, John, The Entertainment of His Most Excellent Majestie Charles II (1662), 37; J Hone, 'Pope and the Politics of Panegyric', The Review of English Studies, 66 (2015), 116–20.

14 A Prospect of the Navy Royal: or, a Panegyrique upon the Fleet. Humbly Addrest to the Most Illustrious Prince Rupert, upon the Occasion of his going as Admiral to the Sea (1673), quoted by T Reimer, 'Before Britannia Ruled the Waves: die Konstruktion einer maritimen Nation', Ludwig-Maximillian's University, Munich, PhD thesis (2006), 248.

15 Winfield, 194.

16 J R Tanner, ed, Further Correspondence of Samuel Pepys 1662–79 (1929), 298: Pepys MS 2854, 146–7, 157, 164–5.

17 TNA SP46/137/231.

18 Keay, Magnificent Monarch, 154, 215.

19 R Endsor, The Restoration Warship: the Design, Construction and Career of a Third Rate of Charles II's Navy (2009), 85. A project has been launched to build a replica of Lenox at Deptford, inspired by Richard Endsor's outstanding book about the ship: www.buildthelenox.org.

20 TNA ADM106/42, Admiralty to Navy Board, 16, 17 June 1679.

21 TNA ADM106/42, Pepys to Navy Board, 14 Apr 1679.

22 TNA ADM106/41, Pepys to Navy Board, 18 Nov 1678.

23 TNA ADM106/40, Pepys to Navy Board, 3 July 1678.

24 TNA ADM106/41, Pepys to Navy Board, 30 March 1679; Pepys MS 2856, p143.

25 TNA ADM106/330/10; Pepys MS 2857, p486. I am grateful to Frank Fox for the point about Loyal London and Royal James.

26 Pepys Diary, 26 Oct 1664.

27 London Gazette, 240 (5 March 1667). I am grateful to Frank Fox for discussion of this point.

28 Pepys Catalogue, III.xlv.

29 Luttrell, I.138.

30 TNA ADM106/342/640.

31 Examples: TNA ADM106/309/405; ADM106/317/30; ADM106/320/284; Pepys MS 2855, pp237, 248.

32 TNA ADM1/3547, p353

33 See eg Pepys Diary, 26 Oct 1664.

34 Rodgers, 'Ship Naming', 223; Endsor, 85.

35 Pett, Autobiography, 83–4; Endsor, 84–7.

36 TNA ADM106/3520, fo2.

37 TNA ADM106/339/237.

38 Evelyn Diary, 8 June 1666.

39 Pepys MS 2856, p88.

40 Pepys MS 2860, pp76–7, 83.

41 W Hunt, rev J Spain, 'Beauclerk, Charles, first Duke of St Albans (1670–1726), army officer', ODNB.

42 M Goldie, ed, The Entring Book of Roger Morrice 1677–91 (Woodbridge, 2009), IV.57.

43 Pepys MS 2860, pp60, 83.

44 The same class originally included an HMS Grafton, too, but after less than ten years' service, she became a Blairite defence cut in 2006, when she was transferred to Chile.

45 TNA ADM1/16113; B Warlow, Shore Establishments of the Royal Navy (Liskeard, 2000 edn), 120–2.

Chapter 4

1 J R Jones, The Anglo-Dutch Wars of the Seventeenth Century (1996), 61–2.

2 BL Sloane MS 2754, fo1. The author of this tract was Sir Henry Shere (1641–1710), engineer of the Tangier mole.

3 Knighton, 35.

4 Pett, Autobiography, 156–7; H Todd, 'Charles, James and the Re-creation of the Royal Navy, 1660–65', Transactions of the Naval Dockyards Society, 8 (Portsmouth, 2012), 49.

5 CSPVen 1661–4, 7.

6 TNA ADM106/315/275.

7 TNA ADM106/320/288; ADM106/3118, 193. The king had been heavily involved in the decisions about earlier trials of lead sheathing: Catalogue, IV. 162, 181. I am grateful to Richard Endsor for discussion of this matter.

8 Catalogue, IV.500.

9 Luttrell, I.37, 53.

10 For example, TNA ADM106/307/307, 395.

11 TNA ADM/321/100.

12 TNA ADM106/331/1/42.

13 *Naval Minutes*, 394.

14 *The Travels of Peter Mundy in Europe and Asia*, V, ed R C Temple and L M Anstey (Hakluyt Society, second series, LXXVIII, 1936), 136.

15 *Naval Minutes*, 115.

16 Pepys MS 2853, 429.

17 NMM SPB/50. I owe this reference to Richard Endsor. The prominent shipbuilder Sir Henry Johnson was among others who thought 'no-one understood the theory of that art better than the king': *Memoirs of Thomas, Earl of Ailesbury, Written by Himself* (1890), I.97.

18 Quoted by C Mallagh, 'Some Aspects of the Life and Career of William Sutherland', *MM*, 100 (2014), 18.

19 Burnet, I.167.

20 H C Foxcroft, ed, *A Supplement to Burnet's History of My Own Time* (Oxford, 1902), 49.

21 J Franklin, *Navy Board Ship Models 1650–1750* (1989), 2–5; B Lavery & S Stephens, *Ship Models: their Purpose and Development from 1650 to the Present* (1995), 10, 12, 14. As Lavery and Stephens note (p28), there is actually no firm evidence that Charles had his own collection, but it seems highly unlikely that he did not.

22 Franklin, *Ship Models*, 98–101.

23 Franklin, *Ship Models*, 179–81. I am grateful to Frank Fox and Richard Endsor for a discussion of this issue.

24 *Naval Minutes*, 128.

25 Pepys MS 2854, p55. In the same letter, he requested a loan of the yacht's draught from her builder's widow, so that he could study it himself.

26 *CSPVen 1671–2*, 206–7.

27 BL Lansdowne MS 1236, fo170.

28 TNA ADM2/1753, p49.

29 Guildhall Library, London, MS 30,004, Trinity House minutes, 97. Sir William Penn, the Master, tactfully compromised by ordering ships sunk at both locations.

30 NMM SPB/16, item 7; *Samuel Pepys and the Second Dutch War*, 27; Pepys Diary 1 February 1664.

31 Evelyn 22 Dec 1664; NMM SPB/16, items 23, 25; [Henry, sixth] Marquess of Lansdowne, *The Double Bottom, or Twin-Hulled Ship of Sir William Petty* (Oxford, 1931).

32 BL Lansdowne MS 1236, fo170v.

33 A Marshall, 'Morland, Sir Samuel, first baronet (1625–1695), natural philosopher and diplomat', *ODNB*.

34 *CSPVen 1673–5*, 259, 268.

35 Pepys MS 2856, 95.

36 BL Lansdowne MS 1236, fo171.

37 Pepys MS 2854, 266.

38 Pepys MS 2853, fo207v.

39 Pepys MS 2856, 96. Similarly, in March 1678, Charles surprised Pepys by having a set of sailing orders ready so quickly, and insisting on their immediate despatch, that Pepys had no time to pen a lengthy covering letter: Pepys MS 2854, fo1v.

40 TNA E/M/21/58 (typescript continuation of *Calendar of State Papers, Venetian*, for 1676–8), Sarotti letters to Doge and Senate of 13 and 27 Mar 1676, 6 Nov 1676, 29 Apr 1678.

41 *Naval Minutes*, 16, 220.

42 F Fox, 'The English Naval Shipbuilding Programme of 1664', *MM*, 78 (1992), 287, 289.

43 *Catalogue*, IV.54.

44 *Naval Minutes*, 243.

45 Endsor, *Restoration Warship*, 9.

46 TNA E/M/21/58, Sarotti letter of 13 Mar 1676.

47 Pepys MS 2853, fo230v, fo251v, 255; *Catalogue* IV.518.

48 Winfield, 116–17, 120–1.

49 R C Anderson, 'The Ancestry of the Eighteenth Century Frigate', *MM*, 27 (1941), 158–65.

50 *Catalogue*, IV.126; Endsor, *Restoration Navy*, 9–10.

51 Knighton, 122.

52 *Grey's Debates of the House of Commons*, IV (1769), 21 Feb 1679; online at http://www.british-history.ac.uk/greys-debates/vol4/pp112–130.

53 The great Pepysian scholar J R Tanner confidently assumed that many of the initiatives relating to the Thirty Ships came from Pepys, thus disregarding the Admiralty secretary's own statements that 'His Majesty' was responsible for them: *Catalogue*, IV.xciii, 407, and cf the Appendix to this book.

54 *Catalogue*, IV.407, 414–15.

55 TNA ADM106/42, Pepys to Navy Board, 2 Apr 1679.

56 Pepys MS 2853, 319; *Catalogue*, IV.415, 422–3, 428, 463.

57 Endsor, *Restoration Warship*, 11.

58 *Naval Minutes*, 13; quote from Knighton, 127.

59 Endsor, *Restoration Warship*, 13.

60 Pepys Diary, 26 Oct 1664.

61 Sutherland, *Shipbuilding Unveil'd* (1717), xxvi. F Fox, *Great Ships*, 73–4; Davies, *Pepys's Navy*, 39–40.

62 *Naval Minutes*, 203; Pepys Diary, 22 April 1668; Winfield, 162.

63 *Naval Minutes*, 13–14. In September 1678 Charles acceded to the Navy Board's request that at least one of the new ships with upright stems should be properly tested at sea, and the *Captain* was commissioned as a result: Pepys MS 2855, 116; *Catalogue*, IV.607.

64 *Catalogue*, IV.468.
65 ADM2/1746, fo68v.
66 *CSPVen 1669–70*, 136.
67 TNA ADM106/304/91–4.
68 *Gentlemen and Tarpaulins*, 75.
69 *Catalogue*, IV.238, 257, 274–6.
70 *Catalogue*, IV.279, 286,
71 A Peters, *Ship Decoration 1630–1780* (Barnsley, 2013), 102–15.
72 Pepys Diary, 14 Dec 1663.
73 A M Steere, 'The Evolution of Decorative Work on English Men of War from the 16th to the 19th centuries', MA thesis, Texas A&M University (2005), 37.
74 D Pulvertaft, *Figureheads of the Royal Navy* (Barnsley, 2011), 45–7.
75 Davies, *Pepys's Navy*, 39–40, 45. I am grateful to Frank Fox for a discussion of this point.
76 TNA ADM2/1745, fo114.
77 Table source: *Gentlemen and Tarpaulins*, 10.
78 F Fox, 'The English Naval Shipbuilding Programme of 1664', *MM*, 78 (1992), 277.

Chapter 5

1 Pepys MS 2856, p33.
2 Luttrell, II.6–10.
3 Pepys MS 2856, p81.
4 C G 't Hooft, 'The First English Yachts', *MM*, 5 (1919), 109–14. At much the same time, the king ordered gondolas from Venice for his new canal in St James's Park: *CSPVen 1659–61*, 208, 215, 225, 227, 288, 290, 302; *1661–4*, 34, 38, 40, 42, 45.
5 Pepys Diary, 8 Nov 1660.
6 M Tanner, *Royal Yacht Mary: the Discovery of the First Royal Yacht* (Liverpool, 2008), 7.
7 'T Hooft, 'First English Yachts', 119–23.
8 Pepys Diary, 30 July 1662.
9 Winfield, 253–4.
10 For the finds brought up from the *Mary* wreck site, see Tanner, *Royal Yacht Mary*. Several are on display at Holyhead and Liverpool maritime museums.
11 TNA ADM106/42, 9 May 1679; Pepys MS 2860, pp228–9. By the 1680s, 'spare' yachts were increasingly being employed on ordinary Sixth Rate duties: in May 1682, the *Richmond* and *Monmouth* yachts were based in the Channel Islands, *Portsmouth* in Ireland, and *Anne* at Tangier (ADM8/1; I am grateful to Frank Fox for this point).
12 TNA LS 9/99.
13 *Catalogue*, IV.247, 371. The total costs of two earlier yachts, *Charles* for the king and *Anne* for the Duke of York, were £722 1s 5d and £1,815 2s 4d respectively: *CSPD 1661–2*, 482; cf *CSPD 1663–4*, 161.
14 *Catalogue*, IV.228.
15 H Jacobsen, *Luxury and Power: The Material World of the Stuart Diplomat, 1660–1714* (Oxford, 2011), 136.
16 Endsor, *Restoration Warship*, 268–73.
17 T Dalton, *British Royal Yachts: A Complete Illustrated History* (2001), 37; 't Hooft, 'First English Yachts', 117.
18 *CSPD 1663–4*, 271; Fraser, *Charles II*, 224.
19 Pepys Diary, 17 Aug 1665.
20 Endsor, *Restoration Warship*, 267.
21 *Catalogue*, IV.519–21.
22 Pepys MS 2857, pp305–7; Lincs AO, Jarvis MS 9/1/A/5, 4–7 Feb 1685.
23 W E May, 'The Navy and the Rebellion of the Earl of Argyle', *MM*, 57 (1991), 17–18.
24 R C Anderson, ed, *The Journal of Edward Mountagu, First Earl of Sandwich* (NRS, 1929), 235.
25 TNA ADM51/4265.
26 Lincs AO, Jarvis MS 9/1/A/5.
27 TNA ADM3/277, p46.
28 *CSPD 1661–2*, 545–6; C L Grose, 'The Dunkirk Money, 1662', *Journal of Modern History* 5 (1933), 1–18.
29 Lincs AO, Jarvis MS 9/1/A/2, 9–16 May, 2–4 June 1670.
30 Pepys MS 2853, fos179, 182; Lincs AO, Jarvis MS 9/1/A/4, 8–10 Oct 1677.
31 Keay, *Last Royal Rebel*, 225; Lincs AO, Jarvis MS 9/1/A/5, 16, 24 Feb 1680. In 1683, the *Mary Yacht* also brought over Prince George of Denmark to his marriage with James's younger daughter, Anne.
32 TNA ADM51/3943, 3810; Lincs AO, Jarvis MS 9/1/A/5.
33 Lincs AO, Jarvis MS 9/1/A/5, 14 July 1680.
34 For instance, the voyage of the *Anne Yacht* to the latter in July and August 1675: Lincs AO, Jarvis MS 9/1/A/4.
35 TNA ADM51/4265; *Catalogue*, III.58.
36 BL Egerton MS 3341, fo24.
37 Lincs AO, Jarvis MS 9/1/A/4, 28 Apr 1679.
38 TNA ADM106/287/235.
39 Lincs AO, Jarvis MS 9/1/A/5.
40 Nottingham University Archives, Portland MS PwV 60; J M Rigg, rev M Kilburn, 'FitzRoy [formerly Palmer], George, duke of Northumberland (1665–1716), courtier and army officer', *ODNB*. In 1688, though, it was reported that James had authorised an equally illegal operation by assigning a yacht carrying three 'musquiteers' to snatch Gilbert Burnet from his exile in the Netherlands: *Morrice Entring Book*, 236, 243.
41 Winfield, 253.
42 Winfield, 194.

43 TNA ADM51/345.

44 C M Gavin, *Royal Yachts* (1932), 56–7.

45 Pepys MS 2860, pp148, 154.

46 Lincs AO Jarvis MS IX/1/A/3, 15 Sept 1672; MS IX/1/A/5, 13 June 1682.

47 Fazeby's family preserved a number of the king's orders to him: NMM, OBK/8.

48 Pepys MS 2853, p357 (cf p374).

49 Prob 11/379/351; R E G Cole, *History of the Manor and Township of Doddington* (1897), 196–208.

50 J Y Akerman, ed, *Monies Received and Paid for Secret Services of Charles II and James II* (1851), 207; Prob.11/523/220.

51 TNA ADM106/3540, part 2, 'petitions' folder.

52 Weiser, *Politics of Access,* 179–83. Of course, this figure excludes the many shorter voyages that did not entail overnight stays, or the day voyages to destinations where the king then spent the night ashore.

53 HMC, *Report on the Manuscripts of the late George Allen Finch, Esq., of Burley-on-the-Hill, Rutland* II (1922), 56; Hutton, *Charles II,* 379.

54 Lincs AO, Jarvis MS 9/1/A/5, 29–30 June, 11–13 Sept 1682; HMC, *The Manuscripts of the Earl of Dartmouth* III (1896), 122–4; Weiser, *Politics of Access,* 183.

55 Gavin, *Royal Yachts,* 59–60; O Baldwin and T Wilson, 'Gostling, John (1649/50–1733), singer and Church of England clergyman', *ODNB.*

56 Notes to Hyperion Records, *Purcell: The Complete Anthems and Services,* vol 8 (CDA66686), recorded by Harry Christophers and the Sixteen in 1994.

57 Bod, Rawl MS A189, fo205. This might have been due in part to the introduction of a new 'plaything', the *Fubbs Yacht,* launched in 1682; but the *Fubbs* was only employed on royal voyages twice in 1683/84 (as Pepys reckoned the 'yacht years' between May and May, it is impossible to tell whether Charles or James employed them between May 1684 and May 1685; very few logbooks of the yachts survive to enable a cross-check).

58 Lincs AO, Jarvis MS 9/1/A/5.

59 TNA ADM51/3810, 3876; *Morrice Entring Book,* III.223, 243; *Passages from the Diary of General Patrick Gordon of Auchleuchries* (Aberdeen, 1859), 130. I am grateful to Peter Le Fevre for the latter reference.

60 Bod, Rawl MS A189, fo208.

61 TNA ADM3/278, first section, p87; Pepys MS 2857, p87; MS 2860, p170. However, Tichborne was a staunch Catholic, which might have made James II look kindly on a request for a yacht.

62 TNA ADM51/4265.

63 Pepys MS 2855, p175.

64 TNA ADM51/3810. It is unclear whether these are the same French comedians that the *Kitchen Yacht* brought over in 1677, and took back in the following April: Pepys MS 2853, fo212; Pepys MS 2854, p29. In 1683, the *Fubbs Yacht* brought over some 'Italian players': TNA ADM3/278, third section, p65.

65 Pepys MS 2856, p114.

66 Pepys MS 2856, pp81, 83, 96. Shortly afterwards, a smaller group of Catholics was put aboard the *Cleveland Yacht.* For the religious careers of the ladies in question, see https://wwtn.history.qmul.ac.uk/.

67 Pepys MS 2856, pp86, 99.

68 Pepys MS 2856, pp161–2.

69 R D Gwynn, 'James II in the Light of his Treatment of Huguenot Refugees in England, 1685–6', *English Historical Review,* 92 (1977), 820–33.

70 *Gentlemen and Tarpaulins,* 200.

71 *Catalogue,* IV.284.

72 Bod, Rawl MS A189, fo205. Cf *Naval Minutes,* 250–1.

73 Eg TNA ADM51/3810.

74 Bod, Rawl MS A189, fo208.

Chapter 6

1 Davies, *Pepys's Navy,* 28. 'Parkinson's Law' was based partly on the fact that, as the number of ships and men in the operational navy contracted markedly after World War Two, the numbers employed in the Admiralty bureaucracy steadily increased.

2 A Turnbull, 'The Administration of the Royal Navy from 1660–73', University of Hull PhD thesis (1974), 78.

3 TNA ADM2/1732, fo1.

4 TNA ADM2/1732, fo1.

5 TNA ADM2/1732, fo16v.

6 Pepys Diary, 26, 29 June, 3, 5, 12, 17 July, 6 August 1660.

7 Capp, *Cromwell's Navy,* 371–4; Todd, 'Re-creation', 48.

8 Capp, *Cromwell's Navy,* 374–5; Todd, 'Re-creation', 49.

9 Turnbull, 'Administration', 110–16.

10 Rodger, *Command of the Ocean,* 102.

11 A set of general instructions to captains from 1648 is BL Add MS 9305, fos34–7. For the debate on the extent of James's personal responsibility for the reforms of this period, see Turnbull, 'Administration', 86–91.

12 *Ailesbury Memoirs,* 122. Clarendon's suggestion that, in naval affairs, his son-in-law was essentially just a cipher for his secretary, William Coventry, has more than a whiff of sour grapes about it, while his

account of James's conduct of the Admiralty is strewn with so many errors as to make it nearly worthless: *The Life of Edward, Earl of Clarendon* (Oxford, 1857), II.79–85.

13 Turnbull, 'Administration', 108–9; Callow, 201–2, 212–13.

14 Coventry MS 99, fo7.

15 Alnwick Castle, MS 506 (microfilm Deposit 325 at the British Library), fo120, Charles II to Rupert, 27 Oct (1664? 1665??)

16 *CSPD 1668–9*, 9.

17 Clarke, *Life*, I.434–7; Fraser, *Charles II*, 256–61.

18 *Gentlemen and Tarpaulins*, 134–5.

19 BL Add MS 28,042, fo15.

20 Turnbull, 'Administration', 72, 97–8.

21 R K Hayes-Steuck, 'Emerging from the Shadows: the Life and Career of Arthur Annesley, Earl of Anglesey (1614–86)', University of Florida PhD thesis (2005), 77, 82–5.

22 Knighton, 98–9.

23 Pepys Diary, 29 Oct, 5 Nov 1668; Clarke, *Life of James II*, I.436.

24 *Pepys and the Second Dutch War*, 338, 339–40, 341–3, 347, 350, 365–6, 375, 376, 377, 382–3, 401–2, 422–3, 433.

25 C S Knighton, ed, *Pepys's Later Diaries* (Stroud, 2004), 6–7.

26 *CSPVen 1673–5*, 324.

27 Hutton, *Charles II*, 263.

28 BL Add MS 40,860, fo50; Knighton, 106–7.

29 Alnwick Castle, MS 506 (microfilm Deposit 325 at the British Library), fo118, Charles II to Rupert, 27 June (1665?).

30 TNA ADM8/1, passim; S Hornstein, *The Restoration Navy and English Foreign Trade, 1674–88* (Aldershot, 1991), 60–3.

31 W D Christie, ed, *Letters addressed from London to Sir Joseph Williamson* (1874), I.152–3, 181–2; II.8, 10, 12, 15.

32 TNA ADM106/283/175; ADM106/284/166; ADM106/284/309; ADM106/285/203.

33 Pepys MS 2853, fos195v, 197v.

34 See eg Pepys MS 2853, p350.

35 Eg *Catalogue*, IV.347, 350, 427, 536–7, 570, 613, 655; Pepys Diary, 6 Dec 1661.

36 Pepys MS 2860, p370.

37 Pepys MS 2879, p223.

38 *CSPVen 1673–5*, 73.

39 *Williamson Letters*, I.100, 136. Puckle was the father of the man credited with inventing the first machine gun.

40 The Navy Board of the 1660s has been studied exhaustively, thanks to the presence of Pepys. By contrast, the board of the period 1673–89, especially during the first six years, has been virtually ignored by historians.

41 Pepys MS 2853, p437.

42 Pepys MS 2854, p75.

43 *Catalogue*, III.185–6.

44 BL Add MS 10,115, fos29–31, 53–6, 66–7.

45 TNA ADM106/320/366; *Catalogue*, III.296.

46 Pepys MS 2853, fo223, p319.

47 Pepys MS 2853, p451.

48 TNA ADM2/1746, fo158v.

49 TNA, ADM2/1746, fo148.

50 Murdoch, *Terror of the Seas*, 237–82. James was appointed to the post on 1 February 1673.

51 A J Mann, *James VII: Duke and King of Scots, 1633–1701* (Edinburgh, 2014), 125–6.

52 *Catalogue*, IV.xiii. These figures omit the first six months of the commission's existence, the minutes for which survive in TNA ADM3/275 but were never incorporated into Pepys's bound volumes. Therefore, they escaped the attention of the Admiralty journal's editor, J R Tanner, who always assumed that the entire history of the Restoration navy could be written exclusively from the papers in the care of the Pepys Librarian, namely, himself. During the earlier period, the king attended twenty-eight out of sixty-nine meetings.

53 TNA ADM3/275, pp3, 5.

54 Pepys MS 2855, pp71, 85–6.

55 TNA ADM3/275, 15 October 1673. Once again, therefore, I have taken exactly the opposite position to Ronald Hutton, who claimed (in relation to 1673 alone) that Charles 'rarely attended the commission itself, and the impression is that he was dabbling in such trivial matters partly for a dilettante's pleasure': Hutton, *Charles II*, 302.

56 *Catalogue*, IV.20.

57 *Catalogue*, IV.579.

58 Bod, Rawl MS A214, index at beginning of volume.

59 Eg NMM LRN/5.

60 BL Harleian MS 7504.

61 Pepys MS 2855, p19.

62 *Catalogue*, IV.360–2.

63 Pepys MS 2853, fos187–8, 190.

64 Knighton, 142.

65 *Catalogue*, IV xxxiii–xxxiv, 632–4. Cf the notes made by Williamson, the other secretary of state, who seems not to have been present at either of the meetings described here: TNA SP29/366, fo409.

66 There are a number of extant copies of the Lord High Admiral's instructions in question; I have used NMM AND/30.

67 *Catalogue*, IV.634–5.

68 L C O'Malley, 'The Whig Prince: Prince Rupert and the Court vs Country Factions during the Reign of Charles II', *Albion*, 8 (1976), 333–50; R M Smuts, 'Craven, William, Earl of Craven (bap 1608, d1697), army officer and royal servant', *ODNB*.

69 Quoted by J D Davies, 'The Navy, Parliament and Political Crisis in the Reign of Charles II', *The Historical Journal*, 36 (1993), 271–88 (quotation from p279).

70 NMM LBK/49, p86.

71 Knighton, 132–3.

72 TNA ADM106/42.

73 TNA ADM106/42.

74 J D Davies, '"A Lover of the Sea and Skilful in Shipping": King Charles II and his Navy', *Royal Stuart Papers*, 42 (Huntingdon, 1992), 7.

75 *Tangier Papers*, 309. Cf *Naval Minutes*, 71–2.

76 J D Davies, 'Pepys and the Admiralty Commission of 1679–84', *Historical Research*, 62 (1989), 34–53.

77 Leicestershire Record Office, DG7/PP148, fo4.

78 Hornstein, *Restoration Navy*, 134–54.

79 Davies, 'Admiralty Commission', 39.

80 TNA SP 44/63, pp31–2, 34.

81 TNA ADM51/3863; TNA SP 44/63, p36.

82 Miller, *James II*, 113–19.

83 TNA SP 44/63, pp31–2.

84 TNA SP 44/63, pp36, 51, 58, 59

85 NMM, ADM/L/W/137, *Woolwich* log, 25 May 1683. The squadron that Grafton brought round from the Thames to Spithead consisted of three Third Rates, *Grafton*, *Henrietta* and *Montague*, and three Fourths, *St David*, *Oxford* and *Woolwich*: TNA ADM8/1, 1 June 1683.

86 TNA ADM51/407; Luttrell, I.272.

87 J D Davies, 'The Birth of the Imperial Navy? Aspects of Maritime Strategy, c1650–90', *Parameters of British Naval Power 1650–1850*, ed M Duffy (Exeter, 1992), 19.

88 G de la Bédoyère, ed, *Particular Friends: the Correspondence of Samuel Pepys and John Evelyn* (Woodbridge, 1997), 141.

89 *Tangier Papers*, 34–5; M Lincoln, 'Samuel Pepys and Tangier, 1662–1684', *Huntington Library Quarterly*, 77 (2014), 417–34.

90 Gentlemen and Tarpaulins, 195–8.

91 Bod, Carte MS 216, fo498v.

92 From N Thompson, *A Collection of 120 Loyal Songs, all of them Written since the Two Late Plots* (1685), 220.

93 *CSPD 1684–5*, 152.

94 Pepys MS 2857, pp67, 95–6, 99, 163, 218, 227, 300

95 Burnet, *History*, II.419.

96 H C Foxcroft, *The Life and Letters of Sir George Savile, Bart, First Marquis of Halifax* (1898), II.351.

97 Pepys MS 2857, pp300–1, 305–7.

98 NMM SPB/16, item 25.

Chapter 7

1 His father later claimed that Francis first went to sea under Sir John Lawson, so he might have served under that officer in the Mediterranean in the early 1660s; however, he is known to have been with Lawson at the battle of Lowestoft in June 1665, so might not have gone to sea until that year. HMC, *Supplementary Report on the Manuscripts of the Late Montagu Bertie, Twelfth Earl of Lindsey* (1942), 181; TNA ADM2/1745, fo132.

2 See their respective entries in *ODNB*.

3 *Gentlemen and Tarpaulins*, 128–30.

4 *Naval Minutes*, 33–4.

5 Hyde: Longleat, Coventry MS 98, fos52–3; Finch: J Charnock, *Biographia Navalis* (1794), I.56.

6 *Gentlemen and Tarpaulins*, 29–32.

7 Anon, *The Three Establishments Concerning the Pay of Sea-Officers* (1705), xiii.

8 Burnet, *History*, I.298.

9 *Gentlemen and Tarpaulins*, 36, 53, 232–3.

10 R E Glass, 'The Image of the Sea Officer in English Literature, 1660–1710', *Albion*, 26 (1994), 583–99.

11 Wiltshire and Swindon History Centre, MS 1332/1/5/11.

12 http://www.historyofparliamentonline.org/volume/1660-1690/member/darcy-hon-conyers-1622-92, accessed 4 Sept 2016.

13 http://www.historyofparliamentonline.org/volume/1660-1690/member/courtenay-sir-william-1628-1702, accessed 7 August 2016.

14 Original document at Sherborne Castle, published by D Ellison, 'Lend Me a Frigate', *MM*, 68 (1982), 81.

15 TNA ADM51/605, 26 Apr 1678.

16 BL Add MS 88980, passim.

17 Bod, Rawl MS A174, fo191.

18 BL Add MS 29554, fo386.

19 BL Add MS 28053, fos291–2.

20 Pepys Diary, 28 Jan 1666.

21 Lincs AO, Jarvis MS IX/1/A/5, 1 Oct 1682.

22 *Tangier Papers*, 247. Cf *Naval Minutes*, 194.

23 *Gentlemen and Tarpaulins*, 50–1, 179–84.

24 J D Davies, 'Munden, Sir Richard (1639/40?–1680), naval officer', *ODNB*; E Bateson et al, *A History of Northumberland*, II (1893), 189–91.

25 HMC *Finch* MSS, II.167.

26 Luttrell, I.117.

27 HoP, *House of Lords 1660–1715*, II.192, 215.

28 *Catalogue*, IV.609.

29 *Tangier Papers*, 218.

30 Pepys MS 2856, pp22, 63.
31 P Le Neve Foster, *The Le Neves of Norfolk* (1969), 6–7; *Further Correspondence*, 298.
32 Pepys MS 2853, p352.
33 TNA ADM6/425, pp80–1; ADM6/428, lieutenants' list for 1673–9, no. 18; *Catalogue*, IV.51.
34 Pepys MS 2853, fo195.
35 NMM ADL/L/3.
36 Pepys MS 2853, p291.
37 TNA SP 44/63, p63.
38 *Grammont Memoirs*, 113.
39 Pepys MS 2854, p192. Mansel must have served as a midshipman extraordinary, as John Crofts was the sole lieutenant of the ship in 1678.
40 J D Davies, 'Berkeley, Sir William (1639–1666), naval officer', *ODNB*.
41 J Hattendorf, 'Herbert, Arthur, earl of Torrington (1648–1716), naval officer and politician', *ODNB*.
42 Magalotti, 99; H McDonnell, 'Irishmen in the Stuart Navy, 1660–90', *Irish Sword*, 16 (1985), 102–3.
43 M D Sankey, 'Sheffield, John, first duke of Buckingham and Normanby (1647–1721), politician and author', *ODNB*.
44 TNA ADM3/277, p119.
45 Callow, 173.
46 Pepys MS 1490, p29.
47 Lincs AO, Jarvis MS 9/1/A/5, Gunman's 'record to my posterity', 13 June 1682; TNA SP 44/63, p41.
48 *CSPD 1665–6*, 591; TNA ADM3/277, pp4–5; Pepys MS 2854, p45.
49 *Grammont Memoirs*, 216; *CSPD 1670*, pp178, 690–1.
50 Pepys Diary, 13 June 1666, 4 Apr 1667; J R Powell and E K Timings, eds, *The Rupert and Monck Letterbook* (NRS, 1969), 71.
51 A Marvell, *Third Advice to a Painter* (1666).
52 G E Aylmer, 'Slavery under Charles II: the Mediterranean and Tangier', *English Historical Review*, 114 (1999), 380.
53 D F Allen, 'Charles II, Louis XIV and the Order of Malta', *European History Quarterly*, 20 (1990), 332–6, although Allen is in error on a number of points.
54 TNA, Prob 11/350/292; ADM106/3537, pt 1, 'Captains' Petitions'.
55 *Tangier Papers*, 221.
56 Coventry MS 104, fo19.
57 TNA ADM2/1750, pp222, 223, 228.
58 TNA ADM 1/3546, pp311, 319.
59 HMC *Le Fleming*, 44.
60 Pepys MS 2853, fo193r.
61 Bod, Rawl MS D18, fos1, 35.
62 TNA ADM8/1, disposition list of 1 Sept. 1677.
63 *Catalogue*, IV.493–4. For the establishment of 1676 and the issues it caused, see *Catalogue*, I.214–15,

64 Bod, Rawl MS A190, fo236.
65 Pepys MS 2853, fo231v.
66 Pepys MS 2853, fo232v.
67 Pepys MS 2853, p264.
68 Pepys MS 2853, fo256.
69 J Sugden, *Nelson: A Dream of Glory* (2004), 112–13.
70 *Catalogue*, IV.535–6.
71 *Catalogue*, IV.543–5; Bod, Rawl MS A191, fo153.
72 *Catalogue*, IV.569.
73 R D Merriman, 'Captain George St Lo', *MM*, 31 (1945), 14–15.
74 Pepys MS 2855, p207; the quotation is from Andrew Lambert, Laughton Professor of Naval History at King's College, London, giving the E G R Taylor memorial lecture on 13 October 2016 (albeit speaking of a different context, ie Sir John Barrow and Arctic exploration).
75 Knighton, 115.
76 *Catalogue*, IV.477–89.
77 W E May, 'Midshipmen Ordinary and Extraordinary', *MM*, 59 (1973), 189.
78 J Miller, *James II: A Study in Kingship* (1989 edn), 80.
79 *Catalogue*, IV.544.
80 'Bastard breed': Pepys MS 2854, fo17v.
81 See eg J R Tanner in *Catalogue*, I.202, A Bryant, *Samuel Pepys: the Years of Peril* (1945 edn), 186–7; C Tomalin, *Samuel Pepys: the Unequalled Self* (2002), 303.
82 R Ollard, *Pepys: A Biography* (1991 edn), 252.
83 NMRN MS 121/12, pp129, 135–6, 149; *G&Ts*, 53–4.
84 Knighton, 114–15.
85 NMM LBK/49, pp33, 116.
86 Bod, Rawl MS A170, fo214.
87 W E May, 'Gun Salutes', *MM*, 45 (1959), 326.
88 Pepys MS 2853, p290.
89 Pepys MS 2853, p344.
90 Pepys MS 2856, p14; *G&Ts*, 53.
91 Pepys MS 2855, p206.
92 Disposition list from TNA ADM8/1. For Priestman: Pepys MS 2854, pp113–14; Ollard, *Pepys*, 223.

Chapter 8

1 Bod, Rawl MS A289, fo32.
2 R Johns, 'Antonio Verrio and the Triumph of Painting at the Restoration Court', in M Hallett, N Llewellyn, M Myrone, eds, *Court, Country and City: British Art and Architecture, 1660–1735* (New Haven and London, 2016), 156–9; Sharpe, *Rebranding Rule*, 106–8.
3 Callow, 133–4. For the significance of the portrayal of both Charles and James in Roman garb, see

Sharpe, *Rebranding Rule*, 100–1, 266.

4 Pepys Diary, 22 Apr 1661; *CSPVen 1661–4*, 97; *1664–6*, 266–7.

5 Davies, *Pepys's Navy*, 31.

6 Succession to the Crown (Jersey) Law, 2013: L.14/2013, States of Jersey.

7 Reimer, 'Before Britannia Ruled', 30–7.

8 T W Fulton, *The Sovereignty of the Seas* (1911), 99–104.

9 Quoted by J Crick, 'Edgar, Albion and Insular Dominion', in D Scragg, ed, *Edgar, King of the English 959–975: New Interpretations* (Woodbridge, 2008), 159; D Armitage, *The Ideological Origins of the British Empire* (2000), 105–7.

10 J D Davies, '"Great Neptunes of the Main": Myths, Mangled Histories and "Maritime Monarchy" in the Navy of the Stuarts', in Davies, A James and G Rommelse, eds, *Ideologies of Western Naval Power, 1500–1815* (forthcoming).

11 S I Sobecki, 'Introduction: Edgar's Archipelago', in Sobecki, ed, *The Sea and Englishness in the Middle Ages: Maritime Narratives, Identity and Culture* (Woodbridge, 2011), 7–25.

12 J Burchett, *A Complete History of the Most Remarkable Transactions at Sea* (1720), 36; Fulton, *Sovereignty*, 39–42.

13 N A M Rodger, *The Safeguard of the Sea: A Naval History of Britain 660–1649* (1998), 78.

14 On all of this, see also B Heuser, 'Regina Maris and the Command of the Sea: the Sixteenth Century Origins of Modern Maritime Strategy', *Journal of Strategic Studies*, published online 18 Dec 2015.

15 Rodger, *Safeguard*, 79, 114.

16 NMRN MS 121/1, pp7, 14.

17 I am grateful to Professor Steve Murdoch for this point.

18 Fulton, *Sovereignty*, 118–24; G Chowdharay-Best, 'The King's Chambers', *MM*, 60 (1974), 92–6.

19 J D Alsop, 'William Welwood, Anne of Denmark, and the Sovereignty of the Sea', *Scottish Historical Review*, 59 (1980), 171–4.

20 Fulton, *Sovereignty*, 213; K Sharpe, *Image Wars: Promoting Kings and Commonwealths in England, 1603–60* (2010), 217.

21 Fulton, *Sovereignty*, 367–74.

22 Fulton, *Sovereignty*, 254–6; Rodger, *Safeguard*, 380–3; Armitage, *Empire*, 115–17.

23 R Morieux, *The Channel: England, France and the Construction of a Maritime Border during the Eighteenth Century* (Cambridge 2016), 157–8.

24 Fulton, *Sovereignty*, 400–3.

25 Armitage, *Empire*, 118–19.

26 Pepys Diary, 17 Apr 1663.

27 Sobecki, 'Edgar's Archipelago', 28.

28 Sobecki, 'Edgar's Archipelago', 4.

29 TNA ADM7/729, p116.

30 Pepys Diary, 29 Nov 1661; Callow, 209–10.

31 *CSPD 1661–2*, 236.

32 Guildhall Library, MS 30051, volume 1, pp57–9.

33 NMRN, MS 121/1. Other collections of precedents produced within the Admiralty include TNA ADM7/723–32, Pepys MS 2877; but a potentially valuable volume on the subject, compiled by the Secretary of State Sir Joseph Williamson, is currently missing (TNA SP9/53). Cf Burchett, *Transactions*, 28–39.

34 R Brabander, 'Intersections of *Priyvate Interests in Publick Warr*: A Prosopographical Analysis of Restoration Privateering Enterprise', Brandeis University PhD thesis (2013), 115.

35 C Molloy, *De Jure Maritimo et Navali* (1676), 46, 59.

36 *CSPVen 1661–4*, 105.

37 C H Hartmann, *Charles II and Madame* (1934), 36.

38 Hartmann, *Charles II and Madame*, 38.

39 Hartmann, *Charles II and Madame*, 35–40. However, special arrangements were made in 1672/73, when a combined Anglo-French fleet went to war with the Dutch.

40 Fulton, *Sovereignty*, 464–5, 501–3, 510–11, 514–15.

41 BL Add MS 32094, fos50–2.

42 *Naval Minutes*, 53, 58.

43 *Naval Minutes*, 156; *Petty Papers*, 241–2; Armitage, *Empire*, 123–4, from which the quotation is taken.

44 Armitage, *Empire*, 121–2.

45 Pepys MS 2855, p191; NMRN MS 121/1, p8.

46 W Westergaard, ed, *The First Triple Alliance: The Letters of Christopher Lindenov, Danish Envoy to London, 1668–1672* (1947), 323–4; *CSPD 1667–8*, 336, 422; *CSPD 1671*, 65.

47 Fulton, *Sovereignty*, 476–80; J R Jones, *The Anglo-Dutch Wars of the Seventeenth Century* (1996), 181; K H D Haley, *An English Diplomat in the Low Countries: Sir William Temple and John de Witt 1665–72* (Oxford, 1986), 282.

48 Bodl, Rawl MS A314, fo16v; Pepys MS 2857, p107.

49 Fulton, *Sovereignty*, 464–7.

50 Fulton, *Sovereignty*, 469–70.

51 R C Anderson, ed, *The Journals of Sir Thomas Allin* (NRS), I (1939), 30, 61, 102, 107, 117; II (1940), passim.

52 TNA SP89/11/163.

53 BL Sloane MS 2439, fos21, 31.

54 National Library of Wales, MS 38B, 20 May 1680.

55 Bod, Rawl MS A195, fo235; Lincs AO, Jarvis MS 9/1/A/2. Gunman had avoided a clash on the outward voyage.

56 Fulton, *Sovereignty*, 471–3.

57 C Storrs, *The Resilience of the Spanish Monarchy 1665–1700* (Oxford, 2006), 78–9.

58 Quoted in *Gentlemen and Tarpaulins*, 64.

59 S Harris, *Sir Cloudesley Shovell: Stuart Admiral* (2001), 85–7.

60 *Catalogue*, IV.268, 278–9; Lincs AO MS Jarvis 9/1/A/4.

61 Bod, Rawl MS A477, fos117, 129, 131; HMC *Le Fleming*, 65; *CSPVen 1666–8*, 238; *CSP Ven 1669–70*, 72, 86. For the *Milford* incident, see *CSPD 1668–9*, 292; Pepys Diary, ed R Latham and W Matthews, 26 May 1669.

62 HMC *Le Fleming*, 118. This followed an incident in December 1674 or January 1675, when two French warships failed to salute the *Bonadventure* off Falmouth: *Catalogue*, IV.124.

63 *Catalogue*, IV.449.

64 Pepys MS 2854, p233.

65 Pepys MS 2855, p36; Allin Journals, II.203–4.

66 Luttrell, I.125–6; TNA ADM51/3932.

67 A fuller version of the section that follows appeared in my piece, 'Chatham to Erith via Dover: Charles II's Secret Foreign Policy and the Project for New Royal Dockyards, 1667–72', *Transactions of the Naval Dockyards Society*, 8 (2012), 113–30.

68 D Dessert, *La Royale: Vaisseaux et marins du Roi-Soleil* (Paris, 1996), 301–2.

69 Davies, 'Chatham to Erith', 115.

70 Hartmann, *Charles II and Madame*, 223–4.

71 Hartmann, *Charles II and Madame*, 229.

72 R Hutton, 'The Making of the Secret Treaty of Dover, 1668–70', *Historical Journal*, 29 (1986), 303.

73 Davies, 'Chatham to Erith', 119.

74 P Sonnino, *Louis XIV and the Origins of the Dutch War* (Cambridge, 2003), 147.

75 Miller, *Charles II*, 178–9.

76 Hartmann, *Charles II and Madame,* 278–80.

77 H T Colenbrander, ed, *Bescheiden uit vreemde archieven omtrent de groote Nederlandsche zeeoorlogen* (The Hague, 1919), ii 169; W Troost, *William III: The Stadholder King* (Aldershot, 205), 81.

78 The claim to the Dutch territories was abandoned by Charles only very reluctantly in 1673: Miller, *Charles II*, 206–7.

79 TNA SP 104/177, fo84.

80 Bod, Rawl MS A460, fo39v; *CSPD 1670*, 326, 429, 438, 444, 459, 469.

81 BL Addit MS 9307, fo98.

82 Davies, 'Chatham to Erith', 123–4.

83 J Steerup, 'Danish and Swedish Flag Disputes with the British in the Channel', *Strategy and the Sea: Essays in Honour of John B Hattendorf,* ed N A M Rodger, J R Dancy, B Darnell and E Wilson (Woodbridge, 2016), 29–32. I am grateful to Professor Steve Murdoch for the point about the supplies.

84 Morieux, *The Channel*, 158–9 (quotations from, respectively, Champigny, rear-admiral stationed at Le Havre and Dunkirk in 1714, and Admiral Sir Roger Curtis, d1816, former C-in-C Portsmouth).

85 Steerup, 'Flag Disputes', 33–6.

86 W G Perrin (ed), 'The Salute in the Narrow Seas and the Congress of Vienna', *The Naval Miscellany* III (NRS, 1927), 289–329.

Chapter 9

1 Bod, Rawl MS D147, fo67.

2 A Lambert, *Crusoe's Island: A Rich and Curious History of Pirates, Castaways and Madness* (2016), 53–7.

3 Bod, Rawl MS D147.

4 Quoted by C Stevenson, 'Making Empire Visible at the second Royal Exchange, London', in *Court, Country, City: Essays on British Art and Architecture, 1660–1735*, ed M Hallett, N Llewellyn, M Myrone (New Haven, 2016), 66.

5 G Glickman, 'Conflicting Visions: Foreign Affairs in Domestic Debate 1660–89', in *The Primacy of Foreign Policy in British History, 1660–2000: How Strategic Concerns Shaped Modern Britain*, ed W Mulligan, B Simms (Basingstoke, 2010), 19–20.

6 NMRN MS 121/1, p14.

7 Glickman, 'Conflicting Visions', 19.

8 W L Sachse, ed, *The Diurnal of Thomas Rugg, 1659–61* (1961), 87.

9 M J Braddick, 'The English Government, War, Trade and Settlement 1625–88', 296–301; N C Landsman, 'The Middle Colonies: New Opportunities for Settlement, 1660–1700', both in N Canny, ed, *The Origins of Empire: British Overseas Enterprise to the Close of the Seventeenth Century* (Oxford, 1998), 355–64. For James's role in New York, see Callow, 264–82.

10 G J Ames, 'The Role of Religion in the Transfer and Rise of Bombay, c1661–1687', *Historical Journal*, 46 (2003), 318.

11 BL Add MS 9302, fo172v.

12 G G Harris, 'Ley, James, third earl of Marlborough (1618/19–1665), naval officer', ODNB.

13 HoP, HoL III.701–2.

14 W E May, 'The *Phoenix* in India, 1684–1687', *MM*, 57 (1971), 193–202.

15 BL Add MS 9302, fo172v.

16 TNA ADM8/1; I R Mather, 'The Role of the Royal Navy in the English Atlantic Empire

1660–1720', Oxford University DPhil thesis (1995), 71–5, 95, 99–102, 318–19.

17 Hornstein, *Restoration Navy*, 58–9.

18 T Stein, 'The Mediterranean in the English Empire of Trade, 1660–1748', Harvard University PhD thesis (2012), 1, 16.

19 T Stein, 'Tangier in the Restoration Empire', *Historical Journal*, 54 (2011), 1006.

20 Stein, 'Tangier', 995–8; Glickman, 'Conflicting Visions', 251–5.

21 Charles Fitzcharles, Earl of Plymouth, who had been known all his life as 'Don Carlos'.

22 A R Beach, 'Satirising English Tangier in Samuel Pepys's *Diary* and *Tangier Papers*', *Remapping the Mediterranean World in Early Modern English Writings*, ed G V Stanivukovic (Macmillan, Basingstoke, 2007), 227–44; Glickman, 'Conflicting Visions', 257, 261–77.

23 *Tangier Papers*, 79; Hornstein, *Restoration Navy*, 155–9, 179–94.

24 *Tangier Papers*, 34.

25 E M G Routh, *Tangier, England's Lost Atlantic Outpost* (1912), 264–5.

26 W Pettigrew, *Freedom's Debt: The Royal African Company and the Politics of the Atlantic Slave Trade, 1672–1752* (2013), 11, 22–6; Brabander, 'Privateering', 117–18.

27 Callow, 247.

28 P E H Hair and R Law, 'The English in Western Africa to 1700', *Origins of Empire*, 255–8.

29 Callow, 238–57.

30 Luttrell, I.142; Pepys MS 2855, p137; B Cameron, *This Master Firebrand: A Life of Charles Mordaunt, Third Earl of Peterborough, 1658–1735* (Wilby, 2009), 11–12.

31 J R Jacob, 'Restoration Ideologies and the Royal Society', *History of Science*, XVIII (1980), 26–7.

32 'WG', *In Praise of the Choice Company of Philosophers and Witts, who meet on Wednesdays, Weekly, at Gresham College* (c1662).

33 T Birch, *The History of the Royal Society of London*, I (1756), 7–8.

34 R K Merton, 'Science and the Economy of Seventeenth Century England', *Science and Society*, 3 (1939), 19.

35 Birch, *Royal Society*, I.111–13.

36 Birch, *Royal Society*, I.183–92.

37 Merton, 'Science and the Economy', 20–1.

38 Birch, *Royal Society*, I.477n.

39 F Willmoth, 'Mathematical Sciences and Military Technology: the Ordnance Office in the Reign of Charles II', *Renaissance and Revolution: Humanists, Scholars, Craftsmen and Natural Philosophers in Early*

Modern Europe, ed J V Field & F A J L James (Cambridge 1993), 127–9.

40 S B Bailey, *Prince Rupert's Patent Guns* (Leeds, 2000), 12–13 and passim.

41 L Jardine, 'Never Trust a Pirate: Christian Huygens's Longitude Clocks', in Jardine, *Temptation in the Archives: Essays in Dutch Golden Age Culture* (2015; freely available online at www.ucl.ac.uk/ucl-press), 33–44. Cf Merton, 'Science and the Economy', 12–17.

42 Cited by Brabander, 'Privateering', 178.

43 Pepys Diary, 1 February 1664.

44 Brabander, 'Privateering', 134–58.

45 Fulton, *Sovereignty*, 446–9.

46 *Letters to Williamson*, I.149.

47 Brabander, 'Privateering', 286–91, 307–9.

48 For James and the examples cited here, see Callow, 257–9, 271–82 (especially pp281–2).

49 C Jones, *The Sea and the Sky: the History of the Royal Mathematical School at Christ's Hospital* (Horsham, 2015), 11–19.

50 Jones, *Sea and the Sky*, 18. Pepys claimed (in Pepys MS 2612, p111), that he conceived of the idea, and then persuaded the Earl of Sandwich, who subsequently convinced the king and Duke of York. But, as Clifford Jones points out, Pepys's chronology simply does not match the known sequence of events, and is contradicted entirely by the unassailable alternative evidence of the agency of Clayton and Clifford in the matter.

51 Jones, *Sea and the Sky*, 45–55, 133–44.

52 Fraser, *Charles II*, 193; Jackson, *Charles II*, 5–10.

53 Evelyn Diary, 2 Sept 1680; H Wallis, 'Navigators and Mathematical Practitioners in Samuel Pepys's Day', *Journal of Navigation*, 47 (1994), 3

54 Bod, Rawl MS A171, fo17–20.

55 *Naval Minutes*, 28; Wallis, 'Navigators', 7; C Verner, 'John Seller and the Chart Trade in Seventeenth Century England', *The Compleat Plattmaker: Essays on Chart, Map and Globe Making in England in the Seventeenth and Eighteenth Centuries*, ed N J W Thrower (Berkeley, CA, 1978), 145–6.

56 H M Wallis, '"Geographie is Better than Divinity": Maps, Globes and Cartography in the Days of Samuel Pepys', *The Compleat Plattmaker*, 22–3.

57 F E Dyer, *The Life of Sir John Narbrough* (1931), 58–60.

58 Dyer, *Narbrough*, 70.

59 Dyer, *Narbrough*, 76.

60 Dyer, *Narbrough*, 77.

61 Dyer, *Narbrough*, 79–89.

62 J D Davies, 'Narbrough, Sir John (bap 1640, d1688), naval officer', *ODNB*.

63 *CSPVen 1669–70*, 144.

64 G L Nute, *Caesars in the Wilderness* (1943), 105–30.

65 *Catalogue*, IV.16.

66 TNA ADM2/1745, fo46.

67 TNA ADM106/23, fo29; ADM10/15, p141. Pepys's 'Register of Sea Officers' (*Catalogue*, I.425–6) conflates his career with that of a namesake who might have been his father; the latter's naval career ended after he wrecked *Kent* in 1672.

68 HMC *Le Fleming*, 126. Cf *Catalogue*, IV.291–2.

69 PL MS 3177, p127; D J Hepper, *British Warship Losses in the Age of Sail 1650–1859* (Rotherfield, 1994), 12. Wood's journal is PL 2542.

70 Lincs AO, Jarvis MS 9/1/A/2; G P B Naish, 'Hydrographic Surveys by Officers of the Navy under the Later Stuarts', *Journal of Navigation*, 9 (1956), 52

71 Wallis, 'Navigators', 3–4.

72 TNA ADM2/1, pp12–13; ADM91/1, pp1, 91.

73 NMM CLU8, Narbrough to Hayter, 29 June 1679; NMM ROM2, 17 Sept 1677, 20 Oct 1677.

74 F E Dyer, 'The Journal of Grenvill Collins', *MM*, 14 (1928), 197–219; National Library of Wales, MS 38B.

75 *Naval Minutes*, 188.

76 Quoted by S Mountfield, 'Captain Greenvile Collins and Mr Pepys', *MM* (1970), 91.

77 *Naval Minutes*, 133.

78 Wallis, 'Navigators', 3; Naish, 'Surveys', 47.

79 M Ximena Urbina, 'La sospecha de Ingleses en el extremo sur de Chile, 1669–1683: Actitudes imperiales y locales como consecuencia de la expedición de John Narborough', *Magallania*, 44 (2016), 15–40.

80 Wallis, 'Navigators', 15; Lambert, *Crusoe's Island*, 26–30.

81 Glickman, 'Conflicting Visions', 21–3.

82 S Pincus, *1688: the First Modern Revolution* (New Haven, 2009), 319.

83 Burchett, *Transactions*, 405.

Chapter 10

1 Longleat, Coventry MS 102, fo7.

2 Longleat, Coventry MS 95, fos60–79.

3 Davies, 'Chatham to Erith via Dover', 122–3.

4 Pepys MS 2854, fo12.

5 N A M Rodger, 'The Idea of Naval Strategy in Britain in the Eighteenth and Nineteenth Centuries', in *The Development of British Naval Thinking: Essays in Memory of Bryan Ranft*, ed G Till (Aldershot, 2006), 19–20.

6 Bod, Carte MS 75, fo199.

7 BL Add MS 32094, fo46.

8 Coventry MS 95, fos83–4.

9 *Sandwich Journal*, 201.

10 Coventry MS 95, fos175, 179.

11 TNA SP 104/177, fos88–9.

12 A Bryant, ed, *The Letters of King Charles II* (1968), 253–4.

13 Bryant, *Letters*, 264–70; *Gentlemen and Tarpaulins*, 166–70.

14 BL Lansdowne MS 1236, fo147.

15 F Fox, *The Four Days Battle of 1666: The Greatest Sea Fight in the Age of Sail* (Barnsley, 2009).

16 K Sharpe, '"Thy Longing Country's Darling and Desire": Aesthetics, Sex and Politics in the England of Charles II', in *Politics, Transgression and Representation at the Court of Charles II*, ed Julia Marciari Alexander and C MacLeod (Yale UP, New Haven, 2007), 23–4.

17 Wiltshire and Swindon History Centre, MS 865/410, Bullen Reymes's book of prize ships taken, 1664–5. The uncertainty over numbers is due to the fact that the source is slightly damaged, with the tops of several pages missing.

18 Magalotti, 94.

19 BL Egerton MS 861.

20 Turnbull, 'Administration', 82.

21 BL Harleian MS 1510, fos61v, 63v.

22 BL Add MS 32,094, fo28. Cf Clarendon, *Life*, 88.

23 Knighton, 89.

24 TNA ADM2/1745, fos127–8.

25 TNA ADM2/1745, fo128.

26 NMM CLI/130, p14.

27 TNA ADM2/1745, fos128–9.

28 BL Lansdowne MS 1236, fo139.

29 C Molloy, *De Jure Maritimo et Navali* (1676), 55.

30 R Hatton, 'Louis XIV and his Fellow Monarchs', *Louis XIV and Europe*, ed Hatton (1976), 18–21. Cf F Bluche, tr M Greengrass, *Louis XIV* (Oxford, 1990), 232–4; P Burke, *The Fabrication of Louis XIV* (New Haven, Ct, 1992), especially pp61–83.

31 Bod, Carte MS 47, fo166.

32 In addition to other sources cited, this and the following paragraphs are based on my essay on 'Chatham, 1667' in B Heuser and A Leoussi, eds, *Famous Battles and their Myths* (Barnsley, forthcoming, 2017).

33 BL Sloane MS 1786, fo177v.

34 J Stubbe, *A Justification of the Present War* (1672), 2, 39, 40.

35 J Stubbe, *Justification*, 11–28; id, *A Further Justification of the Present War* (1673), 1–3; W de Britaine, *The Dutch Usurpation* (1672), 1–9; Fulton, *Sovereignty*, 476.

36 W de Britaine, *The Interest of England in the Present War with Holland* (1672), 9–10.

37 *CSPVen 1671–2*, 221.
38 A B Gardiner, 'The Medal that Provoked a War: Charles II's Lasting Indignation over Adolfzoon's Breda Medal', *The Medal*, 17 (1990), 11–15, and rejoinder by M Scharloo, 'A Peace Medal that Caused a War?', *The Medal*, 18 (1991), 11–22 (quotation from p21 of latter).
39 Hartmann, *Charles II and Madame*, 292. For the connection between naval setbacks and domestic discontent, see Davies, *Pepys's Navy*, 35–6.
40 St John's College, Oxford, MS 253, Charles II to the Duke of York, 4 Sept 1672.
41 Knighton, 59.
42 *CSPVen 1664–6*, 91.
43 Evelyn Diary 1 July 1665, 17 June 1666.
44 *CSPVen 1671–2*, 189.
45 Lincs AO, Jarvis MS 9/1/A/3.
46 *Letters to Williamson*, I.91, 110.
47 *Journals and Narratives*, 68, 78–9, 106, 108–9, 146–7, 151–2, 158, 299, 305, 307, 315, 317–18, 324, 326, 332, 337, 340.
48 Clarke, *Life of James II*, I.425.
49 *Sandwich Journal*, 204.
50 TNA, PRO31/3/115, fo55v.
51 *CSPVen 1671–2*, 214.
52 *British Naval Documents 1204–1960*, ed J B Hattendorf et al (NRS 1993), 198.
53 *Journals and Narratives*, 93, 157; Lincs AO, Jarvis MS 9/1/A/3, 15, 16 August 1672; Colenbrander, 93; *Naval Minutes*, 229.
54 *Journals and Narratives*, 95–101, 156–7, 164–184; *CSPD 1672*, 83–97, 163–6; Colenbrander, *Bescheiden*, 109–23; Clarke, *Life of James II*, 461–75; J Sheffield, Earl of Mulgrave, Marquis of Normanby and Duke of Buckingham, *Works* (1740 edn), II.14–16; P de Villette-Mursay, *Mes campagnes de mer sous Louis XIV*, ed M Verge-Franceschi (Paris, 1991), 144–6. Funeral of des Rabesnières: *London Gazette*, 684, 10 June 1672; *CSPD 1672*, 156.
55 Coventry MS 95, fos399–401.
56 *Gentlemen and Tarpaulins*, 162–5
57 *Journals and Narratives*, 14–15.
58 *Journals and Narratives*, 14–15.
59 Eg Coventry MS 95, fo399; BL Addit MS 21,948, fo205; Addit MS 37,951, fos4–5. Intelligence reports: BL Addit MS 21,948, fo205; Lincs AO, Jarvis MS 9/1/A/3, 26 May 1672; Clarke, *James II*, 463.
60 Lincs AO, Jarvis MS 9/1/A/3, 28 May 1672. Cf *Journals and Narratives*, 95.
61 *Journals and Narratives*, 95, 165, 168, 171, 172, 173.
62 *Journals and Narratives*, 175; *CSPVen 1671–2*, 235–7; Clarke, *James II*, I.465–6.
63 Davies, *Pepys's Navy*, 260.

64 Staffordshire Record Office, MS D(W)1778/Ii/ 355.
65 TNA ADM 51/3817.
66 *Letters to Williamson*, I.174.
67 *Letters to Williamson*, I.168–70.
68 *CSPD 1673*, 494, 498, 509, 510.
69 *Letters to Williamson*, I.186.
70 *Letters to Williamson*, I.189–92.
71 *Letters to Williamson*, I.162.
72 Martel's narrative: Colenbrander, *Bescheiden*, 321–5. Dating of narrative: *Letters to Williamson*, I.189–90, II.1. His arrest: ibid, II.20; Colenbrander, *Bescheiden*, 348.
73 *Letters to Williamson*, II, 2; BL Stowe MS 202, fo 337; BL M636/26, Denton to Verney, 4 Sept 1673.
74 *Letters to Williamson*, II.36, 46.
75 Coventry MS 95, fo404.
76 W A Shaw, ed, *Calendar of Treasury Books, 1672–5* (1909), 419.

Chapter 11

1 M Range, *British Royal and State Funerals: Music and Ceremonial since Elizabeth I* (2016), 79–88.
2 Foxcroft, *Halifax*, II.355.
3 J Sheffield, Duke of Buckingham, *Miscellanies* (1933 ed), 56.
4 Evelyn Diary, 6 Feb 1685.
5 M Wenzel, 'The Windsor Beauties by Sir Peter Lely and the collection of paintings at St James's Palace, 1674', *Journal of the History of Collections*, 14 (2002), 205–214. Cf Callow, 127.
6 *Morrice Entring book*, III.195.
7 F Sandford, 99, 125; C A Edie, 'The Public Face of Royal Ritual: Sermons, Medals, and Civic Ceremony in Later Stuart Coronations', *Huntington Library Quarterly*, 53 (1990), 311–336; Callow, 135–7; Sharpe, *Rebranding Rule*, 234–5, 266–8.
8 Pepys MS 2857, pp444, 448.
9 C S Knighton, ed, *Pepys's Later Diaries* (Stroud, 2004), 179–202.
10 C S Knighton, 'A Century On: Pepys and the Elizabethan Navy', *Transactions of the Royal Historical Society*, 14 (2004), 145; Knighton, *Pepys and the Navy*, 148–50.
11 Knighton, *Pepys and the Navy*, 150–4.
12 Bod, Rawl MS 170, fo217.
13 Thus the special commission's claim, in March 1687, that it had sent to sea a Channel Guard stronger than any seen in the last twenty years, was a downright lie: Knighton, 151.
14 Analysis of disposition lists in TNA ADM8/1.
15 A V Coats, 'Portsmouth Dockyard: Contested Buttress of the Navy, Monarchy and Church in the 17th century', in *Les arsenaux de Marine, du XVIe*

siècle à nos jours, editors tbc (Paris, forthcoming in 2017).

16 Knighton, 156; *Gentlemen and Tarpaulins*, 184.

17 Pepys MS 2860, p42; for Young's long service, Pepys MS 2877, pp289, 365.

18 S B Black, 'The Chest at Chatham, 1590–1803', *Archaeologia Cantiana*, 111 (1993), 268–9.

19 Nottingham University Archives, Portland MS PwV 60.

20 Bod, Rawl MS A289, fo43; *Catalogue*, I. 266–95.

21 Bod, Rawl MS A186, fo351.

22 *Gentlemen and Tarpaulins*, 202.

23 Pepys MS 2857, p319; *Gentlemen and Tarpaulins*, 200–2; http://www.historyofparliamentonline. org/volume/1660-1690/member/strickland-sir-roger-1640-1717.

24 NMM FFX6/1/7.

25 *Gentlemen and Tarpaulins*, 202–3.

26 Burnet, *History*, III.95–6.

27 *Gentlemen and Tarpaulins*, 204.

28 *CSPVen 1666–8*, 226.

29 TNA ADM2/1746, fo158v.

30 J Childs, *The Army, James II, and the Glorious Revolution* (Manchester, 1980), 41–2.

31 *CSPD 1687–9*, 198.

32 D F Allen, 'Charles II, Louis XIV and the Order of Malta', *European History Quarterly*, 20 (1990), 325–6.

33 Allen, 'Order of Malta', 336–7; Hornstein, *Restoration Navy*, 160–6.

34 Unless stated otherwise, the following section is based on my essay '"The Strongest Island in the Whole Universe": Aspects of Anglo-Maltese Relations in the Seventeenth and Eighteenth Centuries', *Transactions of the Naval Dockyards Society*, 5, ed R Riley (Portsmouth, 2009).

35 A Fitzroy, *Henry, Duke of Grafton* (1921), 49–54.

36 TNA ADM 51/3873.

37 Pepys MS 2860, p323.

38 TNA ADM 51/957.

39 Ibid; D F Allen, 'Attempts to Revive the Order of Malta in Stuart England', *Historical Journal*, 33 (1990), 949. Cf www.orderofmalta-malta.org.mt/publications/Maltese%20Cross.pdf; I am grateful to Peter Le Fevre for this reference.

40 Bod, Rawl MS C198.

41 D G Pilgrim, 'The Uses and Limitations of French Naval Power in the Reign of Louis XIV: The Administration of the Marquis de Seignelay, 1683–90', Brown University PhD thesis (1969), 283–4, 290–1.

42 Morieux, *The Channel*, 113.

43 Figures for fleet sizes from TNA ADM8/1.

44 *Gentlemen and Tarpaulins*, 203, 205.

45 Pilgrim, 'Seignelay', 310–12, 317–23. Or even three worlds: it was highly unlikely that the French could have provided fifteen or sixteen ships anyway, as their fleet was in an even more shocking state of disrepair than James's had been in 1684–5 (Pilgrim, 'Seignelay', 324–7).

46 *Gentlemen and Tarpaulins*, 205–6.

47 J D Davies, 'James II, William of Orange and the Admirals', *By Force or By Default? The Revolution of 1688–9*, ed E Cruickshanks (Edinburgh, 1989), 100–1.

48 TNA ADM106/384/58.

49 Davies, 'Admirals', 88.

50 Although he had commanded a fleet in two huge battles, he had never actually commanded an army, and would not do so until the day of the Battle of the Boyne: Callow, 64.

51 A P Barclay, 'The Impact of King James II on the Departments of the Royal Household', Cambridge University PhD thesis (1993), 11.

52 Davies, 'Admirals', 83–5.

53 Davies, 'Admirals', 85–93; *Gentlemen and Tarpaulins*, 211–17.

54 NMM ADM/L/C/107, 14 Oct 1688.

55 Pepys MS 2857, p408; HMC *Dartmouth* MSS I.260–1; Clarke, *Life of James II*, II.233–4.

56 Davies, 'Admirals', 88, 94, 101.

57 Clarke, *Life of James II*, II.207–8; Barclay, 'Household', 187–8.

58 Davies, 'Admirals', 101.

59 J Childs, *The Army, James II and the Glorious Revolution* (Manchester, 1980), 1, 180.

60 L Jardine, *Going Dutch: How England Plundered Holland's Glory* (2008), 19.

61 TNA ADM51/4135.

62 For the Irish presence at Portsmouth, and the clashes between these troops and the dockyard workers, see Coats, 'Portsmouth Dockyard'.

63 NMM LBK/49, p150.

64 Bod, Rawl MS A186, fo218.

65 ADM 8/1; *Gentlemen and Tarpaulins*, 218–19.

66 *Particular Friends*, 186n3.

67 What follows is from TNA ADM51/3873, log of the *Isabella Yacht*.

68 NMM LBK/49, pp157–8.

69 NMM LBK/49, p158.

70 Clarke, *Life of James II*, II.251–2.

71 TNA ADM52/3.

72 Barclay, 'Household', 195.

73 Barclay, 'Household', 143.

74 Barclay, 'Household', 192–5

75 HMC *Le Fleming*, 231.

76 Assuming that this story is not a complete invention,

the remarkably tight timetable suggests that messages, perhaps from the King or else from someone in the royal household, were awaiting Lloyd at Plymouth.

77 Bulkeley survived the Revolution, but his brother, the third Viscount Bulkeley, was accused of covert Jacobitism on a number of occasions, and his uncle went into exile at Saint-Germain.

78 J Callow, *King in Exile: James II, Warrior, King and Saint* (Stroud, 2004), 19, 21–3.

79 Callow, *King in Exile*, 23.

Chapter 12

1 However, it seems to have originated with Nelson's brother-in-law, so there may be some element of truth in it. See the note by R W Beale, *MM*, 53 (1967), 383–4. Moreover, there is no inherent reason why Henry and Nelson could not have met when they were both in Sicily over the winter of 1798/99. There is also no foundation to the suggestion that Nelson's refusal in 1788 to celebrate the centenary of the Glorious Revolution was due to latent Jacobitism: it was motivated by purely local Norfolk politics. C Petrie, *The Jacobite Movement: The Last Phase, 1716–1807* (1950), 182; J Sugden, *Nelson: A Dream of Glory* (2004), 387.

2 BL Add 34,990, fo144.

3 Callow, *King in Exile*, 66.

4 S Débarbat, 'Des connoysances de Jacques II d'Angleterre en matière d'astronomie', in *The origins, achievement and influence of the Royal Observatory, Greenwich, 1675–1975: proceedings of the Symposium held at the National Maritime Museum, Greenwich, 13–18 July, 1975 (fourth joint symposium of the International Astronomical Union and the Union internationale d'histoire et de philosophie des sciences)*, 79–80.

5 For these various actions, together with the background to them, see P Aubrey, *The Defeat of James Stuart's Armada* (Leicester, 1979),

6 Callow, *King in Exile*, 200.

7 HMC *Finch MSS*, V.429.

8 Pepys MS 2853, p266.

9 Callow, *King in Exile*, 202.

10 E Cruickshanks, 'Attempts to Restore the Stuarts, 1689–96', *The Stuart Court in Exile and the Jacobites*, ed Cruickshanks and E Corp (1995), 10.

11 E Corp, *A Court in Exile: the Stuarts in France, 1689–1718* (Cambridge, 2004), 108.

12 N Genet-Rouffiac, *Le Grand Exil: Les Jacobites en France, 1688–1715* (Vincennes, 2007), 207.

13 P J Le Fevre, 'Lloyd, David (1642/3–1723), naval officer', *ODNB*.

14 BL Add MS 37,662, fo129; cf fos261–3, 266.

15 Genet-Rouffiac, *Le Grand Exil*, 353; J D Davies, 'Jennens, Sir William (bap 1634, d1704?), naval officer', *ODNB*.

16 HMC *Stuart Papers*, I.69, 88; J S Bromley, *Corsairs and Navies 1660–1760* (1987), 139, 150–2.

17 J LePelley, 'The Jacobite Privateers of James II', *MM*, 30 (1944), 185–93.

18 Bromley, *Corsairs*, 142–3, 144–6; E O Ciardha, *Ireland the Jacobite Cause, 1685–1766: A Fatal Attachment* (Dublin, 2004), 118–19, 126.

19 Bromley, *Corsairs*, 143.

20 Bromley, *Corsairs*, 147.

21 Bromley, *Corsairs*, 149. For Nagle, see also Genet-Rouffiac, *Grand Exil*, 208–9.

22 HMC *Finch MSS*, V.160–1. The government's correspondents invariably described all of these ships as 'French', but a significant number of them would actually have been sailing under Jacobite commissions.

23 BL Add MS 42,586, fos93–4.

24 BL Egerton MS 2621, fo89, 27 June 1690; HMC *Finch MSS*, III.225, 383; *CSPD 1690–1*, 60, 63, 68.

25 J M de Bergerac, 'Memoires d'un Protestant', *MM* 40 (1954), *145–51* (quotation from p151).

26 C Petrie, *The Marshal Duke of Berwick* (1953), 62–3, 157–8 (quotation from p63).

27 J D Davies, 'Camocke, George (c1666–1732), Jacobite naval officer and officer in the Spanish service', *ODNB*.

28 O Ciardha, *Ireland*, 231.

29 B Morgan, 'Osborne, Peregrine, second duke of Leeds (bap 1659, d1729), naval officer', *ODNB*.

30 HMC *Stuart Papers*, II.49, 51–3, 62.

31 HMC *Stuart Papers*, II.310, 454; IV.6.

32 E T Fox, 'Jacobitism and the Golden Age of Piracy, 1715–25', *International Journal of Maritime History*, XXII (2010), 283.

33 A Bialuschewski, 'Jacobite Pirates?', *Histoire social/Social History* 44 (2011), 155–6 and 147–64 passim. For Jacobite names of pirate ships, see also Fox, 'Jacobitism', 287–8.

34 Nicholas Rogers, 'Riot and Popular Jacobitism in Early Hanoverian England', in Eveline Cruickshanks, ed, *Ideology and Conspiracy: Aspects of Jacobitism, 1689–1759* (Edinburgh, 1982), 71; quoted by Fox, 'Jacobitism', 289.

35 HMC *Stuart Papers*, VI.213–15; Fox, 'Jacobitism', 286.

36 Bialuschewski, 'Pirates', 160–1; E Cruickshanks and H Erskine-Hill, *The Atterbury Plot* (Basingstoke, 2004), 149–52. For Ó Morugh, see S Murdoch, 'The Northern Flight: Irish Soldiers in Seventeenth-

century Scandinavia' in T O'Connor and M A Lyons, eds, *The Ulster Earls and Baroque Europe: Refashioning Irish Identities, 1600–1800* (Dublin, 2010), pp88–109. I am grateful to Steve Murdoch for providing me with this reference.

37 S Murdoch, 'Soldiers, Sailors, Jacobite Spy: Russo-Jacobite Relations 1688–1750', *Slavonica*, 3 (1996), 9; R Wills, *The Jacobites and Russia 1715–50* (East Linton, 2002), 23.

38 Wills, *Jacobites and Russia*, 27–8, 52.

39 D Fedosov, 'Under the Saltire: Scots and the Russian Navy, 1690s–1910s', in M Cornwall and M Frame, eds, *Scotland and the Slavs: Cultures in Contact 1500–2000* (St Petersburg, 2001), 26; Wills, *Jacobites and Russia*, 52–5.

40 National Archives of Scotland, GD24/1/944/3, 7, 13.

41 Wills, *Jacobites and Russia*, 175, 179–80.

42 J S Gibson, *Playing the Scottish Card: The Franco-Jacobite Invasion of 1708* (Edinburgh, 1988).

43 E J Graham, *A Maritime History of Scotland 1650–1790* (East Linton 2002), 160–3.

44 M G H Pittock, 'Gordon, Lord Lewis (c1725–54), Jacobite army officer', *ODNB*; TNA ADM8/24 for Gordon's service on, and departure from, the *Dunkirk*.

45 For Walsh's career, see R Cock, 'Walsh, Antoine Vincent, Jacobite first Earl Walsh (bap 1703, d1763), Jacobite naval officer', *ODNB*.

46 F J McLynn, 'Sea Power and the Jacobite Rising of 1745', *MM*, 67 (1981), 163–72.

47 McLynn, 'Sea Power', 166, 171.

48 For which see J S Gibson, *Ships of the '45: The Rescue of the Young Pretender* (1967).

49 J D Davies, 'Adam, Viscount Duncan', *British Admirals of the Napoleonic Wars: The Contemporaries of Nelson*, ed P J Le Fevre and R Harding (2005), 46.

50 Carmarthenshire Archives Service, Stepney papers transferred from Llanelli Library, SE1101.

51 http://www.troublemag.com/a-toast-to-exiled-kings/ (account of exhibition at the National Gallery of Victoria, Australia, 2013), accessed 27 April 2016.

52 M Pittock, *Material Culture and Sedition, 1688–1760: Treacherous Objects, Secret Places* (2013), 129–31.

53 O Ciardha, *Ireland*, 338–40.

54 D Zimmermann, *The Jacobite Movement in Scotland and in Exile, 1746–59* (Basingstoke 2003), 1, 120–58, 167.

55 R Mackay, 'Keppel, Augustus, Viscount Keppel (1725–1786), naval officer and politician', *ODNB*.

56 N Tracy, *The Battle of Quiberon Bay 1759: Hawke and the Defeat of the French Invasion* (Barnsley 2010), 148–9.

Appendix

1 *Catalogue*, IV.331–3.

2 Bod, Rawlinson MS A180, fos352–5.

3 It is unclear what that purpose was. Following his arrest in 1679, one of the charges brought against Samuel was his involvement with a ship called the *Hunter*. But it was a different ship, and the charges related to events during the third Anglo-Dutch War: J & B Long, *The Plot Against Pepys* (2007), 66–7, 70, 72–3, 76, 118–19, 127–9, 231. Perhaps these minutes were preserved in case the two ships somehow became confused by Pepys's opponents; but in any event, the point they make about the problematic nature of the published Admiralty journal remains valid. After all, neither Samuel nor John Pepys were likely to fabricate for their own purposes speeches made by the king and Duke of York, given that the potential consequences of doing so might have been as bad as, if not worse than, the consequences of the actual charges brought against Samuel in 1679.

4 Passing mentions of James being at meetings when his attendance was otherwise unrecorded can be found in *Catalogue*, IV.160, 386, 519.

5 *Catalogue*, IV.330

6 The balance of probabilities suggests that this was the second Marquess of Worcester, who was employed on some confidential duties by King Charles I during the first civil war: S K Roberts, 'Somerset, Edward, second marquess of Worcester (d1667), courtier and scientist', *ODNB*.

Index

Names of ships are given in italics.